THE LAW
OF THE LAND

THE LAW
OF THE LAND

The Evolution
of Our Legal System

CHARLES REMBAR

Harper & Row, Publishers, New York
Cambridge, Grand Rapids, Philadelphia, St. Louis,
San Francisco, London, Singapore, Sydney, Tokyo

A hardcover edition of this book was published in 1980 by Simon and Schuster, a division of Gulf & Western Corporation. It is here reprinted by arrangement with Simon and Schuster.

First PERENNIAL LIBRARY edition published 1989.

Library of Congress Cataloging-in-Publication Data

Rembar, Charles.
  The law of the land.

  Reprint. Originally published: New York: Simon and
Schuster, c1980.
  Includes bibliographical references and index.
  1. Law—United States—History and criticism.
2. Law—Great Britain—History and criticism.   I. Title.
KF352.R45 1989   349.73   88-45942
ISBN 0-06-097219-X   347.3

89 90 91 92 93 LG 10 9 8 7 6 5 4 3 2 1

FOR LANCE AND JIM

Contents

1

The Blessed Man and
the Arguably Admirable Tiger

PROLOGUE

There once was a man blest with an extraordinary ability to enjoy
life. He was strong and skilled and healthy. His body served him
well. His eyesight and hearing were excellent; all his nerve endings—tactile, olfactory, gustatory—were fine-tuned. He began at
a level some of us achieve only on alcohol or drugs or sea air. He
loved trees, mountains, snowflakes, ocean waves, the ruddy turn-
stone, the scarlet tanager (especially the female, who is not scarlet), basketball, soccer (these for playing, not so much for
watching), good fresh bread with good fresh butter, certain
wines, certain paintings, a great variety of music, Maryland crab-
meat, brisket of beef, quite a few books, and several people. He
didn't care much for the Broadway theater or hominy grits, judging the potential in the one case sadly untapped and in the other
somewhat limited, but he allowed that on occasion they could
be interesting, even pleasurable.

This attitude toward the Broadway theater and hominy grits
went to the essence of his character. He could find pleasure in
things which, on the whole, he judged not good. "There will
ordinarily be something that is handsome, or sounds funny, or
increases one's knowledge," he would say, "in the most unlikely
situations." He was not merely being cheery. "I am no foolish
optimist," he would add, when challenged. "What I'm saying
doesn't make everything okay. Things these days are pretty rot-
ten. But nothing is unmixed. Even where the net effect is disagreeable or downright bad, some element may yield aesthetic

pleasure or laughter or enlightenment. This isn't faith or credo; it's just a fact of life. One may as well be open to it." And with his health and strength and splendid sensibilities, he could practice what he preached. He had his share of misfortunes (though his share was smaller than the shares of some), but his misfortunes did not paralyze or blind him. He almost always found a tremor of delight.

One day he was walking in the jungle. He liked the jungle very much. Its dark beauty he thought special, its dangers overrated. Suddenly he spied a tiger, perhaps twenty yards away. At first the tiger, his attention fixed on something elsewhere that seemed interesting, even edible, did not see the man. The man's quick brain spun off some thoughts. "The dangers of the jungle, I have maintained, are exaggerated, but they exist. In this unlucky happenstance I have encountered one of them, the worst perhaps. Here we have a lesson in the weakness of generalization—the ultimate fallacy, from a personal point of view, of statistical analysis. The fallacy is insufficiently recognized, and if I should survive, I shall have an illustration on which to build a chapter, or at least a footnote, in my new book. The chances of getting killed on a jungle walk are less than on a motor trip. Very few people who come here suffer any harm—a tiny minority, really. We must keep in mind, however, that it is hard and often perilous to belong to a minority."

Just about this time the tiger turned, stirred by ideas he felt but could not quite identify. He saw the man, and the man saw that the tiger saw him. "I am finished," thought the man. "I am famished," thought the tiger.

I

The man did not resign, however. He reviewed the possibilities. So did the tiger. "If I make a move," said the man to himself, "my chances will be even less than if I stand here." "I hope he doesn't try to run," said the tiger to himself; "the speed of an undernourished tiger, at any distance more than twenty yards, is less than commonly believed."

The tiger made three long leaps and sprang. "Magnificent," thought the man. "What grace and power! How superior to human athletes, even to ballet dancers. This beast is beautiful, and I have managed to catch him at his best. How many people

have been privileged to witness such a sight? Too bad, I won't
be able to tell anyone about it. Too bad, more broadly, that I
have to die. And probably a painful death. But there's no denying
the experience."

In fact, it was not painful. The tiger's aim was accurate. The
man's neck broke clean. Unconsciousness and death arrived at
once.

I I

Thoughts fly quickly, quicker than a tiger's leap. The man's
thoughts were in the air as the tiger raced. He was not an insensitive tiger. And he was a tiger whose ego, in that season, badly
needed shoring up. His wife had been complaining about the
lack of food around the cave, refusing to concede that these were
times when prey was tight. "You're supposed to be the meat-
winner around here," she would remind him. And then that
smirking line she was so fond of, which he never once considered funny: "You call yourself a tiger."

The last time they had this kind of conversation, the tiger
got so upset he lost his customary dignity. His voice rose in pitch
to petulance. He almost meowed. "I've had a run of bad luck
lately," the tiger said. "Crap," said his wife.

Passing through space that was charged with the man's
thoughts, the tiger felt their substance. He couldn't quite get the
language, but the sense and mood were clear. "Gee," said the
tiger to himself, "here's someone who really likes me. And in
such trying circumstances. How fair of him. What a nice person."
In that split second the tiger decided he would spare the man.
He swerved, and narrowly flew by. Not many landbound creatures would be able to perform that maneuver at such a speed. It
was a close thing, though, and had the tiger not simultaneously
pulled in his claws, there might have been some damage. But as
it was the man felt just a rush of air, and a light brush of fur. "A
pleasant tactile sensation," he observed.

The tiger stopped where his great leap ended, well beyond
the man and off to one side. He turned and tried to smile,
forgetting for the moment that cats cannot smile. But the man
understood, or thought he did. He smiled, and waved his
thanks, and walked away. The farther he walked, the faster he
walked.

I I I

As the tiger, bounding forward, gathered in his target's thoughts, he had some thoughts of his own. "Flattery is a deadly weapon. Even with honest, well-intentioned laudatory statements, one must be on guard. This man is perceptive, and has remarkable detachment—a most extraordinary human—and he's put me in a better mood than I've been in for quite a while. It's a shame he has to die. For myself, I would go hungry longer. I could wait for one of those stupid antelopes, who annoy me with their speed and caution. But I've got to think of the wife and cubs." The tiger kept his course and struck.

I V

The racing tiger reminded himself of the power and danger of flattery, but realized right away they ought to be discounted. "On balance, I'd prefer to see him live. Not only do I like him, but if I let him live he'll talk. This is my chance for immortality, which after all is nobler than a full stomach. As for the wife, she should try to think of it as staying on a diet. As for those pampered cubs, a glimmer of how things were in the Depression will do them good."

And so the tiger swerved, and the man's fine eyes remarked the swerve, and the man survived to tell the tale. He not only told it, but he wrote it, and appeared on television to discuss it. The tiger became one of the most famous tigers that ever lived, a model of kindness and athleticism, a culture hero for a time.

V

The tiger, as he leaped, cut through all these thoughts, rolled them to either side in waves, made a wake of them. He had a duty to his family; he was very hungry himself. It would be unnatural to be diverted. He went straight for the man's throat. As the tiger made his final leap, the man moved slightly to his left—a superb move, nicely timed, just far enough, not gross. The man felt the rush of air but nothing else; the claws, stretched as far as they could go, never touched him.

It happened that the man was standing in front of a sturdy jungle tree—something the tiger had not noticed, or, if he noticed, deemed not pertinent. His urgent lunge carried him head on into it. Only his fine skeletomuscular construction kept the tiger from being killed. He was plenty knocked out.

The man looked around, and saw what happened. "Wow!" he said, his heart going like a runaway pile driver. "What an event! But I'd better be going, fast, before that beast recovers." He sprinted all the way to the edge of the jungle and a far distance out of it.

The tiger after a while came to. He dragged himself home, and got the kind of welcome he had lately come to expect. "Don't put on that tired, injured look," said his mate. "If you think your job is tough, you might try staying home with these wild hungry cubs of yours, and do everything else I have to do besides."

"I've got a headache," said the tiger.

"Oh shut up," said she.

V I

Taken with a fit of kindness and the hope of immortality, the tiger, in midair, tried to change his course. His coordination was not quite good enough. He hit the man, not the direct clean hit he would have made if he hadn't tried to swerve, but just enough to inflict a nasty wound that would deny the man his favorite sports for half a year or more.

The man felt pain, both in his battered flesh and in his disillusioned soul. "What an oaf," he thought. "Not nearly so adept as I imagined. I may expect to be confined, for months and months, to pleasures mainly passive. It is bitter, but, I must admit, enlightening as well: tigers are much better in intention, and less good in execution, than they're supposed to be. But will the beast commence a new assault, now single-minded, furious because he has made so lubberly a move? How far does his animal kindness go?"

There was no new assault. The tiger had no heart for it. To his other woes, which he could reasonably assign to the world about him, he had added one that came only from within. "Everybody can make a mistake," he tried to argue. "The best of us have bad days. Consider Justice Holmes, deciding that organized baseball is not a business. Consider Henry II and Becket." But like all true competitors, he found no comfort in such observations; one-time-at-bat-is-not-a-season is a truth but not a solace. He couldn't bring himself to start from scratch and kill the man he should have killed the first time round or altogether spared. It would just be messy; it had no class; he slunk away.

When the tiger got home, his mate, having sent the cubs to visit and busy cleaning up, turned to greet him: "How many times do I have to tell you not to come in tracking blood? But I take it you finally got us something to eat?" "No, I didn't," answered the tiger miserably.

This time she did not snarl. She searched the tiger's face in a way he wasn't sure he understood. "Well," she said, "I guess things are tough for other families in the jungle too. Prey is tight these days. Don't feel so bad." They were silent for a moment. "C'mere," she said.

EPILOGUE

The book to which the man had fleetingly adverted was a book of history. Immediately after the event described—that is, the event as last described—he resumed his work on it. The publisher, he reflected, had paid him an advance. Suppose he had been eaten by the tiger. He would leave no more than notes and ruminations. His estate would have a hard time keeping the advance. Not to mention the morality of it.

The contemporaneous cogitation the incident provoked had gone to the weakness of statistics and the hazards that minorities confront. But other thoughts, jarred loose from his unconscious, now floated to the surface. "The most prominent, and the least accepted, feature of the universe is its complication," he wrote (in draft). "Nothing is unmixed. There are more factors than we can comprehend, or wish to comprehend, an enormity of factors. Things are neither apocalyptic, as a certain writer is fond of saying, not yet anyway, nor bully, as a certain President was fond of saying. Being wrong," he added, "does not exclude an excellence in writing, though it is a serious disadvantage in a President. Things are just terribly, terribly entangled. Not crazy, not chaotic, but almost insupportably complex. Take the warring schools of history. They may none of them be right; they may, more likely, all of them be right.

"There's something else to learn from what I've just been through," he continued. "Spinoza said—I think he said; I was very young when I read it—there's no such thing as 'possible' or 'likely.' If we had all the facts and made no errors in our logic, we could be sure of what will happen, which is bound to happen anyway. The same for what has happened in the past. The point made by Spinoza—or was it Crescas?—is brilliant, but has not much utility. In the lives we lead, a rigid determinism, whatever its philosophical validity, merely dissipates our energies. For human purposes (or purposes tigrine), it's better to acknowledge this, and not shy away from 'probably' and 'maybe.' Indeed, unless we wish to swindle ourselves, the acknowledgment is necessary. Understanding how things are, or were, must include a range of chances. And speaking of philosophers, I would like Descartes better if he had said, 'I think I think; therefore I think I am.' "

Inspired by the encounter, and chairbound by his injury, the man in a brief few months delivered to his publisher a splendid manuscript. That is, if the tiger missed. Otherwise, the man's secretary took the unfinished material he had written, added a few things of her own, and sent it in. The publisher didn't really care which way it was. "It's how you sell the book that counts," he always said.

2
Battle

Ashford came before the King's Justices and charged Thornton with murder. He swore that Thornton, "not having the fear of God before his eyes, but being moved and seduced by the instigation of the Devil," had raped Ashford's young sister Mary, and then "did take the said Mary Ashford into both hands and cast her into a pit of water," so that she drowned. Thus did Thornton "kill and murder against the peace of our said lord the king his crown and dignity."

The charge was set out in a writing, at the foot of which Ashford put his mark. When it was presented, the Justices ordered the sheriff of Warwickshire to "attach Thornton by his body, according to the law and custom of England, so that we may have him before us on the morrow of All Souls."

The sheriff found Thornton and brought him to court. Ashford was there. The Justices commanded Thornton to plead to the charge. Thornton replied:

Not guilty; and I am ready to defend the same by my body.

"And thereupon," the scribe tells us, "taking his glove off, he threw it upon the floor of the court."

This was a signal that Thornton demanded trial by battle. He would have the truth of Ashford's charge tested in combat between the two of them. If Ashford won the battle, Thornton would be guilty, and (assuming he survived the battle) Thornton would be hanged. If Thornton won, he would be adjudicated innocent, cleared of the charge of having murdered Mary, and of course not liable for the mayhem or killing of his accuser. It would be possible, indeed, for Thornton to have done away with two Ashfords, sister and brother, without legal retribution, the one killed in passion or in fear, the other by due process of law.

Ashford first claimed the circumstances were exceptional, so that Thornton should be denied the right to defend himself by battle. The Justices were not persuaded, and ruled that the established procedure for cases of this kind must be followed— that is, trial by battle.

Ashford then asked for a few days' time. It was granted. On the day appointed, he returned to court and said he would not fight. The judgment, therefore, necessarily, was that Thornton should go free.

□

It was not the age of the Normans or the Plantagenets, or even the Lancastrians. The case arose in the century preceding our own. The year was 1818.

A hundred and fifty years had passed since Newton set forth his *Principia;* in less than a hundred more, we would have Einstein's theory of relativity. The steam engine had been at work for exactly half a century, and had made a locomotive run on rails and a boat go up and down the Hudson. Darwin would soon embark upon his voyage. In sixty years the telephone would ring.

All the Beethoven symphonies except the Ninth had been performed. Jane Austen's life was over. Soon the French Impressionists would be at work. It was the year of Karl Marx's birth. Abraham Lincoln was a tall young boy. The United States Constitution and its Bill of Rights had been in force for almost thirty years. In 1818 Thornton established his innocence with his glove; seventeen years later Mark Twain, who made such things so laughably archaic, was born, and half a dozen after that, the symbol of modern rational jurisprudence, Mr. Justice Holmes.

It is shocking, barely credible, but not so wild as it appears. Before we make a judgment, let us, as judges must, listen to the story, since every case at law is first of all a story.

□

The word "appeal" has had two meanings in the law. There is the one today familiar: review by a higher court of the judgment of a lower. The other is strange now even to attorneys: it was the name of a criminal proceeding brought not by government but by a private citizen. Its roots went deep in English history. For long years before there was prosecution by the state, there was prosecution by the person wronged (or, in case of homicide, his next of kin). The trial of crime had to wait upon the suit of individuals. There was no governmental accusation, no official pressing of the case, no district attorney or king's counsel. Near the end of the twelfth century, public prosecution came into being: indictment by the sworn testimony of neighbors, under the goad of royal justice. But the private suit for crime did not die out. Appeal and indictment existed side by side.

It was appeal that Ashford brought. The ancient forms were followed. Having found "pledges" to guarantee the fines and costs that he must pay if his suit did not succeed, Ashford obtained the writ that sent the sheriff out. The sheriff came back with Thornton, "whose body I have in his Majesty's gaol," and on the day of hearing set the prisoner at the bar. The charge was read. After an adjournment it was read again, this time, as the court directed, "slowly." A few days later, with accuser and accused both standing at the bar, the charge was read a third time, and Thornton was called upon to plead. It was then he threw the gauntlet.

Appeal for some time had not been much employed, and when it was, it led to trial by jury, as official prosecution had done since early in the thirteenth century. That was the long-established practice. But wager of battle, as a mode of trial when an appeal was lodged, had never been formally abolished, either by Act of Parliament or by judicial renunciation.*

We can only speculate on why in Thornton's case an attempt was made to retrieve the ancient mode. Perhaps the lawyer, struggling with a hard and complicated case, mused wistfully aloud upon a simpler age and the purity of battle, and a desperate client seized on the words he heard. Or perhaps some memory of old ways persisted in the working class of Warwickshire (this knightly plea was made by one the writ described as "labourer"), an old wives' tale not of medicine but law, that Thornton knew

---

* *"Battle" and "combat" are used interchangeably for this kind of trial. It is also called "judicial duel." The term "wage battle" refers not to the fighting itself, but to the party's pledge that he will abide by the outcome. The word is close relative to "wager" in the sense of "gamble." The etymology suggests what sport it is to wage war, to lead an army into battle.*

and asked about. But more probably the tactic was an advocate's conception, outlandish but considered. Here was a case that offered an opportunity both to use the law and (as will appear) to change it, to change it for the better. The demand for battle was, I think, a work of legal intuition, the product of a roaming mind.

Given the enticement of creative action, the lawyer had first of all a client to defend. He had to make a cool appraisal, a guess about the outcome of the tactic he would choose. Was Thornton physically the stronger man, likely to win the duel? Or, no matter what his chances man to man, was the evidence so deadly that the odds were better in the field than in the jury room? Or did the lawyer, believing that the charge was false, calculate that Ashford in the fight would wear the awkward clogs of conscience? Or that the fear which must assail the false accuser might silence Ashford altogether? Or did he think Ashford neither a liar nor a coward but simply a sensible man, who would decline to risk his life in such damn foolishness? Whatever reckoning impelled the choice, it worked.

Thornton having demanded battle, Ashford was given leave to counterplead. "After eight days of St. Martin, in Michaelmas term," Ashford's counterplea, to which he swore, was read. Its thesis was that Thornton had no right to battle. This mode of trial, Ashford argued, if indeed it still existed, had never been appropriate where guilt was strongly indicated. And in the present circumstances, "he saith, there were, and still are, the violent and strong presumptions, and proofs following, that he the said Thornton was guilty of murder."*

When Mary's body was taken from the pit, it was "examined in the presence of divers credible witnesses, and it was manifest that the said Mary Ashford had come to her death by drowning." It was manifest also "that recently before the death some man had forcibly had carnal knowledge of the body of her the said Mary Ashford, and that up to the time of such carnal knowledge she had been and was a virgin."

The crime was done, the counterplea continued, in the early morning of the twenty-sixth of May. The evening before, Mary had been at a dance. Thornton was there, and was heard to say "in gross and obscene language, that he would have carnal knowledge of Mary Ashford or die by it."

---

* In quoting the pleadings, some of their language, mostly formal repetitive phrases, is omitted.

Thornton and Mary danced together until midnight, and left together, and were seen together about three hours later. At four o'clock Mary Ashford went to Mary Butler's house to pick up some clothes; she had dressed there for the dance. She stayed about a quarter of an hour, and was observed to be "in good health and in perfect composure of mind." Then she started her journey home, from Erdington to Langley, walking along Bell Lane. What happened next was shown by footsteps and other marks on the dewy grass and freshly harrowed ground, "carefully examined and compared" by the divers credible witnesses—an approach, a flight, pursuit, and violence. The counterplea gave details to support the general statements in the count:

> There appeared upon each of the arms of her the said Mary Ashford, between the shoulder and the elbow of each of the said arms, the mark and impression of a human hand, the said marks and impressions denoting that each of the arms of Mary Ashford had been grasped and held with violence. And there were stains of blood upon the thighs and private parts and upon the clothes and dress of Mary Ashford; and the front part of the shift wherein the said Mary Ashford was clothed was rent and torn. And upon certain grass growing forty yards from the said pit there was the mark and impression of a human figure, from which said mark and impression it was manifest that a human body had been lying there with the arms and legs thereof extended.

Thornton, with the court's permission, then made a "replication," also sworn. To begin with, said Thornton, he was not obliged to note the counterplea at all; he was by dint of law privileged to wage his battle. Moreover, contrary to what Ashford said, there were no "violent and strong presumptions" that he had done the murder. He picked up the story where Mary Ashford left Mary Butler's house. About a quarter past four, a witness saw her, alone, not accompanied by Thornton; again, about a quarter hour later, another witness saw her, still alone. Then Thornton was seen, between half past four and twenty-five to five, "walking very slowly, leisurely, and composedly" along the lane leading to the house of his father, with whom he lived.

This was evidence tending to establish an alibi—a plea of elsewhere. It having been averred that the crime occurred at such a time and such a place, defendant offers proof that at that time he was at another place. Thornton's replication filled out the alibi with facts of time and distance. If his witnesses were telling the truth, he could not have been where he must have been to commit the crime described.*

What does it look like? The alibi is dubiously neat; so many people seem to have had their eyes on clocks. (How many members of the working class in 1818 carried watches?) A man can have friends who will perjure themselves if that will save his life. And beyond a doubt, whatever may have brought them to their union, Mary and Thornton were on that night united. Ashford's counterplea ended by saying that in the morning

> Thornton was searched and stripped in the presence of divers credible witnesses, and the shirt and the breeches of the said Thornton were stained with blood, and Thornton then and there declared that on the then preceding night he had carnal knowledge of the body of the said Mary Ashford by her own consent.

"By her own consent." Thornton did not deny the event, but only that it was forcible. Nor did he deny that, at the dance, he said he would have Mary or die in the attempt.

□

Appeal, as I have mentioned, was older than prosecution by indictment (which began in the late 1100s), and for a while retained a prior place. After jury trial for crime came in, appeal led more often to trial by jury than to trial by battle. In the fourteenth century, it was made subject to a statute of limitation; the private prosecution had to be started within a year and a day of the crime alleged. In deference to appeal's seniority, the Crown would hold back prosecution, by indictment, until the year and a day had passed. But the bringing of an appeal could not be depended on, and it was realized, gradually, that the inhibition of indictment might mean no prosecution at all. After a year, witnesses might be hard to find—in that age of easy violence, gone or dead and gone. So in the sixteenth century new legislation directed that indictment should not wait. But the legislation took pains to

---

The word "alibi" has been dulled down to mean any excuse, and then sharpened up to mean an ego-protecting, semitransparent rationalization for poor performance. For this perversion of meaning we might blame, in part, Ring Lardner and his creature Alibi Ike. If we could ever blame Ring Lardner.

preserve the ancient action, and provided that acquittal on indictment would be no bar to subsequent appeal.

As time went on, personal enforcement of the criminal law
subsided. By the eighteenth century, if wager of battle was unheard of, appeal was at best uncommon. And if battle was terribly
primitive, appeal was terribly unfair. Thornton had once been
tried for the murder of Mary Ashford—indicted and acquitted.
It is wrong that questions of guilt and innocence should turn
on physical contention, but it is an obvious tool of tyranny that
a man tried and found not guilty should be tried all over
again.

In the United States the Constitution forbade double jeopardy, but English law did not. Nor was there in England any
constitutional review, like ours, by which a court could nullify
an Act of Parliament. There is none now. Parliament's last word
on the subject had been that acquittal in public prosecution did
not prevent another trial in appeal. Yet Thornton's lawyer
thought that Thornton, and others caught up by this unreasonable Act, might be saved from double jeopardy by a proper use of
precedent.

Fidelity to precedent has the Latin designation *stare decisis:*
let things decided stand decided. It is fundamental to all law,
but especially our common law. *Stare decisis* was involved in
the three main issues of the case. Was the ancient system of
appeal still part of English law? If so, was trial by battle part of
it? Third, was any exception to the rule of battle applicable in
this case?

As to the first, there could be little question, and Ashford's
lawyer raised none. Although for centuries appeal had been
rarely used, no Act of Parliament had declared it dead, no court
had doubted its existence.

If appeal was still alive, was battle too? Could post-En-
lightenment, highly civilized English judges stomach so savage
a test of truth? In general, our courts will not decide a broad
issue when a narrow one will do. In part this reflects our adversary system: courts are to dispose of the dispute between the
parties, not try to legislate. In part, it is simply the wisest course
in a precedential system: each case is different, and a grand
statement of principle may sound perfect in the case before the
court and foolish when the facts are altered just a bit. So hold
back the question whether trial by battle has entirely vanished
from our law. We shall not have to reach that question if one of

its exceptions shows that at any rate it is not available in the present case.

□

Apart from urging that trial by battle was by this date absurd, Ashford's lawyer could argue that exceptions ate up most of it and that one in particular excluded battle here. From the beginning, eight centuries earlier, there had been exceptions. His opponent conceded some were clear and well established: if the accuser was a woman, or a man too old or a boy too young to fight, or one who had been maimed, or if the defendant had escaped from prison, or where a charter gave a special privilege to a group. (Such a charter relieved accusing Londoners of the need to underwrite their accusations with limb and life.)

A more troublesome exception was the one Ashford's lawyer stressed: a case that at the outset supplied strong evidence of guilt. The venerable authorities gave these instances: a man captured at the scene of murder with a bloody weapon in his hand; a master and a servant who slept in one house, the master found dead in the morning and the servant missing; a thief "taken with mainour"—that is, with the loot in his possession.

In olden days, such evidence of crime led immediately to execution; the accused had no right to battle, or to any other kind of trial. In time, Ashford's lawyer pointed out, the law grew less peremptory; trial by jury came into being, and, instead of facing instant death, the accused could face a jury. It remained the law, however, that trial by battle was by such circumstances ousted. The second trial that appeal afforded would be by a second jury.

Ashford's lawyer cited the revered commentaries of Glanvil, written in the twelfth century, and of Bracton, written in the thirteenth. He also cited Fleta and Britton, who wrote a few years later, and Staunford, a lesser light but more recent, who might be said to represent a relatively modern view. In the sixteenth century Staunford laid it down:

> The reason why a man in an appeal shall be admitted to try by battel, seems to be this, that no evident or probable matter appears against him.

This turned the thing around, and made combat the exception, available where innocence was likely anyway.

Ashford's lawyer, Chitty, was famous; his treatises are still read today. Thornton's lawyer, Tindal, less celebrated, beat him. Tindal went even further back in history. He began by reminding the court that trial by combat was brought to England by the Normans. Therefore, Tindal reasoned, "it seems material to examine into their books on this subject."*

The Norman books emphasized the defendant's right to elect battle, to cast his "gage," or, as Lord Coke some time later put it, "to try it body to body." The election might now be rare, but the right, said Tindal, was firm, the doctrine undiminished. There were exceptions, true, but if the accuser did not wish to fight, he had the legal burden: he must demonstrate that the situation fell among the exceptions.

The report of the case does not tell how Tindal persuaded the court that Ashford failed to bear the burden. Perhaps he began by arguing that the pleadings left room for more than one account of Mary's death. Thornton had declared he wanted Mary, desperately, and she danced with him till midnight, and met him in the fields. But these, the undisputed facts, hardly prove a murder. Thornton's recital of where he was after Mary started home was specific, and fit together. He named the witnesses who would support it, and if they were perjurors, Thornton, for a murderous man, had an extraordinary number of deeply loyal friends. Ashford's counterplea, in contrast, relied heavily on those nameless "divers credible witnesses."

So Thornton did have carnal knowledge of Mary. And she of him. It is as plausible there was tenderness before Mary went to the Butler house as there was rape by Thornton later. The bloody

---

* The steadfast English: in 1818 the Normans still are "they." A people of thoroughly mixed blood who might settle on any one or more of a variety of ancestors—Celtic Britons, Anglo-Saxons, Danes, Viking-French, a touch of Roman; any visitor today can see the different faces and combinations of them—the English deem all but Anglo-Saxons alien. Though in the course of history they have generally been winners, the English accept, indeed insist upon, the livery of a group best known in history for being vanquished. Is it an embarrassment of success, some need to apologize for having done so well, that makes them choose a set of losers? (Their land has not been successfully invaded for nine hundred years; last time it happened it was under Anglo-Saxon management.) Or does their odd allegiance to an ordering of classes create uneasiness, so that Englishmen, remorseful, must introduce themselves as Gurth and Wamba?

garments proved no more than virginity. Chitty thought he helped his client's case by stating that Mary arrived at the Butler house "in good health and in perfect composure of mind." But the statement points the other way as well. Sweetly humming, a witness might have added.

There was evidence of pursuit and violence along the lane from Erdington to Langley. But on our last hypothesis, if it was Thornton Mary met, there was no need for violence. Mary, one judge remarked, might have walked too near the open pit and fallen. Not likely, but granted there was rape and murder, it could have been another man. Thornton might have been the man of Mary's choice; another—envious, repellent—might have followed him.

It could even have been Ashford. We need not posit open incest. Translate it to a passion socially approved, but carried past the measure society allowed. Mary dishonored the name of Ashford, unless there could be a public record that she resisted to the death. If this young virgin lay with another man, she was no longer his sister; she might as well be dead. Vent the rage, simulate the rape, save the family name. This might explain Ashford's obdurate invocation of the law, his not resting with one jury's verdict.

There were, then, other possibilities. The sworn counter-plea was not final proof that Thornton murdered Mary. But did it have to be? How much proof must Ashford offer, to negate the right of combat?

Consider the examples in the commentaries. They denied the right where proof of guilt was far short of what we now would deem conclusive. The one holding the bloody knife might have wrested it from the assailant, who escaped while the hero sought to aid the victim. Or the accused might have found the fallen victim and drawn the weapon in a vain attempt to save his life. The servant could have slumbered soundly through the criminal intrusion, awakened in the early morning to find his master dead, and fled in panic. One with stolen goods in his possession could have come upon them innocently. Yet trial by battle in each such case must be rejected, the authorities proclaimed, authorities who spoke when battle was still familiar. Probability was enough.

So in Thornton's case. He had made his extravagant avowal. He admitted the embrace. There was evidence of violence. And that night Mary died. Other explanations can be imagined, but the plainest is that Thornton murdered her. That there might be other explanations would not have saved the right of combat in the time when Glanvil wrote.

□

Return to *stare decisis*. Our courts by and large are bound to follow precedent. A precedent is a decision on a given set of facts (given by the evidence the litigants present, sifted by the judge and jury). The decision embodies a principle which will govern this set of facts and others similar enough. "Similar enough," of course, is no sharp canon. A cluster of situations, related but diverse, are deemed to be the same, because it is concluded that all of them—for social, political, and/or moral reasons—should be treated in a uniform way.*

If the cluster is too large, the law becomes insensitive, loses touch with justice, and the chances of its working hardship in a given case are high. If it is too small, the law is lost in niceties, people don't know where they stand, and the chances of corruption in a given case are high. A principle by definition must have some generality; it must spread over a number of particulars dissimilar in some respects but alike in essence. How large that number, how broad the rule, what constitutes the essence, where the principle should stop and another principle begin—that is the heart of the law. The answer will vary according to the purpose of the rule, the need it seeks to meet, the problems in administering it, the requirements of fairness.

The process of forming precedent includes description of the instance—the fixing of facts, not in the sense of resolving conflicts in the testimony but, such conflicts settled, in measuring importance. The story that makes a case at law is necessarily composed, not naturally presented. Each person in the case has

---

* *I pause to argue, respectfully, with His Honor Fowler. (Lawyers come to understand the uses, and the weaknesses, of authoritative texts.) Those who scorn "and/or" as legal cant might ponder other ways to convey the meaning. Thus, here, this group of concepts; social reasons; moral reasons; political reasons; reasons social and political; reasons social and moral; reasons political and moral; reasons social, political, and moral. "And/or" permits the use of five words in place of twenty-three. Language developed for legal purposes is sometimes bad, sometimes good. Indiscriminate derision of it is a vulgar substitute for wit, something close to finding a mine of humor in an alien's idiom and accent.*

an infinity of traits. An infinity of events occurs at every moment. What selection should be made? (The historian and the novelist are familiar with the task.) The indications of violence, Thornton's motivation, his opportunity, his alibi—these of course were central. But what else? The fact that Mary Ashford was a virgin? That her death occurred by drowning? That it occurred in Warwickshire? That Thornton was a laborer? The crime committed on the twenty-sixth of May? Committed in 1818? Of these, one had immense significance—the one last mentioned, the year. Part of every case at law is the state of the world at the time the case arises.

The point is insufficiently recognized except in one field of law: we often hear that the Constitution must be adjusted to current conditions. Take, for example, the power given Congress to regulate commerce among the states. This grant has been the basis for a mass of welfare legislation and a national control of our economy which would astonish (for a minute, anyway) the men who wrote the Constitution. But their astonishment would not show that their words had been distorted. In our interrelated economy, where state boundaries are largely an impertinence, the Founding Fathers' words must have a meaning they could not have had when the young states indeed were separate. They intended to give Congress authority over interstate commerce; the times, and not the courts, enlarged the grant. If their intent is to be fulfilled, interstate commerce must be seen as it is at the time when Congress acts, not as it was at the time Congress's charter was drafted.

Take another section of the Constitution: the First Amendment's guarantee of freedom of the press. In 1787 the press, quite literally, the printing press, was the only instrument by which ideas could spread—other than word of mouth, much less efficient, protected by the companion phrase, "freedom of speech." There was no other way to market ideas wholesale. But the framers were concerned with the spread of ideas, not with the particular machinery by which it was done. So films, radio, television, as they come into being, are considered "press" and receive the cover of the guarantee. Such holdings by our courts are not undisciplined extension of the rule the First Amendment states; they are a strict adherence to it.

That the Constitution has been made flexible is a commonplace. What is not generally appreciated is that a similar process, though more constrained, applies throughout the law. Rules are rarely altered by the courts, in 1818 even less than now. But it is principle working on circumstance that yields decision. The set of facts in every case at law includes the world about us. Though the case as the lawyers state it sounds very like the precedent, the decision can be different if the world is now significantly different. These precedent-bending changes go beyond economics and technology. Those that count as significant for the purpose—that lead to different ends while the rule remains the same—may be less palpable. In medieval England the appearance of a crime was enough to hang a man. The reason was not alone the daily cruelty, though that was much of it. People of the Middle Ages were not much bothered by a hanging (of someone else), or by the more horrid death that those in power, secular or clerical, so readily imposed; many people—never all, unquestionably a greater number then than now—found pleasure in the execution. But it was more than that. The medieval mind loved certainty and loathed the contemplation of alternatives. The quantum of evidence that could form a presumption of guilt was by our standards small.

It will upset some readers to hear that human beings have in the last one thousand years improved. But the graph of Western history shows a clear if crooked line—weaving, wayward, but in its main path undeniable—of morality ascending. Whether the line will reach high enough fast enough to save us from destruction is another matter. So is whether one should be disgusted by its current level. But we have come a long way from those centuries when most men of Christendom were slaves, and not just knighthood but the intellectuals of the time, the churchmen, found ecstasy in massacre: ". . . one rode in blood up to the knees and even to the horses' bridles, by the just and marvellous Judgment of God."*

From Glanvil's day to the time of *Ashford versus Thornton,* a great deal more than political shift and industrial revolution

---

* *There has been a recent tendency to rehabilitate the Middle Ages, to tell us they were much better than an earlier generation of liberal historians would have had us believe. To some extent it is religion defending itself. To some extent it reflects the need of those troubled by today's uncertainties to climb back into an Age of Faith. To some extent it is professional: the need of writers (of history as of other things) to say something different from what has been said before. The case is made by ignoring the daily life, and death, of most of those who inhabited the Middle Ages.*

had taken place. People were different inside. They no longer killed so cheerfully. They were less fearful of a complicated universe, a shade less anxious to clutch at simple answers. They could, in law as elsewhere, more readily acknowledge the existence of a doubt. So, in law, the meaning of "presumption" had synchronously changed.

We do not take away a person's life, the Justices decided, or even change his legal rights, on evidence of guilt that would have satisfied the medieval mind. Wager of battle, it is true, will be denied where there is sufficient proof of guilt. However, though what Ashford shows might once have been sufficient, it is not sufficient now. We acknowledge the exception, and we accept its words. But the moral glossary has changed.

The court did not say all this. On the issue to which the lawyers addressed their main energies, the scope of the exception, the opinions hardly went beyond a statement of conclusion: the degree of proof required, they said, had not been demonstrated. The Justices failed to meet, head on, the authorities Chitty cited. But the report of the case discloses the feeling that informed their ruling. Not in his opinion, but by the way of interjection during argument, the Lord Chief Justice Ellenborough said:

> It certainly makes one retire with a degree of horror from the consideration of such laws, which prevented a man from explaining circumstances which, after all, were only prima facie, and not conclusive evidence against him.

It is true that Ellenborough's words relate to an earlier time, when denial of the right to battle meant no trial at all. Ashford was not asking that; he was only asking that Thornton go before another jury, to which Thornton could explain away the implications. But he had explained them once already, and been acquitted, and to put him through a second trial offended the nineteenth-century sense of justice more deeply than no-trial-at-all offended the sense of justice of the Middle Ages.

□

So much for the exception. How about the rule itself? Could it still be law that defense could be by battle, that guilt or innocence should turn on formal violence? If time works changes in law, could the court really hold, at this late date, that might made right?

Here the judicial task was different. "Interstate commerce," "the press," "presumption" are words that have large loose legal meanings. When the court was dealing with the presumption, it was dealing with definition and degree: how strong must be appearances to amount to a presumption? But once the presumption was out of the case, the unabolished, unaltered old law of appeal called for trial by battle. The fact that in recent centuries defendants had waived the right, and chosen trial by jury instead, did not deny the right. Trial by jury cannot be called trial by battle except in metaphor. The law often uses metaphor, but not to negate a rule in so flat and simple a way.

Yet even where degree and definition do not provide the vehicle, courts can move the law. It was open to this court to say that combat was no longer part of English law, that it had gradually been shed. Staunford's statement marked its vitiation, and that had been three hundred years before. The common law comes from sanctioned custom—custom so ancient, the old texts tell us, that "man's memory runneth not to the contrary." But custom must at some date be born, and must eventually die. Trial by duel had long since fallen into disuse, was now thoroughly unaccustomed. If a rationale was needed, the court might have pointed out that judicial combat had a strong religious element —God, in theory, chose the winner—and it had come into the law when England was under the Church of Rome. Having grown independent of that Church, and abandoned its theology, England could cast aside its legal relics too.

It was open to the court, but not obligatory. *Stare decisis* should ordinarily mean what it appears to mean, so that the law is decently reliable, comprehensible to the average person advised by his average lawyer. Some issues (like the scope of the exception Chitty cited) demand a change, or what seems to be a change. Some changes are more abrupt than that, and yet are justified by social need and policy. The tensile toughness of our law has made it live and work where a more brittle structure would by now have crumbled into powder. There are situations that offer judges a choice (intelligent judges, not those who feel free to go one way or another because they hardly know which way to go). A departure can be justified; so can a clinging to the past. Thus trial by battle. There was sufficient warrant for judicial declaration of its demise. On the other hand, the court was not obliged to take the step; no case or authority had yet cast doubt on the existence of that mode of trial. *Stare decisis,* on this issue, gave the court an option.

Let me suggest that these judges, for good if inexplicit reason, did not want to rule that trial by battle had vanished from the law. The reason was that on the action of appeal itself they had no option; they could not by judicial decision abolish it. Yet they felt, rightly, that the law should be rid of appeal.

Arguments can be made in favor of appeal. It can be said that the assaulted victim, or the dead man's widow, or the dead girl's brother, should have the right to ask the courts to act upon the crime. Suppose prosecuting officials are lax, or incompetent, or corrupt. But the arguments the other way are better. Even if double jeopardy is not involved, appeal should not be part of the legal plan. Paranoid accusers are too many and too ready, the hardship on innocent defendants is too great. There is opportunity for cynical extortion. And though the wish to prosecute be honest, it is an ugly notion that the law should for its enforcement tap the springs of private vengeance. Administration of the criminal law is best left in public hands.

The abolition of appeal, however, was the kind of change our legal system puts beyond the reach of judges. Though it had its origin in the common law, appeal had gotten Parliamentary sanction. Parliament (once King-in-Parliament, before that King-in-Council) is in British law supreme, just as here, in proper legislative matters, Congress is supreme (a point some Congressmen can hardly bear to face). The fourteenth-century statute had made appeal statutory, no longer part of the pliant common law. The extinction of appeal, if it was to be extinguished, had to come from another statute. The courts can, and often do, interpret legislation; they must in concrete situations give the statutory words their meaning. But they cannot simply overrule the statute. (Unless, in the United States, they find conflict with the Constitution; in no event in Britain.) So though the Justices had an option on whether to keep battle, they had no option on appeal. Parliament had endowed appeal with legislative standing. If it was to disappear, Parliament would have to make it go.

But the Justices might unsettle Parliament. If you insist on keeping this procedure, now unwise, they silently proclaimed, take it with all its thorns. We cannot abolish appeal, but we can choose not to abolish combat. We will be immovable conservatives and thus, perhaps, induce some movement in the law. We will carry adherence to the past to its unpalatable extreme. However abhorrent a trial by force of arms may be, we hold it an unavoidable part of the action of appeal. Archaism counters archaism.

Thornton might be saved from double jeopardy—and, much more important, the oppression of the statute might be lifted—by stubborn application of a primitive procedure. The judges had to be brave enough, counsel having been persuasive enough, to declare barbaric ridiculous trial by combat still prevailing law. They had to be prepared to face the shallow criticism (which came) that they were living in the past. The court managed. The Lord Chief Justice announced, unblinking, that in any action of appeal, battle was "the usual and constitutional mode of trial."

□

One of his brethren on the bench came closer to expressing the underlying thought. Justice Bayley, delivering his opinion, said:

> This mode of proceeding, by appeal, is unusual in our law, being brought, not for the benefit of the public, but for that of the party, and being a private suit, wholly under his control. It ought, therefore, to be watched very narrowly by the court; for it may take place after trial and acquittal on an indictment at the suit of the King; and the execution under it is entirely at the option of the party suing, whose sole object it may be to obtain a pecuniary satisfaction.

Having made his comment on appeal and the kind of person who would bring it, the Justice allowed a bit of feeling to emerge, and drove home the holding of the court with some pardonable relish:

> One inconvenience attending this mode of proceeding is, that the party who institutes it must be willing, if required, to stake his life in support of his accusation.

An English inconvenience.

The Lord Chief Justice, drier, returned to sum it up:

> The general law of the land is in favour of the wager of battle, and it is our duty to pronounce the law as it is, and not as we may wish it to be. Whatever prejudices therefore may justly exist against this mode of trial, still as it is the law of the land, the Court must pronounce judgement for it.

So sorry, Lord Ellenborough was saying. Wager of battle is beastly. But there is nothing we can do about it; it remains the law. (Unless, though I will not say so, you legislators change it.)

There was a loud outcry against the atavistic ruling, loud enough to wake up Parliament. The next year, 1819, a statute ended trial by battle. And while Parliament had its mind upon the matter, it ended appeal as well.

3

Taxonomy

The law, like other intellectual products that we impose on nature, is arranged in classes. Rules and precedents are grouped, for argument in court and for decision, for study of the law, and for common understanding. The design is sometimes given institutional expression: separate courts for different kinds of cases.

This, of course, is not remarkable. What is remarkable is how lissome the arrangement is; and how, as the law grows more sophisticated, the design keeps getting dimmer.

To some extent, the classification follows nature, the law reflecting varieties of human conduct and transaction. To some extent, it is jurisprudential, the work of those who undertake to analyze the law. For the most part, though, it is history's improvisation.

In the beginning, categories hardly mattered. Later, commentators fell in love with them, constructing an ontology, and those who practiced law obediently followed. But the lines of demarcation were never altogether clear, and in the course of time, in recent years especially, they have become less clear. Often they are not lines so much as swampy separations, with interpenetrating ebb and flow. Yet they are convenient. This chapter will describe the principal divisions.

And incidentally give some glossary. Not much; the law has not the need of special language most laymen think it has. The law has not the need, but lawyers tend to act as though it did. This is in part incompetence—it is easier to repeat a baggy formula than find words that really fit—and in part exploitation of man's liability to magic. For centuries our lawyers, a priestly caste, used a mysterious tongue, composed of Latin, French, English, incantation and a bit of mumbling. These continue, more or less, to the present day—Latin less, English more, French absorbed, incantation down a bit, mumbling steady.

CRIMINAL LAW AND CIVIL LAW

Criminal law has to do with relations between the misbehaving individual and his government, civil law with relations among individuals. "Individuals" here includes groups treated by the law as entities (not all the time, not all to the same extent): corporations, unions, partnerships, some other forms of association.

The criminal law establishes rules of conduct; their breach, if prosecuted and if conviction follows, results in punishment. The government then takes away the convict's freedom, or his money, or some of each, or (hardly ever nowadays) kills him. In earlier centuries there were other penalties: maiming, torture, abjuration of the realm, forfeiture of property (not in order of horror necessarily, as rated by contemporaries).

In a criminal case, the government is a litigating party, "the prosecution"—in Great Britain the King or Queen, in the United States the People. Judge and jury are also government, but, dishonesty aside, there is no collegial consequence. The judging officers of the government, unless they themselves are criminal, show no favor to the prosecuting officers. (You see the importance of an independent judiciary, independent of the rest of government. The independence, not yet entire, is relatively new. It has been a long hard fight, largely won but not yet over. Franklin Roosevelt was obtuse about it, and Nixon fought on the other side.)*

---

* The needed next step is an institution independent even of the judiciary—a powerful, skeptical office that can watch, indict and prosecute (in a separate court) all three branches of the government. The Special Prosecutor of the Nixon Administration provides a sort of shanty antecedent, much like other jerry-built beginnings of certain legal institutions. Partly because of its dubious provenance—a shotgun marriage of a most reluctant groom (the President proposed, Congress prodding)

The civil law seeks to enforce the claims of individuals upon each other. The government is present only as judge and jury (except to the extent, not significant in this context, that lawyers are looked upon as officers of the court). The outcome of a civil case, in form at least, is usually not punishment; it is a remedy. The successful plaintiff obtains a sum of money, called "damages," which theoretically repairs his hurt—a translation of injury into dollars when there is a tort, of disappointed expectations when there is a breach of contract. Or, in special situations, instead of money a decree forbidding the defendant to repeat his depredation or commanding him to keep his promise.

The criminal law, on the other hand, is not directed to redress of the victim's loss. It used to be. Its main interest now is collective, the safety of society at large. It may bring money to the government (in the form of fines), but not to the person from whom the goods or cash were taken. Restitution is an occasional byproduct, but restitution is a voluntary act of the defendant, tribute to his conscience (rarely) or an effort to obtain a lighter sentence (ordinarily).

The criminal law establishes prohibitions thought necessary or beneficial and through penalties tries to enforce them. It tries in several ways. It seeks to teach the miscreant, by jailing him, the unwisdom of recidivism, and more realistically (the didactic effort doubtful) to close his opportunities for a while. Looking beyond the individual who is prosecuted, the criminal law, by advertising the possibility of penalty, aims to deter all of us from engaging in the disapproved behavior. Two other goals of the

---

and a hesitant bride (Leon Jaworski never really seemed to like what he was called upon to do)—the office functioned poorly on a patently strong case. Consider Jaworski's ex cathedra pronouncement that a President cannot be indicted, and his reduction of the charge against Kleindienst, an Attorney General who, under oath, lied on a question of the gravest import, and then received a minimal sentence, and even that suspended. (This is no disparagement of Jaworski's staff, which did well considering its handicaps.) Contrast it with the work of Senator Sam Ervin, who with fewer legal weapons and less staff, but with greater wisdom and a better understanding of the Constitution, contributed much more.

There is no satisfactory model in our own history, but the Swedes have given us a fine one in their ombudsman.

criminal law are one of them ostensibly archaic and the other mainly hopeful: vengeance, which we now disclaim, and rehabilitation, which has recently lost credit. Then there is the widely held, and dearly held, idea of retribution (which in my view is vengeance in the mask of justice). And, finally, the criminal law has indirect effects, which I will come to in a moment.*

With its characteristic disdain for nice categories, our law provides for civil suits by government, to collect its taxes, for example, or to try to dismember monopolies. Reciprocally, in certain actions between private parties—libel, for example— there is once in a while an additional award, called "exemplary" or "punitive," whose main purpose is not to compensate but punish. And quite apart from the exceptional case in which such an award is imposed, the civil law generates its own deterrence. One may be impelled to honor a contract not because honor is involved, but because a court may make it costly not to. One may hesitate to hurl an insult because a libel action can make it extravagant indulgence. Even when plaintiff's claim is weak, defending a civil suit is usually expensive, and for most of us unpleasant. There are lawyers' fees, other charges (stenographers' recording of depositions, for example), and, for many litigants the most expensive element, the drain on time and energy.

In the United States, the "costs" the winner ordinarily gets are far from reimbursement; they are nominal. There are statutory exceptions: the Copyright Act, for instance, provides that the loser in an infringement suit may in aggravated circumstances—a willful infringement by defendant, a frivolous claim by plaintiff—be ordered to pay counsel fees and other expenses to the winner, but the amount the court awards is almost always smaller than the lawyer's bill. There are other statutes that establish a legal right and authorize recovery of litigation expense when the right is successfully sued on, and at least one court has asserted a general judicial power to award legal fees whenever a claim is baseless and badly motivated. Usually, however, the litigant in this country must bear his own expenses, no matter how emphatic his victory. In England, the situation is different: the courts have broad discretionary power to impose actual costs, and exercise it vigorously. For example, the Scientologists sued

---

* The terms "private law" and "public law," used more by Continental jurists than our own, correspond roughly to the civil– criminal division, though their emphasis is more on what is regulated than on how the regulation is effected.

a Member of Parliament for libel. He had made his charges in a broadcast, outside the shelter of Parliamentary debate. Nevertheless, the plaintiffs lost, and, in addition to the award of damages, they were ordered to pay the defendant £27,000 for his expenses, and the pound was worth more then.

Neither the American nor the English system works. The American departure from the English tradition was a populist manifestation: the impecunious plaintiff, it was felt, should not have to face the prospect of double fees. But he has to pay his own, no matter how valid his claim, which means he gets less than his due. As for the English litigant, although he may recover his own expenses if he wins, he may have to pay both sides' expenses if he loses. Since litigation is always risky, the English plaintiff is inhibited by the thought of double fees. Correlative considerations affect defendants.*

The expenses of litigation deny justice, partially or completely. A plaintiff is advised to relinquish a valid claim because it will cost too much to sue; a defendant is advised to pay a groundless claim because it will cost too much to defend. If the case is brought to court, neither party, no matter how successful, can count on perfect justice. A victorious plaintiff does not get an amount that compensates his injury or loss, but only that amount minus his expenses. A victorious defendant comes away not whole, but poorer by the cost of proving he owed nothing to the plaintiff.

This led me to suggest, some years ago, that lawyers in litigation should be paid not by their clients but by the government. Lawyers are theoretically officers of the court, and their services in our adversary system are as much a part of the attempt to achieve justice as the services of judges, clerks and bailiffs. The theory should be given real effect, and lawyers should get their compensation from the judicial institution rather than from those who find the need to use it. I will speak of this in more detail in a later chapter.

The suggestion aroused no enthusiasm. Lawyers are afraid they would have smaller incomes. Legislators hate to spend

---

*Another difference gives the American plaintiff an advantage over the English plaintiff. America has the contingent fee, an arrangement under which the plaintiff's lawyer is paid only if successful, usually by a share in the award. It is common in this country—especially in personal-injury cases—and forbidden in Great Britain.

money for abstract justice—that is, for justice which no particular power group demands. There are also some legitimate objections.

□

The categories, I have warned, are not sharp and solid. The civil law, as we have seen, can serve a public rather than a private purpose, and deter misconduct. The criminal law, on the other hand, is not always a deterrent. There are individuals whose psychic structure is such that the prospect of punishment does not deter, and some for whom it may even be inducement. And on a more rational, and more odious, level, corporate management often regards a fine imposed in a criminal prosecution as no cause for shame, merely an item of expense in the operating statement. Conscious violation of environmental regulations provides examples, and, in 1972 especially, violation of election laws. Corporations cannot go to jail, and the prospective fine (a dim prospect usually) is less than management estimates the gain will be.

But the distinction between the deterrent effects of criminal and civil law exists, psychologically at least, and therefore practically. A postulate of civilization is that rules be generally observed. Citizens must have a habit of obedience to law, must respect the rules, must ordinarily follow them even when they expect a breach will not be found or punished.

This is plainly not a universal habit; there are many wicked people, or, if you prefer, psychopaths. (Rarely perfect psychopaths, but often in a measure—from murderers down to bribers, or, in damage to society, from bribers down to murderers.) But the habit of obedience to law is present; it is present to the extent that we are civilized, and the extent is obviously large. If it were not, society would not exist. We could not feed or shelter ourselves without the products of a peaceable economy. Most people are most of the time law-abiding. If they were not, this intricate delicate machinery in which we live would stop. After some unimportant violence, nearly everyone would die.

We are apt to separate morality and the law, and for certain purposes the separation is valid. But it is hugely overworked, and in a fundamental sense invalid. If the survival of society has value, obedience to the law is itself a moral need. This is felt, if not recognized, by most people most of the time.

The kind of law to which this habit of obedience is directed is usually the criminal law. It carries a higher charge of moral sanction than the civil law. We have one sort of accustomed response where conduct is declared a crime, another where its only consequence is civil liability. There is less moral feeling about breaching contracts or doing harm not designated criminal.

An engaging school of jurisprudence divorces civil law from morals altogether. The idea is that the civil law merely sets alternatives. Assuming no criminal behavior is involved—no criminal fraud, no willful assault, no robbery or perjury—the law of tort and contract, it has been said, does no more than put a price on violation. Take breach of contract. You sign a paper saying you will furnish goods or services. Does the law demand you do? Or does it only say that if you don't, and if the other party sues, and if he is successful, you will have to pay him money? To put this jurisprudence in the bluntest terms, one's promise in the law is the taking of an option: one may either keep the promise or run the risk of judgment—not moral judgment, simply a dispassionate court order to pay money. The same analysis can be applied to torts. (A tort is a legal wrong for which there is civil liability, one of a large and varied class; we can define the class, simply, as the residue left when we subtract breach of contract from the totality of civil wrongs.) Thus negligence, the commonest tort: we are free to be as careless as we like (short of the gross recklessness that may amount to crime) so long as we are willing to assume the cost of the damage that we do. Or a rather special kind of tort, copyright infringement: the amount a court may make you pay for your plagiarism is in effect a permissions fee —higher than what you might have bargained for, but not certain to be exacted.*

This jurisprudence, broached in the late nineteenth century, went counter to the way people had thought about the law. It was luminous, and intriguing, as any idea new and graceful is intriguing, and nicely unsentimental. Its principal early proponent was Oliver Wendell Holmes (the lawyer, not the literary doctor; later Justice Holmes). It is part of the school of jurisprudence now known as "legal realism." There is no connection with Platonic realism; on the contrary, the bias is empirical, and the concepts uncongenial to the philosophy of Plato.

But legal realism in its strictest form is not altogether realis-

---

* A similar analysis might be made of the criminal law: you have the option of obeying or running the risk of punishment. But here it would have less validity, because of our different feelings about civil and criminal law.

tic. Courts are not that sharp in their analysis. They continue to get the law and morality all mixed up. When legal doctrine leaves them room, as it often does, they react unfavorably to shabby dealing and to inconsiderate behavior. They are inclined to regard a promise as a promise, in the law or out of it. This tendency to fold morality into the law has grown stronger in the course of legal history. While our legal philosophers become more acute, the courts, in this respect, get fuzzier. Thank the Lord.

COMMON LAW AND STATUTE

The term "civil law" has another, quite different meaning. It designates the legal systems, existing mainly on the continent of Europe, that derive from Roman law. In this sense, "civil law" is distinguished not from "criminal law" but from "common law" —the Roman system from the Anglo-American. And a civilian, in this context, is an expert in the Roman law, in or out of uniform (the uniform in this instance being vestment).

"Common law" too has other meanings. They depend on what it is opposed to. In the paragraph above, it is opposed to the law of other countries; in the paragraphs that follow—within the Anglo-American system, and whether the law is criminal or civil—it is opposed to statute. Here the distinguishing feature is the source of the law. This is a second important division.

Legal scholars have differed on the essence of the common law. At first it was thought to be, and pretty much was, an expression of custom and usage. The early common lawyers regarded it as pre-existing: it is the law because it always was the law. In later centuries the common law was seen not as part of history, but as part of Nature, or Divinity, or Reason. In either of these views, the common law dwells outside of court, and the judge's obligation is to find it and declare it, not presume that he can make it.

Statutory law, on the other hand, is unquestionably made. It is produced by legislative bodies: Congress, state assemblies, Parliament, once King-in-Council. When these bodies legislate, something new is added to the law or something old is put away. This is done by deliberate act, at a given moment. A statute, as the etymology informs us, is a thing set up, constructed, made to stand.

The common law, in contrast, is continuous and pervasive; its parts are not discrete. It is not designed; it is only applied, to familiar situations (here we have "settled law") or to new ones (here it makes a biological adjustment). It lives a freer life.

Statutes appear in specific written form; the common law does not. Statutes have a certain textual rigidity—not as much as may appear, but the common law has none. Judges, in their opinions, can undertake to state the common law, as can scholars in their writings, but the words have no political authority. Opinions (and, with less force, some nonjudicial scholarly comment) have considerable effect on cases that come later, but it is only "holdings"—how in fact the courts decide the cases put before them—that achieve the force of precedent. And even precedents, according to the older views, are not themselves the common law; rather, they bear witness to it.

□

Here is a place for some vocabulary. A trial is a way of ascertaining facts; to that end it uses examination and cross-examination of witnesses and the study of physical evidence, most prominently documents. The law to be applied is determined by the judge, after hearing, or reading, argument. A brief is an argument written out. Pleading is not legal argument, although, in a use not yet correct, it has taken on that meaning; it is the formal written statement of the litigants' positions. Once pleading had huge significance in the law, and tiny mistakes were fatal; its main modern function is to chart the area of dispute.*

The jury's job is to fix the facts; where there is no jury, the judge takes that job too. A verdict is a jury's doing; a judge's determination, of law or fact, is a decision. The final exercise of judicial power on behalf of one party or the other is a judgment —an acquittal or conviction in a criminal case, a dismissal of the claim or the granting of damages or other remedy in a civil case. A motion is a party's request that something be done in the course of the litigation. An intermediate exercise of judicial power is an order (though there are some judgments known as "final orders").

Certain judgments are called decrees. "Judgment" was orig-

---

* In England all argument to the court is oral, and "brief" has a different meaning. It is the educating memorandum given the barrister, to prepare him for trial or appeal, by the solicitor, who has the primary contact with the client.

inally a word belonging to the courts of common law, and meant, in civil cases, an award of money or a declaration of title or possession. "Decree" is from the courts of Chancery, also known as courts of equity, a direction to the losing side to do something or, more frequently, to refrain from doing something. A jurisdiction is a political space in which a judicial system operates, the state of Minnesota, for example, all of England, for another. In a different sense, jurisdiction means power unrelated to geography: subject-matter jurisdiction (power to deal with certain kinds of cases) and personal jurisdiction (power to force those reached by writ to obey the court's command).

Judgments, decrees and orders are the courts' effective acts. Opinions give their reasons. A holding is a judgment, or an order or decree, together with the chain of reasoning on which it hangs, viewed in the context of the case's facts. Everything else in an opinion is dictum, short for *obiter dictum,* a thing said by the way. A dictum can be persuasive in future cases—depending on the level of the court and the reputation of the judge who voiced it—but persuasive only. The holding is the precedent.

□

The traditional views of the common law have in this century been challenged. The challenge comes from the legal realists, whose basic tenet is that the law is only that which comes to pass when we go to court. The older jurisprudence sees the happenings in court as phenomena of an overarching presence. The newer sees the happenings in court as all there is, and, by way of corollary, stresses heavily what courts do as distinguished from what they say.

In giving reasons for their decisions, judges like to speak of "rules" and "principles." But their declarations sometimes vary oddly from the net effect of their decisions, and so the legal realists suggest we pay attention to results rather than to stated reasons. Meanwhile, subscribers to the older doctrine accept as ultimate neither the results nor the judicial statements (though they give the latter more respect than realists do). As they see it, both are accident opposed to essence, both can be mistaken applications of the law, and so not the law at all. This, for them, resolves the paradox of a fixed abiding law and what seems to be its periodic alteration by the courts.

The older doctrine reached its portliest form in Blackstone's *Commentaries.* Blackstone, unsuccessful as a lawyer, shrewdly turned to teaching law, and his lectures became the volumes published in the 1760s. They had immediate success. Though soon enough, and brilliantly, attacked by Jeremy Bentham ("rhetorical nonsense," he called the *Commentaries,* "nonsense upon stilts"), they survived and dominated most of legal study until fairly recent days. They had particular force in the new United States, where the law was part of a frontier culture starved of reading matter. The *Commentaries* pervaded not only the thought of lawyers but the lay idea of law as well, so durably that in American films of the 1940s the guardhouse lawyer is called "Blackstone" by his buddies.*

Blackstone and those who shared his view—and until the twentieth century most judges and lawyers did share his view—conceived of the common law as an *a priori* set of "eternal, immutable" rules (his words) from which the proper resolution of all disputes could be deduced. The courts had merely to contemplate the noble edifice and lodge the case in one of its apartments.

The *a priori* view of law has had a variety of adherents, changing in the course of time. The earliest were those who simply saw the common law as pre-existing. Their conception was essentially historical, not supernatural (saving the supernatural element that pervades all medieval institutions). The law is law because that's the way things are and ever have been. Though the theory never fit the facts, even as contemporaries saw them, this jurisprudence prevailed for more than a millennium. Blackstone made it grander. The common law is not merely immemorial custom, but something necessary in nature. He was not the first to think so, but, as often happens with a propagandist, he became the most renowned of those who thought so. The common law is a thing transcendent, which judges try to grasp and bring to bear on the clay of specific controversy, though judges sometimes fail. Blackstone had it both ways, rational and super-rational: this common law "the Creator has enabled human reason to discover." The divinely reasonable system was embodied "in a peculiar and emphatical manner" in

---

* *Blackstone's career would be difficult now. Our law schools draw their teachers from those distinguished as students or in practice. Some observers of American college and graduate faculties have said that law school teaching is the most interesting and (subject matter aside) the most enlightening of all.*

the law of England. The Creator was apparently less eager to reveal it to those who were not English.*

In the twentieth century, a related belief has been held by "natural law" adherents, coming mostly from the law schools of the Roman Catholic universities. Here again the law exists independent of the courts, outside the minds of lawyers and of judges. Decisions that do not fit the scheme are errors. For all of these—early common lawyers, Blackstone and his followers, modern natural-law philosophers—the function of the courts is not to invent the law but discover it, whether in custom or in logic or in revelation.

Contemporary legal philosophy, in the main, takes the more secular, empirical approach: the common law is only what the courts have made it. It may be one thing or another depending on which judge is sitting; its principles are best stated as a set of predictions of what the courts will do in future cases.

The controversy is in my opinion splendid, but somewhat less important than the pleasurable philosophy may make it seem. "Natural law," for example, and its cousin "natural rights" were used in the eighteenth century by those who wanted change, who rebelled against established power. But in the 1930s these same slogans were held aloft by those who resisted the Roosevelt revolution, which took some wealth and power from where they were stored and spread them out more widely. The New Deal social and economic legislation, opponents argued, transgressed the natural rights of man in property and contract. Natural law had moved from left to right.

Even conceptually the differences between the warring philosophers are not so great as they appear. Empirical as the modern realists wish to be, they cannot dispense with principle. There is no law unless some number of specific instances, somehow related, are dealt with in a uniform way. Once this is recognized, we have a rule of law, whether we call it an abstraction from a group of judgments, a prediction of results in future cases, a declaration of pre-existing law, or a transcendental truth. And the contrast between the common law and legislation remains, though it is less vivid in the dusty pigments that the realists use.

---

* *The doctrine paid little attention to legislation. A parallel doctrine could, however, be applied, if the legislators' function is analogized to that ascribed to judges: the legislators' function is to discover the true law; bad statutes are just mistakes.*

The differences between the schools of jurisprudence are even smaller if the natural-law proponents are understood to be speaking not of what the law is, but of what law ought to be. It is then a matter of emphasis, and a natural-law philosophy becomes one whose main attention rests not on rules that fallible man has made, but on right rules of law, which will be found in divinity or reason, according to where our faith lies.

□

Yet ideologies have their influence, in the law and out of it. They have consequences that depend not on whether they are true, but on whether they are taken to be true. Today it is accepted that the prime function of legislation is to make changes in the law. For centuries, however, the idea of law as timeless was so strong that legislation introduced itself apologetically, disclaiming all intent to do much more than give expression to existing law.

Thus a statute of William the Conqueror begins: "This I will and order: that all shall have and hold the law of King Edward as to lands and all other things with these additions which I have established for the good of the English people." Similarly, a statute of Henry I: "I give you back King Edward's law with those improvements whereby my father improved it by the counsel of his barons." The old law is still in the law, these kings announce, with a little touch-up here and there.*

These Norman kings in fact were altering the law considerably, else there was no need to mention additions and improvements. But to gain acceptance for their changes they thought it best to say they weren't really making any, hardly. And the prevailing concept affected more than the form of the legislation; it inhibited its substance and extent. William and Henry might

---

* *The Edward referred to is Edward the Confessor, the Anglo-Saxon king who immediately preceded the Harold who lost at Hastings. He had gained a great reputation for holiness, which on the evidence available may have been no more than sexual impairment, and a great reputation as a man of law, which I believe resulted from the fact that the Norman kings felt it necessary to hark back to something. Since William claimed that Harold had no right to kingship, the most recent reign he could cite was that of sainted Edward. Accordingly, right up to 1688, every English monarch at his coronation swore to maintain "the laws of Edward the Confessor," although Edward made none.*

have ignored the past and, backed by force of arms, proclaimed they were establishing new law. They chose not to, and as their practicality is famous, the choice suggests the ideology had weight, and that the changes were somewhat less than these monarchs might have wished.

They did not abandon Anglo-Saxon customs and devices (or Danish; Canute had been there), but rather used them—this despite the fact that they employed intellectuals trained in the more sophisticated Roman law. (Here, as elsewhere, the Norman kings were practical. Their appreciation of the uses of intellect in a barbarous age is the answer, I suggest, to the riddle of how an unpromising dukedom gained such strength so fast.) Their main minister was Lanfranc, a lawyer-cleric from Lombardy, a scholar. He and his assistants and successors must have found the Anglo-Saxon idea of law annoying—though not the Anglo-Saxon respect for it—but the deferential way they wrote the statutes shows they recognized its force.

They also must have found annoying the need to deal with the strongmen who made up the aristocracy (often not even the strongmen, but sons and grandsons and great-grandsons of strongmen, who inherited land and status without inheriting the strengths that won them). Take *Durham's Case*, in 1088, one of the earliest judicial proceedings we have record of. Important people accused of crime were tried in *curia regis*, the king's court, an assembly of the magnates of the realm. Durham, both a bishop and a baron, held his fief at the edge of the realm, and was powerful and fractious. He was also brighter than most of the other nobles. Charged with rebellion against the Conqueror's son, King William Rufus, Durham said the court lacked jurisdiction. He was a bishop, he argued, and hence he must be tried in an ecclesiastical court, with a right of appeal to the Pope. Lanfranc, for the King, pointed out that Durham was charged not with dereliction as a cleric, but with treason as a vassal; his clerical office had nothing to do with his secular obligations to a secular superior. The report tells us that Lanfranc was directed to return a number of times while the great men were consulting; they had to hear the distinction more than twice before they got the point. If they ever did. At any rate, the challenge to the jurisdiction was denied and Durham was held guilty. William Rufus was still the boss, that much the barons knew.*

---

* *"Baron" then was a title for the highest vassals, those who held their lands directly of the king. Now it designates the low-*

The ideological clash—between the English concept that the law had always been and must always be the law and the late-Roman concept that the law is a conscious manufacture of political authority—was a product not of racial characteristics, but of time, the difference between a young legal culture and one with a longer history. The more sophisticated the law becomes, the more it is regarded as something made, not found. The Roman law itself displays the same development. In the end, it was a matter of imperial legislation and produced the codified kind of law now known as Roman. But during the republican period the concept of a pre-existing law, merely translated by those who wrote it down, was dominant. The documents of Roman legal history begin with the Law of the Twelve Tables; these were, expressly, an attempt to put in written form established customs.*

This deep deference to a half-remembered, half-imagined ancient law endured to recent times, and, not quite so deep, is with us still. Its influence has not always been reactionary, if by reaction we mean a reaching back to things less good. It was republican Rome, a healthy progressive Rome, that produced the retrospective Twelve Tables. Magna Carta, which, cleaned of the sentiment smeared upon it, remains an important document in the progress of the law, looked only to the past. "The cry," says Maitland—the cry which, though it came from feudal throats, drove England a step toward freedom—was "not that the law should be altered, but that it should be observed . . ." †

Later, Edward Coke fought his king by citing (and misciting) old precedents. And then—manifestation most remarkable—come the argument and exhortation that gave the American Revolution its rationale. In the flood of writing which prepared the way, there is scarcely any urging that something new be tried, any call to progress. Most of the agitators are ostentatiously conservative: King George and his ministers have abandoned the

---

est rank of nobles, an example of the usual historical debasement of words of social distinction.

* *England's Alfred, who lived in the ninth century, a very early time in English culture, was deliberately innovative, but in the law as in other things he was extraordinary.*

† *Frederic William Maitland is, by acclamation, the great historian of our law. I join in the acclaim, and wish to add, to the tribute to his scholarship, a tribute to his writing. He did his main work around the turn of the century.*

British Constitution, the law has been corrupted, we demand return to the good old days (which, of course, had never been). With a steadfast backward gaze, the American rebels take up arms. In the name of precedent, they effect a revolution and create a set of political rights the world has not seen before.

The new jurisprudence of the legal realists also has its uses. Released from the notion of a common law fully formed and perduring, courts find it easier to make revisions that are needed. Easier, note, a comparative: there never was a time when courts could not find a way to make changes in the common law, and they do not make them cavalierly now.

□

The United States Supreme Court, which almost from the start undertook a political function, is in this respect unlike the rest of the judicial system. Concerned mainly with the Constitution, and regarding it as organic in more than a single sense, the Supreme Court has a looser loyalty to precedent. The Court was always influenced, as Mr. Dooley said, by the results of the last election (though not always in the way that Mr. Dooley meant; the conservative half of the bench in the 1930s did its best to undo the last elections). The "activist Warren Court" was readier to make changes than most of its predecessors, though not so eager to abandon past decisions as its critics, and some of its fans, have said.

As elsewhere in the law and politics, abstract concepts supplied the lyrics of debate while the music was hardly heard. Richard Nixon said he was appointing "strict constructionists." In fact he wanted to create a revisionist majority, prepared to fracture precedent. Neither Nixon nor his opponents on this issue were really concerned with "strict construction," which means a reading of the Constitution tending toward the literal. (Tending merely: only the simplest documents can be taken literally.) Nixon's opponents wanted decisions that favored personal liberties, advanced the status of minorities, and gave more protection to the criminally accused. Nixon wanted the reverse. "Strict construction" has connotations of the "conservative" view of these issues, but the connotations are misleading. Justices Black and Douglas, for example, deduced their "liberal" view of free speech and press from what they claimed was a literal reading of the First Amendment.

A similar subversion of real issues occurred during the New Deal, when Roosevelt's opponents were shrill about "states' rights." What was at stake was not the growing power of central government, but welfare programs, aid to unions, and business regulation. The power of the central government would inevitably grow (though perhaps a shade more slowly if conservatives prevailed). The interconnected growth of our economy had for the most important purposes erased state lines. (Some cultural relevance remained, but in the past forty years it too has nearly disappeared—not because of central government, but because of films and television, hotel and fast-food chains, the death of local beers, and other devastations. It is free enterprise, not government control, that has homogenized the nation.) State legislation could not effectively manage the things that had run wild, and those who benefited from the wildness cried for retention of power in the necessarily powerless states.*

All courts knead the law to fit new situations, but only rarely do they abandon precedent (the Supreme Court on Constitutional points excepted). Even more rarely do they confess abandonment. It used to be they never would, but the new jurisprudence has made them franker. The House of Lords (that is, the part of the House of Lords which sits as Britain's highest court) recently announced that it would overrule precedents "in a proper case"—a liberty American courts had for some while silently assumed. But a "proper case" will not frequently arise. Ordinarily, if a court regards the precedents as unfair or impractical, but cannot find a way around them, it will leave it to the legislature to enact new law. Nevertheless, the difference in attitude and emphasis is significant. The new jurisprudence has

---

* *Outside the Constitutional sphere, the same sort of deceptive slogans were used in the conflict between the "isolationists" and the "interventionists"—deceptive even to most of those who shouted them. Ostensibly, the debate had to do with the extent to which the United States should become involved in the affairs of other countries. In fact, adherence to one or the other of these concepts of foreign policy was dictated by the purpose of the involvement. In the 1930s, the interventionists were those who hated Hitler and fascism more, the isolationists those who hated them less. In the postwar period, it was a matter of who hated Soviet Communism more or less, and people had little trouble switching from intervention to isolation, or the other way around; they passed each other in opposite directions without so much as a nod.*

limbered up the courts. The value of precedent, and its function, are now better understood. It is respected rather than adored.

This social utility—the reasons, as I understand them, why even contemporary courts are not likely to change their ways very much at a time—was stated in The End of Obscenity. With apologies to readers who saw the passage there, I repeat it:

(1) *Stare decisis* is an anticorruption device. If courts are not bound by external rules, if they are not called upon to explain their decisions in terms of precedent, corruption is made easier. "What is right" in a particular case too readily becomes what is right for the particular judge or his friends. There should be a single set of laws for rich and poor alike; that much is easy. There should also be one set of laws for those who helped the judge get on the bench and those who opposed, for those who have good stock-market information to give the judge and those who don't, for the political clubhouse and the rest of the neighborhood, for the organized group and the unattached private citizen. *Stare decisis* does not insure this. But it makes it complicated and awkward for the judge to be dishonest. His decision must appear consistent with what has been done in the past, and more than an appearance of consistency is necessary to avoid reversal on appeal. A system in which he was bound only to achieve a "just result" would be a breeze for the crooked judge. There are considerations, he would tell you, that are not immediately apparent; one must not be too technical.

(2) More broadly—whether or not what stands in the way is corruption—fairness demands that people in similar situations should be treated in a similar way.

(3) Society implies order, and order implies not only a uniform application of law at any moment, but also a strong continuity from moment to moment. There must be a given pattern for each instant in time, and the pattern must hold still—reasonably still—as times goes by. . . . Nothing in the heavens ordains, for example, that a contract for the sale of real estate must be written and signed, but the economy will not function if in one season the courts demand the writing and in the next they do not. Indeed, sometimes the good of society requires more urgently that there be a rule than that the rule be good. It may be argued that cars should be driven on the left of the road rather than the right; the point does

not seem important. But it is very important that they keep to one side or the other, and that the rule not be subject to frequent change.

(4) There is a practical utility in *stare decisis* that is not confined to the law. Habit has its defects, but it is economical. The search for precedent goes on everywhere: in the business office, when a difficult question comes up, we head for the files; how was it handled the last time? The law is not involved; there is no external compulsion. But we know that last time thought and effort went into the problem, and it seems a good idea to have the benefit of that thought and effort now. The past has banked its wisdom, and it is foolish not to draw on it.*

□

An example of how jurisprudence can have a practical effect: About thirty years ago the highest New York court was presented with the question whether a defamatory radio broadcast constituted slander or libel. Except where the statement fell into one of four defined classes, which the defamation in this case did not, slander entitled the injured party to a verdict only if he could prove a measurable monetary loss. In libel, on the other hand, the same statement would at the time give plaintiff whatever sum the jury felt appropriate, whether or not he had evidence of loss.†

In the pronunciation used by lawyers, the letters of Latin words are given English, not classic Latin, sounds. Thus certiorari *is* "sershorary," *not* "kairtiorahry"; *subpoena is* "subpeena," *not* "subpo-ayna." *And the phrase above is* "starey desighsis," *not* "starry daykisses."

† *The United States Supreme Court has since revised the law of libel, in ways too complicated and uncertain to permit of treatment here.*

The four kinds of slander deemed so serious that proof of financial damage could be dispensed with make a comment on the rapid movement of history in the last half century. They were (and in treatises still are) statements accusing the plaintiff of (1) commission of a crime, (2) having a loathsome disease, (3) departure from proper standards of business or professional conduct, and (4), if the plaintiff was a woman, unchastity. The first and third probably still have that effect, the second perhaps, the fourth most likely not.

Slander is oral defamation, libel is written. There is no plainer proposition of the common law. The New York Court of Appeals, which felt the victim of this sort of obloquy ought to win despite the lack of proof of monetary loss, decided that the broadcast was a libel rather than a slander. Six of the seven judges, caught in the speech-and-writing hobble, held that some sort of writing must be involved if the plaintiff was to have redress and found it in the script that the broadcaster had used. This was playing with precedent in an illogical, invalid way. (Suppose in an ordinary slander case, the defendant, not trusting his extemporaneity, had made some notes and memorized them.)

The seventh was Stanley Fuld, later Chief Judge of the court, one of our best judicial minds. He agreed with the result —the plaintiff should recover—but he could not accept his colleagues' reasoning. His own reasoning would make all defamatory radio broadcasts libel, whether script-read or memorized or ad-lib.

The action for libel had developed in the seventeenth century, long after the action for slander. The invention of printing created the need for it. The courts expressed the distinction between slander and libel in terms of their obvious physical characteristics: the audible versus the visible. Their opinions became the "authorities." The underlying policy, however, largely unexpressed, has to do not with physical form, but with capacity to injure. Books and pamphlets could travel farther, reach more people, and work greater injury than spoken words. If the good reason, rather than the stated reason, for the different legal consequences of slander and libel is understood, radio and television belong to the part of the law harder on defamers and kinder to their victims, to libel rather than slander. Broadcasting represents a technological development analogous to printing, and the damage it can do resembles—indeed, surpasses—what is done by books and papers.

Fuld's opinion makes more sense and comes closer to justice's demands. Was it too far a departure from precedent, a violation of the common law? Not at all, I think. On the contrary, it was in the tradition of the common law, a closer adherence to *stare decisis*. Consider the sense of the precedents, instead of the majority's literal translation of past opinions. But the new jurisprudence helped. Without it, Fuld might not have been so bold. For one thing, the shift in emphasis from what courts say to what they do permitted a less slavish reading of the old opinions. For another, if common law is a social tool rather than authoritarian mystery, we can ask why courts acted as they did, and direct our loyalty to the law's real reasons rather than its formulas. (Since the date of that decision, the Fuld view has been adopted by most courts: script or no, defamatory radio and television broadcasts are now treated as libel rather than as slander.)

☐

Returning to where we started: whether we deem it judge-found law or judge-made law, the common law comes, immediately at least, from courts; statutes come from legislatures.

"Judge-made" is a phrase the realists use. In fact it is more often lawyer-made. Though it gains the force of law only through the rulings of the courts, a new idea originates usually in an advocate's head. This is not because lawyers lose intelligence when they ascend the bench. It is because the air is thinner at that elevation; there is not the rich atmosphere of the need to win. The lawyer-as-champion faced with adverse precedent is apt to respond with more imagination than the lawyer-as-arbiter sitting neutrally in judgment. Not that judges contribute no creative thought. They contribute much; but not as much.

Moreover, the lawyer-as-counselor, hardly moving from his desk, has his own effect upon the law. The course he counsels where the law is not yet clear, repeated by other lawyers and other clients, may become a practice. Custom can no longer itself amount to law—not in recent centuries—but a judge presented with a novel question tends to look at how things are done in the world outside. "Trade practice" is a recognized source of illumination, and the practice is often shaped by the lawyers for the trade. When a lawyer gives advice based on his estimate of what the courts will do or ought to do, he feeds the chance the courts will do it.

☐

In the beginning, we have seen, statutes are presented as declarations of existing law, with a few polite embellishments. But by the fourteenth century legislation is frankly new-made law. Meanwhile the legislative body begins to change from King-in-Council to King-in-Parliament; that is, from the king acting with the advice of his chief assistants and his most important vassals to the king acting with the consent of a majority of the lords and of the representatives of the rural gentry and some wealthy urban merchants. Those representatives are called the Commons, but it is not till later that the Commons speak for common folk.

This shift of power—from the king together with his intimate advisers (and those he does not count as chums but whose strength he has to reckon) to the king plus an elected assembly —is aided, paradoxically (or what would be paradoxically if it were not history we are dealing with), by a succession of unusually forceful monarchs. The consent of Parliament springs freely under royal pressure. The two Henry Tudors and Elizabeth so dominate Parliament they can get what they want by Act of Parliament almost as readily as by fiat. Other things being equal, any sensible ruler, however near to absolute his power, is interested in quieting the cranks and hardheads who are always present and eager to make trouble. Accordingly, the Tudors choose to act through Parliament rather than around it.

But here again ideology and precedent take hold, and in struggles with later kings less powerful, Parliament asserts an authority it never had—authority which, for their own purposes, the Tudors made believe it had. In the struggles of the seventeenth century, Parliament makes good its arrogation. By the end of that century, the monarch has legislative influence, but little final power; two centuries later, hardly any influence; now no influence at all.

Parliament subjugated the Crown; did it subjugate the common law as well? Early in the 1600s, Lord Justice Coke declared that neither king nor Parliament could transgress fundamental principles of common law. In time the proposition was true enough for king (also, academic: he himself could make no law, fundamental or trivial), but it has never held for Parliament; no one in office followed Coke along this line, not even Coke himself. Removed from the bench, he entered the House of Commons, and fought the Stuarts there. In the last stage of his long career, Coke asserted the utter supremacy of Parliament, an assertion which by the century's end had become the constitutional law of England.*

---

*Coke's change of position was characteristic. Celebrated in the history of the law and in the history of freedom, he was a man whose motives are even less clear than those of most historical figures. He first gained eminence as the chief prosecuting officer of the Crown, and in that office showed neither love of law (except as a weapon to destroy the accused) nor the least

Like most conquerors, though, legislation is infused with much of what it conquers. Doctrine is vulnerable to the thought and feeling of those who put the doctrine into practice. For centuries, English freemen had been immersed in the common law; Henry II offered litigation in the royal courts as a substitute for private wars, and made sure his offer was accepted. Knights of the shire, and their successors the gentry, spent a good part of their days as jurymen and local Justices. At the same time commerce grew, and commerce, once it passes barter, lives on law —then, in the main, a customary law. With primogeniture established, the practice of law became the premier calling for landless younger sons. (Ecclesiastical careers were less attractive when English monarchs drew away from Rome, and the military as a profession hardly existed in England until later times.) What they practiced was mostly the common law. So Parliament's statute-making is tempered by its common-law inheritance. M.P.s behave, ordinarily, as though Lord Justice Coke had won his point.

In America, statutes are explicitly made supreme, subject only to the Constitution, itself a statute of a grander kind. But it was settled very early that the courts should tell us what the Constitution means, and judges are lawyers trained in the common law. In the last third of the nineteenth century and the first third of the twentieth, the Supreme Court struck down Acts of Congress and state legislation on the ground they contravened the basic tenets of the common law, which, the Justices said, was incorporated in the Constitution, mainly in the due-process clauses of the Bill of Rights.

In contrast to the situation in which Coke advanced the same idea, the thrust was conservative, not liberal: the Court found that legislation to improve the workers' lot interfered with "free-

---

regard for fairness. As a judge, he was quite different: he used the common law, superbly, as in instrument of liberty, and incidentally—but nobody knows which was incidental—to build the power of the courts. Finally, as a member of Parliament, he made a brave fight against the Crown; he was one of the chief instigators of the struggle that ended in a more democratic government (a long way from real democracy, but a long way too from monarchy). Note how his principles always seemed to take on the color of his personal position. Note also that while he held public office he became a very wealthy man. Yet he did great good.

dom of contract" between employer and employee, and that welfare legislation in general violated the hallowed right of property. This seems to have little to do with the procedural safeguards suggested by the words "due process," but those Justices were not inhibited by regard for language. Nor by regard for history: the contract concept was a late addition to the common law. The court announced it was invoking those good old "eternal, immutable" principles, the immemorial ways and customs. The short-order cooks who graced the bench whipped up tradition in an instant.

In the middle of the twentieth century, the common law continues its insurgency, but now more quietly, and with a different aim. The courts, no longer interested in defending property against welfare, are intensely interested in other aspects of the Bill of Rights—protection of the accused, free speech, equality. These guarantees were put into the Constitution by men who had the common law in mind, an idealized common law, to be sure, but in part historical reality. There would have been no Bill of Rights without that heritage. And here the courts' decisions make more sense: they do not have to mutilate the language of the Bill. "Free speech" seems to mean free speech; "equal" equals equal; "due process" is the fair and even court procedure that is our due, not a guarantee that children may be made to work the mills and mines.*

□

There seems a plain enough distinction. The common law (whether "found" or "made") is unwritten law announced by judges, and only when disputes are brought before them. A statute is law established by vote of an assembly in response to political demand, and then formally inscribed. But as with nearly everything in law, things are mixed, degree determines. Statutes are affected, as we have just seen, by the substance of the common law. Also by its method. Stern as they appear in statute

---

* We have been taught to think of courts as essentially conservative, but in some periods of history—the thirteenth century for one example and the mid-twentieth for another—the courts have fostered change. Nevertheless, there is characteristically a hanging back, not political (there the courts have varied) but rooted in professional habits. Hence judges have diminished the effect of various statutes by holding them to be only "declaratory of the common law."

books, statutes are not self-enforcing. If they are not obeyed, someone must go to court. And the court not only has to issue a judgment or an order, but also very often determine what the legislation means.

Canute commands the sea to stay away. The sea pays no attention. Here is unrecorded sequel: The matter devolves upon the royal ministers. They suggest Canute did not mean the tides should cease—this is not a reasonable interpretation—but rather that something should be done to contain the damage tides can do. The ministers construe the decree as a command to build a sea wall, and render judgment that it be built, and direct their men-at-arms to see that it is done. Some of the shore, formerly wet, will now usually be dry. The ministers apply and enforce the King's command, and, in doing so, interpret it. The royal utterance alone was not much use.

Enactment of a statute is not enough. Two further things are needed: interpretation of its language in concrete cases, and judicial action to enforce it. When a citizen ignores or violates legislation that carries a criminal sanction, some officer must prosecute. If the legislation grants a private right, the one denied the right must commence a lawsuit. In either case, we come before a court.

The legislature has declared its will, but declarations consist of words, and words, this sort especially, seldom have a single meaning. So it is left to the courts to tell us what the statute means, to enforce the legislative declaration as they, the judges, understand it. "A word is not a crystal, transparent and unchanged," said Justice Holmes, "it is the skin of living thought." The thought that gives shape and color to the word, our democratic doctrine tells us, is the thought of our assembled representatives. But often it is difficult to ascertain their thought, and sometimes one may fairly doubt they had a thought at all. The best of statutes do not apply with ease to every situation; most legislation trudges through a muck of ambiguity.

The court must meet the problem, and does it in accustomed style, the style of the common law. Encountering a question of common law, judges search for the applicable rule. Encountering a statutory question, they search for correct interpretation. The materials of the inquiry are somewhat different. When a statute is involved, the judges have a text before them. And they can draw on extrinsic aids: statements of the statute's aims by those who sought its passage, the proceedings of committees and the reports they made, the record of the floor debate. These are called the "legislative history." The grail the judges seek is "the legislative intent," but the quest can be illusory: often the legislators had no intent except to vote the party line, sometimes even less than that, no consciousness at all of the implications of their voting. And even where the legislators did a good and honest job, the situation before the court may not have been envisaged; no draftsman can anticipate the multiplicity of circumstance on which his statute will impinge.*

Twentieth-century Acts of Congress are luxuriantly encased in legislative history: printed committee hearings, committee reports, debates in the House and Senate. Indeed, much of it is deliberately created to give content or definition to the language of the statute—by the committee staff, by government agencies interested in the legislation, by private groups promoting it or seeking to limit its effect. Purposes are made explicit. Concrete examples of the intended application of the statute, inappropriate in the statute itself, are spelled out. Among the state legislatures, the record is spottier: extrinsic evidence is often negligible or simply nonexistent.

But legislative history is supplementary only, for two good reasons. One is that it can itself be equivocal; different legislators who voted for the bill had different things in mind. The other is that generally the language of the statute is all that those affected by the statute ought to be required to take into account. We should be able to rely on the content of the statute books,

---

* *The legislators' ignorance of what they are doing, especially in the state houses, results all too often from incapacity, laziness, dishonesty, or some combination of the three. Sometimes, though, it is attributable to the difficulty of what they deal with and a lack of time. The United States Senate is by far the best American legislature (pay a visit to your state capitol). When the 1975 tax bill was in his Finance Committee, Senator Russell Long said, "If every man insists on knowing what he's voting for before he votes, we're not going to get a bill reported [on time]." This was only the committee, note, a relatively small group of specialist senators, not the full Senate. On some of their work, much more complicated than what their predecessors did a hundred years ago, the best-intentioned legislators have little choice but to vote as they are told by their leaders or their unelected staffs.*

without having to engage in research to discover what it was that stammering legislators meant to say but were unable to make plain.

In any case, the courts must come to a decision. And they do it very much the way they do when there is no statute and the case is governed by the common law. Looking at the facts before them, they listen to the statute's words and strain to hear their meaning, much as they do with authoritative statements of a rule of common law. There will usually be precedents to follow. In most cases, the statute will have been to court before. If this particular statute has not already been construed, decisions on other similar statutes may offer precedents, or at least illumination. And, overriding, whether said or left unsaid: what makes good sense here? At common law, what is the purpose of the rule? With legislation, the purpose of the statute? As to either, what is fair and beneficial in this case? The court, considering all these things, announces that the legislature intended this or that —or, if the court would speak more frankly, that the legislature must have.

The decision makes another precedent, one other courts will follow when the statute is invoked in later cases. They will follow it to just about the same extent they follow precedents of common law; they feel bound but not completely bound, restraint but not restriction (unless the precedent, precise, comes from a higher court). They regard context and the color of the case at bar as critical; the statute's words in different situations may be given somewhat different meanings. But the principle of *stare decisis*—though it be a tolerant principle—is present and effective. Judges do not readily depart from precedents of statutory interpretation any more than they do from precedents of common law.

In one set of circumstances even less. After a series of consistent decisions construing ambiguous statutory language, or one Supreme Court decision on the point, the legislature may for some reason reenact the statute. The original may have by its terms expired, or the legislature may decide to do it over, with improvements, while the part judicially interpreted is left untouched. The courts then deem the reenactment a "legislative ratification," confirmation that the judge-invented meaning is the one the legislature wants. The courts act on the theory—wrong, I think—that the legislators, letting the judicial construction stand, signify that this is what they intended all along. It is wrong because all that usually happens is that the legislators, having roused themselves to pass the original statute, now sleepily say "Uh huh."

□

This mode of statutory interpretation led to the strange immunity from antitrust laws the business of sports once had, and which has only recently been modified. Among the rare foolish judgments of the magnificent Holmes was a 1922 opinion, for a unanimous Supreme Court, holding that the corporations that operated professional baseball teams were not engaged in interstate commerce, and hence were free to enjoy their monopoly without regard to federal law. A little later, at the same term of court, another antitrust suit came up, and Holmes spoke for a unanimous bench again. This time the alleged monopoly was of vaudeville rather than baseball, and this time the Court sustained the prosecution. In the baseball case, justifying his conclusion that interstate commerce was not involved, Holmes had said:

> The transport [in interstate commerce] is a mere incident, not the essential thing. That to which it is incident, the exhibition, although made for money, would not be called trade or commerce in the commonly accepted use of those words. As it is put by the defendant, personal effort, not related to production, is not a subject of commerce.

In the vaudeville case, reaching an opposite conclusion and therefore compelled to distinguish the baseball case, Holmes said:

> . . . in the transportation of vaudeville acts the apparatus is sometimes more important than the performers . . .

Holmes's distinction is of course insulting to the performers. (Vaudeville may have died of hurt feelings.) And it assigns a peculiarly diminished role to the apparatus of baseball. The two decisions make sense together only on the assumption that the traveling baseball team can leave its equipment home. This contemplates games in which the visitors play without their bats or gloves, the catcher without his mask. Perhaps this explained to Holmes why the home team usually wins. In the 1970s—a half century later—the newspapers were full of cases created by those dotty Holmes decisions. The best of us have bad days.

COMMON LAW AND EQUITY, AND SOME OTHER JURISDICTIONS

The term "common law" had no egalitarian origin, although it was used, by the English in the seventeenth century and by the Americans in the eighteenth, for an egalitarian end. It got its name because it was common to all of England—something different from the local law of parts of England, from the law of particular organizations (church law, for example) and from the law of particular activities (the law merchant, for example).

There were, in the beginning, different legal systems for different areas of England, sovereignties that seem to us ridiculously small. Americans now travel greater distances for an evening's pleasure than the length of each such realm, and there is a larger population at an English football match. England, only part of an island that included Wales and Scotland and a great deal of uninhabited woods and fen, consisted in Anglo-Saxon times of a number of separate "kingdoms." In the days of Bede, England's first historian (near 700), there was the kingdom of Lindsey, the kingdom of East Anglia, the kingdom of the East Saxons (that one included London), the kingdom of Kent, the kingdom of the South Saxons, the kingdom of the West Saxons, the kingdom of Mercia, and the kingdom of Northumbria (which sometimes was two kingdoms). Except on the rare occasion when one or another was able to gain hegemony, each king was sovereign, and each kingdom had its separate legal system.

The first English laws put in writing were probably those of Ethelbert, King of Kent; that was about 600. It was almost half the time from then till now before it could be said there was a consistent legal system throughout all of England. As late as the twelfth century, differences among the law of the Mercians, the law of the West Saxons, and the law of the Danes (who were present long enough to leave a bit of law) were given recognition in the royal courts.

Legal systems developed by social or economic groups for their own purposes lasted even longer, some of them down to the present day. Thus the law of admiralty—the law governing what happens at sea—continues to have rules of its own. When ships collide, for instance, the damages awarded can be divided between the owners of the vessels; not so, under the common-law rule, when motorcars collide. In cases arising out of auto accidents—our most fecund source of litigation during the past half century—the court must blame one party or the other, and impose liability on an all-or-none basis (except when both are found at fault, in which case the court will let the losses lie where they have fallen; and except as recent statutes 'have changed the common-law rule). In contrast, if the clash occurs on sea instead of land, admiralty law for about eight hundred years required equal division of the loss, on the theory that collision was "a peril of the sea—a common misfortune." In 1975 the Supreme Court changed the admiralty rule, but it is still different from the common law: now there is, in admiralty, apportionment of fault, and with it apportionment of loss.

The word "admiralty," incidentally, is a product of the ignorant confusion of sound and meaning that increasingly assails our language. Its origin is Arabic, a designation of somebody important, an *emir*. The "d" got in because Latin was the tongue of intellectuals and would-be intellectuals. (The "would-be" is unnecessary if we indulge a current practice and define an intellectual as one who wishes to be thought of as an intellectual.) A person of power was an estimable person, the Latin being *admirabilis*.*

---

* *The phenomenon is rank these days, probably because more than ever we extend our social competition to the realm of erudition, and there is a hasty reaching out for words that have not previously been part of common speech. Thus "shambles," sounding like "rubble" and carrying the disorderly connotations of a shambling gait, has come to be used for anything shattered or even badly disorganized. Properly, it denotes not just ruin but bloody ruin; the primary meaning is "butcher's block." Again, "tortuous," which means "twisting, winding," is taken to mean "tortured," and a newspaper known for caring about its language tells us of a mountaineering effort made difficult by a "sheer, straight and tortuous climb."*

"Stultify" means, literally, "make foolish" and, by reasonable extension, "render useless," "reduce to futility." So far so good: a strong and special word. But people tend to assume, more or less consciously, some connection with "stunt," as in "stunt your growth," and it also sounds a bit like "stifle." Hence we hear it where "nip in the bud" or "smother" is meant.

Not long after the common law had established its dominion over local law, there grew up alongside it a mighty rival, another judge-proclaimed system of rights and remedies. It developed from the Chancellor's meddling in actions brought in the courts of common law. The Chancellor was a clergyman, a high official of the Crown and usually a high official of the Church as well. He intervened at the suit of those who suffered from the common law's rigidity. The common law had earlier been supple, and would again become so, but in the fourteenth century it had hardened into a number of castlike complicated forms. If the grievance did not fit any of these forms, those aggrieved could get no help from the courts of common law. So they began to tell it to the chaplain. Not so to speak, but literally. Unlike the chaplains of World War II, this one could, and would, give them more than sympathy. By the end of the fourteenth century, the Chan-

---

Consider "reticent," which means only "to be silent" or, by very close connection, "disinclined to speak." But it gets mixed up with "reluctant" and with "diffident," having a visual resemblance to the one and a loosely rhyming relation to the other. Accordingly, a writer wonders at another's "reticence to attack those things one expected him to attack." We shall be silent to make trouble.

The maltreatment of "tendentious" is less unwelcome. A pompous word of recent manufacture (1900, says the Oxford English Dictionary*), it is probably getting what it deserves: misuse, where sententious or contentious is the thought intentious.*

Perhaps the most distraught is "sloe-eyed." The sloe is a dark purplish plumlike fruit, and someone, sometime, used it to describe the color of a pair of eyes, eyes he dreamt of, likely. But Orientals have eyes both dark and slanted, and "sloe" and "slanted" go well together. "Slinky" may also have had something to do with it; our silent-movie vamps were quasi-Oriental. Meanwhile, "slow" suggests a mildness. The process, in these days of wide and shallow learning, moves so fast a recent dictionary, one of our very best, defines "sloe-eyed" as "having soft, slanted, dark eyes." It may be added that a plum is neither slanted nor unslanted and assuming (overcharitably) that "elliptical" is meant, a plum is nearer round than the most Occidental eyes (eyes, that is, not eyeballs).

Error, persisted in long enough, must be accepted in the language. But there is no need to hurry.

cellor maintained a regular court to hear such suits, the Court of Chancery. What was initially a series of improvisations became a pattern of stated rules. It was called "equity" and was separate from the common law. It was, in fact, quite as common and quite as much the law. Yet the differences were considerable; they are left for a later chapter.

Though in the sense just used common law and equity are opposites, the two together make up the common law that is distinguished from the Roman law and its descendants. And in most states and in the federal courts, the two are now conjoined; there is just one judicial system, offering a uniform procedure. Moreover, both are systems of tradition and precedent—law that grows out of judicial action in specific cases—so that both are common law as opposed to legislation. But, these shared features in the background, "common law" means one part of the non-statutory law, distinct from another part called "equity," and the various rights and remedies dealt with by the single set of courts quite plainly show their ancestries.

The unification of the two systems carries with it an official unification of vocabulary, which borrows rather even-handedly from the two. However, where the statutes or rules of court do not themselves supply the words, old differences tend to continue. And if the reference is to the older cases, a redistribution of the melded language is of course appropriate. The terms "legal action" and "action at law" refer to what went on in courts of common law, while "suit in equity" refers to what went on in Chancery. "Judgment" designates the ultimate exercise of judicial power at common law, "decree" in Chancery. Purists would preserve the separate names even now, calling litigation derived from common law an "action" and that derived from Chancery a "suit." This distinction is observed about as often as, say, the distinction between "shall" and "will."

Common law and equity, back far enough, are close relatives. The ancestry of both is royal: the rulings of the kings and their high officials. There were also, in early times, local courts that operated outside the royal justice, enforcing the local law. They were heirs to the separate bodies of law that obtained before England became a single realm, and they also reflected variations in local customs among even tinier parts of the map. They were more (and less, of course) than what we think of as courts. They were the structure of local government, insofar as the word then meant government according to law, rather than government according to the local master's wishes. They had functions we would call administrative and executive in addition to judicial.

Prior to the Conquest, there were two kinds. One was the courts of the "vill" and the "hundred." Vills and hundreds were the smallest settlements, a hundred usually covering several vills. (There are conflicting views on whether the name has anything to do with number.) This kind did not survive much beyond the Conquest. They are called communal courts, which has a better sound than it deserves; it means not much more than that they were run by those who were big in the community.

The other, and more significant, kind of local court was the shire court. The noble at the head of the shire was in Anglo-Saxon times an earl, a word bequeathed to the Anglo-Saxons by the saltatory Scandinavian invaders. The earl generally acted through a "reeve," a ministerial official, like a bailiff or a steward, but in this instance more important. The earl's reeve managed the shire court and supervised the lesser courts throughout the shire and was called the shire reeve, eventually "sheriff." After the Conquest, when William had replaced the Saxon earls with his own lieutenants, the shires came under central control, in theory and pretty much in fact. The sheriff became the direct agent of the king; he usually ran the shire, though the earl was his social superior and collected the money that the court brought in. But even after the sheriff became a royal officer, the law enforced in the shire court was the local customary law.

The Norman-French equivalent of "earl" was "count." Shire became "county" and sheriff became "vice-count." All the terms survived, and were used concomitantly—shire, earl, sheriff, county, count, and viscount. At the time in which the legend is set, Robin Hood's foiled enemy was a very potent person.*

"Viscount," which originally designated someone who had important work to do, became, over the centuries, a hereditary title signifying only status, not administration. Meanwhile, the powerful office of sheriff declined to insignificance, until it was reincarnated, not in England but in nineteenth-century America, where once again it was filled by a man of considerable author-

---

* *Gradations of nobility had not yet been permanently fixed. They would not be, under the Conqueror or Henry I or II. The establishment of a structured aristocracy marked a diminution of royal power.*

ity, much needed to maintain order in small settlements, just like his ancient forebear. The rough-and-ready American frontier sheriff and the elegant English viscount are historical kin.

Since he had no standing organization, the reeve, when he needed help, called upon the residents of his shire. The Latin for this assembled force was *posse comitatus*, "the power of the county." A thousand years later, the Western sheriff in America used the same device, swearing in a "posse," a Latin word and a legal concept now familiar, thanks to films and television, to almost every eight-year-old. A contrasting sort of descendant is the sheriff of New York City; he serves judicial writs, holds property "attached" thereby, and never uses a weapon that is not made of paper.

The Conquest brought another kind of local court. Anglo-Saxon England had not been altogether feudal; the Norman system was. Each lord had his court. The privilege of holding court was an important incident of feudal tenure. For one thing, the power to adjudicate was then the principal expression of political authority, not, as now, just one of three. For another, it was an important source of income. On the criminal side, the fines imposed in the feudal court were paid over to the lord. On the civil side, the lord had a duty to render justice between disputing tenants; he also had the gratifying job of deciding what was just, and what is more got paid for it. It cost money to litigate those days, as it does still, but now the most obvious cost is the lawyer's fee; then it was the fee paid to the lord. "The profits of justice" were a significant part of the value of a fief. The phrase does not mean that favorable judgments were sold. (No doubt they often were, as they too often are today, counting trade of favors, usually political, along with the little black bag.) Selling justice meant selling access to the court, not selling the result. The "filing fee" of modern courts is a tiny remnant of the ancient practice.

The higher the court in the feudal scale, the higher the admission price, the king's court the most expensive. The complaining party bought the ticket, but if he won his opponent might be made to pay for it. Again a remnant: a winning plaintiff in present-day litigation is usually reimbursed by the defendant for his filing fees.

As population centers grew, borough courts appeared, a rough equivalent of their country cousins, the shire courts. The privilege of holding court was part of the royal charter by which the town was made a political entity and the burgesses were granted power. In the later Middle Ages, the court of London was an important center of litigation.

Until the legal revolution of the late twelfth century, most judicial business was handled in these local courts. Royal justice was spotty. The king's court settled controversies among those who were his vassals, took special cases for a fee, and occasionally adjudicated royal rights (when the king thought that allowing argument about a doubtful royal claim might be a good idea). The law of the local courts, even when it was administered by a royal delegate, was the custom of the place, except as the various bits of royal legislation might affect it.

Other courts came into being separately, and later vanished, each leaving a legacy of law. The "law merchant" of the Middle Ages belonged to three sets of courts. One was the borough courts which have been mentioned, for the tradesmen in the towns. Another was at the harbors, where international trade passed through offices the kings maintained. The offices were called "staples," whence our word for certain widely used commodities. (The etymology is "pile" or "pillar," and the offices were probably named for the buildings they occupied, typical waterfront construction.) Disputes that surfaced in the flow of maritime commerce were taken care of there, in what were called, reasonably enough, Courts of the Staple. A third set of mercantile courts functioned at the fairs and markets. These were the Courts of Piepowder. The word was pronounced just as it looks: ready-mix for a confection. Eventually, that is; the name at first was Piepoudre. Pavement having gone out with the Romans, buyers and sellers who came to the fair arrived with dusty feet (Latin *pede pulverosus*, Norman-French *piepoudrous*) and the English worked their usual wonders with words of foreign origin.

The law merchant was a set of rules for a certain kind of activity, rather than for a certain group of people. It governed mercantile transactions no matter who conducted them rather than merchants as a class. Its character was not altogether English; there were cosmopolitan strains. Multinational companies are not a new invention.

The Tudors fostered what are sometimes called the Courts of the Royal Prerogative. Star Chamber is the best known, symbol of tyrannical injustice. They were established by royal order —there existed in the Crown a residuum of undefined judicial power—when the common law appeared (especially to the monarchs) to have become inadequate. By 1500, common-law procedure had, indeed, grown stiff and rusty, and juries had become too vulnerable to local power. Star Chamber at first served more than a selfish royal purpose, and in fact was popular, but later it was turned to evil ends. The prerogative courts had a short life; they disappeared in the seventeenth century, when the monarchs were subdued.

But the most important judicial system outside the courts of common law until Chancery matured—and important still for centuries thereafter—was ecclesiastical. The courts of the Church, when they were fully grown, did not confine themselves to clerical disputes; they ruled much of the life of the laity, material as well as spiritual. Not so in the United States, where their jurisdiction has always been limited to matters properly ecclesiastical. (Hester Prynne lived before there was a United States.) But in England, until the middle of the nineteenth century, they dealt with so mundane a subject as inheritance of goods and money. There are traces in America: certain states have special courts for the administration of inheritance, which have clerical antecedents. They are called probate courts, or surrogate's courts, or courts of the ordinary, or bear some other esoteric name.

The New York Surrogate's Courts have created a chronic political issue in New York, where from time to time there have been attempts to end their separate jurisdiction. It is not for the sake of the efficiency that unification might bring; the loss in specialization might reduce efficiency. It is because the Surrogate's Courts, dispensing patronage—awarding easy-money jobs through appointment of fiduciaries—have been factories of corruption. The line of ecclesiastical descent is clear in this reflection of the ancestral churchly peddling of indulgences.*

In the adolescence of the common law, the ecclesiastical judicial system in England was as important as the secular. This fit the medieval concept of twin spheres of sovereignty, spiritual and temporal. The ultimate temporal sovereignty was lodged in the Holy Roman Empire, the spiritual in the Papacy. One sphere was never filled except in theory: the Holy Roman Empire was

---

The last effort at unification in New York was led by Robert Kennedy, and among the things that ended with his murder was the most serious movement to date to remove this vestigial locus of infection. It should be noted that in recent years there have been some uncommonly honest Surrogates.

simply a powerful German kingdom. Its imperial sway was notional, like a modern township plat of streets and lots where nothing but field and wood exists. But the imperial nature of the Church, headed by the Pope in Rome, was quite real. The English secular courts confined themselves to English law, but the English clergy were members of an international organization, the greatest force in Christendom.

In theory, and at first in fact, church courts dealt with churchly matters, and in a churchly way. Their penalties did not include what they called "judgments of blood." They punished by depriving the transgressor of holy function, degrading him from holy orders, or, punishment most awful, anathema. And the offenses they dealt with (again in theory, and in the early period) were spiritual offenses, or violations of canon law, the internal law of the Church. After the Norman Conquest ecclesiastical courts grew stronger. This did not mean the Conqueror gave more allegiance to Rome than his Saxon predecessors did; he gave less.

William the Bastard, Duke of Normandy, carried a papal banner across the English Channel. The Cardinal Hildebrand, soon to become the great Pope Gregory VII, had arranged the holy endorsement. He believed William would be a friend to the Papacy, and a counterbalance to the Holy Roman Emperors with whom the Church contended. William did indeed do much to help the Church in England, but he made it more his church than Rome's. He adopted and translated the Anglo-Saxon tradition of a theocratic kingship, so that he, rather than the Pope, ran the clerical organization. Gregory no doubt regretted the moral sanction he had engineered, and in the privacy of papal councils William the Conqueror must have been William Truly the Bastard.

William gave the ecclesiastical courts a clear jurisdiction of their own, something they had not had before. But it was a limited jurisdiction, limited mainly to clerical matters, and governed by the king. A churchman's rights and duties outside the Church, both civil and criminal, remained part of the secular law. Then, toward the end of the eleventh century, the Church gained greater strength. Gregory led two marches that, for him, were parallel: reform within the Church, and enlargement of its temporal power. This was the progressive movement of the period, an attempt by those who had intellect and morality on their side —relative to the time and place—to dominate the lay nobility.

Where Normans ruled, the penetration of papal power into

secular affairs went more slowly, and not as far. But after William's death, the troubled Rufus could not maintain his father's iron governance, and his successor-brother Henry I, though he was a strong king, found it expedient to yield a bit to Rome. The clerical courts made further gains during the Matilda–Stephen contest for the throne that followed, when central secular government nearly disappeared. Then, in 1154, came Henry II. He dug in. Thomas à Becket's attempt to take the clergy beyond the reach of royal law led to his celebrated conflict with this second Henry, and by a crooked road to sainthood.

The most prominent issue between them, and the most significant for the history of the law, was the issue of the "criminous clerks"—whether churchmen who violated secular law should be prosecuted in secular courts. Becket's position was that the Church must always judge its own. It was not the only issue in their struggle, and on others Henry had less logic, and less justice, on his side. Here his demand was modest, more modest than by right it should have been: only that after a clerical culprit had been tried by a court of the Church, and there found guilty of a secular crime, he be turned over to the secular government for punishment, the same punishment as other men might suffer for that crime. It fitted Henry's effort to establish the rule of law in England. About one person of every six was then in holy orders, and ordination did not take a person out of ordinary daily life. (Or nightly: adherence to the vow of chastity was occasion for remark.) Becket was in effect contending that a large part of the population be allowed to live outside the law that governed the lives of the rest.

Becket's cause made huge profit from his murder. The Martyr Becket accomplished much that the Archbishop Becket could not. The outcome was a compromise on all the issues, a compromise more favorable to the Church than it would have been if the four brave knights had been less stupid or less drunk. The privileges and obligations of landholding in the feudal system, which then made up the bulk of what we would call civil law, would be the business of the royal courts. But crimes committed by that clerical sixth of the population would in the main be handled by the church courts, along with a large part of the civil law that did not directly relate to land.

The issue of the criminous clerks was one on which Henry would probably have prevailed but for Becket's death. Becket's predecessor, Archbishop Theobald, had sought to be flexible in the matter, and the wisest of Becket's bishops counseled restraint and resilience. But the only element of compromise on this point was that the secular courts would in the first instance decide whether the accused was a churchman; if they found he was, they could do nothing to him. For reasons history does not make explicit, this initial jurisdiction never amounted to much. We may guess that as the punishments of the secular courts grew more brutal after Henry's time, there was a search for ways to avoid them; we have an analog in the search by eighteenth-century juries and twentieth-century judges for ways to avoid imposing capital punishment.

The exemption from the secular criminal law is the famous "benefit of clergy." And a great benefit it was. Though the Church's punishments became less spiritual, they remained considerably milder than those of the secular courts: whipping, for example, instead of mutilation, and, when imprisonment became a penalty, shorter prison terms. The reach of the benefit began to grow at the same time that dead Becket's image began to grow. The thoroughly worldly Becket—sexually chaste but fond of pomp and riches, in love with power and its trappings, inordinately its trappings—became an object of worship, the most revered Saint Thomas. Meanwhile, the benefit of clergy, whose origin was probably in part an honest effort to protect the Church itself from lay control, became a device for outrageously unequal law enforcement.

Becket's mortuary cosmetizing—which twentieth-century playwrights and entertainers, in London, Paris and Hollywood, have recently refreshed—occurred almost immediately. He became a saint just two years after his death. (The canonization of a far worthier Thomas—Aquinas—took half a century.) The benefit of clergy needed longer to attain full size. It was gradually extended to those outside the Church whose jobs required them to read and write, that is, to clerks in the modern sense as well as clerics—history often does its work with puns—and eventually to anyone who could read. But intellect has hardly ever held advantage over status. By the middle of the sixteenth century, every nobleman could claim the clerkly privilege, including those who counted on their fingers and could not read at all. Their crimes, in the misshapen word that came into use, were "clergyable."

Except for one important felony. If the crime alleged was against the king himself—when there was not merely violence of one subject on another, but a threat to the royal power—the king's own courts took over. A man accused of high treason could not avoid secular prosecution, no matter how clerical he might be.

In time the benefit became less beneficial. While it flooded out beyond the clergy, the judicial power of the Church bit by bit receded. Though many more could claim the benefit, it applied to fewer crimes. After Henry VIII broke with Rome, specific Acts of Parliament hemmed it in. Not until 1837, though, was the loathsome privilege wholly gone.

□

On the civil side, inheritance of personal property has been mentioned; there was a good deal more. The Church, of course, assumed the burden of preserving the soul of every man and woman, clerical or not, and it is hard to say where behavior merely troubling to society leaves off and behavior that risks eternal hell begins. Ecclesiastical courts adjudicated not only the incidents of private life—marriage, legitimacy, divorce, personal possessions—but also a large part of trade. The courts of common law had very little law of contract before the sixteenth century; meanwhile, the Church's concern with sin naturally extended to the swearing of oaths and could thus accommodate pledges of commercial faith, and did to some extent. The law of defamation also had a root here: slander was declared a form of sin, and its redress remained for quite a while a business of the church courts.*

The two legal systems inevitably mixed elbows. After Henry II made his peace with the Church, ecclesiastical rule in matters matrimonial was unquestioned; so was secular rule over land. But the decision on ownership of land often turned on whether there had been a valid marriage. Was the woman demanding dower the decedent's lawful wife? Was the son who claimed the land the lawful heir or just another poor bastard? Having to resolve such questions, the secular courts built up doctrine on what constituted marriage. As time went on, their doctrine became rigid and their requirements more formal. Common-law judges insisted on ceremony to make a marriage valid, and finally decided that at the ceremony an ordained clergyman must be present. The ecclesiastical courts, in sweet contrast, de-

---

* *Judicial power so broad as this had not been conceded to the Church in earlier times. Before the twelfth century, for example, the secular courts entertained some actions on inheritance of personal property.*

manded no such rites. They did not require that one of their own officiate; they did not even ask for ceremony. Canon law made consent the test for marriage; it was very much like what was to become the modern law of contract. Laymen (as distinguished from lawyers) tend to be legalistic; laymen (as distinguished from theologians) tend to be liturgical. There were also practical reasons: the more elaborate the event, the easier it is to determine whether or not it occurred.*

In addition to handling civil matters important to everyone, and in addition to their criminal jurisdiction whenever there was benefit of clergy, the ecclesiastical courts punished the laity's offenses against morals and religion. The early disclaimer of blood punishments was abandoned as the Church progressed. They burned heretics, and punished somewhat less severely those who committed lesser sins, such as sorcery, witchcraft, incest, and plain incontinency. (Witch-burning was a later practice.) They also heard, and punished when they found the charges true, accusations known as Haunting Taverns and Ploughing Up the Churchpath.

The break with Rome was not an instant revolution. It was a long time in the making, nearly four centuries from Second Henry's declaration of semi-independence to Eighth Henry's final Act. Nor did the break immediately oust the Church from secular affairs. The church courts continued as before, except that the Crown, rather than the Pope, became the ultimate authority, and statutes could control the clergy. Gradually it was accepted that the old independent jurisdiction should not continue independent, and Parliament slowly whittled it away. Very slowly: prosecution for perjury was not taken from the church courts until 1823, and not till 1855 did all civil suits for defamation go over to the courts of common law. It was only on the eve of the twentieth century that the ecclesiastical courts of England were at last confined to things ecclesiastical.

---

* The situation the common law called "special bastardy"—a child born out of wedlock whose parents married afterward—affords another illustration of the tendency of the courts of common law to put greater store on sacrament than the church courts did. The ecclesiastics held the child legitimate; the secular courts held not. The conflict was settled in favor of the common-law view by a statute enacted in 1236, which remained in effect for six hundred and ninety years. In 1926, Parliament yielded to the liberality of the medieval Church.

This, as I have said, was England. The United States has never let the church courts' power reach outside the churches. The writers of our constitutions, state and federal, were careful to make that clear.

SUBSTANCE AND PROCEDURE

These juxtaposed concepts are less definite than formerly supposed. Nevertheless, they remain useful, even attractive, so long as their vague and tender edges are understood and treated kindly.

Substantive law consists of the rights we are said to have and the duties we are told we must accept. Procedural law is the set of instructions prescribing how we redress a violated right, how our neglected duties are imposed. In the absence of a will, widow and children take the land: this is a rule of substantive law. The defendant has twenty days in which to answer plaintiff's complaint: this is a rule of procedure. Another pair of words used to mark the same distinction is "right and remedy." Sometimes, in Bentham's felicitous phrase, procedure is called "the adjective law."

You make a contract to buy a house and at the date of closing stand ready with the price; the seller reneges and will not deliver the deed. Next day, on the way back from the supermarket, you stop at a sporting-goods store, select a pair of skis, pay cash, and, loaded down with groceries, ask that they be sent; they never come. That night, for the sake of your health, you take a walk around the block. An angry neighbor creeps up and flattens you with a good sneak punch, from which you suffer a deviated septum. (He has had considerable neighborly provocation. Not from you, of course; there has been a terrible mistake.) You have a right to have the deed delivered. You have a right to get the skis. You have a right to use the sidewalks unmolested.

What can be done about it? That is, assuming you are willing to go to law. Usually you do something else first. Get up and take a swing at the neighbor. Berate the store and threaten to tell your friends. Or, at the failed closing, look helplessly at your lawyer (who may look helplessly back) and then reproach the seller for his lack of moral fiber. But if all these extralegal measures fail, how do you enforce your rights? The "how" is the law of procedure, the path that must be followed to give effect to what the law has promised you. The "what"—the statement of legal rights and duties—is the substantive law.

This seems clear enough, the two categories separate and distinct enough. But there are difficulties: conceptual, historical, and in application.

Going to court is difficult and expensive, and usually in situations such as these no attempt is made. Even assuming it is worth your while to make the trip, there is no assurance you will win your case. Unless you win, does your right have any meaning? Even if you win, the gain from litigation may not match the cost in time and money. Or the defendant may be insolvent, so that what you gain is nothing. If you do not wish to go to court, or if despite the justice of your claim you lose, or if you win less than you spend—in all these common circumstances, what substance has the substantive law? Do you really have legal right, or just a sense of outrage?

If on the other hand the litigation is successful, it is because the following has taken place (not always all of it, but always some of it, and often more than this): You have brought your opponent into court by service of a summons. You have filed the pleadings and survived all the court's pre-trial demands. You have gained a verdict in a trial hemmed in by synthetic rules of evidence. You have obtained a judgment based on the verdict, and the judgment has survived appeal. With the sheriff's aid, you have found assets of your opponent sufficient to satisfy the judgment. Only then—after you have gone through all these paces of procedure—does the right you thought you had take on real meaning. So, it may be said, the substance of substance is procedure.

This analysis is companion to the definition of the law as prophecy of what the courts will do. Since the law will do nothing for you unless you go to court and successfully employ the court's procedures, what is right but remedy? One of the most brilliant of the legal realists, Karl Llewellyn, called the distinction an illusion. "A right," said Llewellyn, "is as big, precisely, as what the courts will do." Your right to have the house you think you bought, for instance, does not exist unless a court will order delivery of the deed, after you have successfully employed the procedural device called "an action for specific performance." The perfidious seller may give you the deed before you go to court, but only because he thinks you mean it when you threaten suit, and his lawyer tells him he will probably get beat.

If the right does not draw its breath from the action of a court, it draws it from the prospect of such action.

The analysis, in my view, is sound, so far as it goes. But it does not go far enough. It is useful in lawyer's work: in evaluating precedents, in appraising assurances and threats, and in counseling a course. And it is refreshing jurisprudence, a bringing down to earth of airy Blackstone common law and the rootless jurisprudence (except as rooted in the sky) of some natural-law proponents. But the real world is more complicated than either school allows.

Llewellyn was realist enough to concede that "the prevalence of this illusion (as of any other) has results in human behavior." That understates the matter. People act on the assumption that they have rights, and (less cheerfully) that others have rights too. There is an undefined compulsion to observe those rights, whether or not a lawsuit starts. Sellers of houses usually deliver the deed, as stores deliver the goods. The neighbor, appalled at his mistake, will make amends, by paying doctors' bills, and in other ways. If these things happen only because there is anticipation of specific judicial action and appraisal of its consequences, then Llewellyn has said enough. But I suggest that there is more.

The law, even when no litigation is foreseen or under way, conditions our behavior. It is at once effect and cause of moral standards. That one should discharge one's legal obligations is an imperative recognized by most people most of the time. Correlatively, one expects that others will recognize one's proper legal claims. The law by its very existence and our awareness of it affects the way we live—without the use of the courts, or the threat of their use, or even the thought of their use. The process does not require us to entertain illusion.

Functioning in this silent way, the law is a powerful agent. And when it does this fundamental work, it is a law of substance, not procedure—a law of rights and duties, not a law of how to make good service of a summons, where to file the papers, how to pick a jury, when it is too late to make a motion.

I mentioned earlier that civilization hangs on the habit of obedience to the criminal law. Respect for the civil law is much less deep and much less constant, but not less necessary. The civil law is often honored only in the breach, but most of the time it is honored truly. People act toward each other, to the extent required to make things work, as though legal claims and obligations exist outside the courthouse. If they acted otherwise, things would be a mess. The courts, labored as they are already, could not keep up, could not come close. The expectation that rights will commonly be recognized and duties commonly discharged, without resort to litigation, is the fundament of our economy. The goings-on in court are not the entire law, only the half of it.

So the conceptual difficulty of "substance and procedure" is somewhat different from what full realist theory makes it. It is not that the distinction does not exist, but rather that it is not nearly so well marked as lawyers and judges and some historians have in the past assumed. The realists are correct in insisting on the blood relationship of substance and procedure. They are not correct when, in the flush of intellectual achievement, they reject the categories altogether.

□

The categorization encounters historical difficulty too. In teaching law, it is useful to set up different courses in substance and procedure, and in writing legal history it may be well to speak of them in different chapters. But in their actual development they are inseparable, especially in the formative years of the common law. For the moment accept Sir Henry Maine's perception that "substantive law has at first the look of being gradually secreted in the interstices of procedure."

Finally, there is the difficulty of application. That one must deliver merchandise sold or else make good the buyer's loss is a plainly substantive rule; that one may serve a notice of deposition along with the answer to the complaint is a plainly procedural rule. But there are questions whose answers are not so easy, and some whose answers are not what the concepts seem to call for. Take the statutes of limitation mentioned in the "Battle" chapter. There they had to do with crime; the civil law has them, too. An action for breach of contract must usually be commenced within six years from the date of breach; for most torts, within three years from the date the damage is done, excepting defamation, which has a one-year limit in most jurisdictions. Equity has, instead of specific limitations, the flexible doctrine of laches, which means the Chancellor does not allow the suitor to slumber on his rights too long, "too long" depending on all the circumstances of the case. Are these restrictions procedural, announcements of how long the judicial mechanism is available to give sanction to an everlasting right? Or are they substantive

—the right has a finite life, and when its term is over the right does not exist? And what difference does it make?

Usually they are thought of as procedural, which conforms to our natural notions of right and remedy. A broken promise is not repaired by the passage of a period. False words that stain a name are not made true because twelve months go by. Pain may recede in memory, but that does not mean it was not suffered when the victim was assaulted. If these things are recognized as deserving reparation, they deserve it no less the day after the term is reached than they did the day before. Time does not heal all wounds; the homily is fatuous.

Thus limitation appears to be not a matter of substantive right but a practical device. It is difficult to deal with an event long after it has happened. Memories fade, witnesses die, documents vanish, proof one way or the other is hard to find. Moreover, even with all the evidence at hand, the outcome of a lawsuit will not necessarily coincide with truth. Much depends on the hazards of litigation: on the wisdom and honesty of judges and jurors, the skill of lawyers, the luck of testimony. Hence it is only reasonable that the alleged wrongdoer (in most instances we will not be certain he did wrong) should one day be entitled to repose. Finally—most important and scarcely ever mentioned —if all disputes were kept alive forever, there would be an infinity of litigation. In the management of a polity, there needs to be an end of things.

None of these considerations has to do with substance. They have to do with whether, given the weaknesses of litigation and the interests of good government, the courthouse doors should continue to stay open. The right itself exists outside of time, but there comes a day when courts will not enforce it. They will not enforce it for very good reasons unrelated to the final justice of the matter (if its justice could be known).

And the designation brings benefits. Viewing the limitation as "procedural merely"—somehow procedure appears to have less dignity than substance—makes it easier for courts to extend the period when in a particular case its effect becomes too harsh. If a person has a just claim, it seems unfair that he should lose it only because he gets to court a moment later than the statute says he should. His lawyer may have been a slob, or out to lunch, or spring may have come to town that day.

Courts have been ingenious to give the statutes elasticity. In some situations the courts have made them stretch considerably. Suppose, for example, there has been a wrong so crafty that the victim is not at first aware he has been wronged; plaintiff has not understood defendant's machinations. Assume the statute provides a three-year term running from the date the wrong occurred. The statute says nothing about ignorance, fraud, or concealment. Four years later, the gull finds out that he was gulled. If the limitation is substantive, a natural end to the right itself, he is simply stuck. He can complain to anyone who will listen, but the judges will not listen. The right was born when the wrong was done and endured for three years after, and then the right expired. Nothing can bring it back to life.

If, however, the statute is viewed as procedural, the judges may be receptive. They can emphasize the heinous conduct and wonder whether the law's majesty is powerless to help. Courts ought to be able to regulate their own procedures, unless an act of the legislature explicitly forbids. This brings the issue within the scope of what judges regard as malleable. There are certain things deemed subject to "inherent judicial power." Disclaiming authority to create new substantive law, a court can claim a proper interest in how it keeps its house. Part of the domestic operation of a court may be the granting or denial of admission. And, as we have seen, statutes are always, more or less, subject to construction, including statutes of repose.

In the situation just described—a tort concealed—the "procedural" approach opens the way to interpretation: the legislature could not have meant to charge the plaintiff with indolence when there was nothing he could do, nor give defendant a reward for fraudulent behavior. So courts have ruled that the plaintiff's lack of knowledge keeps the clock from running. During the period of his ignorance, the limitation is said to be "tolled." The time is counted from the moment the deed that caused the damage is discovered, not from the moment the deed was done.*

Courts are less inclined to embroider statutes of limitation than they have been in the past; this is part of the contemporary judicial tendency to pay somewhat more attention to what the legislatures say. And many statutes of limitation now explicitly incorporate these court-invented variations. On the other hand, a legislature may make the limitations substantive; there is no constitutional guarantee of any length of time within which one may go to court. (Unless the time prescribed were so ridiculously short as to deny due process; this, so far as I know, has never happened.) Most statutes of limitation are drawn in general terms and apply to classes of actions created by common

So it appears both conceptually congenial and suited to the ends of justice (whatever analytical jurisprudence may assert) to treat limitations as procedural.

Move to the federal courts. They have jurisdiction of "federal question" cases; that is , cases involving Acts of Congress or the Constitution. They also have "diversity jurisdiction," of cases between citizens of different states, whether or not a federal question is involved. It used to be that the federal courts had their own collective substantive common law, while each of them followed the procedure of the state in which it sat. (No federal district takes in more than a single state; some states have several districts.) So far as substance was concerned, most lawyers and judges, nurtured on Blackstone, thought of the common law as something independent of what particular courts might decide in particular cases. Hence federal judges felt free to disagree with state-court precedents on matters of substance, and a "federal common law" developed—that is, the common law as seen by the federal judges, who on various points saw it differently from the state-court judges. Procedure—the practice in the different courts—was something else, less transcendent; it could vary from state to state, and the federal courts could go along. Habit coincided with prevailing doctrine: the substantive common law is a field for intellectual exploration, while lawyers tend to accept procedural rules as arbitrary but unshakable, and federal judges were lawyers trained in the procedure of their own state courts.*

---

law or by other legislation, so that the flexibility of the "procedural" approach is available. Occasionally, however, a statute will create a new right with its own time limit on it, expressed in such a way that the limit has the look of substance. The legislature deliberately designs a transient right. Usually the reason is the very fact that the right is newly created, not part of the well-established pattern that people regard as their moral due. World War II's treble-damage action for price-ceiling violations is an example. (This peculiar bit of legislation is dealt with in another chapter.)

* Congress, which has certain constitutional powers to regulate the jurisdiction of the federal courts, has set minimum money limits on diversity cases. Ten thousand dollars or more must be at stake to gain the federal courts' attention. The requirement was raised from three thousand dollars in 1958. In the beginning, it was five hundred dollars; from 1887 to 1911, two thou-

In a single year, 1938, the pattern was turned inside out. Pursuant to an Act of Congress, the Supreme Court established a uniform procedure for all the federal courts. At almost the same moment, in a case called *Erie Railroad v. Tompkins*—a familiar railroad-accident type of case in which federal judges had used federal common law a thousand times—the Court abandoned its own precedents. It held that in diversity litigation a federal court must follow the substantive law of the state in which it sits. "Federal common law" was ended.

---

sand dollars. The rise is not only recognition of inflation; the aim, in part, is to keep the federal courts unclogged, a dubious policy, most recently embraced by Chief Justice Burger, the result of which is that state courts get worse clogged.

The accepted reason why the Constitution created diversity jurisdiction is that the colonies had been separate enough, and chauvinist enough, so that there was a real chance a Carolinian, for example, might not get full justice in Connecticut. This was thought less likely to happen if he could enter a court run by a judge who owed his office not to the state but to the central government. In an early case, John Marshall described the situation in a rich example of the one-sentence essay:

However true the facts may be, that the tribunal of the states will administer justice as impartially as those of the nation, to parties of every description, it is not less true that the Constitution itself either entertains apprehensions on this subject, or views with such indulgence the possible fears and apprehensions of suitors, that it has established national tribunals for the decision of controversies between aliens and a citizen, or between citizens of different states.

There is some evidence that Marshall's explanation is incomplete. The framers of the Constitution may have had in mind not only state-court judges, but also state legislatures. Separation of powers was not yet axiomatic, and, for some time after the adoption of the Constitution, state legislatures, like ancient Parliament, exercised judicial powers. They "freely vacated judicial proceedings, suspended judicial actions, annulled or modified judgments, cancelled executions, reopened controversies, authorized appeals, granted exemptions from the standing law, expounded the law for pending cases, and even determined the merits of disputes."

Seven years later a case called *Guaranty Trust Co. v. York,* begun in a federal district court on diversity jurisdiction, came to the Supreme Court. The question was whether a state statute of limitations should apply, or a more liberal limitation that the federal courts had used before 1938. The state period had expired by the time the suit began; the federal period had not. The plaintiff contended that, in the absence of specific legislative instructions to the contrary, limitations had always been regarded as procedural, and so the federal courts should apply their own. The majority of the Court rejected the contention— and the precedents—and held for the defendant. The majority opinion was written by Felix Frankfurter, famous teacher of the law and prominent Justice of the Court.*

Frankfurter spoke in the tones of the latest jurisprudence. Law is not a brooding omnipresence. We must look at practical effects. *Erie v. Tompkins,* he said, reversed the unrealistic old notions, and achieved the sensible result that one's rights and duties should not depend on whether the plaintiff, by the accident of residence, can choose a federal or a state tribunal. A statute of limitations effectively ends a right, and when that right arises from the law of a particular state, as it does in this diversity case, that state's law must govern, including its limitations. Whether the defendant will suffer a judgment should not turn on the adventitious fact that the plaintiff lives in another state. Definitions ought to be functional; the law's words can have different meanings, according to the purpose to be served. So with "substance" and "procedure." The traditional labeling of limitations as procedural, Frankfurter argued, must not defeat the sound policy of *Erie v. Tompkins.*

These were the ideas, and the language, of the legal realists, of the jurisprudential "liberals," who were by and large political liberals too, and were centered at the law schools of Columbia and Yale. Frankfurter came from Harvard, which for a while had

---

* *Guaranty Trust was the defendant. In the title of a case, the plaintiff's name usually goes first, but in certain appellate situations, where the old form of petition for review is prescribed, the name of the petitioner—the party seeking review—goes first, whether the petitioner is plaintiff or defendant. Thus in the familiar "certiorari"—short for* volumus certiorari: *"we wish [the record] to be certified"—where the Court is responding to the request of the party seeking review.*

been in the still waters rather than the current of advancing legal thought, and he was conservative on the bench.* Yet Frankfurter made thorough use of the realist analysis:

> Matters of "substance" and matters of "procedure" are much talked about in the books as though they defined a great divide cutting across the whole domain of law. But, of course, "substance" and "procedure" are the same key-words of very different problems. Neither "substance" nor "procedure" represents the same invariants. Each implies different variables depending upon the particular problem for which it is used. . . .
> . . . And so the question is not whether a statute of limitations is deemed a matter of "procedure" in some sense. The question is whether . . . such statutory limitation is a matter of substance in the aspect that alone is relevant to our problem, namely, does it significantly affect the result . . . ?

Semantically sophisticated, sharply analytical—a model of the most progressive judicial thought.

But consider the facts of the case, and the larger issues it presented. It grew out of the corporate finance of the pre-Roosevelt period, the public-be-damned attitude that contributed so much to the pain of the Great Depression. Thirty million dollars' worth of bonds—these were 1930 dollars—had been issued by the Van Sweringen Corporation. (The name is famous from the time when railroads were the hard-riding bullies of our economy—not, as now, mistreated derelicts that might, if sobered up and worked into shape, attain respectability and help a bit on energy and pollution problems.) Corporate bonds are issued through a trustee, almost always a bank, here the Guaranty Trust Company of New York. The trustee is supposed to guard the interests of people who buy the bonds. More often, in those days, the trustee guarded the interests of the corporation that issued the bonds, and others who belonged to the exclusive club

---

* The right-wing politicians and the right-wing press (most of the press at the time) kept on attacking Frankfurter as a radical long after he had become the most articulate voice on the conservative part of the Court. They were confused by his brave role in the Sacco-Vanzetti case, and resented the large presence of Harvard Law School graduates in the New Deal. There was also more than a touch of anti-Semitism: Brandeis and Cardozo were enough.

of high finance. The plaintiff owned six thousand dollars in face amount of the bonds, worth much less at the time of suit. She brought a "class action" on behalf of herself and "others similarly situated."*

The plaintiff alleged that the Guaranty Trust Company had breached its trust in various ways, to the damage of herself and other bondholders. Such a confidence-inspiring name. But there seems to have been confusion, if the allegations could be proved, on which way the Guaranty ran, and who should be the beneficiaries of the Trust. (This, of course, was forty years ago, and none of it relates to the present management of Guaranty's successor.) Plaintiff lost in the district court, but won on appeal in the circuit court, by a two-to-one decision. The circuit court held that where, as here, a plaintiff sought a remedy derived from equity, a federal court was not required to apply the state statute of limitations; it could use the easier federal standard. Guaranty Trust then went to the Supreme Court, where it won by five to two, two Justices not participating.

On the particular facts, fairness would seem to require that the issue before the Court be decided in plaintiff's favor: the people who bought the bonds should have had a chance to prove, if they could, that there had been chicane. But that alone does not make Frankfurter wrong; good rules of law (it bears reiteration) can work injustice in specific cases. So let us consider the rule the Court laid down, the broader effects of its holding.

We have seen that viewing limitations as procedural enables courts to loosen them up (which would have happened here) and that this usually serves justice (which would have been served here). Was there some overriding policy that went the other way?

---

* *This is a kind of litigation where one person sues for all those who find themselves in the same fix, and the lawyers for the plaintiff, if successful, are compensated by the court out of the amount they win—a useful, necessary device where financial pygmies go out to battle financial giants. Lawyers for the giants like to call class actions "strike suits," meaning that the lawyers for the plaintiffs stir them up in order to be bought off by a settlement from which the lawyers get a fee. Sometimes they are, but on the whole—along with its relative, the "stockholder's derivative action," in which a stockholder sues management, in a similar way, for the benefit of the corporation and all its stockholders—the class action has served both individual justice and the public welfare.*

("Policy" in the law can best be understood as justice on a larger scale.) Was there some need to maintain the logic of the law, or some need of practical administration, that dictated the decision?

There was not. Wiley Rutledge, a Justice who should be better known, a very good one, dissented. Various Acts of Congress, he pointed out, conferred equity jurisdiction on the federal courts, and all through the history of equity there had been an unbroken maxim that statutes of limitation should not be rigidly applied. The right asserted here was born in the courts of equity. True, "substance" and "procedure" should not be talismanic, but where the division is unclear, why go against tradition to reach a wrong result?

Between 1930, when these bonds were issued, and 1945, when the Supreme Court heard the case, the country had decided that the money barons' old thievery ought to be discouraged—decided in the securities legislation that Congress passed and in the acceptance of new financial standards not only by the public but by most of Wall Street too. Public security-holders were now to be given some protection against those who by reason of position had inside information and other special strengths. The new social policy and the ancient Chancery rule on limitations pointed in the same direction. Why abandon precedents that serve a contemporary end?

If the goal was symmetry in law—the lessening of discrepancies that result from our fifty-one separate systems (then forty-nine: the federal–state duality, and the differences among the states)—the decision was hardly the forward step the majority purported to be taking. Not infrequently the main questions of a case are resolved according to the law of a state other than the one in which the action is brought. (Roughly, when the transaction has taken place in that other state.) When this happens, the court hearing the case, the "forum," is free to use its own statute of limitations rather than that of the state whose substantive law is applied. The *Guaranty Trust* decision, addressed to federal matters, did not affect that rule. So it could not eliminate the evil of forum-shopping (assuming it is an evil); a choice among state courts might still be made. In fact, if the goal was to frustrate those who sought to take advantage of different rules of the law in different jurisdictions, the decision in one respect lost more than it gained. Corporations might choose trustees located in a state whose law, including its statute of limitations, would afford the best defenses.

Put aside the particular kind of controversy, the public

security-holder against a castle of corporate finance, and consider the majority's proclaimed goal of federal–state uniformity. The decision scarcely makes a dent in the varying benefits and detriments of state and federal actions. Every litigating lawyer will weigh them, and try to get into one court or the other depending on where he thinks his client has the better chance. His choice will be controlled by a number of things unquestionably procedural. One example: pre-trial "depositions"—that is, the gathering of information in advance of trial by examining people under oath. This is an item indubitably procedural; no federal judge would dream of holding that the taking of depositions in a federal action is subject to state law rather than the rules of the federal courts. These depositions are more readily available, and more extensive, and generally much more useful, in the federal courts than in most state courts. Since they critically affect the amount and kind of evidence offered at the trial, they can easily make the difference between victory and defeat. Their nonavailability or inadequacy can bar the "right" as effectively as any statute of limitations.

So can any other element of "remedy" which in actual litigation makes the remedy unattainable. Frankfurter's definition of "substance" as those things that will "significantly affect the result" is not as sensible as it first appears. All but the most trivial matters of procedure can significantly affect the result, and very often do.

The case—apart from the light it sheds on substance and procedure, a light that makes the murkiness all the more apparent—is interesting for another point mentioned earlier in this chapter. Frankfurter, invoking the most progressive jurisprudence, achieved a regressive result. Meanwhile Rutledge, citing judicial precedents, old Acts of Congress, and a tradition going back to the fourteenth-century beginnings of the Court of Chancery, used a conservative view of law to reach a liberal result. So did the barons at Runnymede, and the seventeenth-century English common lawyers, and the American revolutionists, and the Lord Justices who decided *Ashford versus Thornton*.

☐

The realists' critique of "substance" and "procedure," and of other lumpish legal concepts, though itself not wholly realistic, has made great contribution to the law. Lawyers and judges have given too much life to what is essentially a set of tools. They forget that, convenient as a taxonomy may be, it is a manufacture.

Our ideas about rights and duties, as I have said, are important in themselves. Without conscious reference to how or whether a judge and jury will enforce them, they have profound effect on how we act. But this does not mean they are not meshed with what goes on in court. Litigation, whose expression is procedure, is a goad to duty, the last resort of right, a primer and a lexicography of standards of behavior.

4

The Hue and Cry, the Feud, Ordeal and Compurgation

We start with Anglo-Saxon times. Half a millennium of Roman occupation did nothing for our law. The Roman legal contribution came later, indirectly, from the work of scholars, when Rome as a political entity was long gone. By then the English law had passed its infancy and formed its elemental character. The long dominion of the Romans left remarkably little trace: their main bequests to England were a system of roads and bridges, which had lasting consequences, and some baths, which had none. As for the contribution to our law made by others who lived in England before the Anglo-Saxons—the natives so to speak, the Celts who killed the Beaker Folk who killed the earlier Iberians —not much is known, and what is known suggests it be ignored.

The Teutonic invasions of England began a few years after the Romans went away. They went because other Teutonic invasions were threatening Rome itself. The native Celts, beneficiaries of the Pax Romana, had forgotten how to fight and offered little opposition. They made something of a comeback against the Teutons under a leader who was either Celtic or Roman or some of each, and whose career may have been the source of the legend of Arthur. But by the year 600 the heathen Anglo-Saxons —the Romans had Christianized the Celts—thoroughly dominated England. There seem to have been some Jutes along with the Angles and the Saxons, but apparently just a few; we probably hear of them because medieval historians liked to speak of trinities. In any case, the conquerors were groups of tribes that did not think of themselves as nations. In the sixth and seventh centuries these heathens were converted, first by missionaries from Ireland (at the forefront then of Christian culture) and later by missionaries from the Holy See.

□

The administration of most of early Anglo-Saxon law was committed to two institutions: the blood feud and lynching. They are not peculiar to the Anglo-Saxons. Primitive societies typically use family-fighting to redress certain kinds of misbehavior, and mob execution for others. As the society gets stronger, it devises better methods, and finally declares unlawful what were once the law's respected implements.*

The legal evolution of ancient England had extralegal recapitulation in the young United States. Huckleberry Finn presents both feud and lynching in his story. By Huck's time, of course, these ways of righting wrongs had long since been forbidden. Their governmental function gone, they were down to the ugly human drives that are their core. But in ancient Anglo-Saxon England they were entirely legal; they were all the law there was.†

---

* The term "blood feud" in origin probably refers not so much to the blood that is shed as to the ties of kinship that defined the participants.

† Mark Twain, characteristically, at once gives them their due prominence and exposes their shabbiness. An unarmed member of a feuding family, pursued, sees flight is hopeless. He turns to face his enemy. This is not a final bold and hopeful action. It is an attempt to fabricate some evidence that he did not flee but stood his ground, a tainted testament: "'. . . at last Bud seen it warn't any use, so he stopped and faced around so as to have the bullet-holes in front, you know, and the old man he rode up and shot him down. . . .'"

In another passage, a mob has come to lynch a man called Sherburn, who, out of nothing more than irritation (or, as he might put it, offended sensibilities), has murdered an old insulting drunk. Sherburn, however, is a clear-sighted man whose strange mixture of values was probably not so strange, in a large part of the United States, a hundred and thirty years ago. He defeats the mob with a combination of bravery and ridicule:

"The idea of you lynching anybody! It's amusing. . . . The average man's a coward. . . . Why don't your juries hang murderers? Because they're afraid the man's friends will

The feud and lynching are distinct from unorganized homicide, which does not require the existence of society, and from war, which does. Along with slaking thirst for blood, they had the aim of maintaining order within a community; war has the aim of imposing the will of one community upon another. The feud and lynching were responses to the breach of accepted rules of conduct, and sought, in their simpleminded way, to enforce such law as then existed. War has nothing to do with law. It is in fact its contradiction.

□

"Lynch" was not part of the language in the time I speak of. The word did not come into being until the act had existed for millennia, and for centuries had been illegal. (It comes from the surname of an eighteenth-century Virginian, a Justice of the Peace less interested in justice than in peace.)

"Lynch" denotes an organized killing outside the law. "Execute without due process of law," says one dictionary. But in Anglo-Saxon England lynching was not only legal; it was obligatory. If a criminal act was seen to occur, the community was duty bound to chase the culprit and when it caught him kill him. Anyone who witnessed the crime was expected to call on those available to join in a pursuit, and if the quarry beat the pack to the communal boundary, the next settlement was expected to take over. It was a sort of relay race, with a human baton slightly out of reach until the end. At the end was execution.

It was more than sport; it was an instrument of government. But it was also sport, and there has probably never been a more popular one. Here was homicide without risk—either from its victim, he being so outnumbered, or from the law, which did not scold, but instead approved, indeed demanded, so that conscience could not spoil the fun.

---

shoot them in the back, in the dark . . . So they always acquit; and then a man goes in the night, with a hundred masked cowards at his back, and lynches the rascal. Your mistake is, that you didn't bring a man with you; that's one mistake, and the other is that you didn't come in the dark and fetch your masks. . . . If any real lynching going's to be done it will be done in the dark, Southern fashion; and when they come they'll bring their masks, and fetch a man along. Now leave . . ."

It came to be known as "the hue and cry." "Hue" means "cry." Those people would never use one word where two would do. (But unlike many lawyers of later centuries, of whom the same can be said, those who named the hue and cry had euphony on their side.) The one who saw the crime let out the yell. At least he did if help was handy. Anyone who heard the yell was supposed to join the chase. The persistence of the ancient phrase (in our language, not our law) suggests how deeply planted the institution was.*

That was all the trial there had to be: a victim and a runaway, and the evidence of one person's cry. In most instances, probably, there was guilt, but there must have been a few mistakes, and likely now and then a frameup. It would take no great imagination for the miscreant to start a hue and cry against an innocent bystander. There seems to be no recorded case in which the quarry, at length run down, denied the crime. But nobody was bothering to keep records, and it obviously must have happened. When it did, those dominant in the group (whether by force of number or of muscle or of weapon) made their on-the-spot decision. Considering weak vision and weak judgment and weak character, it may be properly assumed that often there was execution of the innocent. It was a quick procedure, though. Those who complain about the law's delays might ruminate.

We are inclined to be more disturbed by frustration than by injustice. That is, we are more readily petulant than wholesomely angered. Thus the common criticism of the law is not that it works badly but that it works slowly. Shakespeare's best-known phrase about the law is "the law's delay." Slowly can of course be badly, but there are other things that should concern us more.

A journalist ordinarily superb on legal topics points out that litigation in England moves more quickly than in the United States; he deplores the slowness here. He is right in part: it is in the main deplorable. But some of what seems sluggishness is the

---

* Modern innovations, such as currency, have given the quarry a better chance. The New York Times of February 9, 1971, reported the following from Kenya: "When a robber fleeing from a shop with about £1,150 ($2,760) began scattering notes and silver as his pursuers gained on him, more than half the crowd abandoned the chase and began helping themselves. The robber made his getaway."

measured grant of things we prize. Our Constitution decrees a solicitous regard for defendants' rights, and that takes time.

Moreover, we should separate delays in bringing on a trial from delays between conviction and the punishment. The latter comes usually from appellate reconsideration of the case, at the instance of the accused. (Ralph Ginzburg was convicted of publishing obscenity in 1963, but did not go to prison until 1972; there it was the Citizens for Decent Literature who muttered about the law's delay.) And in civil litigation, there are usually difficult questions that cannot quickly be resolved; if the answers were apparent, there would likely be no litigation. A great deal of what seems ponderous in the law comes from the need to ponder. Speedy justice is not the ultimate aim; just justice is. Think about the hue and cry.

☐

A much faster system than we have, which would sacrifice nothing of justice, would be easy to achieve, given two things that are hard to get. One is willingness to spend more money on the administration of justice: more and better judges, clerks, government lawyers, more of the physical appurtenances. It is a branch of the familiar problem of allocation of resources. Would you rather see quicker and more evenhanded justice, or would you rather see men on the moon? (Put aside the things on which nothing should be spent at all.) The other is honesty: both the absence of corruption and a good day's work for a good day's pay. Most judges work hard and honestly; many do not, far too many.

I mentioned our Constitution's solicitous regard for defendants' rights. It is perhaps not quite so solicitous as judicial decisions of the 1960s have taken it to be. It is a hard fact to face, but perfect protection of the accused means imperfect protection of society, insufficient law enforcement. A system of justice that has no miscarriages of justice is not a workable system of justice. We need to strike a balance, and in that balance some individuals will suffer, both innocent defendants and innocent victims of crime. But our Constitution, clearly, gives much greater protection to the accused than is given by the law of other countries, especially those with the newest governments, and even including England.

☐

Lynching is instantaneous, but the feud was long, and sometimes needed careful nursing. The blood could cool; there remained the demands of convention. In some instances at least, it must have been a chore, perhaps in many; and as the society became less rude, perhaps in most. There could not have been such love for one's every relative that the savage affair was always welcome. (Old Egbert's bragged just once too often and he's finally got clobbered. Hand me down the goddam sword. I won't be home for dinner.) The slaying of Egbert's slayer provoked response, and the response in turn required retribution, and the thing swung back and forth. There was no fixed end to it, short of a clan's extinction. Each killing imposed a moral obligation to get even, and the natural tendency is to want to get ahead. One Anglo-Saxon feud went on for twenty years. While it was raging, the Norman Conquest happened; the families scarcely noticed.

The fair and open fight was dealt with by the feud, and the assault not fair and open by the hue and cry; theft might be dealt with either way. Both institutions were unsatisfactory. The hue and cry was beautifully efficient. When it was done it was done. But it was unruly, and troubling to the instinct for justice that resides, in some degree, in almost all of us. The feud, on the other hand, though in one sense just—it followed an admitted act of violence—was disastrously inefficient.

Neither did the job that good government requires. There must have been unwitnessed crimes. There must have been crimes, though witnessed, where the culprit looked too formidable, so that the cry stuck in the throat. And on occasion there must have been individuals who doubted the accuser, or were inclined to credit the quarry's plea, or were disdainful of the pack. As for the feud, the administration of government is difficult when important citizens are busy killing off each other. Anglo-Saxon society began to think there ought to be a way to deal with crime through some regular procedure instead of one man's cry, and, where the assault was forthright, to temper the honorable but debilitating feud.

So it developed judicial institutions, crude institutions but judicial, official methods to determine guilt or innocence, and to impose punishments in accordance with established rules. The hue and cry with instant execution went out of the law at an early date, the blood feud somewhat later. (In one of its functions, the hue and cry continued: it remained a police mechanism, a procedure for apprehending criminals though no longer a procedure for imposing punishment.)

Not that legal lynching disappeared suddenly and completely. In 1212—a date by which the English judicial system had grown elaborate—there was a recorded instance of official execution without a trial. It is the Case of the Deacon and the Jewess. Perhaps for love of the girl, perhaps for reasons of the mind, probably for both, the deacon had given up belief in Christ, and circumcised himself. An ecclesiastical tribunal declared apostasy. That done, the Church was finished with him, and turned him over to the sheriff, who might have brought him to trial in the secular courts (though for what, is hard to say). But no trial for secular crime was held; there was no judicial action at all. The deacon was put to death immediately.

There are various accounts of the case, but all agree on what has just been stated, and none raises any question about there being execution without a trial. (They also all agree that the weather was very bad in the year 1212—an adventitious, but, for legal history, unusually solid bit of information.) It may be thought remarkable that at this late date, late in terms of the establishment of the judicial system, the fact of official punishment without adjudication went unremarked. There was no inquiry into whether the deacon had committed any secular crime, and the only ecclesiastical decision had been expulsion from the Church. Nor was this the action of a mob; the matter was handled by high officialdom.

But then, of course, there is from time to time conduct so immoral that the need for retribution is evident. Passionate love of woman and denial of the Faith make an abhorrent mixture, and those in charge, supported we can be sure by a popular majority, would only have been annoyed if the disposition of the case had been delayed by some pettifogging lawyer.

□

For the feud a substitute was offered, money payment to take the place of vengeance, the *wergeld* system (or *wergild*; it is spelled both ways). The first syllable means "man," the second "money." There was payment for the man, if killed, or for some part of him if he was merely injured. In the latter case, the proper word is *bot*, not *wer*; *wergeld*, strictly, was something the surviving kin collected.

There were different sums for different kinds of injury and different kinds of men. The law read like a cannibal's menu: so much *bot* for the loss of an eye, so much for the loss of an ear, so much for an arm, a leg, a hand, even for a toenail. The payments varied also according to the victim's status: high for an *eorl*, less for a *ceorl*, little for a slave (in which case payment went not to the victim or his family but to his owner). There was even a *wergeld* for the king, thoughtfully set so high no one could afford to pay it.

The original aim was appeasement of the family of the killed or injured man. For a long while the *wergeld* system was not compulsory; it was offered only as an option. "Buy off the spear or bear it" survived as an English proverb. Officials might urge acceptance of the payment, but if the family felt like fighting there was no law to make them take the cash and let the credit go.

By the time the Anglo-Saxon era ended, *wergeld* was compulsory. (Theoretically and generally, that is. We must not suppose universal application of any rule of law in such an age; in fact, in any age, but then even less than now.) No more choice of pay or fight; the killer had to pay and the family had to quiet down. If the killer failed to pay, the sanction was outlawry.

There has been a subtle but substantial alteration in the meaning of outlawry. In the legend of the Western film (now spread to other contexts), the outlaw is a man who sets himself against the law, who fights it, usually from a strong position, a man whose crimes our cinematic wisemen ask us to admire. In the legend of Robin Hood, outlawry is a way of life at once ethical and pleasant. In each, the outlaw has both dignity and a kind of freedom. In history, he had neither. The outlaw of ancient England was no sporty anarchist. He did not choose to live beyond the law; he had been put beyond the law's protection.

Law is shelter, and the sentence of outlawry was exposure. The outlaw was like the nonperson of some modern states, except he was not merely shorn of privileges; if it pleased the one who found him, he might be murdered, and his murderer had done well. Outlawry was defenselessness, the outlaw's state of life was dread. The merry men of Robin Hood could not have frequently been merry.

Most of England was then a wilderness of bog and forest. It could contain, and did, a large outlaw population. There were so many that a stranger was presumed to be an outlaw unless he plainly made his presence known. In some parts of England, he had to sound a horn as he made his way along the road; if the unfamiliar figure moved silently, he could be slain on sight.

When we speak of courts in Anglo-Saxon times, we mean the local courts. They operated very much on their own. The royal "laws" were largely precatory, advice rather than command, an early form of jawboning about as effective as the present one. Anglo-Saxon kings sometimes urged that justice should be done, and set up guidelines for it, but the administration of justice was seldom a royal function until the Normans entered.

Some of the advice, however, deserves esteem. For a while, royalty consisted, for the most part, of the better sort of people. Alfred's laws are famous; and probably were heeded. Understanding well the use of preamble, Alfred begins his laws with the Ten Commandments, then quotes from other parts of the Bible, relates a bit of history, and at last lays down his precepts. (This sort of helpful introduction is what Whereases are supposed to be, but lawyers less talented than Alfred do not use them so well.)

The other outstanding early English king was Danish. The Laws of Canute say this:

> And we command that Christian men be not on any account for altogether too little condemned to death; but rather let gentle punishments be decreed, for the benefit of the people.

This was not the majority view. The majority took pleasure in cruelty. So much so that when William the Conqueror arrived, one of his innovations was a reduction in the number of offenses for which the penalty was death. William, known to us for harshness, was probably criticized—privately—as a liberal with no regard for law and order. William was harsh indeed, but his harshness was not for pleasure, nor was it random; it usually had a rational end. His restriction of capital punishment was no doubt unpopular, but William was not much interested in popularity.

Alfred and Canute and the Conqueror were not ordinary men. They could be admired and respected without being widely understood. Their subjects would follow them in battle, but not always in their thought. Most people had no use for "gentle punishments." Most people, by our standards, were not bright. There is no reason to congratulate ourselves; our standards are built on the bequests of prior generations.*

---

* Most warfare of the times was simple conquest, and conquerors secured their gains by wiping out the opposition. The moral test of the invaders' chief was not so much how he established his dominion as how he ruled when it was done. There is something similar in present-day elections. The test is not how the

□

Throughout the Anglo-Saxon period, the open homicide remained entirely moral, at first an occasion for revenge though not disapprobation. Then compensation was substituted for revenge, as the government (such as it was) discouraged feuds, though it never stamped them out. It was the furtive assault on person or on property, where the accusation could be denied, that supplied the principal legal problem. Mob execution became illegal (but not uncommon), and communal courts took on the task of deciding guilt or innocence. The law still sanctioned a bit of personally handled criminal law, called *infangthief*: a man who had been attacked and injured had the right to kill whoever injured him, a notion the great state of Texas has conserved for the benefit of cuckolds. Apart from *infangthief*, however, the government tried to take over. There were two modes of trial: ordeal and compurgation.

The earlier words were *urtheil* (ordeal) and *adfultum* (compurgation). *Adfultum* was "oath-help." The accused brought oath-helpers into court. The trial consisted of his swearing he was innocent and then ushering in his claque. They were not there to give evidence; they said nothing at all about what had happened. They came only to say the defendant was a man of good repute, that his oath was "clean." That was enough for the court. There was no inquiry into the facts. The defense was that the defendant denied the charge, and that he was a man who would not lie.

Compurgation in the abstract has an air of rationality. When methods of gathering evidence are rudimentary or nonexistent, an appraisal of the credibility of the accused seems a fair alternative. (Finding the facts is still today, a millennium later, a

---

candidate gains the office, but how he acts after the inauguration. No President since the earliest ones has run a truthful campaign. Franklin Roosevelt's pre-election speeches were stripped down to naked inconsistency by Walter Lippmann, but few remain who do not think the country fortunate that Roosevelt was elected. A more egregious inconsistency was displayed in 1976, but this was largely a failure of imagination. Carter could well conceive how to become President, but he could not conceive the Presidency. Neither could Gerald Ford. For each, imagination was exhausted in imagining how to get elected. Elected to what?—for each that was the mystery.

difficult task for the courts.) It stands to reason that if pillars of the community swear a man is truthful, he is probably telling the truth. But compurgation as it was practiced did not stand to reason. The statement the compurgators had to make was purely formal. No one weighed the validity of what these warrantors were saying; the court was interested only in how they said it. They had to follow a brittle form. If a single oath-helper forgot some part of the prescribed recital, or if his tongue tripped on the way, the defendant was found guilty. God had made the compurgator stammer.

The formula itself, and the number who must repeat it, varied from place to place and time to time, but the general rule remained the same: if the compurgators were too few, or if they recited poorly, it was held defendant's oath had "burst" and he was guilty. Otherwise he went free.

□

But compurgation was for the upper classes only. Most of those accused of crime had to face ordeal.

It was a nasty form of class distinction. A man in the upper levels of society might get away with murder (except against a person higher in the social scale) so long as he was not brought down by honesty, or by fear of penalty in an afterlife. (If there was attack on someone who ranked higher, it is futile to talk of law at all in this early age.) It is hardly likely that simple honesty played a part in such a situation, and thought of punishment in another world would not frequently outweigh a present threat of punishment in this one. Gathering the oath-helpers could not have been difficult. They did not have to say the accused did not do the deed; they only had to say he was not a man who would lie about it. And members of a minority—here a dominant minority—characteristically unite to defend their own.

This kind of class distortion of the law—not the ever present use of power and prestige which contravenes the law, but an explicit aspect of the legal system—reappears in colonial America. A white settler, by his own Christian oath, could clear himself of a charge leveled by a heathen Indian. Later there was another, similar rule of credibility, this time barely left unstated: this one was applied, especially in our Southern states, when the accused was white and the accuser black. (Those who like to say that racism in the North has been as bad as it was in the South have short memories.) These parallels are not exact, however. Compurgation could be used not only where the victim held a lower place in the social scale, but also where accuser and accused were of equal status. And compurgation was no sure thing; a faltering was fatal.

It was very different for those of the lower classes—by far a larger number—and for those who were "ill-famed," that is, those who already had a bad reputation. These were no doubt overlapping groups; ill-repute (that is, harsh criticism commonly expressed) is not easily assigned to the rich and powerful. For the greater part of the population, trial was by ordeal.*

Ordeal was frankly supernatural. It is part of the larger notion of trial by divination, a symptom of a pitiful human weakness, distrust of our minds and senses. Guilt or innocence is determined by some sign. England by then a Christian country, the sign was sought from God. Elsewhere, from God or Someone.

Australian aborigines, in case of murder, ask the corpse, carried on a bier, to identify the killer. If the murdered man has been a victim of sorcery, he will cause the bier to move around and touch the sorcerer who killed him. A recent Secretary General of the United Nations comes from a country—Burma—which in this century has decided lawsuits by having litigants light candles; the one whose candle burned the longer won the case. Justice was served by making sure the candles were cut to equal size and lighted simultaneously. Borneo in this same recent period had a jollier procedure. Each party put a shellfish on a plate, over which a lime was squeezed. Judgment was rendered in favor of the party whose creature, annoyed by the citric acid, wiggled first. It was well to know some irritable mollusks. A clam happy as a clam was not much use.

Trial by ordeal in Western Christendom was less trial than tribulation. The principal ordeals were these: carry hot iron in bare hands, dip the arm in boiling water, be bound and plunged into a pond or stream. The first two turned on medical consequence. After several days had passed, the injury was inspected. If the burn was healed, the accused was innocent; if it festered,

---

* *The harder procedure for those ill-famed suggests the modern test of liability when an animal does damage. The owner is usually not considered negligent and therefore is usually not liable, unless the animal has previously been a rogue. This has given rise to the legal adage: every dog is allowed one bite. It is about as reliable as other adages.*

he was guilty. The third, called ordeal by water, turned on whether the accused sank or floated. If he sank, he was innocent; if he floated, guilty.

Sinking does not necessarily mean drowning, but if one could not swim, ordeal by water seems a no-win game. But there have been justifications. One, contemporaneous, was put poetically: only the pure would be accepted by the water. If you were innocent and you died, you could count on going to heaven. Another, looking back from the present day, is that the purpose was to grant opportunity for honorable suicide, an analog of hara-kiri. You could let yourself drown and be remembered as an innocent, *de jure* if not *de facto.* *

Other modern scholars are more analytical. The courts of the time, they say, were insecure; there were not the methods of ascertaining facts that exist today. Moreover,

---

* *Hindu law in the millennium before the birth of Christ contains a forecast of what was later done in England, mixed with some pleasanter Asiatic notions.*

> *He whom the blazing fire burns not, whom the water forces not up, or who meets with no speedy misfortune must be held veracious in his testimony on oath.*

The situations in which ordeal was used were those in which

> *an offense has been committed in a solitary forest, at night, in the interior of a house; and in cases of violence; and of denial of a deposit.*

An interesting list, taking in some rough misconduct, together with a delicate breach of commercial practice.

Fire, water, poison, sacred libation and "the balance" were the tests. The last was, literally, a weighing of the defendant, twice. The judge addressed the scales of justice:

> *O balance, thou only knowest what mortals do not comprehend. This man being arraigned in a cause is weighed upon thee. Therefore mayest thou deliver him lawfully from his perplexity.*

If the defendant registered more at the second weighing, he was guilty; if he was lighter or the same, he was innocent. The defendant, it appears, had to sweat it out.

The business of deciding other men's disputes has never been a comfortable one; those charged with judicial functions have in all ages sought means of minimizing their personal responsibility for the decision rendered. The modern judge is likely to depict himself as an inert conduit through which the force of statutes and precedents is communicated.

The explanation is, I think, too reasonable, and overbroad. Some people shrink from handling the disputes of others, but most enjoy the exercise of power involved in rendering legal judgment (though they may not like the heavy load of work that should precede the judgment). Any lawyer who goes to court in civil cases knows that judges generally get some satisfaction from rendering decision. As they are entitled to, if they are serious judges and have struggled to reach the right decision. Wielding power over other people's lives is to some of us uncomfortable, to most of us a mixture of pain and pleasure, to many a pleasure unalloyed.*

Criminal cases are another matter, but those who were likely to be officials in the age we speak of would not have felt much pain. There was pomp and power in holding court, and little to make it troubling. Lives and bodies were extremely cheap, and as for the judge's soul, so long as he followed the rules of

---

* There can be no other accounting for the fact that the occupation of officiating at athletic contests never wants for candidates. Referees of international soccer matches put their lives in jeopardy. The American football referee and baseball umpire do not run such risks (America, we keep telling ourselves, and keep getting told by others, is the most violent country in the world), but they are targets of abuse, and even when good-naturedly indulged they are seen as clownish figures. Consider the jester's uniforms worn by football referees and linesmen, and the baseball umpires' ignominious dusting off the plate, and the willingness of all of them to be made fools of by television's instant replay. What remains, what draws them to their work, is that their word is law, and that they do indeed have power over the lives of other men. (The job used to have another attraction, when professional baseball was played in the afternoon, and games went much faster than they do now, and other forms of labor were more arduous than now. One old-time umpire, asked why he engaged in his line of work, gave a famous answer: "You can't beat them hours.")

the Church he ran no risk of damnation. What was the cost of a few mistakes, of sending an innocent or two to death or mutilation?

Maitland makes a statement about ordeal that rests not so much on reluctance to make decisions as on an inability to. It is simpler than the others, and beautifully neat, and by the test of Occam's Razor, probably the best. "The case is too hard for man," he says, "so it is left to the judgment of God." *

All these explanations fit the structure of ordeal, which to us seems upside down: the judges finish judging before the trial begins. Our present notion (not quite right) is that legal judgment comes after trial; to the people of the period, it was something that came first. Once it was established that the defendant must be tried, and the appropriate mode determined, the judges had done everything required of them. Rules of law were the rules that governed to that point. What happened next was not man's law, nor the work of man at all. This being so, there was no need for scribes to make a record of the trial. Omniscience has no need of files. Hence there is little specific information on the conduct of ordeals or the results.

The wistful efforts of the scholars to see a decent rationale in the ordeal are probably partly valid, but only partly. Theoretically, ordeal might represent a wish to avoid the responsibility of judgment, or it might be thought of as a plea to heaven to answer questions for which no earthly tests of truth had been devised. Or, a theory more pragmatic, ordeal by water might offer an opportunity for suicide to those for whom there was no hope. But the main reasons for its existence, I suggest, were more primitive. The idea of God among these people was not the same as that of modern theologians. Ordeal was the prevailing criminal legal process for the mass of men principally because the mass of men guided their lives in hope of miracle and fear of demonry. It is, again, a matter of degree. We are still

---

* The principle of the Razor, put most briefly, is that the least explanation is the best explanation (a principle useful not only in philosophy, but also, in a somewhat different sense, in social contretemps). More precisely, where there are several ways to account for things, the theory that involves the fewest hypotheses is to be preferred. William of Occam, or Ockham, is honored by having the principle named for him, but wrongly, it seems: Duns Scotus, a little older (both lived around 1300), was its creator.

affected by that hope and fear, still enormously, but a good deal less than those who lived in England at the time.

Whatever else it may have been, one thing I think is clear: ordeal was institutionalized sadism. If it were only the appeal to heaven of an unsophisticated folk, if the judgment was humbly left to God, the procedures were peculiar. God has innumerable ways of signaling His decision without demanding burning flesh or the horror of a drowning. The case could be as well decided by the toss of a coin. (A penny, perhaps, the coin named for Penda, the last pagan king of Mercia, which might have made it inappropriate, except the provenance was by these Christian times probably forgotten.) Surely it is as easy for God to make the coin come up one way or the other as it is for Him to scorch the flesh without allowing it to fester.

Ordeal served a purpose in the law—it served it badly—and it had these other uses too. It was an expression of the piety of the time, and an occasion for communal viciousness. What happened happened; it was God's will, and exciting to attend. For festive cruelty, we now have films instead, winners of acclaim and excellent money-makers. We are told they are obviously art, because the audience is not unaffected. Neither was the audience for a hanging or a mutilation. We may have made some progress, though. Vicarious sadism, by and large, is preferable to the real thing.

All through history people have enjoyed inflicting pain, enjoyed it more or less—more people or fewer people, openly or with their pleasure masked, enjoyed it freely or with their pleasure somewhat spoiled by guilt. They seem, mostly, to get less joy from it today than formerly. The Nazis are regarded, correctly, as not representative of the modern world, a proposition with which we may comfort ourselves as we prepare to make the planet uninhabitable. We are about to breed ourselves to death, or deaden the world with poisons, or—quicker and cleaner— simply blow it up, thus demonstrating that masochism is gaining ground on sadism. This is perhaps a moral gain. The point is arguable, but being cruel to oneself seems less reprehensible than being cruel to others. Hence we can feel a certain saintliness in arranging our demise.

□

The sadism, naturally, had a high sexual content. A disproportionate number of the reported cases had to do with women. We may assume that many more crimes of violence were committed by men than by women—and, except for stealth, nearly all the crimes were violent—yet the records of ordeal abound in cases in which the accused was a woman.*

The sexual element was quite plain in the witchcraft trials, in which the usual test was ordeal by water. It was a regular part of the procedure that the defendant have her clothes removed before she was immersed. Remember that the medieval conception of the witch was nothing like our Halloween cartoon. The witches of early fantasy were not ugly, nor, in all likelihood, were the women accused of witchcraft. Often, it is safe to say, the accuser was a bested rival, or a rejected suitor or discarded lover. The accused was likely to have an allure not supernatural at all. Our pleasant words like "charming," "enchanting" and "entrancing," and (by way of Scotland) "glamourous," are in origin the words of witchcraft.

□

In every age there are great differences among those who administer law. Some are superstitious, some subscribe to reason; some are honest, some corrupt; there are some who care, some unheeding. (Consider the contradictory appraisals of the way the law works now. So much depends on individual experience—what court, what judge, what lawyers one has seen.)

---

* *One of the many examples comes late in the history of ordeal, near the year 1200:*

> *Roll of the Iter of Wiltshire, 10 Rich. 1.—The Jurors said that Radulphus Parmentarius was found dead with his neck broken, and they suspect one Cristiana, who was formerly the wife of Ernaldus de Knabbewell, of his death, because Radulphus sued Cristiana in the ecclesiastical court for breach of a promise of marriage she had made to him, and after the death of her husband Ernaldus, Reginald, a clerk, frequented her and took her away from Radulphus, and Reginald and Cristiana hated Radulphus for suing her, and on account of that hatred the jurors suspect her and the clerk of his death. And the country says it suspects her. Therefore it is considered that the clerk and Cristiana appear on Friday, and that Cristiana purge herself by fire.*

Note that Cristiana, and not the clerk, went to the ordeal. Probably he had the benefit of clergy despite his tendency to frequent. We do not know what happened next.

There must have been variations from place to place, from time to time, and from man to man: that is, the man who on the particular occasion was running the proceedings. Those in charge were more or less intelligent, more or less humane, more or less in charge. The utter illogic of the ordeal must have been at times indulged, at other times outwitted.

We know there was at least one important man who had sense enough to see the foolishness of ordeal. William Rufus, the red-haired William, the second William, who ruled just after the Conqueror, is usually placed among the lesser kings. Yet he was perceptive. He said one day, of the ordeal, that God ought not be bothered with such problems; he, the king, would take the burden of decision off His overburdened hands. The King's contemporaries did not appreciate the irony; if they understood it, they rejected it. The bid was not accepted; the Crown was not then strong enough.

We can reasonably assume that the management of ordeal and compurgation was now and then diverted from the hand of God to the mind of man. It is not difficult to imagine openings for the intrusion of reality, or of mercy, or corruption. Let the iron cool a bit; don't bring the water to a rolling boil; if the accused establishes innocence by sinking in the stream, pull her out before she drowns. Probably such things happened; to what extent we do not know. So far as legal records go, they usually tell us only what occurred before the trial began, infrequently its outcome. But in one such instance a surviving record of a certain local court, about the year 1100, shows that every single one of fifty defendants put to ordeal was found innocent. It is a statistic that must owe something to human interference.

☐

Trial by battle is usually listed as a species of ordeal. This makes a larger category, and thus satisfies the craving for simple classification. There is, of course, connection: battle too was ornamented with the theory that God would give a sign, would make the righteous one the winner. But battle was different from ordeal (or, if you wish, from other kinds of ordeal). It was different historically, legally, psychologically. It was brought to England by the Normans, as Thornton's lawyer pointed out, at a date when ordeal had been in use in England for several hundred years. And lasted longer, as Thornton's justices agreed.

Ordeal was for criminal cases only. Battle, like compurgation, was for both criminal and civil cases. (Champions could be used only in civil disputes; those appealed of crime, and those appealing, had to do their own fighting.) The early law did not make the criminal–civil distinction that we make today, but a difference in the nature of the cases can be discerned and the modern words applied.

And the people viewed ordeal and battle differently. Battle, though it endured, was not popular. The reason historians give is that it was a Norman importation. There is probably another reason. Battle, more than ordeal, was vulnerable to skepticism. Ignorance of physical causes welcomed supernatural explanation. Who could say what it was, if not God's doing, that caused the flesh to heal or fester? In contrast, the causes of victory in combat, if not the justice of it, would commend themselves to reason. They fit the everyday experience of a society built on fighting. Onlookers might listen to the piety that God would judge the truth of the dispute; meanwhile they themselves could judge which combatant was the quicker, stronger, more skilled in the use of weapons. It must have been difficult to resist the message of the senses: that such lawsuits were decided not by Godly intervention, but by the litigants' abilities, or the wherewithal to buy the abilities of a champion. When there is presented to our eyes an obvious explanation for what is happening, we are less inclined to credit the announcement that unseen forces are at work. Even in medieval Christendom. So battle might have been regarded as patently unjust, while ordeal— well, who could tell?

To modern eyes, at least to these, battle seems the better. The human tendencies that lead to combat are different from those that lead to the ordeal, less dark, less ugly. Neither mode of trial belongs in a decent legal system, but combat has some association with qualities we can approve: competence and valor. Ordeal, in contrast, leaves the case to accident, in which there is nothing to respect. And it is more purely cruel, inflicting pain and fright without the joy of battle.*

---

*There is some moral value in rewarding winners, though a noisy part of our current culture will not have it so. There are, I think, several reasons why the antihero has become so prominent. One is that it is a good deal easier to be clever about a loser. (Consider jokes about the schlemiel, a minor Yiddish art form; the schlemiel is a cultural predecessor of the antihero, though an object of contempt, not approbation.) Another is that the present is, in many ways, a bad time for intellect; hence

Trial by battle has its modern counterparts. Contemporary litigation, to a large extent, goes according to the skill and strength of the advocates who engage in it. And outside the courts, trial by battle continues in our conduct and our fantasy.

The impulse has to do with order more than law. (Law and order are in our speech too often joined. A dictator imposes order with no regard for law. A lawful society can tolerate a certain amount of disorder.) Our response to controversy, when we ourselves are not involved, is not altogether a wish that justice should be done. Much of what we feel is mere annoyance: we simply want to calm things down, to get rid of the friction one way or another. And so we push the adversaries into combat. It is their quarrel; they are disturbing things; let them settle things by fighting. Within conventional limits, of course: "a fair fight" is the ideal (though not frequently the fact). Otherwise, the conflict may spill over, bring allies into it, be prolonged. Trial by battle may have helped to end the blood feud.

The schoolyard is frequently the scene of such a trial, something different from unregulated violence; at least it was some years ago. Two boys edge into hot dispute. One, at least, feels wronged. There is not much effort by their peers to determine who is right. The solution, rather, is a formal duel. The boys are encouraged—pressured, really—to fight it out. It is not anarchic brawl. There are usually fixed ways in which the thing is done, analog of rules of court. Often one party does not want the combat; sometimes neither wants it. But they usually feel the social pressure and yield to the convention.*

---

many intellectuals think of themselves as losers. It is comforting to mumble to oneself that the world is full of brothers; it is also comforting to think of oneself as the central figure of a work of art. A third reason is that Americans during the past quarter century have lost their marvelous old self-confidence, a fact reflected in the character of our principal comedians. Keaton, Chaplin, Harpo, Chico, Groucho, Fields—they were indomitable, in the end triumphant (except occasionally Chaplin, who was English). Our leading comedian of the moment, Woody Allen, though richly endowed with talent, has built a career on abasement. (Not ironic modesty, as, for example, Will Rogers, but thorough deprecation.)

* As in court, the procedure does not always work well. I recall a case involving one boy in the fourth grade, the other in the third. The fourth-grader, relatively bright, had been put ahead,

The underlying fantasy is so well rooted that trial by battle still constitutes the core of the principal American art form (if, as fairly may be said, "principal" in this context is that which chiefly interests the public). The Western is our most popular fiction, as well as our most ritualized. The villain has done wrong, but no human judge or jury, no human arbiter at all, determines guilt. The hero's cause prevails only because there is ritual battle and the hero comes out the winner. The appeal to the supernatural that marks the medieval battle is even plainer here than in the clash of knights. The matter is made to turn on a minute and special thing: the one whose gun leaves its holster first is the one who gains the verdict. Here the hand of God needs only the lightest touch.*

□

Minor offenses, at least toward the end of the period we speak of, were treated differently. The proceeding was perfunctory.

---

had "skipped." The third-grader, a different type, had been "left back." So the fourth-grader, eight years old, was two years younger than his opponent, an enormous physical disparity at that age. The community nevertheless decided that the battle must proceed: the grade, and not the age, controlled, and so the younger one was deemed not overmatched. The case, however, never came to trial. The bell sounded the end of recess while the parties and those presiding were still enmeshed in pre-trial proceedings. The eight-year-old, conscious of the timing, held things up with temporizing argument, the equivalent of what the courts call dilatory motions. When they were older, and two years made less difference, the younger, now ready to go to trial, sought the older out. But neither could summon up the faded enmity, and there was peace.

* The crux is the speed of the draw. Marksmanship is taken for granted; so is the accuracy of the nineteenth-century revolver. A superb parody, by one successful television series of another, Maverick of Gunsmoke, opens with the classic gun duel. In the main street of the town, the heroic frontier marshal confronts the villainous opponent (presumably villainous in this case, not actually). Both fire. Both remain standing. The hero is distraught. His opponent asks, politely, "Shall I stand a little closer, Marshal?"

But myth is holy, and tampering is sacrilege; Gunsmoke outlasted Maverick by several years.

The court, presented with the accusation and a bit of evidence, pronounced its judgment quickly. It was perfunctory but rational. The punishment was usually a money penalty or public degradation, not death or mutilation. For these minor crimes, people were content with a mundane appraisal of guilt. Not so if the crime was grave; then appeal to mystery was needed.

This, I think, was direct reflection of the respective roles we still assign to the natural and the supernatural (though their size has altered). In most of everyday life we automatically rely on what we see and hear and feel able to figure out, and this is how it must have been in most of everyday medieval life. We till the soil on the basis of experience and what our senses tell us, though we also now and then perform a rain dance. We trust to our eyes when crossing streets, not to amulets, because in infancy we learn that two objects cannot without some damage simultaneously occupy a single space, though at times we act on the assumption that demons enter bodies.

The baseball player may make the sign of the cross as he enters the batter's box; he has time to. But in the field when a wicked grounder comes his way, his every move is sense-directed and realistic; he has no time for piety. Most of our ordinary judgments are made practically, and in accordance with the facts as our minds present them. It is only when there is leisure for indulgence, or the matter seems beyond our powers, that we forsake reality. Thus, even in the time of ordeal and compurgation, it was accepted that for workaday breaches of the law a workaday sort of mental process would suffice. But not where more important offenses and more important punishments were in question; there the people of the age we speak of could not attain that level of self-reliance.

□

Compurgation in criminal cases began to disappear by the end of the twelfth century. A statute of 1166 is said to contain an "implied prohibition" of compurgation for the graver violations. Express or implied, it would not matter. This was the reign of Henry II, and Henry was not one to allow those charged with crimes against the Crown to escape through licensed perjury, however hallowed the license may have been. It continued, though, in the local courts. And for certain civil suits in the royal courts, compurgation remained the mode of trial a long time after. With the development of new "forms of action" (a subject we will come to later), the use of it diminished, but compurgation lived on to an astonishing old age, and was not formally abolished until 1833.

Ordeal went suddenly. It was the most directly sacral of the modes of trial, and the Church was very much involved. A question must be put to God, and the laity had no access to His ear. It was necessary that a clergyman be present. So the Church could end ordeal, and in 1215 it did.

The Fourth Lateran Council, dominated by the famous Innocent III, was a busy body. The Council announced as dogma that transubstantiation—literally, concretely—occurred in the Eucharist; whether this was so had theretofore been a subject of theological contention. The Council also proclaimed that nobody outside the Church could possibly escape damnation. It decreed that Jews and Saracens must wear identifying badges, this to guard against integration. (One may query whether the identification impeded or promoted the genetic mixtures that we see today.) It took measures against the spread of heresy, including a declaration of war upon the Albigensians, a war that exterminated the heretics so thoroughly that we are not sure now exactly what their heresy was. The Council also ended trial by ordeal as a juridical procedure. It did this by forbidding churchmen to take part.*

Here were a Pope and a Council gathered to do important things that were the opposite of what is now thought liberal. Why did they take this one liberal step? Were they indulging some impulse toward the humane? If so, it was a discordant note in an otherwise harmonious meeting. There must have been other reasons. We can guess.

There was probably secular pressure for the change. For those who had a government to run, ordeal was not a satisfactory law-enforcement tool. God could not be trusted in such matters. The judgment might be unacceptable from a political or admin-

---

* *The year 1215 was a big one; it was also the year of Magna Carta (that is, the first of the several editions of Magna Carta). There are some years like that; 1776, for example, saw the making of the Declaration of Independence, the publication of Adam Smith's* Wealth of Nations *and the first volume of Gibbon's* Decline and Fall, *and the first commercial use of James Watt's steam engine, an event that better than any other signals the commencement of the Industrial Revolution.*

istrative point of view. (Never mind the justice of it.) Ordeal, if my guesses are correct, gave local officials openings to manage things in ways the Crown might not approve.

And the Church had its own need to deal effectively with crime. The crime Rome had in mind was not murder, rape, or robbery. It was heresy. The definition of heresy was made in Rome, but its punishment was often remitted to secular authorities, whose performance probably failed to satisfy the Church. Ordeal was an unreliable way to deal with heresy, unless, of course, one had faith enough to believe that God adjusted the buoyancy of the accused or the recovery rate of scorched tissue. Pope Innocent and the other leaders of the Church, naturally, would not have had that faith. Heresy, whatever it might have meant for the soul, was a worldly threat to the Church. If ordeal determined the result, the true believer might be punished, the troublemaker might go free. The Church did not mind nonsense —indeed, approved of it, when it served a purpose. But it served no purpose here; on the contrary, it worked against the Church's aim. Since ordeal was chancy, it must go, and since it was a religious ceremony, requiring the presence of a priest, the Church could make it go.

And ordeal may have been theologically impolitic. It might have looked as though God was spreading Himself too thin. It could create skepticism to insist that the Almighty went to court, to many courts, each day. Could He have been that interested? In theory, of course. But in practice? How were those who saw the practice struck by it? Did it suit the dignity of God? Some few, but those few influential, might think it brought no honor to the Church.

Finally, a personal factor—accidental, one might say, but great events sometimes turn on such specific things rather than on the large abstractions we are pleased to attribute them to. Innocent III was very much a lawyer, some say the greatest of his age. Ordeal is distasteful to a lawyer, and not only for its cruelty. It does not suit the legal reach for reason. Besides, once ordeal is chosen as the mode of trial, what is left for a lawyer to do?

In any case, the pronouncement had the effect intended. Within three or four years the King of England (then Henry III) sent out the writs that declared ordeal abolished. Maitland writes: ". . . the ordeal was abolished at once and forever. Flourishing in the last records of John's reign, we can not find it in any later rolls." (John ruled until 1216.) The end was not as sharp and clean as Maitland's words suggest. Though ordeal was finished as official trial procedure, the idea did not disappear. In later cases, though the request is each time denied, we hear defendants in the royal courts asking that they be put to the ordeal. Probably these were cases where the accused saw that the evidence, or popular feeling, was so strong against him that he preferred the luck of the painful test. And it lingered as an unofficial community event. For centuries after, those accused as witches were made to suffer the ordeal. (Lynching once again, here illegal but permitted.) And even some intellectuals were shocked by the abrupt departure from the good old ways. At the end of the thirteenth century, when judicial ordeal had been gone for fifty years or more, a writer on the law protested:

It is an abuse . . . that proofs and purgations are not made by miracle of God where no other proof can be had.

But as a court procedure, ordeal was gone, if not immediately in 1215, then within a few years after.

In the royal courts, for a short while, the judges floundered. No compurgation, no ordeal, not much battle. How are these cases to be decided? The answer was trial by jury.

5

The Start
of Trial by Jury

Three features mark the Anglo-American legal system as different from all others. One is the extent to which our law is formed in litigation. Cases in court do more than what would seem their normal function, which is to settle specific controversies by applying rules of law. They also in large measure generate the rules. Our law comes not just from Parliament or Congress speaking broadcast to the body politic; it comes also from judges speaking to the litigants before them (though everyone had better listen). Another peculiar feature is the way we conduct these cases: we pit antagonists against each other, to cast up from their struggle the material of decision. A third—and largest in the public consciousness—is the trial by jury.

The question of its origin has built a stage for virtuoso scholars. The question is confused because, at various points in history, jury trial has had political significance far beyond its value (or impedance) as a litigating mechanism. This was true in seventeenth-century England, in eighteenth-century America, and again right now. Political ends can distract even the most brilliant scholars. But despite the virtuosity, and despite the betrayal of intellect that commitment feeds, we have a fair idea of where the jury comes from.

It had more than a single source. This has contributed to the melee of scholarship. The main one seems to be the royal inquest that the Normans brought across the Channel. They probably learned it from a practice of the Frankish kings, who themselves may have got the idea from some Roman or Teutonic antecedents. Wherever the Normans got it, it is known they used it. The king would now and then direct a group of inhabitants to make a statement, a sworn statement, on some question that concerned him. The fact that they were made to take an oath gave the thing its name. *Jurare* means "to swear." The king or his emissaries would ask the jurors whether crimes had been committed in the neighborhood, or how the king's subordinates were behaving, or which of two disputing claimants had the better right, or even whether certain land was owned directly by the king or only as suzerain of another lord.

The last two questions, in rudimentary form, are civil litigation. As to the very last, it may seem odd a monarch would litigate at all. Why should rulers mighty as the Frankish kings or the Conqueror submit their wealth to the judgment of their subjects? One important factor, probably, is that the Church was mighty, too, and various clerical institutions had various claims to land. Especially on smaller questions, great rivals may prefer to shun a test of strength. Let a jury, in equal dread of worldly and otherworldly power, decide the matter for them.

Then there was the magnates' strength. The temporal authority of a feudal king was rarely absolute; he both depended on, and contended with, the armed power of his vassals. A sovereign may on occasion prefer a lawsuit to a war.

It is a fair guess, too, that even when lesser men asserted rights, the king might hesitate to push aside their claims. A bank of resentment built up against the throne could eventually cause trouble. Though the king might once in a while lose some land he otherwise would hold, it would be politic, when there was not too much at stake, to yield to local sentiment, to allow the local freemen to render judgment based on local understanding.

Given the willingness to submit to adjudication, one may then ask why this mode was chosen—the jury instead of professionals, the jury instead of divination. These medieval rulers did not, of course, have in mind the founding of a democratic institution. There is the highest comedy in the fact they did. They chose this method of resolving questions, we may surmise, for several related reasons. A favorable verdict could express support among the people for the royal claims in general. Or it could manifest a fear of royal vengeance, which might be just as good. Again, the jury verdict is a mundane method of deciding rights, as distinguished from appeal to the supernatural; secular rulers might wish to promote a procedure that would reflect earthly power, as distinguished from divine. And the method was not strange; something like a jury seems to have been part of old Teutonic folkways.

Later they permitted certain subjects to employ the royal mechanism for disputes among themselves. The privilege was granted to those they chose to favor, such as laymen who could pay money for it or churchmen who had tickets to heaven to issue in exchange. When William crossed the Channel and subjugated England, he brought these precedents along.*

□

William the Conqueror was not merely a powerful and ruthless warrior; he was also a powerful and ruthless accountant. Twenty years after Hastings, fifteen years after all opponents were defeated, he took inventory. He wanted to know exactly what his Conquest brought him, exactly what he had to rule, what there was for him to tax. He found out through the celebrated Domesday Survey. To make it, he and his talented bureaucracy used every governmental institution in the land, but at bottom was the inquest. Assemblages of residents were directed to give sworn answers to questions prepared by royal clerks. In triplicate, so to speak: "Three times over, namely, in the time of King Edward, when King William gave it out, and how it is now."

Who owned the land? they were asked. What did it consist of? What had been built on it? "How much woods, how much meadow, how many pastures, how many mills, how many fish ponds, how much has been added to or taken away, how much it was worth altogether, and how much now?" What number of peasants lived on the manor, how many burghers in the town?

---

* *Charles de Gaulle, who hated Americans but shared with many of them (indeed surpassed them in it) the vulgar habit of hollering "We are Number One!" may have taken pleasure in the thought that the institution which is a point of pride to those he called "the Anglo-Saxons" was given them by Frenchmen. Not exactly, however. Another, though less important, root of the jury system had already taken hold in England. And what came across the Channel was brought not by proper Frenchmen but by mongrel Scandinavians—the Normans, briefly resident in France, who had only lately learned to speak French, and very likely spoke it with abominable accents. Finally, the earlier users of the device were not Gallic but Teutonic. The Franks moved in from Germany; Charlemagne was Karl.*

What were the local customs? What privileges existed? And—most striking—could better use be made of the land?

It was a glorious census. Historians have a clearer picture of that England than of any England for many centuries after. The results were listed in the famous Domesday Book. (The original is still available, if you want to be absolutely sure of who owned what in 1086.*)

"Domesday Book" is the same as "Doomsday Book." But "doom" did not then have the connotations it has now. It meant "law" or "judgment." The etymology is found in words that mean a thing laid down or put in place (somewhat like the etymology of "statute," except Germanic rather than Latin), so that it came to designate both the cap of a building and a law or judgment. The two spellings diverged; the one with the double o gradually became a word of dread. The Day of the Last Judgment is the Day of Doom, a terrifying day. This is probably because people tend to expect that any judgment will be painful and condemnatory. But a judgment, in the law at least, is not necessarily to be feared. On the contrary, the one who wins a lawsuit is said to "get a judgment." In William's time, "doom" had the older, pagan meaning, "law" rather than "punishment," though for those who held their lands not rightfully, and might expect to have their trespasses undone, the Domesday Book may indeed have borne a modern connotation.

There was resentment. The survey was a precocious sample of the conflict between a government and its people on the government's need to know. (The people's need to know about the government is another matter.) An efficient government must have information. Giving the information annoys the citizen. The process is full of friction, even taking each side at its best: the citizen law-abiding but jealous of his privacy, the government intruding only for the common weal. The conflict may be less innocent: the citizen concerned not about the preservation of a decent privacy but about concealment of a crime, the government seeking information in order to impose a tyranny or simply keep itself in power. But both sides may be acting properly and

---

* *The handwriting in the Domesday Book is in the Italian fashion. Britain has never been as tight a little isle as it is said to be. Lanfranc, the foremost intellectual in William's court, his principal adviser, came from Lombardy, and brought other Italian lawyers with him.*

with good will, and yet there can be conflict. Invasion of privacy was felt and protested at this early date. A contemporary wrote:

> It is shame to tell, though he thought it no shame to do. So very narrowly he caused it to be traced out that there was not one single hide or yard of land, not even an ox, nor a cow, nor a swine, that was not set down in writing.

It goes on today. Unreasonable search and seizure, which are prohibited by our Constitution, have given the courts a great deal of their recent work. And even honest taxpayers (there are some) find the income tax return an awful nuisance. Much of the objection, of course, comes from those who have committed crimes they want to cover, but the framers of our Bill of Rights decided that intrusion must be limited, even if it means the government is handicapped and many evildoers never brought to justice. On the other hand, the totally ignorant government is no government at all. William was going to give the island the start of sensible rule. He needed information, and he got it. England was no longer in the hands of the dear but sloppy Saxons.*

The survey included ownership disputes, and apparently settled some. But its main business was not adjudication. The first step was to find out what the claims were, and get other information. The inquest, for a century or so, was administrative rather than judicial, a device to gather data that the government required.

William had little need of inquest to validate his personal rights; he was not much interested in asking anybody what they thought he held. His monarchy came nearer to absolute than any

---

*We are often told about our "Anglo-Saxon legal heritage," even by sophisticated writers. There is very little that is Anglo-Saxon in our legal heritage. The great developments came after 1066, and the most important figure in the establishment of the common law was, as we shall see, Henry Plantagenet—half French and one quarter Scandinavian by blood, and Norman in his culture. The error may be due to confusion with "Anglo-American," but even if the proper phrase is used, we should keep in mind that the "Anglo" in this context is in significant measure Norman.

other England has had. But he and his successors wanted ownership—that is, ownership subject to their super-ownership—to be straightened out and manageable. And perhaps they wanted justice for its own sake; most people do, though it is an instinct that yields readily to others. No one knows exactly what went on in those Norman heads. But we do know that to rule they had to keep things ruly. So the next step was to adjudicate disputes, through institutions centrally controlled.

That step, however, was a slow one. The royal courts were established only gradually, the king's administrative assistants taking on judicial functions. Our word "court," the judicial institution, originally meant "court," the king and those in his hall. It took time for the various parts of government to separate, and for the word to take on separate meanings.

At this date, the king's official court—the *curia regis*—was actually two different bodies. Strictly, it was the Great Council, the assembly of chief vassals summoned several times a year to give advice and consent. With William it was advice more than consent; consent was usually taken for granted. But not always. Recalcitrance, even halfheartedness, was something to be reckoned with. Disaffection can become rebellion. Then there was a smaller group, ministers resident with the king, theoretically a sort of permanent committee of the Great Council; these were the men who, under William and his successors, made up the central government. They sent out the officials who took the inquest.

□

The root of "court" is a word that means enclosure. Then, metonymically, the place comes to mean those grouped within it, the adjutants of the leader in whose house they meet. (Hence not only court, but also cohort, courtesy, curtsy, courtesan, and curtain.) This royal inner group has been said to be much the same as the "household" of the Roman emperors. Much, but not quite. The Roman advisers were closer to domestic servants. They were usually slaves or ex-slaves, and though they had great influence, the status must have had some effect upon the function. At their most influential, we may picture, among the less impressive emperors, a Bertie Wooster (not so benign) with his Jeeves (not so omnicompetent).

The Norman ministers, though not often nobles, were more like the modern cabinet. The word "cabinet," like "court," indicates the coziness of the group, a group that in the time we speak of had more power, usually, than most highly titled personages outside the royal household. In recent years, in the United States, the highly titled department heads have themselves lost power to a "household." The process is nearly replicated: a group of White House advisers becomes a cabinet that vies for power with the Cabinet.*

The sending of commissioners for administrative purposes could, with no conceptual wrench, slide into the sending of commissioners for purposes of litigation. These traveling surrogates of the king had experience with the inquest; it would not be strange for them to use it for other governmental purposes. The practice of asking people in the neighborhood eventually replaced all earlier methods of trial.

In the pre-Conquest tribunals—the shire and hundred courts; the Anglo-Saxons had no royal courts—there was something called (in our translation) "recognition." Sometimes, in a dispute, a number of neighbors of the antagonists were called upon to make a statement on what they thought about the matter. Distinguish this from compurgation: they were summoned not just to swear the defendant was a truthful man; they came to report the facts. Some scholars consider the recognition to be of prime importance (perhaps because the word survived). It does not seem so to me. The main modes of trial in the shire and the hundred were ordeal and compurgation; trial by recognition was exceptional. Moreover, it was in the royal courts, not the local courts, that trial by jury as we know it was developed. The flow from the Norman administrative inquest to our trial by jury is continuous and clear. Yet the Anglo-Saxon recognition probably

---

* When Richard Nixon depreciated his Cabinet, and operated mainly through those he took into the White House—Haldeman, Ehrlichman, Colson; at another level, Kissinger (Mitchell was the only close adviser who held a Cabinet post until Kissinger, having taken the power of the Secretary of State, took his title too)—he was creating an approximation of twelfth-century royal administration. The reasons, of course, were different. Henry II functioned in this way because his country and his government were by our measures small, and this system suited. That is, for reasons of state. Nixon functioned this way to thwart the Constitution, and for reasons of stealth; our Senate must consent to Cabinet appointments, and the protesting resignation of a Cabinet official is a noisy public event.

contributed. The method of the invaders was not altogether foreign; that always helps.

□

The Conqueror was succeeded by two better-than-average kings. Victorious invaders generally constitute themselves an aristocracy, both politically (they govern) and socially (they are snobbish toward the beaten locals). The Conqueror and his sons had more sense; they were interested only in the substance. They wanted to secure a power, not create a social gulf. There were, in fact, fewer aristocrats in England under William I than before or ever afterward. He thought it best not to have too many, and he was strong enough to keep the number down. "They are noble," Maitland says, "whom he treats as such."

The realism of the Norman kings has been remarked. They had not been a dynasty long enough to suffer the debilitating effects of prolonged high status, which seems to deplete the brain. The Conqueror, on his father's side, was a near descendant of a Scandinavian pirate. ("Pirate" is a word commonly applied to marauders from the sea until they arrive in force; then they are "invaders.") The Conqueror's mother was a local tanner's daughter not wedded to his father. Thus he was only partly noble, and wholly illegitimate.

To promote the royal power, William II—William Rufus—used words, and he was good at it. He called the people "his Englishmen." He threatened his opponents with the Anglo-Saxon appellation *nithing*, which meant exactly what it sounds like. He was followed by his younger brother Henry, the first King Henry. (The name became so common among rulers of France and England in the next four hundred years as to be not just confusing but a bore.) Henry took an Anglo-Saxon wife. In his reign some useful statements of law were written down, the *Leges Henrici Primi*. These were in theory the Anglo-Saxon precepts of Edward the Confessor, which the Conqueror had said he would preserve, but actually, as we have noted, they added new things to the law.

Better-than-average kings, but not necessarily nice people. Circumstances suggest Henry I gained the throne by having his brother William Rufus murdered, and Rufus could be monstrously unpleasant. There are sides to this second William, though, that are unusually appealing. He was an open homosexual, thus setting himself apart from other kings less candid (including, in the view of some, the Lion-Hearted Richard). This openness goes with his frank and clear-sighted political statements. It added, however, to the opposition he faced. He was also kind to the Jews, and the combination was too much for the Church to bear.*

Some writers have made these brothers, along with Henry II, the objects of reproachful criticism, on the ground they breached the feudal code, the sacred vows given by lord to man and man to lord (in this case, king and nobles). Admirers of the Middle Ages tell us over and over again about the ties of fealty —honorable, reciprocal. The words are dandy: loyalty to those above, responsibility to those below. But the evidence that the stated ideals had great effect is not impressive. The movement of medieval history has to do with disregard of what the lord is said to owe the man (as in the progress toward a working government made by the Norman kings and Henry II) and disregard of what the man is said to owe the lord (small steps along the way to freedom).

An eminent historian says: "The very basis of feudal society was the sanctity of the plighted word . . ." It was hardly basic. Whenever anything thought to be of value was at stake, the plighted word was ignored. Lies and broken promises pervade the history of the time. The society was built not on honor but

---

* There is no direct evidence that Richard the Lion-Hearted was homosexual, and it may well be that he had no heart for sex of any kind. He may have been a twelfth-century version of a mother's boy; certainly he did what Mother wanted. Either hypothesis suits his long betrothal to Alice, Princess of France. Alice was sweet, sweet enough that Richard's father, Henry II, kept her close for years and years while Richard was away in Aquitaine. Dad explained, each year, that the boy was not yet ready for marriage. The betrothal-at-a-distance, and Alice's residence at Henry's court, lasted as long as Henry lived, until Richard was almost twice the age at which a prince might marry. Richard complained, often and loudly, but his complaints came from a longing for Alice's dowry, not her person. He renounced the betrothal after his father died, when he was at odds with Alice's brother, then King of France. Richard's primary interests were battle, slaughter, and religion, the perfect combination for the most celebrated Crusader of them all. He massacred more than two thousand Saracen prisoners at Acre. Dieu et Mon Droit, the peculiarly selfish royal motto, is sometimes attributed to him.

on military force and religious dread, with intermittent injections of reason and the idea of law.

The fond theory of feudal reciprocation has a moment's superficial moral glow; then it is enraging. Even if it had been carried out in fact, where is the justice of it? All people (or almost all) would rather have the privileges and comforts of high station than the privations and indignities of the low. And high station was usually not earned but born to. Balancing the obligations of man to lord with those of lord to man is a dreamy bit of nonsense; the reality was often nightmare.

□

Matilda, the daughter of Henry I, and his nephew, Stephen, competed for the throne. The barons joined the struggle, on one side or the other, or on one side and the other. It was a time of civil war (assuming that the nobles' grabs for real estate can be described in terms so grand). Stephen won, sort of.

Matilda had been the wife of the Holy Roman Emperor, but had no children by him. When the Emperor died, she married Geoffrey the Handsome, Count of Anjou; their eldest son became Henry II. This Henry crossed to England at least four times before he became its king. When he was nine, Geoffrey sent him over for several years, possibly to supply a symbol of male succession to aid Matilda's cause. Meanwhile Geoffrey campaigned successfully in Normandy. Stephen managed to stay ahead of Matilda in England, but had to give up Normandy.

When he was fourteen, Henry, on his own, with "a few companions and a small party of mercenaries, hired on credit," went back to England and attacked some castles. Boldness alone never works, and some lords on Stephen's side, as soon as they found out how little they had to contend with, pressed the toy army hard. So Henry applied for help to Uncle Stephen. (Alliances and enmities kept changing all the time.) Stephen gave him money to pay the soldiers and go on home.*

---

*It has been pointed out that the medieval castle was functional rather than storybook splendid, an uncomfortable fighting place rather than a stately dwelling. What is perhaps not generally known is that before the end of the twelfth century the usual castle was not the stone fortress that we think of—with massive masonry, high crenellated towers, moat, drawbridge, and portcullis—but something close to the stockade used against Indian attack on the American frontier. Most castles at the time young

Stephen, in this instance, was probably neither fond nor foolish, nor in any other way avuncular, but thought it well to show a tolerant confidence. If he was actually confident, he was making a bad mistake. When Henry was sixteen, he returned to Britain, ostensibly to be knighted by King David of Scotland. This time, when Stephen's men attacked, Henry, at the head of some anti-Stephen forces, achieved a reputation as a military leader, and then judiciously withdrew to Normandy. He was no longer an imprudent child.

When he was eighteen, Henry's father named him Duke of Normandy. A few weeks later, his father died, and Henry became Count of Anjou as well. He then made what seemed to be a clever marriage. It was to Eleanor, Duchess of Aquitaine, and former Queen of France, not only beautiful but rich. She had been married to King Louis VII for fourteen years. Louis had the marriage annulled, possibly because she had given him daughters but no sons. The wedding of Eleanor and Henry took place two months after the French clergy approved the annulment.*

There are suggestions in the chronicles that they had been having a romance. Whether Henry married Eleanor for love or policy, it was a major error. Eleanor brought Aquitaine and more to his dominions. But Henry had land enough with Anjou, Normandy and, soon after, England. As time went on, it became quite clear that Henry would have done much better if, like the father of the earlier cross-Channel conqueror, he had found, instead of a duchess, the daughter of a tanner.

In the year after his marriage, at the age of twenty, Henry crossed again to England, this time prepared to fight for it. Ste-

---

Henry engaged in his rash raid consisted of an earthen mound topped by a wooden tower, connected to a level space within a wooden palisade, the whole thing surrounded by a ditch. There were also rectangular forts built of stone, called donjon in French and "keep" in English, but far fewer of these. Settler-versus-Indian films provide a better model of the castle during much of the Middle Ages than films about Arthur or Ivanhoe.

* The ground of the annulment was consanguinity. There wasn't much of it. Robert the Pious, Eleanor's great-great-great-grandfather, was Louis' great-great-grandfather. Robert the Pious was also Henry's great-great-great-grandfather. No objection was made to the Henry–Eleanor marriage. The Church evidently was able to discover sanctity in the marriage of fourth cousins, incest in the marriage of third cousins once removed.

phen didn't fight. He agreed that Henry should succeed him. Nine months later, as though eager to make good the bargain, Stephen died, not in battle but in bed. Henry was already lord of Normandy, Anjou, Brittany, Maine, Poitou, Guienne and Gascony—about half of modern France, including regions relatively civilized and regions of delightful climate. Yet for the rest of his life Henry devoted his best energies to, of all places, England. This half-Frenchman quarter-Norman quarter-Anglo-Saxon, who spoke very little English, gave Englishmen a central part of their character by giving them the common law.*

☐

King Stephen was, to his contemporaries, a model of the feudal knight—courteous, brave in battle, excellent in tournaments. He gave England as poor a rule as it has ever had. The civil war was largely local raids, dispossession, robbery, extortion—extortion in the most literal sense: torture to get money, by "the devils in the castles."

For the development of the law, the most significant aspect of the anarchy was dispossession, the fighting over land. Land defined relationships. But simple robbery was also rife, especially in the knightly class. An example appears in an official report, made about three quarters of a century after the facts recounted:

In the wars of King Stephen there was a certain honest, wandering knight called Warin of Walccotc, and as he journeyed and fought he came at length to the house of Robert of Shuckburgh, who had a daughter called Isabel, and he fell in love with her and asked her father to give her to him, but both Robert and his son William refused. But William, who was also a knight, went out to the wars and was killed; and Warin, hearing of this, came with an armed band and carried off Isabel against her father's will and kept her for a long time.

But at last King Stephen died and the peace of King Henry was proclaimed, and Warin fell into poverty because he could no longer rob as he used to do; yet he could not abstain from robbery, and went robbing far and wide. And

---

* His native tongue was French, and he was a Latin scholar. When he was in England, he tried hard to communicate with those of his subjects who had no French, in royal broken English.

King Henry, hearing complaints of him, ordered him to be seized; and they went out after him and took him hiding in a swamp, and he was brought before the king, who, wishing to make an example of him, that others might keep the peace, commanded him to be put in the pillory, and there he died. And Isabel returned to her father's house with her child; and her father took her back because she had gone against her will, and later she married and had another son.

Note he was an "honest knight." That is, he was honestly a knight, doing what came naturally, just trying to make a living in those troubled times. The establishment of law by Henry II plunged Warin into poverty; what had been a recognized way of life abruptly became illegal (in fact as well as theory). It is as though the Nixon administration had been replaced by one interested in the law, all the law, not just parts of it, and Warin was one of the buccaneering businessmen the White House had smiled upon.*

When Henry gained the throne, he sent out his men to try to establish order. The most important thing, as I have said, was dominion over land. It would be impractical, if not impossible, to determine "ownership," to trace what we call "title" for a hundred years or more. The best that could be done was put things back the way they were before the riotous reign of Stephen. So Henry directed his officials to discover what had happened lately. Find out who had been thrown out of where and restore him to place. To help them get the facts, the King's men —in this context one would call them Justices—summoned local people. That is, they used a jury. The person claiming he was dispossessed had his claim decided by his neighbors, who gave

---

An irrepressibly bright-eyed historian, a chauvinistic Englishwoman (she is a good historian, and the chauvinism is attractive, though it must make us wary) tells us that things were not so bad in Stephen's time. For example ". . . great earls made treaties limiting the armaments they would use against each other . . ." This is presented as an effort "to minimise the horrors of civil war." More likely it was an effort to cut down the cost. In any case, it was about as effective as the disarmament treaties that nations made between the two world wars. We can hope that such efforts will be more successful in the future, but nothing up to now supports the hope. It is superior law—law enforced—that puts down major violence, not agreements between parties who regard themselves as sovereign.

sworn answers to the royal emissary. The order creating the judicial action, the council from which the order issued, and the judicial action itself all shared a single lilting name: the Assize of Novel Disseisin.

The word "novel" referred not to the newness of the procedure, but to the fact that the ouster had been recent. "Seisin" is a concept different from title, more like possession than ownership. There is some dispute as to how far beyond mere possession the idea of seisin went. My guess is that the precise differences in concept have more interest for historians than they had for contemporaries. It was just too difficult to deal with ultimate title, and, considering what ownership was based on, not morally important.

It was not the jury as we know it. It was a body of neighbors who acted on their own knowledge of the facts, as did the juries of the Domesday Book. They did not sit and listen to the evidence; they brought the evidence to court themselves, inside their heads. The idea of proving a case in court came later, and later yet the idea that to make the trial a fair one the jurors should have no preconception of the verdict they will render. The very thing that then was looked for in a juror is now good reason to reject him. The ultimate function of the jury is the same, determination of the facts, but the present method is antipodal to what it was when the jury system started.

There had been instances of the use of inquest for judicial purposes under both the Williams and Henry I. The hardheaded Normans, contemning compurgation and ordeal, had displayed an irreligious interest in the facts. But before this ordinance of Henry II it was a rare and special event, invoked for special cases, where the applicant happened to be a person whose power, military or religious, was important to the king, or one who paid good money for the favor at a negotiated price. Now it became a regular procedure, available to every freeman at a standard fee, set relatively low. And so the trial by jury is launched on its career.

☐

We may pause to consider the man, since it is to him more than any other that we owe the common law. Accounts differ. (As they almost always do: *videlicet Tiger*.) He was "small" and "not physically imposing," says one historian. He was "handsome ... with a tremendous physique," says another. "No stories were ever told of his personal prowess on the battlefield," says the one. "He commanded that physical prowess and skill in war which the magnates admired," says the other. Well, anyway, everyone agrees he wasn't tall, even for the time, when the average height was a good head less than it is today, and that he had physical strength and skills and enormous energy. It seems that he had the natural endowments of a first-rate front-line captain, though he rarely thought it necessary to occupy that role. We may fairly envision a quick, strong, balanced, driving athlete —the perfect halfback, if he hadn't more important things to do. When he had declined in health and spirits, he could still surprise his enemies by the distance he rode in a day.*

As for prowess on the field of battle, it seems to have been about as important for a general then as now. Not a single one of the principal figures in the French and English military history of this period was killed in clash of arms. Nor very many from the echelons below, down through the knightly class. (Lower-class mortality was quite another matter.) This despite the fact that knighthood was in flower, or maybe that's why knighthood was in flower. Of the high-ranking men who spent their lives in warfare, two or three, careless about wearing the heavy armor when things were quiet, got hit by distant arrows. Richard the Lion-Hearted died that way. Another, in a siege, tore his hand scaling the wall and succumbed to fever—tetanus, probably.†

The foremost knight of the time was Sir William Marshal, mightiest in warfare, mightiest in tournament, mightiest in knowledge of the feudal code, purest in his loyalty. The last two go together, since it took a kind of Talmudic learning to know to whom one's loyalty was owed. For example, an actual example: to the king's son, to whom the king had sent the knight for service, or to the king who sent him, when the son made war upon the king? Answer: it depends on the circumstances (as any student of any kind of law can tell you). We are informed of Sir William's qualities by what would now be called an authorized

---

Evidence of medieval stature comes both from bones and from suits of armor. The Vikings were, to an Arab observer who saw them on the Volga, "tall as trees." An existing skeleton of a Viking king shows him to have been five feet six. The trees of Araby must have been shrubs.

†*Perhaps chain mail had developed to the stage where those who wore it could hardly hurt each other, while missile weapons were not yet as effective as they became two centuries later. Perhaps it was a matter of how they used the common soldier.*

biography, so we cannot be certain, but external evidence appears to confirm at least the outlines of the character it draws. Item: when he was seventy, give or take a year or two, Marshal led the charge against the forces of the King of France, who was then invading England. And other incidents seem to show that he was exceptionally formidable, and exceptionally devoted to honor. (If you aim to be the latter, it helps to be the former.)

During the period when Henry and his sons were fighting on the Continent—sometimes against the King of France and sometimes against each other—a fierce battler on the French side built up a reputation. His name was Renault de Nevers. The inevitable single combat was arranged. As usual, nobody got killed or even badly hurt, but Sir William came riding back with Sir Renault draped across his horse's neck; he had by main strength simply dragged Renault off the French champion's charger. The King of France may have been the first man to swear he would never buy another Renault.

□

There was in Henry's character a combination of terrifying power and a humaneness alien to the age. His manic rages paralyzed people in his presence, but he did not often carry them to violence. In an age when the main occupation of the ruling class was war, Henry, once he had matured, came to detest both war and the play at war nobility was so fond of. Yet until his sad last days he was the most successful warrior in Christendom.*

By the standards of the time (are any other pertinent?) his actions and decisions were strangely gentle, kindly. The words seem out of joint. "Chickenhearted" might fit better, to contemporaries. The punishments he set for crime were much less harsh than those employed during both earlier reigns and later. In an age when the handling of prisoners was extra brutal, "not a single captive of any importance died in any of his prisons." (If the captive was not important, history would not know, either way.)

Born into the highest aristocracy, Henry cared nothing for its trappings—"indifferent to rank, impatient of pomp, careless of his appearance." Even on great occasions, he wore clothes

---

* Contrary to the frequently expressed sagacity, one does not have to love one's work to be good at it. One of the aptest pupils I knew in an Air Force group being taught to fly was almost every day reluctant to go up. (Whether out of fear or boredom I never ascertained.)

that were clearly out of fashion. Worse yet, he tended to be bookish—that is, when he sat still.

He was the first of the Plantagenet kings, also known as Angevin because Henry came from Anjou. The dynasty lasted more than three hundred years, from Henry's taking over in 1154 until Bosworth Field in 1485. At first Plantagenet was a nickname. It was not adopted as a formal surname until the fifteenth century, by the Richard of York who was the father of Richard III, who was the last of the line. It started with Henry's father, Geoffrey, an early conservationist. Geoffrey was devoted to the hunt, and the fields of Anjou were rather bare. To foster the species he liked to kill, Geoffrey planted the fields. He planted them with a bush called *genesta* in Latin and something close to that in Old French of the time. Hence Plantagenet. Geoffrey wore a sprig of it in his helmet, so that he would be recognized even when armor obscured his handsome face. The English word for the plant is "broom." It grows in Europe and in Asia, not in America, but it gives us the name of our household implement, which was originally a stick fastened to any kind of twigs, very often broom. Henry cleared away the mess made by Stephen and Matilda and their warring barons; a new broom, naturally, swept clean.

The counts of Anjou were an unusual line. One of them had said, "A king without letters is a crowned ass." Henry inherited not only this ancestor's lands, but the attitude as well. Despite his huge exploits, he found time for academic learning. A great part of the legal invention of his reign seems to have been his own. This King was a creative ruler, something more than one of those (though we should be thankful for them too) with sense enough to choose good minds to serve them. His court, when not at work, was a place of scholarly discussion. He respected ideas, and he had ideas, and he had the words to express them.

Henry had troubles with the Church other than the one involving Becket. During the first five years of Henry's reign, for the only time in history, the Pope in Rome was an Englishman. He was Adrian IV, formerly Nicholas Breakspear, born in Hertfordshire. In 1155, one year after he gained England, Henry asked permission to take suzerainty of Ireland, by then fallen from its early glory. Adrian refused. The reason Adrian gave was that it would be contrary to the papal claim to Ireland, a claim based on the Donation of Constantine. The "Donation" of the Roman Emperor turned out to be a forgery, but the fraud was not discovered until several centuries later. In 1171, rather halfheartedly, possibly to stay out of town while Adrian's successor was seeking to call Henry to account for Becket's murder, Henry went ahead and conquered Ireland anyway. More precisely, Henry sat in Ireland while some of his vassals killed the native king and such others as resisted. Here Henry did not rise above the standards of the age. This was one time he should have listened to the Pope, as the next eight hundred years made clear, and as is now being cruelly confirmed.*

□

We are told by most of those who write about the period that Henry was very much disliked. They usually fail to say exactly who disliked him. It was the nobles and high clergy. Those lower in the social scale never gave him trouble, despite the strictness of his rule. On the contrary, his noble opposition collapsed because it had no underpinning. Only in France, where except for Normandy he did not rule directly, did Henry have to fight.

Good government, at least till one gets used to it, is appreciated, and the parlous days of Stephen and Matilda were fresh in memory. The opposite of law is not freedom; it is subjection to those who can establish power through arms or wealth or what passes for religion. The common folk (to the extent they could see through the haze in which they lived), the middle class (to the extent it existed) and the men of intellect (the few there were) would naturally approve of Henry. But just as naturally those who profited from bad government would disapprove.

Henry viewed the decrees and ritual of the Church not as the embodiment of truth, but as implements of political force, to be both fought and used. He is said to have greatly enjoyed the music of the Church. Certainly he was not fond of anything else it offered. "All his life he neglected the sacraments" and "very seldom made his confession."

---

* Adrian is interesting mainly for his surname. Was some ancestor a brave warrior who would shatter a lance in a worthy cause, or a clumsy slob who ruined the ordnance he was issued? (For that matter, was our Poet-Playwright descended from one unusually combative, quick to anger and full of threats, who kept brandishing his weapons, or from one so frightened that he could not hold them steady?)

... it irked him to hear a priest decide that some of his most sensible actions, done solely for the good of his dominions, were in themselves sinful. Sometimes he would argue the point and lose his temper, and in the end be denied absolution.

Most of those who write the history of the times concentrate on magnates. You tend to work with the materials you have, and records of what the lesser people did or said are meager. So far as the magnates were concerned there was much to hate in Henry. He had a better brain than they. He preferred scholarship to tournament. He wanted everybody, not just the lower classes, to obey the law. He was disrespectful of claims of noble birth. And in this particular disrespect, not generally but in one important instance, he found his greatest trouble.

Henry chose his administrators according to ability rather than social station, and it usually served him well. He took a clerk of undistinguished family, for example, and gave him the rule of Brittany (theoretically under Geoffrey, one of Henry's sons, but Geoffrey was much more interested in tournament than government). Henry's most celebrated choice, however, ended in disaster. It was one a king who set greater store on birth would not have made. Henry raised Thomas à Becket to become his Chancellor and then Archbishop of Canterbury. Becket's father was a London burgher, and burgher in that day meant less than it meant later. It was not clear, indeed, that the ordinary burgher held the status of a freeman.

☐

The political science of the Middle Ages put everybody into three fundamental classes: those who fight, those who pray, those who work. The first consisted of the nobles and their knights and other military men; the second was the ecclesiastics; the third was mostly serfs. It was poor political science. "Those who fight" were not a class. There was a considerable distance between the barons (who later became the peers of England) and the ordinary knights (who became the landed gentry), and between the knights and the brutish, pillaging, unspeakable (and not much spoken of) mercenaries, recruited from the lower orders. And, since "work" meant manual labor, the categories had no room for the wealthier merchants or for the administrators surrounding the king; these two groups had power enough that their omission made the classification silly. Nor did the categories account for resident aliens, outlaws, excommunicates, idiots, lunatics, lepers, Jews and women, or those fictitious but important persons: corporations. (Idiots and lunatics seem to have been numerous; despite the reputed advantages of an ordered society, there is no good reason to suppose psychic disturbance was then in shorter supply than now.)

"Those who work" were nearly all the people, though they get scant notice in most histories. (Nor in the tales of the time, nor in later dramas looking back, including our most admired.) By far the largest number of Englishmen were serfs; there were also the laborers in the towns and armies and the many household servants. (We hear nothing of a help problem until two centuries later, after the Black Death had created a shortage much deplored.)

Serfs were slaves. We are told, by admirers of the Middle Ages, that there are distinctions between "serfdom" and "chattel slavery"—that a chattel slave was personal property, whereas a serf was not, and that serfs had recognized legal rights. As to legal rights, Maitland says:

> In relation to his lord the general rule makes him rightless ...the state is concerned to see [only] that no one shall make an ill use of his property. Our modern statutes which prohibit cruelty do not give rights to dogs and horses ...

As to the property point, serfs in fact were bought and sold. Despite the paucity of records, there are recorded instances. Moreover, a serf was not allowed to move from the soil he tilled; he could be shifted from one master to another by the fortunes of local war or the peaceful conveyance of land. The word "slave" does not appear in Bracton's thirteenth-century treatise, only "serf." Maitland explains it: Bracton "used the worst word that he had got, the word which, as he well knew, had described the Roman slave whom his owner might kill." Slave comes from "Slav." Large numbers of Slavs had been conquered and brought into Western Europe to fill the role the word describes, but the word "slave" as we know it was not yet part of the language.

The condition of workers who occupied some status other than serfdom was not a great deal better. The best estimate is that, one way or another, four fifths of the population were unfree. Today we are reminded frequently—and properly—that twenty percent of America is poor. Contemplate a society in which the figures are the other way around, and the difference between being poor and being rich is not only in material wants, but in whether you can move about and whether you can speak, and what if any recourse you have against injustice. Quite apart from economics, there was an outrageous difference in how life was lived by those who were free and those who were not. Most were not.

The theory, as I have said, fails to account for certain groups, groups (besides the lepers, Jews and women) somewhere in between. It was from those shadowy intermediate depths that Henry II raised up Thomas à Becket to the highest office in the land. "Was not your father my villein?" Henry once asked Becket, exaggerating slightly.

□

The Archbishop and the King set out on separate courses that converged and brought them into head-on conflict. Becket became a thoroughgoing churchman; Henry aimed all along at the construction of a pervasive secular government. The chief specific issue, as we have seen, was the jurisdiction of the church courts. As the struggle wore on, each man showed the worst (along with the best) of his character. Henry got petty; Becket got nutty. Henry at times confused his idea of what belonged to Henry with the rule of law. Becket at times confused Becket with Jesus Christ.

We know much about the murder of Saint Thomas, that it was done by royal henchmen, that it took place in a cathedral (a terribly important circumstance in an age when symbols were even more pernicious than they are now), that it stirred up Church and people, and became Henry's albatross. One of the things we do not know is whether, or to what extent, Henry bore responsibility for the crime.

"I could kill the son of a bitch," Henry might have said in one of his famous fits of temper. It does not mean that the speaker will, or is asking others to. This, of course, is translation, across eight hundred years. But the commonly accepted "Will no one rid me of this turbulent priest?" is translation equidistant. It is a fine English sentence, but Henry could not speak fine English, would not have spoken English to his court, would surely not have used that unfamiliar tongue in a moment of high wrath. Morality aside, we cannot suppose Henry to have been blind to the consequences of killing a churchman so influential. Moreover, murder simply wasn't Henry's style.

Nevertheless, he acknowledged responsibility, and did

great and dramatic public penance: he had himself scourged by the monks of Canterbury. The penance was in all likelihood a political rather than a religious act, a step along the path that made the dead Becket a saint and kept the living Henry the strongest man in Western Christendom, albatross and all.

A similar outburst is reported several years before, and, with Henry's intemperate temper, it is not at all unlikely he said such things on more than one occasion. What Henry may be blamed for is forgetting, in his rage, that there were stupidly ambitious courtiers who might take him at his word. But murder as deliberate plan made no sense—certainly not at this point; the conflict was very close to a negotiated end.

The two men had in common their notable intelligence. In other ways they were different. Becket, selective in his holiness, apparently held to his vow of chastity, but lived in the utmost pomp and luxury. Henry cared nothing for pomp, and could do without luxury, but he could not do without women. Or would not.

Canonized kings excepted, Becket must have been the richest saint in history. We are told that inhibition of the sexual drive results in sublimation, the diversion of energy to things the world regards as good, such as arts and letters. It also results in things less good: aggrandizement and hoarding. Thus *Das Rheingold:* the gnomes, rejected by the maidens, turn to high finance; that is, they go for the gold. Becket's continence was undoubtedly a factor in making him a saint, and possibly in making him as wealthy as he was.

Henry's passion for the sex, and his passion for orderly administration, combined to yield some information rather more solid than the period typically gives us. There are records of his grants of land to the families of those to whom he was attached, and the royal accounts include a reference to a sum spent on clothes for a recipient named Bellebelle.*

□

About the famously beautiful Eleanor, history leaves us in some doubt. There is no doubt she was beautiful. Nor is there doubt

---

* *One writer mentions, as another expenditure listed, sheets for the bed of Bellebelle. I have been unable to find supporting documentation. Assuming authenticity, it is not possible to say whether this was an expression of delicate affection, or of Henry's interest in his own comfort, or both. Both, probably.*

about her vigor: eleven years older than Henry, she bore him eight children (after two by Louis of France) and then outlived him fifteen years. The doubt has to do with character. She did not, as Henry did, rise above the cruelty of her time. She was a chief promoter of the new cult of aristocracy, with all its chivalric foolishness. She seems to have regarded her relationship with Henry as a dynastic competition, and to have treated him more as rival than as lover, childbearing notwithstanding. Perhaps not notwithstanding. The brood became an anti-Henry army, and maybe she meant it should.

Given the circumstances and the standards of times, Henry treated her well. She was the Lady of his House, the Queen of England. Henry introduced no woman to his court whose presence might displease her. That is, not until Eleanor, in alliance with their sons and the King of France, made war on him. Then she was sent away, and Henry openly took a mistress, the Fair Rosamund of romance. Rosamund died soon after, poisoned, it is said but there is no proof, by Eleanor.

After the uxorial-patricidal war began, Henry kept Eleanor confined, except when on formal occasions she came to court to play the role of queen. Her actions, of course, had been palpable treason. Queens have been beheaded for much less. Henry's punishment of Eleanor was mild. It was hardly punishment at all; rather, a practical safety measure. Hot-tempered Henry was not vengeful. He made her imprisonment comfortable and elegant.*

Hollywood, naturally, could not resist doing a movie about these two, nor resist giving itself prizes for the effort, nor resist inane miscasting. Eleanor, dark-eyed, black-haired, her lovely body built of curves, is played by light-haired, light-eyed, geometric Katharine Hepburn. Henry—stocky, powerful Henry—is played by tall, thin, untough Peter O'Toole, who is given lines to declaim that would drive Henry, if he went beyond a sneer, into one of his carpet-chewing rages. (The carpet-chewing is

---

* This is attested by the fact that when Henry died, and Eleanor had her son and ally Richard on the throne, no punishment was visited on Ranulf de Glanvil, who had been her warden. His is a famous name in the history of our law, because the first great treatise on English law is known as "Glanvil," though he probably did not write it. A middling landowner, he became one of Henry's military chieftains, one of his justices, and then Chief Justiciar, the top official in the realm.

reported as literally occurring. One might guess that intelligent Henry, aware of his own capacity for impolitic statements when the anger was upon him, might have stuffed his mouth with whatever was handy, including the rushes on the floor.)

Four sons made war on him. It is a strange story. Not because dynastic sons tried to kill their father—that is a commonplace in history—but because the father never responded in kind. Henry was a doting parent, anxious that each of the sons should have sufficient land, and he had land enough to carry out his purpose. But the elder three were not satisfied, and fought him whenever they could. They were encouraged by their mother, but each was fighting for himself, not for mother or brother.

Since hereditary monarchy was not yet thoroughly established, Henry took the unusual step of having his oldest living son, Henry, crowned joint king with himself. Henry the Younger, after warring on his father in a mean and treacherous way, died of dysentery. (He was a king without a number; Henry III is someone else.) The second son, Geoffrey, is said to have been the least likable of the lot, which is saying something indeed. He did not, however, surpass the others in treachery. (In this quality, it is hard to choose among the four.) The third was Richard, whose sadism was not confined to infidels; within his own Aquitaine, he had prisoners "drowned, butchered, or blinded." Richard—hail the power of entertainment—became vulgar history's hero. The fourth son, John, too young to participate earlier, managed to make the team in the final moments, when he delivered the ultimate double-cross. One of history's villains, he was the brightest of the brood, and apparently had some charm, which is hard to find in his loutish older brothers.

No matter how many times Henry defeated and then pardoned them, his sons would try again. The fighting took place in Henry's French dominions. There were battles, sieges, reconciliations, shifting alliances, new battles, new sieges—altogether a disgusting muddle. Throughout, Henry was forgiving, and almost to the very end victorious. But his forgiveness only gave the enemy-sons new opportunities. At last Richard did him in, with the considerable aid of Philip of France and the treachery of Henry's other sons, and, probably most telling, Henry's fatal illness. Yet—or maybe "And"; it is not so paradoxical—Richard at his own request was buried at Henry's feet.

We do not know what Henry's illness was. It might well have been what the twentieth century calls psychosomatic. Or one can say, more plainly, that Henry died of a broken heart.

The events recall David and rebellious Absalom, though David, unlike Henry, was the victor. But the story in the Bible is cleaner, closer to us though much farther off in time. After Absalom's defeat and death:

> Ahimaaz called, and said unto the king, All is well. And the king said, Is the young man Absalom safe?
>
> And, behold, Cushi came; and Cushi said, Tidings, my lord the king: for the Lord hath avenged thee this day of all them that rose up against thee. And the king said unto Cushi, Is the young man Absalom safe? And Cushi answered, The enemies of my lord the king, and all that rise against thee to do thee hurt, be as that young man is.
>
> And the king was much moved, and went up to the chamber over the gate, and wept: and as he went, thus he said, O my son Absalom, my son, my son Absalom! would God I had died for thee, O Absalom, my son, my son!
>
> And it was told Joab, Behold, the king weepeth and mourneth for Absalom. And the victory that day was turned into mourning unto all the people: for the people heard say that day how the king was grieved for his son. And the people gat them by stealth that day into the city, as people being ashamed steal away when they flee in battle. But the king covered his face, and the king cried with a loud voice, O my son Absalom, O Absalom, my son, my son.

But David was the head of state, and had obligations to his people more important than his feelings for his child. We are touched by David's grief, but a better king would not have shown his grief. Joab, wise and loyal, both field commander and adviser, was not afraid to point this out, forcefully and bitterly:

> And Joab came into the house to the king, and said, Thou hast shamed this day the faces of all thy servants, which this day have saved thy life, and the lives of thy sons and of thy daughters, and the lives of thy wives, and the lives of thy concubines;
>
> In that thou lovest thine enemies, and hatest thy friends. For thou hast declared this day, that thou regardest neither princes nor servants: for this day I perceive, that if Absalom had lived, and all we had died this day, then it had pleased thee well.

Henry had no Joab.

6

Grand and Petty

Whatever the private joys and sadnesses of Henry's life, they did not keep him from bringing peace to England and working great things in its law. The contribution of any individual to the building of the law is necessarily minuscule in relation to the whole. "Thou shalt not bear false witness" no doubt was thought a sensible rule before Moses came down from Sinai. The law at every stage is a product of its history, even when the stage is revolutionary. But measured against what was done at other times and places, the accomplishments on Sinai, in Hammurabi's Babylon, and at Philadelphia in 1787 were enormous. So were those in England in the time of Henry II.*

We cannot say with certainty to what extent the new ideas of Henry's reign were Henry's own. Certainly his advisers helped, even the lowest clerk consulted. Historians find it convenient to speak in terms of what a monarch did, even though chances are someone else had the idea, made the decision, or carried out the plan. Henry, as we have noted, had more respect for mind than rank, and would recognize a good idea no matter what its source.

Today, when a brief is filed by a government department or

---

* It is said that when the Bolsheviks came to power, one of their leaders declared in council that the first class scheduled for liquidation should be the lawyers, to which Lenin replied, "And then we will issue our first decree and we will have a whole new class of lawyers." Apocryphal perhaps, but the point is plain, and the new lawyers would draw on old experience.

by a large law firm, there are usually several names subscribed. Sometimes the bottom name belongs to a junior who contributed more in concept or expression than anyone standing higher. Nothing in the record reveals this, and it is rarely known outside the office (the junior's spouse excepted). Another confusion of authorship occurs at a later stage. Whoever wrote the brief, when its words or thought find their way into the court's opinion, history records them as the judge's own. The true advocate does not mind. Indeed, he hopes the court will steal his product. The only consequence is misdirected praise (or blame), which interests him less than the decision he wants—especially, if he happens to care about the law, in a case whose rule he thinks may do some good.

A more serious plagiarism occurs in another branch of government. Historians and journalists do not hesitate to attribute fine sentences to a President when it is doubtful that the President created them, even when it should be obvious that the man has insufficient intellect to be the author of the words he speaks. Here the consequence is distortion of the voter's understanding. Ideas apart, style itself is one index of a person's mind and character, not by any means infallible but certainly evidentiary. We can be misled when the words are not the speaker's own. Intellect, whatever its failures, is generally desirable in a leader, and the electorate should be cognizant of its presence or its absence. (Under an alias, of course; it has to bear another name, which varies from time to time—practical judgment, good vibrations, savvy, common sense. Intellect by any other name smells sweeter to the voters of America.)

It might do something for the quality of our government if the press, instead of reporting that the President in his speech said this or that, reported that he selected this or that from what was offered him to say. Better still, the Constitution should be amended to require that the President must write, unaided, at least sixty percent of each speech he makes. Then, perhaps, in time, we might get Presidents like Jefferson or Lincoln instead of what we have.

But from what we know of Henry, it is likely his contributions were substantial, not just in action and decision but also in creation. He had the traits a lawyer ought to have: impatience with ritual, a talent for expression, eagerness for innovation bound to respect for precedent, a commitment to reason, an unreasoning commitment to justice. Each of these traits appears in the record of his actions. The record also shows the less attractive traits of lawyers. In his politics, Henry used devices attorneys use to defeat the law: evasion and delay. And there were instances of duplicity, though whether Henry was more duplicitous than those with whom he dealt is unlikely.

He saw to it his courts were excellent. A prominent cleric of the time, whose writing has come down to us, reports a conversation with Ranulf de Glanvil. The churchman remarked he was impressed with a certain case in the royal courts, a case in which a poor plaintiff got fast relief against a rich defendant.

> Yes, said the Justiciar, we are quicker about our business than your bishops are. Very true, replied the cleric, but you would be as dilatory as they are if the king were as far away from you as the pope is from the bishops.

Glanvil smiled, says Maitland.

There is another example, spectacular, of the respect accorded Henry's legal system. The King of Castile and the King of Navarre had a quarrel over boundaries. Instead of following the prevailing course—war or negotiated treaty—these august princes decided to litigate in the distant English courts. It was not merely arbitration by another king; it was a regular lawsuit according to Henry's set precedures, handled like other civil litigation. It went off on a point of pleading that produced a sensible result, as proper pleading often does. There were cross-complaints, each king alleging that the other had wrongfully seized part of his domain. Neither denied this allegation with sufficient specificity. The court decided that the denials were insufficient, and each complaint should be taken to be true. The judgment was that each king give back what he had allegedly—and, as his shabby denials indicated, no doubt actually—seized by force of arms.

☐

Law is one of the verbal arts. Good language does not itself produce good law, but there is no good law without it. Henry's sensitivity to words appears both in the phrases he chose and in the phrases he objected to. On the issue of the criminous clerks, Henry first argued canon law, and seems to have had the better of the argument with his canonical opponents. But Becket would not yield. So Henry invoked secular law, the customs of the realm. Becket and his bishops went into conference. They came out saying they would abide by the customs of the realm *salvo ordine*—"saving their order." Did this mean that Becket would abide by the customs of the realm so long as they did not conflict with what the Church demanded? If so, the statement conceded nothing. If *salvo ordine* meant something less, what did it mean? Becket repeated the phrase several times, never defining it: he would obey the law of England "saving his order."

Henry insisted on definition. A lawyer wants to know the meaning of the words proposed. Or the several things they mean, if ambiguity is the practical solution. Or that the words mean little or nothing if it serves the situation best to leave the point obscure. In any case he wants to know. Here Henry needed clarity, and *salvo ordine* gave him none. "Poison," said Henry, "lay in that phrase."

☐

Henry referred so often to "my rights"—the perquisites of the king of England "in the time of my grandfather Henry"—that we may ask whether he was interested in justice for all of England or justice for Henry only. But often an individual's anger at personal wrongs can be inherent in, or can become, an anger at all injustice. It is clear that Henry, the young Henry anyway, drove hard for personal power, but power was not all he sought. From such evidence as we have, from what in fact was done in Henry's reign (all dubious reporting and interpretation laid aside), from Henry's open actions (discounting what adherents and detractors said about things not clearly known), it is close to certain he intended to improve the law and foster justice in his realm, intended and succeeded.

Henry moved the law a long stretch of the way from magic to reality. And he made it clear to Englishmen that most of the law, the important law, would issue from a single source, from a government strong enough and bright enough to render it large in their lives. It would operate throughout the land. The common law took hold.

With it the jury system. The Norman inquest, as we have seen, was a multipurpose tool, available for any royal service it might suit. In the Domesday Survey, it had been administrative mainly. It had also been used, once in a while, for litigation— the king's own litigation, and, when the king gave out the privilege, for private litigation.

For certain disputes between his subjects, Henry made jury trial a constant legal right instead of occasional boon. It was the kind of litigation we would today call civil. At the very same time he brought the jury into criminal law. It was done at Clarendon, at an assize held in 1166, nicely enough a century after Hastings.

The society's existing responses to crime could not serve a central government that wanted a rule of law. They were deficient both in getting the criminal process going and in the ways they determined guilt. The hue and cry did both at once, very badly. In a single sweep, it began the prosecution and convicted the defendant (and simultaneously accomplished the third part of the criminal process—execution). But it operated beyond the government's control. The other principal way to set the criminal law in motion was appeal—that is, private accusation. Though appeal took place in court, it did not suit the needs of government much better than the hue and cry. It depended for commencement on a private party's wishes; the crime would go unheeded unless the victim (or in case of homicide, his kin) undertook its prosecution. And even when this crotchety machinery had started up the criminal process, the result was left to tests not rationally related to guilt or innocence—to compurgation, battle, or ordeal. There also must have been other ways, of which we have less record, in which proceedings ending in punishment were begun and carried forward. We can probably assume some communal accusation followed by a local trial of some sort or another; there were, as I have mentioned, local variations. And there were processes we can call criminal within the feudal system. Certainly the lord or his men could charge the serf, and the higher lord the lower. But this was not the kind of justice Henry wished to foster; it was the kind he wished to end.

He wanted a realm-wide system of law enforcement, at any rate for major crimes, and a method of initiating prosecution that did not depend on hot pursuit or the vengefulness or daring of the person wronged, and a method of preventing escape from punishment through the leaky tests of guilt. It is a very good guess that he also aimed to give protection to the innocent; Henry was egregiously humane, and, in colder terms, frequent punishment of those not guilty dilutes respect for government. Finally, for both criminal law and civil, he aimed at a single law for England, not subject to the varying ideas of justice of the various communities, or to the outright denial of justice by unrestricted local lords. Hence the Assize of Clarendon.

A specific bit of evidence of what we might reasonably suppose the natural inclination of most local lords, and of how a central legal system might thwart it, is supplied by a reported case that came a little later, in the year 1221. (Before the thirteenth century cases were very seldom reported.) A lowly freeman named William was charged with having stolen a cow belonging to his lord; the damning proof was the carcass, discovered in William's barn. This was a charge of felony, and conviction for a felony meant not only death, but also punishment of the family: the felon's land would be forfeited to the lord. By this date there was a royal court to hear the case. William, obviously desperate—there was nothing more to lose—protested that his lord, with forfeiture in mind, had killed the animal himself and planted it in William's barn. The court found this was so. William was acquitted; the lord was punished. The report does not tell us everything that led to this remarkable result, but one item was that the deputy who seized William, evidently awed by the visiting royal power more than by his lord's, confessed he had been told to make the arrest by the lady of the manor. What odds on the outcome if the case had stayed in the lord's own court?

□

The procedure decreed at Clarendon was fundamentally the same as had been used for Domesday: the king sends round his officers—in this capacity they are Justices—and they ask questions of a group drawn from the neighborhood. This time, though, the makeup of the jury is explicitly provided. A number of knights are summoned from the hundred, a number of "good and lawful men" are summoned from the vills, to function as the jurors. (Vills, as mentioned, were small settlements within the hundred; "village" is close enough in meaning.) The men of the vill report to the knights; the knights report to the Justices.

It will be convenient to call it the Clarendon jury, though that is not its name in history or in histories. At first it has no special name; a century later it is called "grand jury." The jurors hear no witnesses. They can act on personal knowledge, and they can also act without it. They can simply repeat what people say—and this, apparently, is the usual form of their report—that such a one, by common repute, is believed to have done an evil deed. The jurors do not even have to state that they themselves believe him guilty. Hearsay is sufficient.

The jury having reported, those accused must go to trial. The trial will be ordeal. Compurgation in criminal cases is abolished, apparently at the same assize. No explicit words of abolition have been found, but the new system appears to exclude it; at any rate, about this time it vanishes from the trial of crime.

Battle is appropriate only where the accusation comes from the victim or the next of kin. Ordeal is left.*

The ostensible function of the Clarendon jury is the same as that of our grand jury: to level a charge that leads to trial. And this is the way historians see it; they call this assemblage "an accusatory body." But there is another feature of the new procedure, which, I think, has had insufficient emphasis. If one accused by the Clarendon jury succeeds in the ordeal—if the traditional signals show him innocent—he must nevertheless "abjure the realm." If at the port there is no ship to take him, he must stay until one comes, and every day wade into the sea—up to his knees, say some reports; up to his neck, say others—to demonstrate his readiness to go. If he takes too long to reach the port, or if he strays from the route prescribed, he is outlaw, prey to anyone.

This itself is fearful punishment. In the old ordeal, those lucky enough to pass the test—whether truly innocent or guilty —were adjudicated innocent, and escaped all punishment. (Except, of course, the pain of the test itself, but that is inescapable; defendants today must undergo the considerable pain of trial.) After 1166, success in the ordeal is not enough. Found not guilty by the ancient test, the Clarendon-accused must nevertheless leave family, friends, home, possessions—everything he knows and values. And where shall he go? And how shall he live, in the ordered society of feudal Christendom, a stranger in an alien land? He cannot (except in the rarest cases) even speak the language of the place where the ship will set him down.

I have not been able to find records, relating to this period, of what happened to those compelled to abjure after they left England. A noble with land or connections overseas would suffer less, but nobles were not usually involved in the kind of crime the Clarendon jury acted on. (Their crimes toward those below them, if deemed crimes at all, would usually be ignored, and

* Battle will remain a possibility where there is private accusation, but in the next century, after trial by jury is established, the defendant may, if he wishes, put the case to a jury rather than the hazards of the duel. That is, the accuser can no longer insist on battle; the accused has an option. There is inducement to exercise the option; the royal Justices favor jury trial, and it is not wise to cross them. Besides, battle is not popular with Englishmen. So gradually trial by battle is just about forgotten, until Thornton reminds a startled nation that it still exists.

their crimes toward the king were treason, which made a special case.) A knight might find employment as a mercenary. For others, save perhaps a few with special skills, the plight was close to hopeless. For them exile meant impoverishment, and quite possibly death, unless, perhaps, they were taken into slavery. There are reports of attempts to disappear while on the way to port; if the escape was successful, the man became an outlaw. The danger and hardship an outlaw had to face underscore the fearfulness of abjuration. Excepting the forfeiture of lands which was part of the punishment for felony (which would not affect the landless), failure in the ordeal was barely worse than success.

There is today a dread of banishment that seems in part race memory. The danger now, of course, is nothing like it was in the Middle Ages. Yet in 1958 four Justices of the Supreme Court declared that expatriation, which Congress had made a penalty for wartime desertion, was a "cruel and unusual punishment" under the Eighth Amendment. (A fifth Justice, on other grounds, joined the four to nullify the Act.) At that date the penalty of death was not deemed cruel and unusual within the meaning of the Constitution. Denationalization, said Chief Justice Warren, may involve no physical mistreatment, but it means "the total destruction of the individual's status in organized society . . ." One who is banished and thus becomes a stateless person "has lost the right to have rights." This is too much, the Supreme Court held.

The Chief Justice was overstating the perils of contemporary exile; the description makes a better fit with ancient outlawry. And for the same offense—wartime desertion—the defendant might, quite constitutionally, have been made to stand before a firing squad. The decision, whose effect is to raise citizenship up above life itself, seems mighty patriotic. The ghost of Philip Nolan wanders the corridors of the Court.*

□

Our historians mislead us, I suggest, when they call this use of inquest an accusatory mechanism, or dwell on its resemblance to the present-day grand jury—when they divide the Clarendon

---

* *The dear dichotomy of "liberal–conservative" fails once again. The conservative four who dissented were apparently not much moved by the glories of United States citizenship; the opinion of the liberal four seems to hum "America the Beautiful."*

procedure, symmetrically, into accusation by the jury and trial by the ordeal. They are, I think, too much influenced by the later system of indictment followed by a jury trial; the antiquarians are not antiquarian enough.

Henry, it is safe to say, did not take the ordeal seriously. Sophisticates did not. Great-Uncle William Rufus had been wittily scornful of it. It would be utterly uncongenial to a man of Henry's temperament. We may reasonably imagine that Henry met the matter practically. He would preserve the filthy institution to comfort those who might be troubled by his changes. Another ancient mode of trial—compurgation—was being done away with; Henry would be careful not to make a custom-loving populace swallow too much at a gulp. So, I suggest, this was his plan: he would keep ordeal, but render its outcome unimportant. The ritual could be performed for the many who were interested in ritual, but once the Clarendon jury had lodged its "accusation," the case for governmental purposes was done.

Killers who failed in the ordeal were hanged; other felons lost a hand or foot or both, at once marked as having committed crime and disadvantaged in its repetition. Those who succeeded in the ordeal must abjure the realm. Whichever way it went, the two main aims of a practical criminal law were served. Either way, the possibility that the miscreant would continue his misdeeds was altogether gone or very much diminished, by death or identifying disablement, or by expulsion from society. And either way there was deterrence. The presumed malefactor was punished; the realm was rid of him; the deterrent was made plain.

Except as public relations, ordeal itself had lost its meaning. When the Clarendon jury was done, the "accused" was in fact condemned, if not to death or maiming, then to a deadly banishment. It was the classic game of heads-we-win, tails-you-lose, turned to a better purpose. So the jury's report was far more than accusation; it was (if my dissent is right) effectively the trial itself. A fundamental point is missed when this new establishment is thought of only as a young grand jury. Our present-day grand jury, though descended from the Clarendon jury, has a much more limited function. It inquires and indicts, and leaves conviction or acquittal to another institution. Given the effects of expulsion, the Clarendon jury was both accuser and tribunal. What it did was all, or very nearly all. Henry and his advisers must have consciously arranged this.

When we view its judging function, the procedure may offend us. Condemnation rested often on evidence our present law rejects. But it was a vast improvement over earlier procedures which rested on no evidence at all. Recall that when Henry came to England crime was epidemic and punishment hit-or-miss, the innocent easily hit and most of the guilty missed.

Haphazard ways of commencing prosecution (hue and cry, appeal) and distinguishing guilt from innocence (ordeal, battle, compurgation) could neither serve justice nor establish order. The hue and cry was uncontrolled. Private prosecution opened doors to malice. Compurgation released murderers whose friends or debtors, or others intimidated or obliged, came to court to make the ritual recitation. In trial by battle, the strong and skilled defendant could readily go free; for the physically weak defendant, innocence did not matter. Nor did it matter in ordeal, unless there was some brave and kindly human hand to parry the hand of God. The hearsay method was far better than the methods it replaced.

It was a solemn process, and elaborate. Over the centuries the details changed, but in Henry's time the work of the Clarendon jury seems to have gone like this: Four lawful men of each of the four vills that surround the scene of the crime tell their stories to the twelve knights who represent the hundred. If twelve knights are not available, freeholders will do; members of a landowning class, they are not too low in the social scale. We do not know just what goes on in this assemblage, but it is probably safe to say that after the villagers tell what they have heard or think they know, they are interrogated by the knights. The statements of the villagers are put in writing. The knights make their decision. If the first twelve knights do not agree, others are added to the jury until there are twelve who do agree, one way or the other.*

Now the king's Justices go to work. They examine the reporting knights, then turn to the villagers. Any inconsistency may bring down punishment. The jurors must either have direct knowledge of the facts, to which they swear, or else must swear that the accused is by common repute the perpetrator of a crime.

---

* *The size of the group might vary, but it was typically twenty-eight (sixteen men of the vills plus the twelve knights). The present-day grand jury's size—twenty-three—is not much different. Twenty-three became the total because the test of indictment became majority vote and the indicting number stayed at twelve.*

The display of strength that marks the process must impress the jurors. The knights are "sword-girt knights," chosen usually by others of their class, who themselves are chosen (usually, again) by the sheriff. The sheriff, in this age a most important officer, in effect a provincial governor, is overseeing things. The king's Justices come to the shire as the embodiment of the royal power. Judging is not all they do; they are often warriors as well: Glanvil, for example. A twelfth-century royal Justice is different from the modern judge, distinguished only by his robe and the elevation of his bench (though they are impressive too). The Justice is a monarch's viceroy.

The symbol-ridden Middle Ages were skilled in pageantry. The coming of the royal Justices was probably announced by trumpet flare. All the local dignitaries would be out to meet them. The procession was full of color; the Justices' gowns were rich. Everything was at once rigidly formal and spectacular and awesome.

Consider the solemnity and ceremony in a solemn, ceremonious time. Consider the number who must agree. Consider the threat of punishment hanging in the air. Though the jurors speak more often of ill-repute than of the deed itself and this of course is hearsay, it is something more than back-fence gossip. The word "rumor"—used by several historians when they talk about the Clarendon Assize—is inappropriate. What everybody knows is frequently untrue, but, put through this rigorous process, it took far better aim at truth than ordeal or compurgation. Hearsay in these circumstances was not the bad word that it is today. It was not, in fact, a word at all; it was invented centuries later. Discerning minds might be skeptical of secondhand reports, but those same minds would think them better evidence, thus tested, than buoyancy or infection.

Moreover, "repute" that one has committed a crime is not achieved too easily. It is community consensus to which the villagers swear when they have not witnessed the crime themselves. The community can be wrong, of course, but we are moving from the random to the probable. The number of jurors who take part, the questioning, the double distillation—these all guard against mistakes. And deliberate lying is dangerous. A juror who has falsely sworn forfeits all his goods and chattels; he goes to prison for a year or more. He is no longer a "lawful man." (This is not outlawry, but deprivation of important rights. He is "forever infamous.") The jurors will come to their decision gravely. There is not only the specific threat of punishment;

there is also the awareness that they are delegates of government, a government which in this reign has shown itself concerned with justice.

Clarendon was nowhere near our concept of due process, but it was a movement toward it. Solicitude for the accused is very much a modern notion. Even after jury trial had replaced ordeal, most of the period from then till now would pass before one charged with crime could demand to be confronted by his accusers; or call witnesses of his own (though there were witnesses against him); or have a lawyer to defend him (though the prosecutor was a lawyer highly trained). It was later still that the requirement of proof beyond a reasonable doubt would enter, and, indeed, that the presumption of the trial would be changed from guilt to innocence. Meanwhile focus on the fact that the king compelled these semi-savages to accept reason in their law.

□

Justice, of course, is a two-sided thing. Part of us—part of all of us and usually part of each of us—thinks of justice as fairness to those accused, while the other part thinks of it as law enforcement and retribution. The former uses phrases such as "what is fair" and "what is just," while the latter uses phrases such as "bring to justice" and "just deserts" and names our chief prosecuting agency the Department of Justice. Half the citizenry calls for law and order while the other half denounces prisons and shudders at the death cell, and most of us are members of both halves.

One side of justice is the guarding of society and the people who compose it. This plain and simple proposition has been so mutilated by candidates for office that good people sometimes fail to give it recognition. We are also influenced by our entertainments. The interaction of the criminal and his pursuer is the common stuff of drama. We may disapprove the crime itself, but as audience we come to know the malefactor and the lawman, and often—to some extent, more or less, according to our psyches—identify with one or both. We rarely identify with the victim, who arouses not much more interest than a stagehand, and whose function in this fantasy is just about the same.

But peace and order are good, not bad, and a working system of punishments is one way to attain them. Attain in decent measure, that is. Perfect peace and order are heavenly, heavenly exclusively. Henry aimed at a rule of law; it was the chief thing England needed. He advanced the civil law, and drove hard to see that crimes were punished. He was also concerned, the record of his actions shows, to avoid punishment of the innocent. Henry was one of the eccentrics of that time who took no pleasure in barbarity toward the helpless. His punishments were milder, much, than those of reigns preceding his, and, for half a millennium, of the reigns that followed. But they were much more steadily visited than in England they had ever been.*

In the context of the slow development of defendants' rights, the Assize of Clarendon was a considerable improvement. Like most inventions, it was made up of components ready to hand. Ill-fame was a familiar Anglo-Saxon concept. The inquest was a known device. Ordeal was ancient; so was exile. But the filtering and refinement and the organization into a whole—these created something wholly new. Clarendon at a single stroke diminished both England's rampant violence and the condemnation of the innocent by bad luck and superstition. One would now be punished or set free by the test of evidence—evidence by our standards often unacceptable, but evidence nonetheless.

Under Henry's rule, if order was not perfectly established, at least chaos was dispelled. Clarendon was important to the peace that Henry brought to England, vastly more efficient than the older methods and at the same time fairer.

I have mentioned the strength of the concept that the law is settled, the law is fixed, the customs of the realm should not be tampered with. It is concept set upon feeling, not dogma imposed from above, a very strong structure indeed. The law exists, it is not legislated, it is essentially immutable. Kings present their statements of law as declaratory only, expressions of established principle. Then how about the explicit innovations Henry made?

It has been said they were merely procedural. Respected historians have said it: "Henry did not set out to make new laws; he only offered new procedures . . ." This is distinction without a difference, precisely the sort of thing laymen charge lawyers with. The person quoted is not a lawyer; an historian of high

---

* *We can, of course, conceive of other ways to promote peace and order, which, if successful, would be far better than punishments. But up to now these better ways have been nonexistent or insufficient. Currently, some people are questioning whether the prospect of punishment reduces crime. A tiny bit of imagination supplies the answer to the question: suppose there were no punishments at all.*

scholarship, but in law an amateur, supplying in this instance a fine example of amateur seduced by professional arcana.*

The quoted statement relies on a classification useful, as we have seen, in some other contexts. But it is useless here. The fact is that the law was greatly changed. The "substantive law" (the concept was, of course, developed later) might retain its theoretical chastity under these reforms. Murder was still murder, mayhem mayhem, rape was rape and theft was theft. But who was punished and who escaped would be effectively decided by the Clarendon jury, not by ordeal or compurgation or the duel. To the guilty and the innocent, to the government and the governed, these things were fundamental. And the new actions in the royal courts afforded redress that had not existed before, and so created new rights. The distinction between substance and procedure, in situations of this kind, might impress lawyers, but it would not impress the students at today's good law schools, nor the twelfth-century litigants to whose advantage or detriment the new provisions worked.

That last cannot be documented, because there was little reporting of cases then. The next century, though, supplies an instance that is close enough in time and culture. A case arose in which the king's Justices ordered that answers, of a kind which theretofore had been unsworn, be given under oath. This, according to the concepts, is thoroughly "procedural." The magnates who were questioned refused to take the oath. They declared it was unheard of; their ancestors had never, in such a situation, been compelled to swear. It was not part of *lex et consuetudo*, the established law and custom. "And thereupon many times was the book held out to them, but they refused." The conflict seems to have been left unresolved. Apparently, the case in modern terms was "settled"; like many another interesting legal question, this one never reached decision because the parties compromised. But, for present purposes, it makes the point. When the law is changed, it does not matter to those who benefit or suffer how the change is classified; it is the result they care about. The resistance can be as stubborn when the change is labeled procedure "merely" as when it is labeled substance.

---

* *The present writer, venturing outside his own profession, is in a position precisely converse. So while the work of the historians is splendidly attractive, one must be wary of seduction. I am in this too wary, I can count on being told. Perhaps.*

And for the history of the law the change can be as significant in the one instance as the other.

□

Henry's death did not halt the progress of the jury system. The bureaucracy he had fostered continued to manage things. ("Bureaucracy" is a word that invites indiscriminate disparagement. Some discrimination is needed. It is foolish to expect a government to govern without a staff.) The title of the highest bureaucrat was sometimes Chancellor, sometimes Chief Justiciar, depending loosely on whether he was of the Church or not. With Angevin kings so often absent from the realm, the man who held the office was for considerable periods England's actual ruler. Becket held the office as Chancellor. Later Ranulf de Glanvil, Henry's captain and Eleanor's keeper, was Chief Justiciar.

Richard was hardly ever in England—about six months of his ten-year reign—a fortunate thing for England and its law. The rest of the time he spent crusading, or in his French dominions, or, for a time, unwillingly, in Germany. Stumbling back from a Crusade, King Richard, despite a disguise or perhaps because of it, got himself captured by Leopold, an Austrian duke to whom he had given insult in the Holy Land. The Holy Roman Emperor took Leopold's prize away, and held the King for ransom. This led to another advance in governance: the means employed to raise the ransom from the English people was the origin of our personal property tax.

Richard's regent, Longchamp, was overbearing; some of the nobles, backed by the wealthy citizens of London, put Longchamp out of office. It is interesting they could do it; nothing of the sort could have happened under Henry. It is even more interesting that they did it as a court, not as an army or a mob; they sat in judgment on Longchamp, decided he had violated the customary law, and judged he be deposed.

Hubert Walter, Glanvil's nephew, became Chief Justiciar. It was the least nepotistic advancement of a nephew that ever has been made. Later he was made Chancellor and Archbishop, but he was much more lawyer than priest, and a very good lawyer indeed. He had been an assistant in his uncle's time, and was probably the author of the commentary that bears his uncle's name. (He had a curiously modern name; there must be dozens of people named Hubert Walter; or anyway Hubert, Walter.)

In the next reign, that of John, came Magna Carta, or rather the first of a series of documents collectively known as Magna Carta. They were—in several reigns, all through the thirteenth century—issued, withdrawn, reissued, repudiated, revised, and finally confirmed. The first Great Charter came in 1215, when the nobles confronted John at Runnymede. That is also the year of the Fourth Lateran Council. Both assemblies, in their separate ways, helped trial by jury grow.

A decree of the Lateran Council, as we have seen, destroyed ordeal. By this time ordeal had been for half a century the mechanism that completed the Clarendon criminal process. For a while, English officialdom wondered what to do. But not for long. The solution was a second jury. The Clarendon jury would make the accusation; another, smaller jury would take the place earlier held by God.

Some writers express amazement at the speed of the transition from ordeal to trial by jury. It seems to me they needn't. Compurgation had all but vanished in 1166, battle was limited to private accusation, and now ordeal was gone. English royal judges, unlike those who followed the Roman system, were unaccustomed to deciding the facts themselves. The jury was a ready-made, close-at-hand solution. It had already been employed in the trial of certain civil actions. It had entered the criminal law at Clarendon. It could readily be turned to one more use.*

So the final verdict would come not from divine displays, but from the minds of men. This was a doctrinal difference indeed, but not much of a practical shift. Trial by jury then bore very small resemblance to trial by jury as we know it. If my view of Clarendon is fair, there already was acceptance of the idea that punishment, of one kind or another, might follow from the action of a jury. The transition was eased by the practice of drawing the trial jury, partly or entirely, from the Clarendon assemblage.

Given the indictment, acquittal at the trial must have been unlikely. In both their functions the jurors acted on the selfsame data: what they had heard in the community and what they may

---

There is evidence from 1219 that the government still was groping, but it appears to have settled on jury trial very soon thereafter. Given the state of communications, a total change in five or ten years' time was virtually instantaneous.

have known directly. They were not apt to change their minds. "I was right the first time" is a natural response. And much more than ego was involved: there was the fear of punishment for false swearing—not just the danger to the soul, which presumably was not a danger when an altered view was honest, but a painful temporal sting. The punishment for perjury was harsh, and if the verdict of the trial jury differed from that of the indicting jury, was not one oath or the other false?

Maitland describes the jury of the early thirteenth century as having a real function in trials of crime. He writes that since the larger jury need say no more than that defendant was reputed to have done the deed, the smaller jury could arrive at a verdict of innocence. This is one of the few points on which Maitland is not persuasive. The smaller jury could conceivably reach a different verdict, but that is hardly likely. As we have seen, the ill-fame the Clarendon jury acted on between 1166 and 1215 was no simple rumor; it meant the community harbored a strong impression that the charge was true. It is unrealistic to imagine the Clarendon jurors saying, "This is what the community believes, but we disagree." It is even less realistic to imagine some of their number, serving as the petty jury, having no further evidence before them, announcing that they had changed their minds.

We are talking of the start. Later on, when the personnel of the two juries was disjoined, the system, though it stayed the same in form, would be much different in effect. But in this early period acquittal is improbable. (Except perhaps in the rare case where someone other than the accused came forward with a confession, or the ostensibly murdered man showed up alive and well, or there was some other unlikely happening that demonstrated innocence.) The work of the larger jury remained the important thing. For fifty years its "accusation" had led to punishment of one sort or another, its action had for practical purposes been the final verdict. People could not be shocked to see its members play a double role. Those who condemned could condemn again.

Not until the trial jury became in fact a separate group would there be a reasonable chance of acquittal. Then the trial jurors might say—with less fear of punishment for perjury and without appearing irresolute—that the defendant was in fact innocent; the others, the accusing jurors, may have believed the defendant guilty, but we do not. At the same time, and as part of the same process, the larger jury, since its report no longer meant certain punishment, could with less to go on send a man to trial; now their work could more accurately be labeled accusation.

By the time the two kinds of jury became totally distinct—about the middle of the fourteenth century—they had got their separate titles. The jury of accusation, being the larger body, was given the name "grand jury." The trial jury, relatively small, was named the "petit jury" or the "petty jury," depending on how adulterated with English the writer chose to have his French. Pronounced alike, then and now, both spellings are still in use.

☐

Abjuration faded away. It continued briefly as a penalty prescribed for certain crimes, and as an incident of sanctuary: if the accused left the holy house, he had to leave the country too. If my estimate is right, in the beginning of the period of jury trial the government saw no need to expel those who were acquitted because not many were acquitted. Later, as the grand and petty juries grew apart and acquittal grew more frequent, punishment in every case of ill-repute seems to have been no longer needed in the maintenance of order. This, perhaps, was because in the thirteenth century punishments became so severe that deterrence was achieved without it. Or—more comforting—perhaps as time went on the jury trial became a more respected test than ordeal had been; hence it was felt that the acquittal of the defendant should make him altogether free. Some of each, I would say.

Crimes considered minor were not part of the royal courts' work till toward the middle of the thirteenth century, and not a large part then. Meanwhile, on both sides of 1215, they were handled in the local courts, where, as suggested a chapter back, the sacral modes could be dispensed with. The lord rather than the Lord could render the decision.

When the royal courts began to handle minor crimes, the grand jury's presentment was usually enough; a further trial was rare. Here the explanation is probably the same. These things were simply not of a nature to require high formality and the mystic element appropriate to felonies. The punishment was "amercement," a money payment to the king.

☐

The transition to the jury trial sounds progressive, and in a significant measure it was, but keep in mind the level it progressed from. It is a common mistake, a bad mistake, a mistake compounded by much of our history-writing and almost all our historical novels, to assume that the people we are speaking of were people "just like us," that "human beings are human beings," that thirteenth-century Englishmen were the same as twentieth-century Englishmen, and that only the technology and accumulated knowledge differ. In fact their minds were different. Again, as always, there are exceptions: there were modern minds in the year 1200 (though a small proportion of the whole), and there are medieval minds right now (a considerably larger proportion). But most people of the Middle Ages were disinclined to examine concepts that were handed to them, whether by the Church or by pagan custom, and they were—in relation to their far descendants—immensely cruel to helpless victims. They were frightened of mentality and not much moved by others' pain.

Primitive modes of thought run through the development of the jury system. In the beginning, the rulers, secular and clerical, were far ahead of the people. The people preferred ordeal and protested its abandonment. The protests came both from those accused, because acquittal was improbable, and from the community itself, which lost not only a tradition but also an entertainment. At the end of the thirteenth century, they were still protesting, including some who were learned, even one who wrote a book, as we saw in an earlier chapter.

The resistance to reason affected the character of the petty jury. We will accept the new procedure, but it must carry a charge of magic. For example, the number of jurors. In the beginning, it might vary from case to case, but before very long it was fixed at twelve. Why twelve?

No one seems to know, but we can speculate. The Clarendon jury acted on the agreement of twelve men, whether or not they were a majority of those who served. This furnished a handy precedent for the petty jury, but it only moves our question one step back.

Twelve was not impractical. The group was large enough to yield an impressive consensus, yet not so large as to be unwieldy. Beyond this, it is hard to see reason in the choice. The number, of course, has a general utility. There is no rounder number in its range; it is divisible by more other numbers than any up to twenty. So it makes a very good measure. We have twelve months in our year, two twelve-hour periods in our day; we have our dozens and our grosses. We find the number so useful we have given it a second name, one of the very few thus honored (apart from Latin equivalents and slang). Twenty has Score, two has Brace, and one has Ace, none of them as much in use as Dozen.*

But the admirable divisibility of twelve has nothing to do with the size of a group expected to act as a whole. Things less rational seem to have fixed the size of the jury. Odd numbers seem to frighten us; round numbers seem to comfort us. Seven and eleven are granted supernatural powers. Trinities are awesome. The solar year is close to thirteen lunar cycles, yet we insist it have twelve months. Modern elevators, demonstrating how precocious we are in technology and how retarded in philosophy, stop unaided, precisely and with flourish, at Floors Fourteen and Twelve, forsaking Thirteen altogether.

Like other magic-infested notions, the size of the jury became an article of religion. A seventeenth-century legal treatise stated:

> And first as to their [the jury's] number twelve: and this number is no less esteemed by our law than by Holy Writ. If the twelve apostles on their twelve thrones must try us in our eternal state, good reason hath the law to appoint the number of twelve to try our temporal. The tribes of Israel were twelve, the patriarchs were twelve, and Solomon's officers were twelve.

---

* *A number system based on twelve would probably make more sense than the one we have, with its base of ten. That is, the single-figure numbers would go to eleven, the first double-figure number would be twelve. Two more symbols would be needed: 0, 1, 2, 3, 4, 5, 6, 7, 8, 9, #, §; "10" would signify a dozen, and "100" would be a gross. The use of ten as the basis of our numbering—the decimal system—has no rationale other than the fact that we have our hands before our eyes. Our digits are our digits. We could easily have decided on five instead of ten, or even twenty (in the warmer climates). Some animals would probably prefer eight or four. Horses and other ungulates whose hoofs are not cloven might favor the same binary system that our computers use.*

Fingers were man's first computer, with exactly a computer's intelligence. They did what people's minds told them to. Fingers cannot reckon with anything like the computer's speed, but computation is the least of their abilities. They have other wonders to perform: play a piano, throw a curve, declare affection, extend a mooring to a child.

The writer, Duncomb, having neglected the Twelve Tables of Roman law, then moved on to England:

> Therefore not only matters of fact were tried by twelve, but of ancient times twelve judges were to try matters in law, in the Exchequer Chamber, and there were twelve councillors of state for matters of state; and he that wageth his law must have eleven others with him who believe he says true. And the law is so precise in this number of twelve, that if the trial be by more or less, it is a mistrial.

"Ancient times," when Duncomb wrote, were not so very ancient, about as far from him as he from us. He was wrong on the specifics: the number of oath-helpers on a wager of law, for example—that is, compurgation—varied from case to case. (This error was recently given a further injection of authority by the Supreme Court, which is fond of legal history and often gets it wrong.) But Duncomb was right on the general feeling. As Edward Coke, a bit earlier, had put it, "The law delighteth herself in the number of twelve." *

Then there was the rule that the petty jury must be unanimous, which existed almost from the start. There were a few instances of majority verdicts in the thirteenth century, but they were seen as aberrations, and the rule of unanimity soon took on the accouterments of axiom. The rule went unchallenged for almost seven centuries. About halfway through that time, trial by jury came to be regarded as a fundamental right, and unanimity a principal feature. No conviction of a serious crime could occur in courts of common law except by a solid twelve-man verdict. Very recently, there has been retreat. Though the right to jury trial is included in our Bill of Rights, the Supreme Court has held that, where state statutes so provide, ten votes out of twelve are sufficient for conviction and a jury of six may be used (with five votes out of six decisive). So far as civil cases are concerned,

---

* *Recently Lord Devlin, citing the twelve pence that make up a shilling, has mentioned "an early English abhorrence of the decimal system." The abhorrence (lately overcome) hardly seems genetic. Is it to be traced, then, to hatred of the subjugating Romans, who were so fond of decimals? Or to hatred of the tithing? Or are the twelve pence (apart from the magic) to be explained by the easy divisibility, as are the twenty shillings of the pound?*

the states, if they wish, may forget the jury altogether; England just about has.

We think of the jury as a device to guard the innocent, and in present fact it is. But the jury in its conception was no such thing. People of the thirteenth century—not just those in power, but also those they governed—had little interest in what we would call the rights of the accused. In civil matters, remember, the early jury was something plaintiffs wanted. When it was introduced to trials of crime, defendants must have seen it as an engine of the prosecution. So long as grand and petty juries had interlocking membership (if the thoughts expressed some pages back are sound) the trial was close to meaningless; and even when the two bodies had become distinct, a defendant might well have had a better chance with the older modes of trial.

Nor was its main feature, the requirement of unanimity, what we now regard it—an effort to make sure no innocent will be convicted. This is made clear by the disregard of any such goal in other aspects of the treatment given the accused. What was it then, this demand for unanimity? A product, I would say, of the immaturity of the law and the psyche of the time and place. It is characteristic of a rudimentary legal system, and it suits the medieval mind, which has no room for doubt. There is a need to deal in absolutes; there is paralysis without them. Possibilities, probabilities, diverging views of truth—these are notions alien to these people, difficult, disturbing. A thing is so or else not so, and if it is so then everyone must know it.

The older modes of trial fulfilled the need. No one was obliged—or dared—to doubt divine decisions. Humans were not expected to undertake burdens such as estimating credibility and weighing contradictory evidence. Now, in the later Middle Ages, when the job of judgment is shifted onto men, the old ways of thought and feeling will take a while to recede. The yearning for the absolute remains. If the accused is guilty, he is guilty; all the jury must know it. The same if he is innocent. The jury has one voice to speak with, only one.

When the accused went before the petty jury, he was said to "put himself on the country." The law Latin was *patria,* but the word did not refer, of course, to the nation-state, a concept yet to come. (Its concomitant "patriotism" did not enter our language until the seventeenth century; loyalty was to lord, not to "country" as we use the word.) It meant the place where the defendant lived, the community or group of communities, the surrounding countryside, the neighborhood from which the Clarendon jury was drawn. In the older trials, God had judged directly. Now God made his will manifest indirectly, through the minds of men. *Vox populi* was the medium for *vox Dei.**

Here again we see the impulse toward unanimity; it would be the verdict of the country, not the verdict of twelve men. The judgment came from a single throat; there was no discordant babble. Nevertheless, since it had to be assumed that God's voice was everywhere, the formula was double: the accused declared that he would be tried "by God and my country." This recitation continued to be used at the start of criminal trials in English courts well into the twentieth century.

The demand for unanimity is found in primitive societies today: the tribal council does not take a vote, but talks till everyone agrees. And, not surprisingly, it is found in primitive political institutions: the Security Council of the United Nations, for example, which cannot act if one permanent member disagrees. It appears also at more sophisticated levels—refined, in absolutist philosophies (a life of doubt and degree is too uncomfortable to live), and, brutal, in absolutist political systems (a government that allows dissent is too difficult to manage).

□

These features of the infant jury were irrational but harmless, and as time went on they proved beneficent. They found a function inconsistent with their genesis. When, after several centuries, the idea took hold that it is better to let several guilty go unscathed than to penalize one innocent, the large size of the jury and the requirement of unanimity were suited to the purpose.

---

* *"Vox populi vox Dei" is usually attributed to Alcuin, the Anglo-Saxon scholar, who expressed the thought in this form—the form in which we usually see it—in a letter he wrote to Charlemagne in the year 800. It is a wry attribution. Alcuin's letter to Charlemagne does indeed contain the maxim, but only to deny it. Alcuin's point was that the voice of the people was not the voice of God. On the contrary: "We would not listen to those who were wont to say the voice of the people is the voice of God, for the tumult of the mob is always close to madness." Seneca had been one who was wont to say it, and did, to his fellow Romans. Hesiod, with perfect Grecian moderation, had taken a middle position. "The voice of the people," Hesiod said, "is in some ways divine."*

But another bit of mysticism in the early thought about the jury was less wholesome. Jury trial was not, in law, obligatory. The accused had a choice: he could refuse to face a jury. It was an option that led to horror.

Why the option existed has little surviving contemporary explanation. Precedent seems part of it: the jury up to this time had been something that a litigant asked for. But precedent of this kind does not itself supply an explanation. Here again, I suggest, there was a clinging to the older notions. Man is insufficient; God alone can know the truth. No one may be condemned by the verdict of mere mortals, unless he makes that choice, and takes upon himself the responsibility of submitting life and limb to so fallible a judgment. He must give express consent.

All through this period—through every period, including ours, but this one more than most—practical needs and mystical urges interpenetrate. There is no known way to complete the Clarendon procedure except the verdict of a second jury. Ordeal is gone; compurgation is gone; battle is available only when, infrequently, a private party brings appeal. The royal Justices cannot do the job themselves; these judges do not judge the facts.*

So unless the case is submitted to the petty jury, malefactors will go unpunished. The Justices will not let that happen. They will try to talk the accused into making his election, in favor of a jury trial. If suasion fails, they will torture him until he says he wants a jury trial, or until the torture kills him.

It took a while to set things straight. There were instances in which the accused, entitled to a trial by jury, would not accept it, and was forthwith executed without any trial, in the old style or the new. At the same time, there were instances in which royal Justices themselves were punished for decreeing this procedure (or, more accurately, absence of procedure). But the general rule was soon established: no punishment without a trial by

---

* Except so far as minor offenses were concerned, as mentioned earlier. For the grave offenses, there were two situations that presented no problem, either before or after 1215, because trial was deemed superfluous. One was the case of confession. The other was the case where the miscreant appeared too obviously guilty, as when captured immediately after he had killed or wounded his victim. (The phrase, though not the law, remains: "caught red-handed.")

jury, no trial by jury without consent. So was the ultimate method of getting consent: the notorious *peine forte et dure*.

It means punishment strong and hard—not punishment for having committed crime, but punishment to meet the crazy logic that demanded an accord. It was normally preceded by an effort to coax consent. Thirteenth-century instructional manuals have come down to us; they contain a model for the Justices:

> "William, now answer me by what device thou camest by this mare; for at least thou canst not deny that she was found with thee, and that thou didst avow her for thine own."
>
> "Sire, I disavow this mare, and never saw I her until now."
>
> "Then, William, thou canst right boldly put thyself upon the good folk of this vill that never thou didst steal her."
>
> "Nay, sir, for these men have their hearts big against me and hate me much because of this ill report which is surmised against me."
>
> "Thinkest thou, William, that there be any who would commend his body and soul to the devils for thee or for love or for hatred of thee? Nay, verily, they are good folk and lawful, and thou canst oust from among them all those whom thou suspectest of desiring thy condemnation. But do thou what is right and have God before thine eyes, and confess the truth of this thing and the other things that thou hast done, and give not thyself wholly to the enticement of the devil, but confess the truth and thou shalt find us the more merciful."

But if the fear of God and the suggestion of leniency did not persuade, the court was not at a loss. In later years, *peine forte et dure* was "pressing"—piling stones on the body of the accused, one by one, until he gave consent or died. In the beginning, the torture was slower, less dramatic, and there were variations. The recalcitrant might be imprisoned

> barefooted, ungirt and bareheaded, in the worst place in the prison, upon the bare ground continually night and day; that he eat only bread made of barley or bran . . . and that he be put in irons.

(We may note that what was once an item in a list of torments has now become a health food.) The jailer might be directed to give the prisoner water that was disagreeable and probably polluted—"neither from fountain or river" but "from the water running next the prison." Hunger and thirst might be part of it: the prisoner could have no bread on the day he drank water and no water the day he ate bread.

Things got more barbarous, not less, in the centuries that followed the death of Henry II. *Peine forte et dure* had its greatest vogue in Tudor times, around 1500. By that time the method had become regular: the torture of the stones. It was not uncommon that the accused persisted in his obstinate refusal until life was crushed out of him. There was a reason. Conviction of a felony included in its penalty the forfeiture of property. So if there was a guilty verdict, the accused would lose not just his life but also his estate. But if he died beneath the stones, his guilt had not been proven. No forfeiture would follow. His heirs would then inherit. A man convinced he had no chance to win the verdict might choose the certain agony and death of *peine* in order to hand down his land and goods. It might be love of wife and children; it might be the drive to dynasty that was so large in the culture.*

□

The drive is with us still, milder, manifest chiefly in the contortions rich men perform to minimize estate tax. It is something different from the wish to care for those we love; it is a wish to leave behind some potency, an extension of one's self, a scraping clutch at immortality. It comes from the fear of death, the same force that built the pyramids. Land served the purpose in the time we speak of. Now money is the vessel available to most. (A few can use fame, or good works: tangible—a useful building, a vaccine, in the nineteenth century a railroad; intangible—works of art and works of thought, a tiny push on history.)

But "creating an estate"—that is, leaving accumulated wealth—is the common means. So rich men pay lavish fees to tax advisers to preserve a fund they will not be here to enjoy, a fund that goes to heirs they may not like, or even know (as when

---

* *This same drive probably contributed to the establishment of primogeniture—inheritance of land by the eldest male to the exclusion of other heirs—a system useful in this period. It was useful politically because the units of feudal administration would otherwise have become inefficiently numerous, and useful economically because the landed estate served as the main form of accumulated capital.*

a trust ends in the bank accounts of remote descendants). The making of gifts to one's heirs during one's lifetime is a simple way to do it, the gift tax until recently being quite a bit less than the estate tax. This created a situation in which an imperious old man, in an effort to deprive the government of its tax, made gifts of most of his money. He assumed that the recipients, obsequious (up till then), would leave the real control with him. The assumption was unwarranted. Once they had the money, their attitudes changed. The old man, denuded of his wealth, became a miserable dependent. *Peine forte et dure.*

Gradually, the hideous procedure was abandoned. The Justices began to rule that a defendant who refused to consent to trial by jury would be tried by jury anyway. Yet there are instances of torture to induce consent as late as 1734. It was finally abolished by Act of Parliament about the time our Declaration of Independence was taking form. The Act provided that refusing trial by jury equaled pleading guilty. In 1827 Parliament turned it around: a defendant who stood mute would be deemed to plead not guilty. This is the law today. The only known American case of *peine forte et dure* occurred during the Salem witchcraft craze, which was not completely single-gendered: in 1692 a man accused as warlock was pressed to death.

□

"A trial by jury of one's peers": enshrined in Magna Carta, it stirs the democratic piety. It was not meant to.

Magna Carta resulted from a triumph of one part of the aristocracy over another. The reigns of John and his son Henry III were a time of intermittent civil war between the monarch and the leading nobles, other nobles siding with the monarch. If there were democratic issues in the struggle, they were not apparent to the parties. There were personal ambitions, private rivalries, fights for power and for land (the last two pretty much the same). What resulted was not a constitution but a treaty. It was designed for the benefit of the barons who had rebelled against John and obliged him to negotiate, and for their successors who compelled the Charter's reissuance. The victorious magnates, naturally, were thinking of themselves, not of the mass of people. The Charter, nevertheless and marvelously, became the framework of an altogether different structure. An aristocratic barn was converted to a palace of democracy.

The specific provisions of Magna Carta are for the most part not significant. But it is significant that they were specific—detailed statements of various points of law. This reflects the premise of the Charter: things should go according to law. The political victory of the barons was expressed in nice legalities. The nature of the Charter, and the fact of the Charter, gave added strength to the idea of law, the thought that there should be rule by rule rather than rule by ruler. Once this idea was firmly founded, democracy could build; the people were the unintended beneficiaries.

Nisi per legale iudicium parium suorum vel per legem terrae: this is the celebrated clause in Magna Carta which is said to grant our democratic trial by a jury of one's peers, shield of the innocent accused. No such bestowal was intended. At the time of Runnymede, there was no jury trial for crime; it was that same year the Lateran Council, putting an end to ordeal, created the void which a few years later would be filled by jury trial. The Charter speaks of judgment, *iudicium,* rather than of verdict. Juries render verdicts; judgments come from judges.

Moreover, *parium*—"peers" or "equals"—has no democratic implication in this context. "Peers" is one of those curious words that have contradictory meanings. ("Cleave" is another, though more precisely there are two words "cleave" which happen to spell and sound alike.) In our modern jury system it means everyman. In *Burke's Peerage* and the British House of Lords it means aristocracy (that is, the present residue). In Magna Carta it designated those to whom most people were decidedly unequal, those at or near the top of a stratified society. The barons who compelled King John to sign this document insisted they be judged by no one lower in the social scale. They were quite satisfied to be judged by those who held a higher station. This is not a democratic notion. The Charter speaks of equals with a purpose not in any way egalitarian.

The lord could judge the man, but the man could not judge the lord. This is what the barons meant to say and this is what they said. The lower classes could only demand they not be judged by those more wretched than themselves. And that much by implication only: what the baronial victors had in mind was barons.

The magnates wished to be tried by other magnates, not by the royal bureaucrats. The king's Justices were often of lower social origin than those who might be brought before them. That was dangerous: they might care more for the law than for the standing of the litigant. Those clever, bookish bureaucrats— some of them had never carried a lance (or a precinct; compare the conservative politicians' complaint about the clever, bookish New Deal lawyers)—they ought not be rendering decisions that would affect their social betters' lives and fortunes. Think how irksome to be judged by men brighter than yourself and not highborn. When you like to think of yourself as superior, but know you are inferior, and the disparity is given practical effect besides—this is insufferable. Under Henry there was not much the barons could do about it; under John there was.

But history took the mean provision and made it something else. The important words come at the end of the famous sentence: *per legem terrae,* "by the law of the land." Here—and in the numerous provisions that gave the phrase specific application, all those detailed statements of the law spelled out on parchment—is the idea that the law is stronger than any man, even the man called King. It is against the hated John that this political philosophy is made to work, in the interest of the barons. But if the king is not above the law, why, then neither are the barons. Their strength at Runnymede could not possibly carry them that far; it was not conceivable that any one of them was higher than a king. The necessary implication is that everybody, high and low, is subject to the law. The barons' victory in time will do them in, and become the rod and staff of everyman.

Of course, this is legal theory, theory violated then and now, over and over again. But it is rugged theory. It will survive the force of arms; might will rarely ever after quite make right in England or America. It will survive the claims of organized religion; faith in Rome's pronouncements will not win the field of English politics, and the American Constitution will mark the temporal defeat of all our churches. It will beat the Stuart claim to power while across the Channel the Bourbon claim prevails.

The feeling that the law is all-important, that stated principle is preferable to the wisdom of a governor, is the characteristic feature of Anglo-American history. Neither the economic triumphs nor the military prowess of Great Britain and America (in their respective periods) sets these countries apart. Rather, they are extraordinary (except for some few antecedents, the Romans in most of their history, the Hebrews of the Torah) in their deep commitment to law.

Trial of crime by jury, at first a weapon of the prosecution, would in later centuries be highly valued by defendants. "Peers" in this context came to mean "fellow citizens," and a jury of one's peers a group drawn by lot from any segment of society, without regard to class or station or, though these are recent, sex or color. A criminal system under which one's life and freedom are submitted to a group of fellow citizens rather than a monarch or his surrogate became both a symbol and an implement in the Anglo-American revolutions of the seventeenth and eighteenth centuries. So the barons accomplished more than they intended, and much they would have found abhorrent.

The frustration of the barons' wish began almost immediately, if they were not indeed, in this regard, already beaten by their victory. "By judgment of his peers" comes first in the provisions, and then, following the word *vel*, comes "by the law of the land." *Vel*, which in classical Latin means "or," in medieval Latin was often used for "and." The barons meant "and." They had two goals in mind: judgment by no one lower and judgment according to law.

In 1215, however, *"legem terrae"* included the changes that John's father had effected. Possession of property was determined by the assizes Henry II announced, proceedings managed by king's Justices. Recent radical reform, not immemorial custom, governed this most important aspect of the law—not force of habit, but force of Henry. It was the established law of the land, though it had not been established very long.

Since *vel* properly means "or," the provision construed in the purest scholarship would not require that the Justices have equal rank with those they judged if the law of the land was otherwise. The law of the land was otherwise in the possessory assizes. Whether the barons tripped on their bad Latin; whether, having gained their point, they afterward decided that practiced judges could do a better job than their fellow barons; whether they found it just too difficult to replace a working system—we do not know. Whatever the explanation, the king's corps of professionals continued to sit in judgment on the thing dearest to the hearts of the nobles, their dominion over land.

As to crime, it was accepted before Magna Carta that a noble could insist his judges be at least of equal rank. But the most important business of the royal courts, politically, was the trial of felony against the king. In such cases the king was lord; he himself could choose to be chief judge. And there was nothing to prevent the king from keeping his scholars in attendance, or from taking a recess to consult with them, or even from having them speak for him. So both for civil and for criminal matters "judgment of his peers" missed its mark. "Law of the land" became the controlling phrase.

The phrase was put to poor use when, as mentioned in an

earlier chapter, American judges were nullifying social legislation by the use of an invention called "substantive due process" (a neat contradiction in terms). They said they were applying "the law of the land." That is, "due process" was construed to mean not only fundamentally fair procedures, but also certain substantive features of the law, said to be so ancient and imbedded that legislation could not alter them. It was a short-lived abuse of the concept, though. This judicial clinging to a nineteenth-century economic system, which had nothing ancient in it, was made to look foolish by dissenting judges and legal scholars and subsequent decisions. On the whole, in the course of history, the idea of the law of the land has had a leveling effect. That was bound to happen when loyalty to principle displaced loyalty to lord.

7

A Little Writing

Meanwhile, in cases we would now call civil, the petty jury crept in its not so petty pace. In the fifty years before its sudden entry into criminal law, trial by jury became a familiar method of resolving private quarrels.

The local courts, feudal or communal, did not use a jury. Their accepted ways of finding the facts were compurgation, ordeal, or battle. But it might have happened that in the lord's own court he usurped the function, and decided the case himself. This would not fit what we are told about how things were done, but there are hardly any records of what went on in the local courts, and it is not difficult to imagine that an overbearing lord, cowing those before him, might announce he had the word of God, and would transmit it to the parties. In any event, there was much that could be done to impede the course of justice before the trial of facts took place (as there is today). At some date in the twelfth century, probably under Henry I, people disputing title to land began to ask the king to help them out. Title to land was a tremendously important subject, important enough for royal intervention. And the king would want to intervene, to cut down feudal power and enhance his own. And so he issued a writ. It usually went like this:

The King to Eustace, Lord of Winchcombe, greeting. We command you that without delay you do full right to Clement, son of Odo, of one virgate of land with its appurtenances within your manor, which he claims to hold of you by knight's service [or some other feudal tenure] of which one

Giles of Rutherford deforces him. And unless you will do this, let the sheriff do it, that we may hear no more clamour thereupon.

It was a way for the excluded claimant to get an action started; the lord for one reason or another might have been reluctant to give justice to Clement, son of Odo. The writ tells the lord to go forward.

Under Henry II the issuance of such writs becomes more frequent, "the exceptional becomes normal." And a correlative device is used for the defendant; it is established that no man need answer for his freehold—that is, the land he occupies and claims to own—unless the challenger starts his action with a royal writ.*

As these procedures become regular, the writ that starts them is called the Writ of Right. Often Henry will direct the writ not to the lord but to the sheriff (who, remember, was a royal agent) and order that the case be heard not in the lord's court but in the royal court. This violates feudal principles, and is one of the things denounced in Magna Carta (though by that time there will be other procedures by which land disputes are taken into the royal court).

Then Henry makes a radical change. He gives the one who holds the land an option: defendant need not defend by battle. At his request, the king's Justices will summon four knights of

---

There is a point of scholarly dispute here. Maitland says that Henry laid down the rule "in some ordinance lost to us." Van Caenegem concludes that there never was such an ordinance; his research turned up no evidence of one, and he points out that Glanvil says the rule was customary. Maitland's guess strikes me as closer to the mark than Van Caenegem's research. It is hard to imagine the feudal lords yielding jurisdiction without specific royal pressure. Glanvil's statement can easily be one more manifestation of the proclivity to disguise changes in the law. If indeed the rule was "customary," it was a rather sudden custom.

The question draws considerable attention from legal historians, but I think it draws too much. Whether "custom" or "ordinance," the rule would not have become a rule if Henry did not want it to, and could not if the king were weak and the nobles strong. It hardly matters whether Maitland or Van Caenegem is right.

the vicinage who will choose twelve others to say who had the better right. They are not the same as modern jurors. The early jury in trial of crime, as we have seen, acted differently from ours. So did this early civil jury. It did not merely decide the facts; it said who ought to win. In our terms, it was deciding both facts and law. It was called—a fourth use for the word—the Grand Assize. (And trial by such an assize in this kind of case was a possibility in England until 1834.) Until the time of Henry II, the assembling of a jury to determine rival claims had been occasional, not regular. The kings, as we have noted, used it for their own purposes, and once in a while, not often, gave or sold the privilege to a subject. Now it became an established procedure of the king's administration, not a sometime thing.

At about the same time, other regular writs were created that brought other kinds of dispute into the king's own court. They dealt not with land but with goods or money. They were called Debt, Detinue, and Covenant. Here the shock to the feudal system was not so great: we may assume that the nobles, short of prescience, thought this yielding of jurisdiction trivial, the big thing being land.

Covenant in one sense meant no more than agreement, and legal actions resembling the modern contract action existed in some local courts. The resemblance ends when we consider the modes of trial that were used. In the royal court, the Writ of Covenant was soon restricted to claims based on documents under seal. Defendant's seal was proof enough; the document would be enforced according to its terms. But if the defendant protested that the seal was not his seal, this question, on the issuance of the writ, would be tried by combat.

Debt had to do with money—money loaned, for instance, or due upon a sale. Detinue had to do with goods; defendant, it was claimed, wrongfully detained them. Plaintiff did not say that defendant had seized them wrongfully. A claim of wrongful seizure, at that date, would produce a criminal rather than a civil action. These goods might have been borrowed, or rented, or left for safekeeping. The defendant came into their possession lawfully, but he would not give them back, and it was time to. Trial for Debt and Detinue was by compurgation.

The rights asserted in Debt and Detinue were part of a single concept; only the subject matter varied. Today we have separate concepts for the situations to which these writs applied. Money loaned, or payable for goods and services, is now regarded as a sum the debtor is obliged to pay; it is not any particular stack of dollar bills, nothing that belongs specifically to plaintiff. It is simply a number, in currency, that the creditor may demand. On the other hand, if you lend your lawnmower to a neighbor and neighbor fails to bring it back, it is that specific mower which you demand, and, if you ask in the proper way, the court will force the neighbor to return it. This is the distinction, as Maitland says, between "I am owed" and "I own."

Medieval man, however, had little understanding of "owe." The merchants, a sophisticated if ignoble group, might know and use it among themselves, but the dominant class, the landholders, those who are beginning to go to the royal court, do not think of things that way. The Writ of Debt, though it deals with situations quite dissimilar, sounds very like the Writ of Right:

> The King to the sheriff, greeting. Command Hugh of Newbury that justly and without delay he render to Robert Middleton one hundred marks for which Hugh is indebted to him, so Robert says, and of which Robert complains that Hugh deforces him; and if Hugh will not do so, summon him by good summoners to be before me or my justices on the fifth day after Michaelmas to show why he has not done it. And have there the summoners and this writ.

Note "deforces." The idea is a physical withholding of specific coin that belongs to the plaintiff, very much like the forcible occupation of land complained of in the Writ of Right. (Note also "greeting," here and in the other writs, a word that has survived in our present form of subpoena, and in the military draft notice. The long life of the word may have been sustained by irony.)

In part, the similarity of Debt and Detinue was practical: coinage varied so considerably that a particular hundred marks might not equal another hundred marks. But mostly it was an indiscriminate mode of thought, which persists in the way we view our bank accounts. We usually think in terms of "my money in the bank." That is not the law, not now, nor has it been for several hundred years. The law is that the bank merely owes the depositor a certain sum, equal to his deposits minus his withdrawals. If the bank should fail, this point of law can have painful practical effect. When the bank is acting as trustee, the money belongs to the beneficiary of the trust and he can get it back, but the ordinary depositor is only a creditor, and he must take a loss if there is not enough to go around. Government insurance of bank accounts, of course, has made the distinction less important, but it was very important during the Great Depression, out of which the government insurance was born. In the 1930s, depositors discovered, unhappily, that it was not their money in the bank.

In the main, however, the medieval difficulty with "owe" did not survive the Renaissance, which was as remarkable for its finance as for its art. (Herbert Muller—who, I think, speaks with objectivity, since his primary field is literature, not accounting —has said that the Renaissance inventor of double-entry bookkeeping "has probably had much more influence on the human life than has Dante or Michelangelo.") Indeed, the concept of "owe," once it was embraced, was carried much too far. The common use of such phrases as "due to" and "owing to" shows an inclination to make all causality a matter of ledger entry.

Debt, Detinue, and Covenant, leaders though they were in the building of the central legal system, had little to do with the introduction of the jury. Their methods were wager of law for Debt and Detinue, battle for Covenant. (Giles, you say Robert owes you a hundred marks? But Robert says he doesn't and has his compurgators here to say he would not tell a lie. Geoffrey, you say that Ralph has conveyed this land to you, and you claim you have it in writing, with a seal upon the parchment? How about that, Ralph? You say it's not your seal? Okay, Sheriff, bring them in, and let them fight it out.) It was their contemporary, the Writ of Right, that started something like a regular jury trial.

☐

The second regular use of the jury entered through a roundabout corridor. The most prominent issue in the Henry–Becket struggle involved criminal jurisdiction, the trial of criminous clerks. But ecclesiastical courts concerned themselves also with civil matters. One aspect of their activity had to do with land that had been dedicated to the Church's use; the clergy asserted jurisdiction over any dispute relating to that land. But suppose one party to the dispute claimed the land had not been dedicated. The churchmen said their courts should resolve that question; Henry said the lay courts should. In 1164 Henry worked out a sort of compromise. The king's Chief Justiciar would call twelve recognitors to decide not the ultimate controversy but only the prior question of whether the land had been so dedicated. Following their verdict, the case would proceed in the one court or the other. This was the Assize Utrum, *utrum* meaning "whether."

In the beginning, in all actions in the royal court or on royal order in a local court, the writ was custom-made and granted on petition. (Nice that "custom-made" is an antonym of "customary.") The writ issued from the Chancery, the group of clerks, headed by the Chancellor, who were secretaries to the king. As more petitions came along, a writ already fashioned, or something very close to it, might answer to the grievance. Every office has its files. Before long there was a register of standard writs, each adapted to a familiar set of circumstances. To distinguish them from the earlier writs issued specially, these were called "Writs of Course." They could be obtained from the Chancery simply by paying a fee—now fixed, no longer negotiated—without bothering the king himself or his more important officials. This suited Henry's drive to set up regular procedures, part of the larger drive to create a rule of law.

Thus the occasional became regular, the writs became categories, and if the statements in the writ were lent credence by appropriate proof, a judgment of the court would follow. The various writs, with the characteristic procedure and the characteristic remedy that adhered to each of them, became the "forms of action." Afterward, when the writ system had declined, the concept of the form of action remained, and for several hundred years was the Grand Vizier of the common law. In essence, the form of action imposed the set of elements, derived from one or another of the writs, that plaintiff must set forth in his pleading and establish at the trial.

☐

Latin was then the language of government and learning. French was the language spoken by the nobles and most of the lesser lords. Scholars, of course, knew both. The common people spoke English. It was not an English we could understand, any more than a visitor from the States can understand a native Virgin Islander (unless the latter is so courteous as to change his speech for the hearer's benefit) though what he speaks is English. (Henry II, as we have seen, spent most of his childhood in France and had very little English.)

Since the official language of the law was Latin, English words like "writ" were, at the time, informal. The title the document bore was "breve," which meant a short writing, or a letter, or a summary. It was from the Medieval Latin *brevis*, an adjective for "short." The English "writ," which at first meant any piece of writing, took on this special legal meaning.

But since the conquerors spoke French, that language was for a while a second tongue of government. In the law a sort of pidgin French developed, later called "law French." It held its place long after English kings no longer regarded themselves as even partly French, and outside the law the language had been forsaken. In 1362, a statute, reciting that French was little understood in England, directed that all cases should be "debated and judged" in English. But the statute itself was written in French. Lawyers continued to use law French, and write their commentaries in it. In Parliament, Latin and French competed for its statutes and its records, and French defeated Latin. From the middle of the thirteenth century to the middle of the fifteenth, all Acts of Parliament were written in French, even while its members debated them in English. Since then, the statutes and records of Parliament have been written in the language that its members speak. In the courts, pleadings were cast in Latin well into the eighteenth century.*

This preservation of languages that hardly anybody used (except the one in church and law, the other in law alone) probably had three reasons—two bad, one good. One was the wish to mystify indulged by fraternal groups. Another was simple inertia. The third, shared with every discipline, was the sensible use of terms that are more precise because they have fewer connotations. The epithet "jargon" is deserved only when the first and second motives are at work; it is an epithet easily employed, as often as not in ignorance, where special words function properly to transmit special concepts.

Latin and French each left a rich legacy to the vocabulary of law. We can recognize the Latin: certiorari, prima facie, subpoena, for example. But we are less aware how much is French: tort, contract, debt; master, servant, partner; arson, burglary, larceny; marriage, guardian, infant, ward; justice, judge, juror; counsel and attorney; plaintiff, defendant, action, suit, claim, evidence, verdict, judgment, appeal. Though the French, of

---

* The pidgin French grew less French and more pidgin as the date of the Conquest receded. Eventually, it became something very like a Sid Caesar version of a foreign language. For example, in 1631, at the Salisbury Assizes, capital punishment was visited on a wretch who had engaged in criticism of the judiciary, employing what some present-day thinkers would call symbolic speech. The indictment charged that the accused "ject un brickbat a le dit justice que narrowly mist."

course, in an earlier time had come out of Latin, it was French when it entered England. Almost everything in court except the witness and the writ has an Anglicized French name, as does the court itself. Two words, however, the most fundamental in our law, are purely English: right and wrong.

From *brevis* come both our adjective and our noun. Originally, the American legal brief was brief in fact; it was the lawyer's summary of the evidence offered and the legal position taken, something to inform the court of what was coming or remind it of what had passed. Today, the legal brief is hardly ever short and often terribly long; oral argument is ordinarily much briefer than the brief. This is partly because litigation has become more complicated. The procedure has in a sense been simplified, but the issues in litigation—both the facts and the law of the usual lawsuit—have become vastly more elaborate. (If disputes are simple, they are less likely to be litigated.) The change in legal style reflects the elaboration of our economy. There are many more cases than there used to be, and some enormities among them. It takes longer to listen to oral argument than to read a brief. Besides, with the substance of the law grown so large, the judges often have little antecedent knowledge of the particular point at issue; they will have to do their study of the law after oral argument is over. Indeed, the many hours judges sit and listen are largely a waste of time, a judicial archaism, unless they read the briefs beforehand and direct the oral argument to the points that trouble them. Some courts do.*

The advocate can, however, make good use of oral argument if he employs it as a supplement, recognizing that at the present day full presentation is the function of the brief. The argument can do two things. One is to set the mood and tone, to give the court an idea of the personality if one may call it that (I think one can) of the client's case. The other is to stimulate, and try to answer, questions from the bench. Most lawyers dislike having

---

Judges, like ballplayers, jazz musicians, and other such groups, develop their own slang. An appellate court that studies the briefs and the record before the oral argument calls itself a "hot court."

In England, the system is quite different. All argument is oral; no briefs are filed in court. The word is used for the memorandum prepared by the solicitor (who has the primary contact with the client) for the use of the barrister (who presents the case in court).

their organized rhetoric interrupted by the judges' questions. But depending on the lawyer's capacity, intellectual and emotional, to deal with the unexpected, these interruptions are beneficial. Better to have the difficult question hurled while you are there to make some answer, better than to have it come to mind—the judge's mind—later on, when you are gone and have no chance at all to deal with it.

Less time is allotted to oral argument in most lower courts than on appeal, and often the judge will dispense with it altogether, simply taking the briefs. In the case in which William Buckley sued Gore Vidal and Gore Vidal sued William Buckley and Buckley sued the magazine *Esquire* (that last, legally, the main event), the contest, after years of preliminary skirmish, came down to a pre-trial motion. The briefs on the motion, not loosely written, ran to three hundred pages. The court decided to hear no oral argument at all.*

□

Now back to the early writs. Whether the action took place in the king's court or in the lord's court, it was extremely slow. One reason it was slow was that the idea of legal representation had not yet come to English law. Neither plaintiff nor defendant could have another person act for him, except in trial by battle, when champions could argue the case without words. There was no profession of lawyers. There were some men learned in the

---

* *In England, the judges frequently make their ruling from the bench directly after argument is over. Some years ago I watched the English Court of Appeals in action; at the conclusion of the argument one of the three judges got out of his chair and stood behind the other two, and the three, in whispers, came to their conclusion. They heard, among other cases, an appeal from a criminal conviction of robbery, which carried a long prison term. To an American lawyer ignorant of English ways, two things were exceedingly strange. The convicted defendant remained standing, in a prominent box, while his appeal was being argued. In America, he could come to court if he wished, but he would not be made part of a pageant. Even stranger: when the decision went against defendant and the conviction was affirmed, he quietly but distinctly and without a trace of irony said, "Thank you, m'lords," and was taken off to prison. On the first, score one for the United States; on the second, score one—I guess—for Britain.*

law, but these were the king's Justices and administrators and the scholars in the courts ecclesiastic. They were not for hire to private litigants. Nobody practiced law.*

So at each stage of the case the litigants themselves had to be in court. But one or the other might have good reason not to. He might be on a holy pilgrimage; a bridge on the road to court might have been washed out; he might be off crusading; he might be suffering a fever. The litigation would have to wait. A large body of law developed on the subject: it specified the excuses for nonappearance that would be recognized as valid, and how long would be allowed for each. They were called "es-

---

*There had been representation in Roman law, which gives us the word "client." The client was a plebeian economically dependent on a particular patrician, and if the client had a legal problem, the patrician went to court for him. We have an interesting, and unattractive, inversion of the original: lawyers now are economically dependent on their clients, and most of them are willing to play a courtier's role—not only the impecunious lawyer to avoid starvation, but the rich lawyer to get richer. This misshapen relationship is prevalent, of course, throughout our society (and every other), in the large corporate structure most prominently. But it is especially bad in legal practice. It is an ugliness in itself, and greases departures from real ethics. The lawyer's only master should be the law. He is obliged to advance his client's interest, but only so long as that interest is consistent with legal and other social values. If this creates a conflict, and if the client refuses to follow the lawyer's lead, the lawyer should cease to act for him. Or not begin to act for him if insurmountable conflict is apparent from the start. The client ought to remain a client in the Roman sense, and the lawyer ought to recognize that his standards should be higher than those of others. It is this last that makes the dishonest lawyer so contemptible. It is not that lawyers are worse than other groups; it is that they should be better.

To a considerable extent, however, there are strong traces of the old relationship. It is not at all unusual for a client to demand a course of conduct that is unacceptable—it is deceitful, or knowingly illegal, or too cruel to the other side—and then abandon his demand when the lawyer tells him to. It is as though the apparently self-assured client has unexpressed doubts that he wants the lawyer to resolve. Often, in fact, he has.

soins." Since the Writ of Right would determine the most fundamental of matters, the ownership of land, it had the most essoins of all. Illness was good for a year and a day, and if the defendant was willing to stay in bed that long he could keep the plaintiff off the land that long, regardless of the merit of the claim. It might be hard to tell whether he was really ill, but he really had to be in bed. Four knights would be sent to check on his excuse: did he have a transient indisposition or a veritable "languor"? They would report whether they found him up and about or "in bed as befits a man making such excuse, boots off, breeches off, all ungirt, or even naked, *quod plus est*." The Latin hardly needs translation: if he had nothing on at all, that was a plus.*

Then a new action is invented, an action that will employ a jury. Action by Writ of Right is cumbersome, and most Englishmen do not like trial by battle; these things we know. And we may presume that Henry and his advisers deem this new device sound administration, another good way to quiet "clamour" and with the same stroke bring more fees into the royal treasury. We can also see at work Henry's antifeudal, antiformal attitudes.

The unpopularity of trial by battle is clear. The reason is obscure. The other purely sacral mode, ordeal, provokes no such objection (except among those too advanced for their time), so it is not a part of a general protest against the irrational. Nor is it likely that those involved are afraid to fight, land being about as dear as life. Moreover, if fear were the basis of objection, we should expect to hear it from the weaker side, physically or fiscally, balanced by expressions of support from those who for the one reason or the other could expect to do well in duel. It may be resentment of an alien mode: battle has been brought to England by the Normans, who remain a minority. Though the Normans are an oppressing rather than an oppressed minority, most people in England are English. But that would be an unusually long-lived xenophobia; the importation occurred a hundred years before the date we speak of.

In the chapter that dealt with the early modes of trying crime, I suggested as a reason for the English aversion to battle that it seemed not quite divine enough. But battle, though less mysterious than ordeal, has a residue of divinity, and now we are

---

* *The parties to land actions were called "demandant" and "tenant," but "tenant" has misleading connotations and this chapter will anachronistically use "plaintiff" and "defendant."*

dealing with civil matters. When there is crime to punish, these people are content, indeed prefer, to leave the decision to God. But for disputes over the possession of land (for our own time, substitute "money"), they would rather the resolution be more rational, practical, mundane. Handle worldly matters in a worldly way; leave sin and crime to Heaven. It is like the difference in attitudes toward minor and major offenses, suggested some pages back.

The new jury action is called the Assize of Novel Disseisin, mentioned two chapters ago. Its new idea is this: ignore, for present purposes, who has the proprietary "right," and decide only who has lately held the land, who has been "seised" of it. Unlike cases brought by Writ of Right, where defendant has an option, the decision here in every case will be made by jurors.

Seisin, roughly, means possession. There is a fine distinction, but it is not important here. What is important is the difference between the concept of title, absolute and abstract, and the concept of settled occupation of the land, and the procedural difference that follows. This action from start to finish will take place in the royal court. There will be a jury no matter what. As soon as the plaintiff obtains the writ, the sheriff will summon the jurors. The plaintiff says he had seisin of the land when the defendant came and threw him out. If the jurors agree, the defendant will be put off the land and the plaintiff put back on. It will be a rapid remedy; few essoins are permitted.

"Novel," as I have said, refers not to the newness of the writ or concept, but to the fact that plaintiff claims a recent dispossession. The events of which he complains have occurred not long ago. They must have, if the writ is to be obtained; there is a time limit on its issuance. The limiting period is changed by ordinance several times, but in the early days it is never long. One ordinance provides, for example, that the dispossession must have occurred since the last time the king crossed over into Normandy.

Later the period becomes much longer, so much longer that the character of the action is changed from one concerned only with recent possession to one resembling the actions based on title. In the fourteenth century, an Assize of Novel Disseisin can determine who had possession as far back as 1216; such disseisin is hardly novel. But by then all actions relating either to possession or to ownership of land are being replaced by a single later-developed action, which we will come to.

The Assize of Novel Disseisin is announced at the same

Council of Clarendon that in 1166 starts the modern criminal system on its way. Two revolutions are accomplished at one meeting, in the criminal and the civil law. Although, like the new criminal system, it employs elements already known, the new Assize is truly an invention. A commentator in the next century recalls that its creation took much thought. *"Multis vigiliis excogitata et inventa"*—one need not be a classics scholar to feel the strain and toil.*

The new action helps plaintiffs rather than defendants. Its thrust is different from "no man need answer for his freehold unless. . . ." Henry has ruled twelve years; things have been calmed down. The need to keep things orderly no longer requires that the status quo be favored. Civil litigation has become an instrument in the centralization of government. Discourage violent dispossession, hold powerful subjects in check, give small claimants a remedy they can afford, provide a quick and rational legal action in the royal court. Meanwhile, offering new attractive legal ware, enrich the royal treasury. The government can dare to be less conservative, less defendant-minded.†

There is written record of the change in criminal procedure made at the Council, but none of the civil writ. Extrinsic evidence, however, indicates it came out of that same Council. At the time, some things were put on parchment, others not. A few words from the king would do the job. It may well have been no more than this: after a lot of discussion among Henry and his lawyers, Henry said, in French or Latin, "All right. That's how we'll do it." Then the form of the writ was drafted and its existence was made known.

†*In general, conservatism—the word, I think, can only be used in general—is associated with a bias in favor of defendants in civil litigation. Not always, of course; the antiunion injunctions of the late nineteenth and early twentieth centuries were obtained by employer plaintiffs. But the real opponent of the plaintiff in a personal-injury action is a big insurance company. It is usually small business that sues big business in antitrust treble-damage actions. The typical shareholder's suit against the management of a corporation pits an individual who may or may not have some money against those who have a lot.*

Put plaintiff, small, and anti-status-quo together; put defendant, large, and conservative together; you will be more often right than wrong. Throughout history. Henry, as we have seen, was not conservative.

Robert de Mandeville, say, comes back from a stay in Aquitaine and finds Gerald Fitzgerald occupying an English manor that Robert claims is his. In Stephen's time, Robert, if he felt strong enough, would have had his men attack. After Henry takes the throne, there is danger in waging private war, not just from one's opponent but, deadlier, from the King. So Robert litigates. Before 1166, he would go to the court of the noble of whom the land was held. The process would be slow, and, unless Gerald chose to use the Grand Assize, in the end come down to battle. Meanwhile, Gerald would not budge.

Now, however, after Clarendon, Robert can get much faster action in the royal court, and without the hazard of a duel. The jury will say who held the land during the period covered by the writ. If they recall that Robert held the manor until he left for Aquitaine, a leaving that occurred within the period to which the writ is currently restricted, Robert will win the case and go back on the land. If Robert has been gone for a longer time, if Gerald has occupied the manor since before the date prescribed, Gerald will win the case and stay. But, says Robert, I own this land; a vassal of William the Conqueror granted it to my great-great-grandfather, and the line of descent is to me. Then go back to your lord's court, say the royal Justices, and have that solemn question determined in the ancient solemn way. Meanwhile let Gerald be, let things continue as they are, don't make such a fuss.

Or, perhaps, without going to any court, Robert, much the stronger (personally or by reason of retainers), simply throws Gerald out. Gerald then can get the writ, and if he has occupied the manor throughout the limiting period, the judgment will restore him to the land. The same relief is available lower in the feudal scale; it is available to any freeman. The new writ makes it less engaging to try to take over by force.

There is still a way to determine "rightful" ownership, but Henry doesn't seem to care about such things. He is realist enough to know that all title traces to conquest; the oldest ownership is based on theft. He himself will often announce that his royal rights should be no less than they were in the time "of my grandfather Henry," Henry I. But these statements seem more public relations and legal argument than the product of broad conviction. Old title is no better in his view than a recent possession during which the land has been worked in peace and a contribution to the polity made. So the most important part of the law becomes seisin rather than ownership, with emphasis on "novel." The loftiest aristocrat of his time and place, descendant of long-established great houses in France and England, Henry is not impressed with lineage, and has no use—in either sense, esteem or application—for the notion of aristocracy. New status is as good as old; new power is as good as old.*

We still have not learned the lesson Henry teaches. We pay homage, for example, to "old money," deemed more respectable than new. The principal difference between the *nouveaux riches* and the *anciens riches* is the guilt of having benefits one has not earned, which tends to produce a somewhat keener sense of public obligation among the latter—statistically, that is.

☐

Then another form of action is produced, also tried by jury in the royal court, an action that to us seems hardly different but to twelfth-century eyes demands a different writ. These people have just come from many generations of formalism in the law, back to the forests of Germany. Procedural rigidity will not easily diminish. Indeed, after a hundred years' amelioration—marked by the innovations of Henry and his scholars, and their successors Hubert Walter, Pateshull, Raleigh, Bracton, and aides whose names are not recorded—formalism will have a renaissance.

Movement from formalism to flexibility is characteristic of both law and language. If we did not know the history, it would seem it ought to be the other way around. But declensions and conjugations—case endings and sets of verb forms—were used more in dead languages than in our living tongues, and legal

---

* *In one respect, Henry is fighting a losing battle, and the grating incompatibility between Eleanor and Henry shows. The nobles are no longer the companions-in-arms that came with William the Bastard, but the descendants of those buccaneers. They do not have the strength their grandfathers had; Henry's middle-born bureaucrats wield more power than they. So they constitute themselves a social elite, an aristocracy based on bloodlines rather than on competence. Under Eleanor's leadership, they construct a special way of life, which incorporates the code of chivalry and other social costumery which the lower classes do not share. Eleanor triumphs over Henry at least in this one field. She constructs a high society.*

procedure, which is the way the law expresses itself, has meanwhile, with some ups and downs, grown increasingly informal.

Novel Disseisin has been shaped for the man lately expelled from his land. Suppose the plaintiff is not the person who had seisin, but his heir. In the brief period since Father died, and before his own return from foreign wars or wherever else he was, or simply because he was young and weak, someone else has occupied his heritage. Strictly speaking, Novel Disseisin does not apply, since he himself was not disseised, and the Justices speak very strictly. So another writ has to be invented, and though it takes not much invention, it takes ten years to do it. The new writ commands the jurors to say whether what is called the plaintiff's ancestor—his father, mother, brother, sister, uncle or aunt—was seised of the land, and has died within the time limited for obtaining the writ, and whether plaintiff is the heir. If the jurors answer yes to all three questions, the defendant is expelled and the plaintiff is installed. The name of this writ is Mort d'Ancestor. (Which of course sounds like the name of a Hollywood agent. But then Novel Disseisin sounds like a bestselling work of fiction.)

The framers of the writ, however, miss a few people from whom land might descend. There are other relatives, though the cases are rarer. So other writs are devised, with other wonderful names: the Writ of Aiel, the Writ of Besaiel, and the Writ of Cosinage. Aiel is for the case where the plaintiff has inherited directly from his grandfather; Besaiel where he has inherited from his great-grandfather; Cosinage from any other relative. We do not know why these kin were not included in the earlier writ. Two things may explain the omission. One is that the king's lawyers at first respond only to the cases they encounter and fail to let imagination wander, or, more likely, that they take into account the limited imagination of those to whom the new procedures must be made acceptable. In that age most minds tend to be extremely literal when they are not engrossed in magic, and a rational concept, between the swings, is a difficult thing to fix on. (Thus the idea of "the Crown"—regal power, abstract but operating, as distinguished from the person of the king—takes centuries to develop.) Another thing is the reluctance of the nobles to yield further jurisdiction. Each new writ means more business for the royal courts, less for the courts of the lords. This will inhibit both the number of new writs and their scope. Whatever the reason, another three quarters of a century go by before these corollary actions, closer to Mort d'Ancestor than that one was to Novel Disseisin, make their appearance.

□

When we think of modern civil litigation, we usually think of contract or of tort—disputes growing out of trade, or the relationships between employer and employee, or the agreements under which corporations and partnerships are organized and do business with each other and with the public; or actions to compensate for damage negligently done to person or to goods (mostly on the highway or, lately, in the hospital), or intentionally, for fraud, libel, invasion of privacy, infringement of patent or copyright, occasionally assault, and (again lately) deprivation of civil rights. Litigation over possession of land is a tiny part of the labors of the courts today. But in the early time we speak of it was almost all of civil litigation.

There were some writs that had to do with coin and chattels: those already mentioned, Debt, Detinue, and Covenant, and two others, Replevin and Account. Replevin was used where goods had been wrongfully distrained. "Distraint," also called "distress," was the taking of defendant's goods to insure his attendance in court, lawful when done properly but often done improperly. Account was used against the bailiff of a manor who was doing a little skimming (or a lot). But all of these were a minor part of what occupied the courts. The oldest surviving "roll"—the record of cases, on parchment kept rolled up—is from 1194. Nearly every case recorded on that roll relates to title or seisin of land.

In the late twelfth and thirteenth centuries other actions came into being. These are the most important of them: The Writs of Entry, a much used group that lay between Novel Disseisin and Writ of Right, dealt with a recent flaw in title—only a recent flaw, otherwise the Writ of Right must be employed. The Writ of Right of Dower protected the widow's interest in her dead husband's land. The Writ of Darrein Presentment fixed the right to make appointment to ecclesiastical office, a valuable form of patronage. Then there was the Writ de Nativo Habendo, *nativus* meaning serf.

The last had to do with ownership of people, rather than of land, but the people were tied to the land. Like the Writ of Right, it directed that the dispute be settled in the feudal court. However, if the subject matter of the action spoke up and claimed he was a freeman, there was another writ, de Libertate Probanda.

This writ "for proving freedom" instructed the sheriff to bring the case to the royal court and summon those who claimed to own the man. It is significant not because of its prominence in the work of the courts; it seldom appears on the rolls. It is significant because it tells us that already at this early date the infant common law showed some interest in personal liberty.

The procedure is odd. Logically (by feudal logic) and more efficiently, the serf's claim should have been heard in the feudal court in which the claim was made, the court where, pursuant to the Nativo writ, the action was going on. Contemporary records give no explanation for the shift of jurisdiction. The explanation is probably radical Henry and his lawyer-intellectuals. The court where the action started was run by the lord of the contesting underlords. He would prefer to have within his domain as many serfs as possible, whatever underlord they might belong to. Freemen can wander off. Henry and his team had a different inclination. In the next century, the commentator Bracton, looking back and trying to account for this writ, says: "I can assign no reason unless it be in favour of liberty, which is a thing inestimable and not lightly to be trusted to the judgement of those who have but little skill." Bracton's statement is forever pertinent, and often in specific cases fits the advocates on both sides.

8

Transgressions, Parliaments, and Trespass on the Case

Our present-day civil actions are not descended from any of the writs we have been speaking of. Not even the actions relating to land survive, in person or in progeny, despite their great importance in their time, despite the fact they were the blocks on which the common law was built. Some of our legal remedies come from a body of law, afterborn, called equity: injunction, for example. Some are the product of legislation, new actions created by special statute: patent infringement, for example. But most of them are variations of a single writ, a writ not mentioned up to this point because it did not yet exist. It was called the Writ of Trespass.

It is a writ of doubtful parentage, but, according to one view, it probably came from the criminal law. If so, and it seems to me to be so, then our fundamental civil remedies—actions in tort, property actions, even the actions on contract—are seminally criminal.

Early in the thirteenth century, an invasion occurred within the common law that bears a strong resemblance to territorial invasion by force of arms (that last, coincidentally perhaps, a phrase in the writ itself). There was recapitulation, in English legal history, of an old phenomenon in the world's political history. A barbarian horde comes down on a civilized society, conquers it and rules, is in time assimilated, takes on the refinements of the subjugated people, becomes civilized itself. Thus Sumer and Babylon in the Fertile Crescent and the invaders from the bleak outside; Crete and Greece and their north-to-south barbarians; Rome and its waves of Goths; China and the

Mongols; the backward Christian conquerors of cultured Moorish Spain.*

So here. A rugged criminal writ enters civil litigation, subjugates existing civil writs, and then is thoroughly assimilated. The final product, some centuries later, is a new society of forms of action, altogether civil.

We have talked about appeal of felony. Until late in the twelfth century, when Henry added his system of regulated accusation, it had been the premier procedure of the criminal law, an engine of public peace fueled by private vengeance. It continued, in a diminished role, for centuries thereafter. The victim (or his next of kin if the crime wiped out the victim) went to court and made the charge and then carried the matter forward, at first to culmination in a duel, later to the verdict of a jury. The accusation had to follow a form: it had to say the robbery, rape, mayhem, or murder was done "wickedly and feloniously, with force and arms, and in violation of the king's peace." If the accused did not appear, he became an outlaw. If he appeared and was bested in the duel, he suffered the penalty of death (or, under Henry's mitigated punishments, the loss of a hand or foot). This is the procedural progenitor of such genteel contests as, for instance, our action by a seller for the price of goods sold and not timely paid for.

About the middle of the thirteenth century, the Chancellors begin to issue a writ for the benefit of those who want not just revenge but also some compensation. It is not at first the kind of writ that creates a form of action. The proceeding is still the criminal appeal, but the writ adds something to it. It directs that if the appellor wins, the accused, besides suffering the usual punishment, will be made to pay his victim for the hurt.

Meanwhile, the royal court has begun to take jurisdiction of crimes less serious than felony, breaches of the peace that up to now have been left to the local courts. In the thirteenth century, capital punishment has its broad domain restored and then en-

---

History stopped repeating itself, in this respect, when high economics and advanced technology became the principal elements of military prowess. Technology has always been critical, but the simpler technology of early warfare was within the grasp of lower cultures—the bow and arrow, the chariot, the stirrup (that last, medieval Europe's single but important innovation)—while the kind of technology that has mattered in more recent times favors the more sophisticated.

larged, but for these lesser crimes prison and fine are deemed sufficient. They are called transgressions—*transgressiones* in Latin, *trespasses* in law French. (There is no "misdemeanor" in medieval law.) The writ that adds compensation to the appeal applies as well to minor violations. Hence the conduct of which complaint is made need not amount to felony. There must, however, be an allegation of an act of violence, and the rest of the old formula remains: though the violence may be slight, the defendant is said to have used force and arms—*vi et armis* —and to have breached the royal peace—to have acted *contra pacem.**

Supplementary at the start, the Writ of Trespass soon becomes an "original writ," that is, a writ employed to begin a civil action, like the others we have been viewing. (The ones that end it, that enforce the judgment, are "final writs," and those issued in the course of the action are the "mesne writs.")

Trespass—the word itself reflects the chief concern. Here again the medieval emphasis on land. Defendant has "stepped across." He has gone, unwelcome, onto plaintiff's property. But the writ embraces more than that. The transgression can be an assault on neutral ground, or a carrying off of plaintiff's goods: trespass on the person or trespass on his chattels. The requisite violence becomes mild indeed, and even nonexistent. The transgression is simply transgression of the law, one of a group of personal wrongs for which the courts are ready to grant a remedy. The writ can be obtained in situations where there is no physical act at all; here force and arms and breach of peace become allegations that cannot be denied. That is, they are fictions.

They may, however, happen to be true, and in certain descendants of this writ they remain real elements even now; there is physical contact though usually no arms are used and the force employed would hardly raise a sweat. In one context, the idea

---

* *The concept of a "peace" that is a ruler's right goes back to Germanic law. It belonged not only to a king but to each leader in the social structure. Every ruler, naturally enough, wanted order in his group, as do modern governments. The difference is that freedom from disturbance was considered the chieftain's personal privilege, and disorder among those he led was a personal affront. With the strengthening of central rule, the king's peace overrode all others.*

has not changed a bit: this is the very thing "No Trespassing" signs forbid.*

The theory that the Writ of Trespass had its source in criminal appeal was arrived at, independently, by Maitland in England and here by Holmes and James Barr Ames. More recent scholars dispute the theory (although they are not themselves of one mind). At the moment, they appear to have the upper academic hand. Even H. E. Bell, author of an admiring assessment of Maitland's work, says that S. F. C. Milsom "argues convincingly that the *vi et armis* [force and arms], alleged in the writ, was from the first a formality . . . This interpretation overturns Maitland's theory." †

That the action of trespass in its pure primeval form is still with us, and can be put to the most modern use, appeared in the 1976 case of Le Mistral v. CBS. *Le Mistral, a superexpensive New York City restaurant, had been cited for violating the New York City Health Code, a matter of cockroaches partly.* CBS Television News *thought this worth reporting and sent a reporter and a camera crew. They entered the premises "with cameras rolling" and pushed on despite the maître d's objections. "Consternation, the jury was informed, followed" (this from the court's opinion). When the restaurant sued, the network argued the First Amendment, it being a year in which the press—both print and electronic—was given to sanctimony, and reckless in its dilution of First Amendment guarantees. The court, however, held that whatever right the network might have to broadcast information, it had no right to force its way, over protest, onto one's property to get the information. It was trespass, pure and simple.* The New York Times *of June 5, 1976, reported that "lawyers said [the decision] was significant because there have been so few cases on this subject." Probably not more than several hundred thousand.*

†*What Milsom says, in the passage Bell refers to, is: "When, therefore, under Edward I* vi et armis *came regularly to be alleged, it was from the beginning a formality, not the vestige of true complaints in rougher times." If "beginning" refers to the reign described, the first half of the sentence need not be disputed. If the second half of the sentence is addressed to the earliest days of our legal history, the state of things in Edward's time would not answer the question of origin. (I should like to add the note that, despite what may or may not be a disagree-*

The Holmes-Ames-Maitland view commends itself to me. It is not plausible that anything is "from the first a formality." A formality is the empty shell of something that once had content. We nod to an acquaintance because once we bowed, and we bowed because earlier we kneeled, or even lay face down upon the ground. We did those things in the beginning to express, quite literally, surrender; the defeated warrior was prostrate. The nod was not invented suddenly, without meaningful antecedents. Neither was *vi et armis*. The nod is mere courtesy now. It was far from mere when it began. *"Vi et armis"* was mere formality, in many trespass cases, by the end of the fourteenth century. It is hard to believe it was merely formal when the first complaints were heard. It is understandable that an allegation should be retained in conservative legal pleading after it has lost its meaning; surplusage ordinarily doesn't hurt. But why would the very first litigants include an allegation that never had a meaning?

□

In any event, the royal courts soon ceased to require proof of physical violence (soon, as early legal history measures time). There was, of course, the medieval readiness to pretend. Society has always been ready if not eager to pretend, but in this regard the Middle Ages are peerless. The fiction that developed here, of force and arms and breach of peace, was not the only one in medieval law.

And this particular fiction lay very near reality: affronts to property or person, even when not violent in themselves, could in such violent times quickly lead to violence. The law sensibly concerns itself with provocation. Probably the king's Justices found imperceptible the line between an act that ruptured peace and an act that might excite the rupture, or perhaps they chose not to perceive it.

Then, once more, the prime importance of landholding: any uninvited crossing of a boundary was a very serious thing. Given the psychic components, the formula is barely fiction. It is not difficult to imagine the emotion that takes the place of the literal meaning. Whether or not a clash results, this is felt to be an act of violence. Invade my land and you pierce my body.

---

ment, Milsom is, in my opinion, one of the very best historians of our law.)

Finally, the social structure must have made its contribution. The open invader would have to use force or threat of force; the peace was patently breached. But one who stole in stealthily we may suppose to be a poacher, a man of the lower orders, likely a hungry serf. Such a man, it is fair to guess, had often been dealt with summarily, by the owner of the land himself; no bother with legal technicalities here. So why insist on technicalities when we do him the honor of litigating?

□

If these things explain the emptying of the formula and the wandering from the borders of the criminal action to enlarge the ambit of the civil, they do not themselves account for the disappearance of the other writs. Why was Trespass so preferred?

It was preferred, by plaintiffs, because it had splendid practical advantages. In part, these grew out of a fundamental characteristic of our early law, the reluctance to decide. We have noted how in early times the burden of decision was put on the shoulders of God, and when the jury came to the trial of crime, there remained a supernatural element. The same trait was manifest (though to a lesser extent) in civil cases. The notion lingered that no one would be bound by human judgment unless he appeared and agreed to accept it. Hence, for instance, the trouble taken with essoins in the land-title actions. It was something like modern arbitration: no one need arbitrate a dispute unless he has consented to (after a question arises, or in advance, by provision in the contract that governs the relationship).

Default judgment—the granting of relief to plaintiff when defendant does not appear—was not fully a component of our law until the eighteenth century. In the Middle Ages, the law's efforts to deal with the defendant who simply ignored the original writ were in most forms of action confined to making life difficult for him; if those efforts did not succeed, if defendant never came to court, there could not be a judgment. The situation is quite different now. Once a summons is properly served, the wheels of litigation begin to turn and defendant's absence cannot stop them. The case is under way, and if defendant does not come in and defend, plaintiff wins by default.*

There are several ways in which service can now be properly effected. The traditional and most common way is to find the defendant within the territorial jurisdiction of the court and hand the summons to him. The summons, a short, conventional

Default establishes liability. If the complaint is for a fixed amount, as in an action on a promissory note, it can be the end of the case. If the amount owing is not certain, plaintiff will have to prove his damages to the satisfaction of the court, but this is done in a one-sided hearing that goes by the old name "inquest." All this is not quite so rigorous as it sounds: courts are strongly inclined to "open the default" and, despite expense and inconvenience to the plaintiff, allow the tardy defendant to contest the claim if he has any reasonable excuse for his delinquency. But default is a dangerous thing; however light the persuasion needed, the court must be persuaded to give defendant a second chance.

Things were different in the thirteenth century. Most original writs simply told the sheriff to "summon the defendant by good summoners." If the defendant refused to come, the only recourse was a mesne writ. The sheriff might be ordered to seize defendant's chattels. (This was the "distraint" which, if used where it should not have been, could give rise to an action of Replevin.) If that failed to work, another mesne writ might direct the sheriff to seize the defendant rather than the goods—that is, arrest him. The word is pronounced "mean," which was doubtless what defendant felt these writs to be, though from a modern point of view their most notable aspect was, in Maitland's phrase, a "tedious forbearance."

The process was far from foolproof. The defendant might hide his chattels, or even hide himself. Besides, the sheriffs were often lazy or corrupt or shrewdly disobedient. The king's conquest of the jurisdiction of the feudal courts was to some extent at first a hollow victory. The sheriff was usually a powerful local lord. If he could no longer handle these matters in his own court, he could hamper and reduce what happened in the royal court, because he was the man who had to make things happen there. In most common-law actions, there could be no judgment at all

---

document, is a remnant of the ancient writ. The resemblance, over the centuries, is striking, and the summons still is sometimes called a writ, but its only functions are to establish jurisdiction over the defendant and let him know an action is begun. In some jurisdictions, it need not issue from the court. The plaintiff or his lawyer can write it out and have it served; the court does not even hear about it until later in the case. The lawyer generally buys a pad of printed forms from his stationer and fills in names and dates.

unless the sheriff brought the defendant in, and no effective judgment unless the sheriff enforced the final writ.

The use of the Writ of Trespass made things altogether different. Because of the criminal features the halfbreed action bore, defendant's failure to appear made him an outlaw. We have seen the power of that dread sanction; the mesne writs used in other actions to insure appearance, all of which required that the sheriff stir himself, were hardly needed. Moreover, since there were fewer steps to take, the action went more quickly. And since there was less for the sheriff to do, there was less for him to do badly. Delivering the original writ and executing final judgment were his only duties. Then there was the criminal aspect of the judgment itself. A defeated defendant not only had to pay the plaintiff; he also had to pay the king, and maybe go to jail besides. Finally, unlike Debt and Detinue, the defendant in Trespass could not escape liability by bringing in his oath-helpers. Trespass, like other crimes, was tried by jury; lying was not an automatic defense. Altogether a neat proceeding, from plaintiff's point of view.

From plaintiff's point of view. But for every plaintiff there is a defendant, and so we might expect, instead of overwhelming demand for replacement of old writs, something nearer a balance. The triumph of Trespass involves two further factors. One is that the royal courts were looking for business. Since it is plaintiffs who are the customers, an action attractive to plaintiffs is movable merchandise. And it is profitable business: in addition to fees of court, there are fines for the royal treasury. The other factor is that this new action suited the requirements of the society as a whole. Defendants might be disadvantaged, but if the expanding economy was going to function, a faster and more effective mode of litigation was needed.

☐

The first regular writs were created by Henry II and his close advisers. In later reigns, under kings less lawyerlike, new writs came out of the Chancery, which meant the office of the Chancellor, the literate center of the royal court, the place where writs would naturally be written. This issuance of new writs in the king's name—often, likely, a bureaucratic production in which the king did not participate—had always been resented by the barons, an exacerbation of their loss of jurisdiction. Toward the end of the thirteenth century, it came under increasing attack. That was a century of conflict between the magnates and the monarch, first John, then Henry III, then Edward I, a period of intermittent civil war, with the King of France taking an occasional hand against the King of England. The pseudonymous creation of new forms of action was one of the principal points of conflict.

By the end of this same century, England was having regular parliaments. This was not response to popular demand for a voice in government. On the contrary, the summons to assemble elicited more groans than cheers. It was a product of the needs of the king, or of the barons when they were dominant and could call in the assembly—their needs in fighting with one another or against the King of France. The principal need was money.

To some extent, the parliaments served to rally moral and military support. The convocation was an opportunity to explain the leader's position, to be charming and/or scary, to flatter the lesser men by allowing them to rub highborn or celebrated elbows. But warfare was no longer a matter of personal allegiance and private arms. Cash was more important now, to buy equipment, food, and men. Henry II had offered one of his several insults to feudal theory by relying, in his military exploits, on mercenaries more than chevaliers. The money, in the necessary sums, would have to come from the knights, who were evolving into country squires and now would rather give cash than military service, and from the tradesmen of the towns, the "burgesses" or "bourgeois."

A central machinery to gather taxes did not exist, nor did the warring factions have power enough to tax by autocratic fiat. However, the men from time to time on top had strength enough to make cooperation prudent. So representatives of countryside and town were called together, the situation was discussed (thus "parley," "parliament"), and something between a demand and a request was made, tilting one way or the other depending on the power. It was a chore for those who attended, time away from business, alleviated perhaps by the jollity conventions offer. And its product was generally bad news both for those who were present and those whose delegates they were.

It was quite different from our present notion of a representative assembly. The knights and burgesses were gathered less to speak for their constituents than to return and speak to them. They were summoned mainly so that they would listen and carry the message back. Yet there was always a bit of the other in it, and sometimes more than a bit. By feudal culture and present threat these people were in awe of station, but it was plain that in close contests between king and barons their support could tip the balance. And though the parliaments were called for the leaders' purposes, the talk, once under way, could hardly be restricted. The assembly might interest itself in other things. Here—in the need for cash of would-be autocrats, royal or noble —is the seed of modern democratic government. This was not an English phenomenon; it was going on all over Western Europe. But it took better root in England, and in the common law it had a trellis on which to climb.

During the second half of the thirteenth century, it was established there should be three parliaments a year, and part of the agenda should be the expression and redress of grievances. One grievance was the bureaucratic spawning of new writs. Men of property had come to understand that new remedies meant new rights and duties. Probably they understood it from the start, better than we do now. Henry's innovations had made the point painfully obvious, or joyously obvious, depending on whether you suffered the writ or used it.

Although the faster, more effective royal remedies were welcomed by those who wanted judicial aid in their endeavors, they were resented by the lords who were losing jurisdiction and by all who felt alarm at the growth of central power. The magnates were indignant. Compare the reactions of captains of finance and industry to New Deal legislation and the authority it gave to federal agencies, their cries in defense of "states' rights" and "liberty"—meaning "let us exercise our economic power as we please." (State governments being less likely, and much less able, to control economic brutality.) It was a reaction, both in the time we speak of and in the 1930s, at once anti-intellectual and anti-Executive. (Contrasting nicely with the Nixon years, when pro-Executive was anti-intellectual.)

For most of the thirteenth century, starting with the revolt against John that reached its climax in 1215 and ending with the coronation of Edward I in 1272, the English monarchy has been contending with high nobles. The accession of Edward ends the struggle, the rebellious barons are at last defeated, but the monarchy has paid for its victory. Parliament has been established. It is still far from the dominant institution it will become four centuries later, but it exists as a third element in the nation's government, along with the kings and the nobles.

It is now acknowledged doctrine that new law should come from statute—not from the king in private council or from his clerks and judges, but from open legislative operations in which the king himself is visibly active and Parliament takes a hand. (About this time we can begin to spell it with a capital *P*.) That much the vanquished barons have accomplished. The monarchy, though victorious, has lost some of the close-knit power it held in Henry's time. The power has leached through the highest levels and been absorbed by Parliament. But the barons have lost more: not only is the king once again supreme, but the power that lies outside the throne must now, in some degree, be shared with commoners.

□

Historians call Edward I "the English Justinian," Justinian being the emperor who put the final stamp on Roman law. Edward's standing as a lawgiver has hardly better footing than that of his Anglo-Saxon namesake, Edward the Confessor. This much can be said of him: he defeated the centrifugal energies of multipeopled Britain; he set out on an imperial course, with more or less success (Wales more, Scotland less); and he liked and substantially promoted system and organization. Order rather than law was his bent. (Mussolini made the trains run on time, or tried to.) The famous statutes of Edward's reign—the legislative strides that stimulate historians to bestow the appellation—are attributable not to creativity on Edward's part, but rather to the growing strength of Parliament.*

That famous Roman Emperor was not Roman. (It was still the Roman Empire, though its center in his time was Byzantium.) He was "by birth a barbarian," a Slav from what is now Yugoslavia, a barbarian in the language of the time, not necessarily a savage but an outlander who spoke in an outlandish way; he never shed his accent. Justinian became ruler not by conquest from the hinterland but by a combination of blood relationship and personality: his predecessor was an uncle who adopted him. Justinian's Code was a well-edited collation of all of Roman law, an attempt to organize what had then become a sprawl into a single set of written statements. Total integration was not achieved, but it is nonetheless a remarkable redaction. Justinian

---

* *In 1978 Mussolini's problem was solved, with admirable ease, by the Long Island Rail Road. It simply revised its timetables. If the trains do not run on time, then make time attend the trains. One result was that schedules to eastern Long Island that year were slower than they were three quarters of a century earlier.*

did not, of course, write the Code himself. But he initiated the project, chose the scholars, and led them in their work.

Justinian's name is interesting. It might seem to be one earned by its bearer for his celebrated devotion to law and justice, an ex-post-facto recognition. Not so; he was given it at birth, in his family's language. He was called Uprauda, which in Slavonic meant law or justice.*

The great event of Edward's reign was theoretical. The legislation itself was far less significant than the acceptance of the theory that new law should come from statutes, from the representatives of the political community (such as it was, a small fraction of the population) rather than directly from the monarch or the monarch's men. The king would be the most important person in the realm, and, if he could, would simply use Parliament as his rostrum. But whether he worked with the assembly or through it (the preposition varying with the particular monarch's ability to dominate), the main source of law would be the Act of Parliament—not, of course, excluding the power of the courts to change the common law and alter the meaning of statutes in case-by-case adjudication. Edward's extraordinary fiscal needs sealed the constitutional principle. He fought not only to try to keep his lands in France, but also to subjugate Wales and Scotland. That took a lot of money. He also went on a Crusade, which took some more. Besides, he inherited the deficit his father's wars created. Edward had to make deals with Parliament. Magna Carta was reissued once again.

Another product of the thirteenth-century conflict, a related product, important to the barons for the reasons I have stated, had to do with litigation. The machinery for issuing writs began to stiffen. Pressure was put on Chancery to stop the free and easy manufacture of new writs. When the barons, led by Simon de

---

* The name may have determined his career, rather than the other way around. See Roger Price, What Not to Name the Baby, which advances the thesis that a name given at birth strongly influences one's character, unless one has character strong enough to reject an inappropriate name and take another. Some of Price's examples: Harry knows where to get ice. Jim knows where the action is. Bonnie smells good. Name an infant Roger at the time when Price was born and he will wear glasses, become the teacher's pet, and lose Bonnie to an athlete named Lance (and, Price omits to add, grow up to write charming perceptive outrageous books).

Montfort, held the upper hand, they forced Henry III, Edward's father, to accept the Provisions of Oxford. These required the Chancellor to swear he would issue no writs, except those already established, "without the commandment of the King and his Council who shall be present." It seems the day of the clever clerks is over. Or is it? In the same few years, the third quarter of the thirteenth century, there is protest that would-be plaintiffs "have been obliged to depart from the Chancery without getting writs, because there are none which will exactly fit their cases . . ." A growing law feeds on contradictory grievances.

□

Bracton makes a statement that does not seem to suit the history, either of the period when the standard writs developed or of the subsequent period we have now come to. Translated loosely, it is this: "As many writs may be issued as there are situations that call for legal action." Maitland suggests that just when Bracton wrote, in the middle of the thirteenth century, "it may have been possible to argue in this way" because of the freedom Chancery then enjoyed. More likely, though, Bracton was indulging in a practice that writers of legal treatises have never been able to resist: misstating the actual law to suit their notions of a better law, confusing "is" with "ought to be."

The Register of Writs had by this time expanded to include about five hundred standard writs, though only a few were frequently used. Five hundred may seem a great many, but the writs were narrow, and the facts of the case had to fit the form. It is a familiar experience for the practicing lawyer—and for clients who have left their lawyers' offices with frustratingly vague advice—to find that no wholly satisfying precedent exists. New situations are seldom congruent with the facts of a decided case —"on all fours," as lawyers say. Since the Procrustean writ had to be suited precisely, there must have been many situations that not even five hundred could reach. The "must have been" is confirmed both by the statute of 1285 that we will come to in a moment and by the later rise of the Court of Equity.*

---

*Earlier, it had been possible to start an action in the royal court without one of the writs in the Register. This other procedure was called querela, or "plaint." The senior legal historians do not give it much attention, though it was an important procedure in its time. Its existence demonstrates that here, as everywhere in our legal history, things simply are incapable of neat

Usually conflicting demands come from different sections of society; there is conflict but no inconsistency. But often they have a single source. Today we hear that the federal government is too big and interfering, and, from the very same voices, that the federal government should do more. Take the case of our grain farmers, purest Middle America. (Remember Middle America? It was a separate state that existed within the United States, and dominated all the others, from 1968 to 1973, not a territorial state so much as a state of mind. It wasn't really very middle, any more than the Eastern Liberal Establishment was Eastern.) The farmers denounce the government for being soft on Commies, and then, within the blinking of an eye but without the batting of an eyelash, insist we supply those Commies with the grain they badly need. They excoriate the welfare state, and cry for subsidies. Ideology is often powerful, but so is ready cash, and Middle America was never high on ideology.

By Edward's reign, as we have seen, the idea has taken hold that new law should be made by legislators rather than by king or royal bureaucrats, that more of the population—not much, but more—should have a say in government. But it is recognized that rule-by-a-few has a flexibility that rule-by-many cannot match. Both vectors are given play. The bureaucrats must be restrained. Then, having reined them in, Parliament loosens its hold just slightly. A statute of 1285, implicitly denying the clerks power to create new forms of action, allows them to fashion changes in the old ones:

And whensoever from henceforth it shall fortune in the Chancery, that in one case a writ is found, and in like case [in consimili casu] falling under like law, and requiring like remedy, is found none, the clerks of the Chancery shall

---

and systematic exposition. Since in the beginning royal justice was a matter of the king's acting on specific grievances with which his subject might beseech him, it is not surprising that the practice continued while the writs were being regularized. I have not dealt with actions begun by plaint, because they vanished very early and it was the writ system that produced the common law. It may be noted, however, that the equity system, when it came, harked back to the querelae. They leave, in addition, at least one other heritage: though there is no longer any legal action called a plaint, the one who brings our present actions is called, almost universally, the plaintiff.

agree in making the writ; or adjourn the plaintiffs until the next Parliament, and let the cases be written in which they cannot agree, and let them refer them to the next Parliament, and by consent of men learned in the law, a writ shall be made, lest it might happen after that the court should long time fail to minister justice unto complaints.

The date of the statute, 1285, is significant. In the preceding hundred years profound changes have occurred. Both the culture and the economy have advanced and got more complicated. England grows rich on a pastoral commerce; its great export trade in wool has begun. Raising and shearing sheep, collecting and carding wool, are for thirteenth-century England what mines and mills and factories will be for nineteenth-century England. There are changes in town and countryside. Agricultural techniques improve. New towns spring up; old ones enlarge.

Oxford and Cambridge are now called universities. Cathedrals have been built. Hubert Walter has written Glanvil's treatise, Bracton has written Bracton's. Roger Bacon is reaching far beyond the medieval mind. (All this while thousands are being killed for no purpose except royal and aristocratic clutching at land and power, and while the criminal law expands and its punishments grow more horrid.)

So the stiffening of the legal system cannot continue very long. The emergence from a feudal structure renders the existing forms of action inadequate, not only for the sake of individual justice but also for the common weal. A lean and simple legal system will not suit the new society. Big government—that whipping boy of current politics—is exactly what is needed.

There are, among historians of the law, sharply different versions of what happened next. The fact is that the common law continued to expand. New forms of action were developed to meet society's new needs. And it is agreed that they all descended from the Writ of Trespass, which begat another writ called Trespass on the Case, which begat a varied family. But there has been fierce academic struggle over how this came about.

The view shared by the most celebrated names—Blackstone, Maitland (on this agreeing with Sir William), Holdsworth —is that the expansion came by way of the statute of 1285. The story would go something like this:

The longer half of the provision speaks of what Parliament

may do, but the first part confirms the authority of the clerks of Chancery to make new writs in "like cases." (Assuming, says the statute, that the clerks agree, but clerks with appetite for institutional power are not likely to disagree.) People come to Chancery with grievances that ought to have attention. Will they be sent away empty-handed because the case is not really close to any that the standard writs address? What is to be done?

The clerks know. If they have lost their license to invent new writs, they have leave to vary old ones. They can draft new writs "in like cases." They choose to play their variations on the writ that for practical purposes is best. Hence we come to Trespass on the Case, and later on its varied incarnations.

Moreover, as we have seen, our courts and lawyers have a way with legislation. The Anglo-American irreverence toward legal scripture—the spirit of the common law as distinguished from the coded Roman law and its descendants on the Continent —will greet this legislation. Its words leave ample opportunity for construction, and in a field of thought which is the common law's home ground. "Like case" means there will be new kinds of trespass writs to fit the case—writs called Trespass on the Case.

Other scholars, digging hard—T. F. T. Plucknett and E. J. Dix and C. H. S. Fifoot—say it happened differently. The 1285 statute was more a restriction than a license. In fact, their researches seem to show that only two new writs, neither having lasting consequence, were created by the Chancery pursuant to this legislation. There had been actions for "trespass on the special case" before 1285, and, after a pause, there was an expansion of that kind of action in the fourteenth century. The famous men have been misled by the word *casu,* "case." The fact that it appears in this statute, say these more recent writers, has no bearing on the separate development of Trespass on the Case.

Ah, well, ask the Tiger. In any event, it starts with Trespass, and it involves the athletic talents of the common law. Whether or not the statute was the key, there takes place, around this time, another development that will contribute mightily to what follows. A new profession has arisen, a group at first called "pleaders." They are people we would now call barristers in Britain, litigating lawyers in the United States. It has become a profession only at the end of the thirteenth century. Until that time, litigants acted for themselves or had amateur assistance. These pleaders constitute a coterie of avant-garde composers.

The variations they play on Trespass on the Case are numerous and rich. The Justices, many of them now themselves ex-pleaders, are a sympathetic audience.

It takes time—a couple of centuries, and the process does not stop there—but eventually Trespass on the Case becomes the family of actions that will make up almost all the common law: Assumpsit, Ejectment, Trover, Deceit, something simply called Case, Libel, Slander, Battery, Assault, some actions with the old name Trespass. The "force and arms" is dropped by most of them; only the last-named three still involve a breach of boundary or intentional physical harm.

So, whichever group of scholars is correct in this dispute, the fundamental fact remains. Particular statutory actions and equity aside, it is from the rugged Writ of Trespass, criminal genetically, together with the cases likened to it, that our civil law derives. The other writs will leave the courts and be consigned to history.

9

Fiction

Even the writs relating to land, the writs with which the common law began, the haughty doyens of the rolls of court, are in the end displaced. The Writ of Trespass becomes the test of who owns real estate. I single out this part of the growing law because it makes a gaudy illustration of the use of legal fiction, and legal fiction was one of the principal means by which the common law developed.

At first the transfer of land, other than by inheritance, was generally done by a grant for the life of the grantee, later by grant forever (accomplished by giving the land to the grantee "and his heirs," a formula whose utterance was required in England until 1881). In the thirteenth century, the legal device we now call a lease comes into use: owners are renting land for a term of years. What can the lessee do if a third party, stronger, dispossesses him? Not much. He is not entitled to a Writ of Right; he has no title to the land. He is not entitled to Novel Disseisin; he has not been given seisin. To be sure, the intruder has committed a trespass, and for this the lessee may get damages. But to the end of the fourteenth century that is all he gets. He is not put back on his rented land unless the person who has title or seisin, the one from whom he leased, is willing to go to court and bring an action of his own.

Then, just about fifty years later, the lessee is sometimes given a better remedy: the court, upon the lessee's successful trespass action, will restore him to possession. By the end of the fifteenth century it happens all the time. There is no new original writ, there is no new statute, it is simply judicial accommodation to a demonstrated social need. We do not know the rationale, though we can be sure there must have been one, however casuistical. Leases are now useful; leases are now common. They ought to be protected, and all it takes, in the very same trespass action, is another sentence in the final writ that gives the sheriff his instructions.

This still has nothing to do with ownership, only with the lessee's right to occupy the land during the term of his lease. There is another social need. Landholding now is less dynastic. More people buy and sell it. The more frequent such conveyances, the more frequent the disputes. A better, quicker way to settle them is wanted.

Consider not the man who rents, who by this time has an effective remedy, but the man who buys the land or thinks he bought it and cannot get dominion of it. Or the man who occupies the land and thinks he owns it when another comes along and says he bought it (from someone else who really owned it) and threatens to take over. Up to now all the courts can offer is the ancient Writ of Right, with its essoins and risk of trial by battle, or the somewhat younger seisin actions, which are prematurely aged. We are not now talking of leases; this is a controversy between two parties each of whom says he is the owner, one in possession of the land, the other on the outside trying to get in. The lessee's form of action looks good to the outsider, though what he claims is more than a lease. On the other hand, the older actions look good to the man who has possession. Trespass is efficient; trespass is harsh. Its criminal features have not yet faded. If trespass unadorned is to be used to try ownership, the losing defendant, who may be an honest buyer from someone who had no right to sell, can be jailed and fined. So lawyers— "lawyers" in the broad sense, clerks and Justices and pleaders —gradually develop a modification that will determine who really owns the land, efficiently yet without the aches and pains of the primeval trespass action. It is called Trespass in Ejectment, later simply Ejectment. In its final form it involves a complicated fiction. Too much plot, one is tempted to say, except it works.

A fiction in the law is indeed a fiction. It is something made up. If there is correspondence to the facts, that is coincidental. The fiction may, of course, be true in a nonliteral sense. A fantasy can open a window on reality; a legal fiction can amount to truth as the philosopher of pragmatism sees it. In either case, the audience cannot raise a question. Readers of the novel must accept its premises or stop reading. Litigants are not allowed to deny the fictive allegations.

One Gilbert of Newbury claims that land occupied by a certain Alan de Beresford belongs to Gilbert, who has bought it from the rightful owner. John Doe brings a trespass action against Richard Roe, alleging that Gilbert owns the land, that Gilbert has rented it to Doe, and that Roe has trespassed on the land with force and arms and ousted Doe. Doe is called "the tenant." Roe is called the "casual ejector." (Not referring to Roe's style—just happened by and rather liked the place—but to the fact that he makes no claim of ownership.) Gilbert and Alan are real. Doe and Roe and the lease and trespass and ouster are all fantasy.

It is Gilbert, of course, who obtains the writ, in the name of Doe. But since the writ is addressed to Roe, a nonexistent person, how does Alan, the real adversary, find out about the action and obtain his day in court? He is notified by letter, a letter sent by Gilbert though it purports to come from Roe. The letter to Alan is signed "Your loving friend, Richard Roe." (There is now a bond between them. What is going on in court, if Gilbert is successful, will put fictitious Roe in prison and cost real Alan his enjoyment of the land.) Roe's letter says that he himself asserts no interest in the land, but thinks it a good idea that Alan appear in the action and take on friend Roe's defense, else Alan's ownership may be put in jeopardy because Doe is saying that the land is Gilbert's.

When Alan appears, the court informs him it will have the spectral Roe step aside and permit Alan to defend the action, but only on condition. Alan must concede most of the allegations in Doe's declaration to be true: that Gilbert made the lease to Doe, that Doe occupied the land under this lease, and that Doe was then thrown out by Roe. If Alan wishes, however, he may contest Doe's allegation that Gilbert is the owner. That, of course, is what the case is all about. It is only the fiction that cannot be contested.

The older writs would allow Alan more chances for delay, but the court will have none of that. If Alan will not join in the whimsy, the court will proceed without him; it will render judgment for Doe against Roe and thus recognize Gilbert's ownership. But Alan himself is not charged with the crime of trespass —it was Roe who did the evil deed—hence Alan can participate without the risk of fine or prison. So Alan will agree to this procedure. The court then goes on to hear, and decide by jury trial, who really owns the land. That decision is necessary to determine how Doe and Roe come out in their trespass action; Doe would have no claim if he leased the land from one who did not own it. If Doe wins, the court will nevertheless award no damages, even though the forcible ouster of a rightful lessee is now a matter of record. An award of damages would be futile; not even the strongest sheriff can get money out of a ghost. (And, after all, the ejectment was so casual.) But ownership will be settled.

This was not worked out all at once. The older writs continued as alternatives where plaintiff claimed seisin or title, but their use diminished steadily, and by Tudor times an action of ejectment was the standard method to determine ownership of land. It continued in full charade into the nineteenth century; only then did Doe and Roe together leave the scene, their rancor apparently composed.*

□

Another important use of fiction in the early days was to build the jurisdiction of the royal courts. In the long struggle between Crown and aristocracy that marked the Middle Ages, the royal reach for litigation was important as both means and end. Jurisdiction brought in money, and jurisdiction meant political authority. The writs were developed partly to fill felt needs—we can allow this much to the wish to do well for the realm on the part of one or two kings and some of their scholar-advisers—and partly, probably mostly, to establish power. Civil jurisdiction, even more than now, was intertwined with capacity to rule. For one thing, until Parliament came into being, judicial proceed-

---

The names are occasionally used today in other legal contexts: a John Doe warrant for arrest where the suspect's name is not known, and in actions where the court, to save embarrassment or protect the privacy of the parties, keeps their real names out of the open record of the case. Thus some marital matters become Jane Doe v. John Doe, *and a recent litigation in which a plaintiff patient successfully sought to prevent the defendant psychiatrist from publishing her case history is captioned* Doe v. Roe. (*The court gave away the genders—quite unnecessarily—by adding a pair of first names.*)

ings, whether on the manor or at the throne, were the prime expression of government. What is now done by departments and administrative agencies was in those days done in court. For another, deciding ownership of land meant allocating mastery, and thus increasing one's own. Later, when commerce became as important as agriculture, deciding business controversy had similar effects. The fact that the highest official in the realm was called Justiciar shows how close to congruence judging and government were.

At the same time, civil jurisdiction also meant money, quite directly. From the earliest times, holding court was a business. I have mentioned "the profits of justice." "Court costs"—sums payable to the court for its trouble—are at present nominal, a negligible fraction of the funds it takes to maintain our judicial system. In the Middle Ages it was quite the other way: what the court charged litigants for its services was considerable. This was in addition to the fines, amercements, and forfeitures that came from criminal cases.

In the Anglo-Saxon period, the "king's thegns," the warrior nobles, had some judicial powers among their responsibilities and privileges, and from this they took some profits. The Conquest, bringing England a maturer feudalism, enhanced and fixed the system; the money yield of the feudal court was prized, a main incident of tenure. Then the royal courts took over.

The takeover involved the ever present mix of armed might and ideology. The kings of England could not, except by ravishing feudal tradition and at risk of feudal war, simply proclaim: "Stop holding court. We will hold court. Else we will destroy you." Remember the lords who refused to take the book when it was held out to them. They gave as reason that such a thing, for such as they, was not how things were done.*

---

*The importance of ideology has been mentioned in an earlier chapter. One of the most powerful of ideologies, of course, is Marxism, and its most powerful professors have uttered famous anti-ideological pronouncements. Stalin asked how many divisions the Pope had. Mao said, "Political power grows out of the barrel of a gun." (In a New York Times account of his career in the week of Mao's death, that was the only one of his statements quoted.)

Stalin's remark is often cited for the proposition that he was a cynical realist. If he took into his reckoning the Church's

It was accomplished piece by piece; that is, writ by writ. It was done most boldly at the start, in Henry's reign, subject, of course, to the limits politics imposed, which in Henry's case meant mainly those arising from his struggle with the Church. No fiction then was needed. Henry could simply issue a decree, in plain Latin. During the century after his death, kings and their advisers moved more cautiously, but the power of the royal courts expanded: new writs were created, and trespass edged over into civil litigation. Each new writ magnified the royal jurisdiction, took in more of the life and livings of the realm, deprived the feudal courts of power.

The victory of the Crown made the common law supreme, and the instruments employed to gain the victory—the writs and the forms of action we have been speaking of—shaped the content of the law. The triumph of the common law was at first a royal triumph, and then a royal defeat. The ideological armament employed against the Stuarts was the supremacy of the common law, a supremacy over everyone, including the monarch himself. The kings had made a monster that devoured them.*

□

Through the twelfth century "the king's court," the *curia regis*, had no special juridical connotations. It meant, as I have said, the king and those who attended him. A person summoned by a royal writ appeared before Henry himself and such aides as

---

influence on the minds of many people whose efforts in the conflict counted, and was merely emphasizing that the Pope had that if nothing else, the remark was not cynical. If he was trying to make the point that the Pope had no strength at all, it was not realistic.

* The condemnation of monsters, as this instance shows, is indiscriminate. I gave up horror movies long ago, when it became offensively plain that the monster would almost never win. Some monsters were truly evil and deserved to lose, but in many a film the moral issue was not that clear. And now and then the monster was sympathetic, more appealing than his human enemies. All he wanted was the girl. What was so bad about that? And maybe she would rather have had him than that blank-faced fiancé of hers. But the monster got a dirty deal, and succumbed (though bravely) to trickery and numbers. The common law, unsymmetrical and barnacled, is the most lovable of monsters.

Henry thought were needed. If the king was not in England, the Chief Justiciar sat in his place.*

There was little specialization at the top. The king relied on those whose skill and judgment he trusted on all important matters—financial, military, diplomatic, legal. The chief men in the service of the king were not confined to any office; they moved from one responsibility to another as they were needed. There were no particular Ministers, no Secretaries of State, Treasury, Defense, no Attorney General; the Chief Justiciar was several things besides Chief Justice.

Specialization began at the lower levels. The clerks who wrote the royal documents became the Chancery. Those who dealt with financial affairs became the Exchequer. Records began to be kept separately, and this, with the specialization of the clerks, led in the thirteenth century to what can be thought of as separate offices.†

Meanwhile the judicial function, like the administrative in the Chancery and the fiscal in the Exchequer, began to take on

---

* *This does not mean all royal government was conducted at the royal center. The sheriffs, who were agents of the king, operated in their counties. And the king sent out other agents, for two purposes. One was to check on the sheriffs and others who governed locally, especially to see that the king was getting whatever money was due him. The other purpose was judicial, to preside over some of the litigation. These royal emissaries were called Justices in Eyre, "eyre" being a corruption of the Latin* iter, *the root of our "itinerary." Their importance declined as more and more judicial business was taken into the central courts.*

In the young United States, American judges did something similar: they were said to be "riding circuit." This is why the main divisions of the federal system are called "Circuits," instead of, say, "Divisions." Despite the mobility the name implies, most federal courts now stay put. (Some, because they take in large areas, move around a bit.)

† *The Exchequer was so named because when people came to pay what they owed to the king, things were laid out on a checkerboard; it made the calculation easier. The English imported this computer from the Continent, where it had been learned from the Arabs, who, including the Jews comfortably among them at the time, possessed the highest culture in the world, China perhaps excepted.*

separate institutional identity. The gradual transition from "the king's court" (the king in person with his retinue assembled) to "the king's courts" (a group of judicial organizations) occurred mainly in the thirteenth century. Henry II, as we have seen, took a direct hand in judicial business throughout his reign. He was interested, for both practical and intellectual reasons; he was one of the best lawyers in Christendom. Henry delegated, but reserved ultimate power to adjudicate in person, which he exercised in cases legally or politically important.*

Even after the issuance of established writs became a routine Chancery matter, the case itself might have to come before the king; plaintiff and defendant might have to travel to wherever the restless Henry rested. Under Richard, the travel burden lessened. He had much less interest in legal matters, and he was hardly ever in England. His Justiciar could generally be found at Westminster. After Richard's reign, English kings stayed most of the while in England, but they roamed about the country. Litigants naturally liked a fixed place better, and one of the promises John made in Magna Carta was that there would be a court, in the judicial sense, at "some certain place."

Later in the thirteenth century, judging became a full-time office, no longer a part-time function of those who had other duties to perform. The kings seldom took part in person. And jurisdiction was differentiated. For litigation between subject and subject, a group of judges sat regularly at Westminster; this, the Court of Common Pleas, seems to have satisfied the demand of the Charter. Cases involving the king directly, which included the trial of crime, still followed the king around, and the judges who accompanied the king and heard them became the Court of King's Bench. Meanwhile the specialized handling of financial matters created the third of the courts of common law, the Court of the Exchequer. So parts of the royal court, rather than the entire court, began to hear the cases. But the parts were con-

---

* Before Henry's time, it had been the rule that the king himself did not judge (except where he acted as feudal lord to his own vassals). A statement attributed to William Rufus evidences both this early rule and the difficulty in applying it. "Take heed to yourselves," he tells the judges, "for by God's face if you will not condemn [the defendant] as I wish, I will condemn you." Under Henry we hear no more of the rule.

sidered to represent the whole, and kept its name. Hence "court" in the sense in which we commonly use the word.*

During the thirteenth century, and for several centuries after, the number of judges was small, usually no more than a dozen. At first, these shifted from one to another of the royal benches as judicial business required, but by the end of the thirteenth century the benches were on the way to institutional identity. Each had its own staff of clerks and its variations in procedure. There was no longer a Chief Justiciar—that is, an official supreme in all departments including the judicial. Instead there were Chief Justices, that is, the presiding judges of each of the several courts, plus a Chancellor.

Those who sat as judges had other duties as well; they were still counselors to the king. They gradually lost their other functions, and by the sixteenth century they were judges and nothing else. A century later, after the conflict with the Stuarts, the courts achieved firm footing as an independent branch of government. Not independent in the American sense—they could not nullify Acts of Parliament—but independent in that they need look only to the law, not also to the Crown. Since then the courts have been run by judges as we know them, rather than king's men.

Breaches of the king's peace were prosecuted in the Court of King's Bench. As the criminal jurisdiction of the local courts diminished, King's Bench became the criminal court of England (except for minor local crimes). It also heard cases that involved the king as feudal lord, in accordance with the tidy feudal arrangement by which a tenant's complaints against his landlord were decided in the landlord's court. (It was not until late in the

---

* In addition to the continuing use of the word to signify a royal presence, there is a rare third sense which reflects the combined functions of the early court. The Massachusetts constitution calls its legislative assembly a court, The General Court of Massachusetts. Hence the highest judicial body of Massachusetts— the equivalent of Supreme Court or Court of Appeals in other states—is called The Supreme Judicial Court.

It may be noted that King's Bench, now Queen's Bench in the reign of Elizabeth II, remained King's Bench under Elizabeth I. Considering the power of Elizabeth I, she must have wanted it that way. The change was made in the reign of Queen Anne.

fifteenth century that the royal courts began regularly to intervene to protect those lowest in the social scale from ejection by their lords. The end of the Middle Ages can be marked, roughly, at the middle of that century.)

The king's financial disputes with his subjects were settled in the Court of the Exchequer. This court also handled actions for debt between one subject and another, when the claimant was himself indebted to the king and collecting what he was owed would help him pay that debt.

Civil actions generally were handled in the Court of Common Pleas. Trespass, however, because it involved a charge that the king's peace had been breached, could go to King's Bench. Could, but did not have to; it might be brought in Common Pleas, under that court's general jurisdiction over civil actions. So might Debt, though it was Exchequer's specialty.

So the separate parts had some mutual jurisdiction almost as soon as they separated, and then the overlapping grew. Each Court expanded its scope to take in most of what the others did, saving the truly criminal cases which were the province of King's Bench. Common Pleas had civil litigation by original design. King's Bench and Exchequer, each having a bit to start with, used fiction to enlarge it.

Not satisfied with the expansion of business that the expanding trespass action gave it, King's Bench looked around for more. It claimed, successfully, that it could decide all legal questions involving a prisoner in its custody. "Legal questions" included civil lawsuits brought against the prisoner. Next it began to allow a plaintiff to file an action for trespass even though there was no trespass; plaintiff's grievance belonged to one of the other forms of action. Once the trespass case was started, the defendant could be arrested. Once the defendant was arrested, he was a prisoner of King's Bench. Once he was a prisoner, any form of action could be used against him.

Meanwhile, in Exchequer, a plaintiff was allowed to say he owed money to the king even though he didn't. The successful pursuit of any claim he had against defendant would render him better able to pay his fictional debt to the king—a matter of interest to Exchequer. This is different from the older cases where there were real debts to the royal treasury and the jurisdictional mechanism was extrapolation rather than pretense. Here we have pure fiction, which had the good fiscal name *quo minus:* because of defendant's delinquency, plaintiff was minus an amount that he would otherwise pay the king—just supposing he was indebted to the king.

We have seen why the royal court took business away from feudal and communal courts. But why did the three divisions of the royal court take business away from one another? Maitland cites two reasons: both have to do with fees, first fees to courts, then fees to lawyers. The livings of the clerks, and to some extent the livings of the judges, came from the prices the courts charged litigants. The more cases, the better the wages. Then, as the legal profession developed, different groups of lawyers practiced in the different parts. Common Pleas started with the broadest civil jurisdiction, theoretically all the civil jurisdiction. Only "serjeants"—a word related to "servant," here servant of the Crown —were allowed to practice at Common Pleas, and one became a serjeant only by royal leave. Apprentices who had not yet obtained that leave had to practice elsewhere, and so they seized every opportunity to enhance the civil jurisdiction of Exchequer and King's Bench.*

Something might be added to Maitland's explanation. Note that the expansion of one royal court's work did not bring with it diminution of the others'. When the royal courts shouldered into the work of the local courts, the latter eventually perished. But Common Pleas, King's Bench, and Exchequer all grew large together. The economy was getting bigger and more intricate; there was naturally more controversy. Henry had given forceful impetus to the idea that litigation ought to take the place of private war. A more capacious set of forums, offering the royal brand of justice, was wanted. When there is plenty of business for all, competition is less defensive. We are not too troubled by invasions of our markets if we see other markets to invade. The judges, clerks and lawyers were undoubtedly looking for income, but it is doubtful they could have used these fictions so

---

* The title "Serjeant" is still in use in England. The prosecutor of Lady Chatterley's Lover, for example, became Common Serjeant of the City of London, to American ears a dubious reward.

It has long been said that lawyers are "officers of the court." The implication is that they have public responsibilities which go beyond the interests of their clients, that there are standards they should observe other than the simple winning of the case. This is good and useful, though not carried far enough. The concept duty may have entered with the licensing of serjeants.

wantonly had there not been public need for wider avenues of litigation.

□

One more set of fictions by which the legal system was made to meet the times may be mentioned. Criminal prosecution was in theory and in custom a person-to-person affair. When the government prosecuted, it was the king who brought the action. His peace had been violated, or the faith due him as feudal overlord had been breached. By the thirteenth century most important prosecution was the government's. Except where one subject appealed another—a recourse already fading—the king himself was the litigant. To litigate, as we have seen, one had to be physically in court; the court could not proceed unless the parties were before it. No judgment could be given, in any of the numerous sessions of King's Bench, whether it was at a central site or traveling through the country, unless the king was present.

If this theoretical requirement were fulfilled in fact, the king would have no time for any but judicial business, and indeed might have to be in several places simultaneously. We may picture a sweaty royal personage, robes flying, crown askew, scepter getting heavy, rushing here and there in a futile frantic effort to attend all prosecutions. The courts saved the royal dignity. His presence was a fiction that could not be denied. The king was said to be ubiquitous—as omnipresent, for this purpose, as the Lord one rank above him.

□

Thus, by fiction, were the forms of action rendered richer, more available, and more effective, and thus, by fiction, did the king's courts grow. Fictions multiplied as the centuries passed—"contrived," as Maitland says, "to get modern results out of medieval premises . . ." They were maintained well into the nineteenth century, in both Britain and America.

"Fictions are falsehoods," Jeremy Bentham cried, "and the judge who invents a fiction ought to be sent to jail." Bentham's denunciation of legal fictions was radical in its time. Within a century new thinkers were exalting them. Vaihinger, in his "As If" philosophy, and Tourtoulon, in his jurisprudence, made remarkably similar analyses, apparently independently. (Vaihinger seems to have been first, but Tourtoulon did not know about his work, which Vaihinger did not publish until thirty-three years after it was started.) Both treated fictions broadly; legal fictions were only a species. Both distinguished fictions from lies, the latter defined as untrue statements intended to deceive the hearer, and from myths, defined as untrue statements believed by the speaker to be true. Since legal fictions are untrue statements which both speaker and hearer know to be untrue, they are neither lie nor myth.*

So far, so good. But not much good. Vaihinger and Tourtoulon dumped legal fictions into a huge category that included mathematical concepts, classifications, and principles of science. In the law, it would also include stated rules, and such things as corporations. "Fiction" thus defined is too unwieldy to tell us much about legal fictions. Legal fictions are rather special, as the action of ejectment indicates. We would never understand them by studying such concepts as species-genus-family-order, or Boyle's Law, or line or point or surface, all of which fit Vaihinger's and Tourtoulon's definition.

The corporation is no fiction in the legal sense, though one may call it fictive. True, unlike the individual, it has no physical existence. But this scarcely means it does not have a hard reality. Ask anybody who has dealt with one. There is nothing in the corporate concept that is inconsistent with what we know, as there is, for instance, in the assertion that John Doe has a lease and that Richard Roe has run him off the land.

Bentham had had a fine time attacking legal fictions: "...[they are] a syphilis which runs in every vein, and carries into every part of the system the principle of rottenness." He was writing at a date when legal fictions had got so numerous and abstruse that they were putting the law outside the reach of ordinary understanding. Now, the law ought to be a bit beyond the reach of ordinary understanding. It has the difficult job of finding efficient general rules that will not too often cause hardship in specific cases. For this job, just-plain-common-sense will not do. Good law lies somewhere between the obvious and the recondite. Bentham was protesting a legal system that had wandered too far from reality. He was speaking when the time had come—it had come perhaps a hundred years before—to clear away the heap of fictions and formalities, the centuries' legal kitchen midden. Bentham is wrong when his statements are ap-

---

* *This paragraph is in heavy debt to, and the next is in hot dispute with, Jerome Frank's remarks on the subject in his* Law and the Modern Mind.

plied to medieval feasibilities; he is right as of his own day. By then there were better ways to state the law and to effect the needed changes—a more supple use of precedent, a stronger legislative process. Or there would be soon, thanks in part to Bentham's efforts.

With all the reforms, legal fiction is not completely gone. In 1964, the United States Supreme Court announced that the traditional law of defamation hampered freedom of speech and press, so the First Amendment required it be softened. The Court ruled that something said or written about a public official could not give rise to a slander or libel action—no matter how defamatory, no matter how untrue—unless the defendant wrote or said the thing with actual malice toward the plaintiff. (Later the Court would add "or about a public figure," and, for a while, before a new majority retreated, "or on a matter of public interest.")

"Actual malice" was a phrase familiar in the law of libel and slander. It has for quite a while been settled that certain defamatory statements, even if untrue, may ordinarily be made without incurring legal liability, because the subject is one on which uninhibited comment is especially important (comment about the government, for instance, or literary criticism) or because of other special circumstances (reply to what is itself a defamatory attack). The statements are said to be "privileged." But if the court finds that the defendant was acting in bad faith, making the false statement out of hostility toward the plaintiff or with desire to do harm, the privilege will be lost. Such motivation has been called, reasonably enough, "malice" or "actual malice"—with the "actual" added to avoid the dilution suffered by words put to frequent service. The concept is also used in considering the measure of damages, whether or not a privilege is involved; proof of defendant's malevolence can increase the amount awarded to a successful plaintiff.

The 1964 case involved criticism of an Alabama chief of police for his conduct in a racial conflict. This was a situation where, in the established law of libel, a privilege existed, the citizen's privilege to make "fair comment on matters of government." The privilege could be negated, again by established law, if the plaintiff showed that the defendants had made the statement maliciously. The Supreme Court, creating new Constitutional doctrine and trying to draw it into the shelter of existing precedents, thought it found a pulley in the malice concept. But when the Justices turned the concept to their purpose—to narrow the circumstances in which they would allow a public official to win a libel action—they gave "actual malice" a definition it never had before. They said actual malice existed when, and only when, defendant had made the defamatory statement with knowledge of its falsity or in reckless disregard of whether it was true or false.

Neither of these states of mind is synonymous with malice. Its legal sense, as up to then the courts had used the word, was hardly different from its everyday sense. But plain-English malice might be altogether absent in situations where, under the new definition, courts would be bound to find that "actual malice" existed, and altogether present in situations that held no "actual malice" at all. A speaker does not necessarily have ill will toward the object of his obloquy, though he speaks recklessly or even knowing that he lies. His purpose may be something else. Dishonest or grossly careless in his statement, he may be nobly striving toward some vision of the public weal, or ignobly trying to make his journalism salable. The harm to plaintiff is incidental, not a motivating force. Defendant may even be truly sorry the plaintiff has been hurt.

On the other side of the Supreme Court's test, the speaker (or writer; for this purpose they are the same) may make a statement which is perfectly true, but with the single aim of injuring the plaintiff. This of course is malicious in both the ordinary and the traditional legal sense. Yet the plaintiff will not win. In most jurisdictions, truth, no matter how venomous, is a complete defense. The court's including the word "actual" made the definition all the more bizarre; the precedents on which it relied often simply said "malice." This newly minted "actual malice," one must understand, is actually not actual.

As mentioned in an earlier chapter, our system of *stare decisis* allows for change, though not too often, nor too sharply, nor without some linkage to the past. Here the Court was not adept. It tried to maintain a tie to established law by using an established concept, but the concept, turned to the Court's desired goal, was nowhere near reality. "Actual malice," in this context, was close kin to Richard Roe's expulsion of John Doe.

It was not only fiction; it was improvident fiction, and contrasts with the sage fantasies of the early common law. It creates confusion in the public understanding of the law, and opens opportunities to those for whom confusion is a weapon. Thus Governor George Wallace, interviewed on network television when he was still important in the 1976 Presidential campaign, disposed of certain charges by saying they were libelous. He added that he could not sue—the implication being that otherwise he would—because of the Court's decisions. The law, he pointed out, now demanded that a public figure prove actual malice, and the people who published these scurrilous libels were going around saying that George Wallace was personally a nice fellow and they really liked him. In the face of such friendly disclaimers of personal ill will, Wallace asked his interviewer, how could he ever prove malice?

□

I said some paragraphs ago that the modern corporation is no fiction. Yet some aspects of its conduct suggest the use of fiction. Theoretically, corporate management is controlled by stockholders voting democratically. In fact stockholders of a large corporation exercise very little independent judgment. Management is inhibited—to the extent it is inhibited—by the law directly (Securities Acts and Antitrust Acts most prominently), by the threat of corporate raiders (another group seeking to replace the group ensconced, through winning the votes of the generally ignorant stockholders in a "proxy fight"), and by class actions and stockholders' suits. But this negation of corporate theory—the divorce of management from ownership—is not the same as the legal fictions we have been speaking of. It is not an open indulgence in make-believe to reach a worthy end. It goes against the law, not with it. It often comes close to fraud, and sometimes gets there, though not nearly so often as it used to fifty years ago.

Something more like ancient fiction appears in the conduct of small corporations, through which most small business is done. It is common practice to "write up the minutes" of a directors' or stockholders' meeting when in fact there was no meeting. There are usually two or three or four stockholders, those who run the business and their spouses or other relatives, and the same people, or some of them, act as the directors. The principals are too busy to have a formal meeting. A trip in from the suburbs by the spouses to hear what they already know is a nuisance. Nobody wants to bother. So the lawyer writes the minutes of the meeting as though it were actually held, with a quorum present, and the secretary of the corporation signs them.

This is innocent enough if a majority, at a given date, agreed on what is written in the minute book; *Robert's Rules of Order* is not sacred. The practice can become fraudulent when the

whole thing is an afterthought: in order to accomplish some desired result, agreement must be said to have been reached at an
earlier time, and the minutes are predated to record a decision
that was never made, formally or informally. The fraud may be
upon minority stockholders—hostility within a corporate family
which is also a family by blood or marriage is not uncommon—
or upon business creditors, or upon the Internal Revenue Service (compare Nixon's predating of his gift of papers). However,
when there is in fact a meeting of minds if not a meeting of
bodies, the writing up of minutes does no harm, saves some time,
and is loyal to the tradition of the salutary legal fiction. In some
states there are statutes specifically authorizing the practice, thus
turning the fiction into nonfiction.*

Finally, there is the fiction involved in the stockholder's
suit. It is brought for the benefit of the corporation against the
corporate officers and directors and people with whom they have
dealt. Any judgment obtained by the stockholder will go not to
him but to the corporation. (He benefits, of course, to the extent
of his share of the corporation—tiny, ordinarily—and his lawyers
from fees awarded by the court out of the judgment gained.) The
corporation should be the plaintiff. But those against whom the
claim is made control the corporation; they will not sue themselves. The courts have solved the problem by allowing the
stockholder to name the corporation as defendant. Thus it becomes a party to the litigation, and any party can have a judgment
in its favor. This is genuine old-fashioned fiction, judicially approved contradiction of reality. Here a defendant gets the pro-
ceeds if, and only if, the court gives judgment for the plaintiff.

---

* "Corporate family," as suggested above, is more than legal
metaphor. The stockholders of a small company are often husband and wife and children, and, in addition, there is the recent
increase of less sanctified relationships. A new client, describing
his company, referred several times with obvious affection to
"my wife," the person who owned half the stock and ran the
business with him. As we got better acquainted, and he gave me
more of the facts, he mentioned that he and his co-manager were
not legally married. "Just incorporated," he said.

10

Pleading

Over the years, common-law procedure got cranky and tyrannical. The plaintiff had to find the single form of action proper to his case. The defendant had to make the proper answer. To the naked eye, any one of several forms might seem to suit the facts, but plaintiff had to pick the right one, else he could not stay in court. Or he might discover that there was no form of action for his grievance, though it seemed in common justice he had been wronged.

Plaintiff and defendant then engaged in a pleading joust. Pleading in the law, except in the earliest days, has been the parties' formal statement of position, not argument addressed to judge or jury. It constitutes the first stage of a litigation; at common law it led directly to the trial. Each such formal statement is called "a pleading," and the activity itself is called "pleading." In the courts of common law, pleading quickly grew elaborate, and mysterious, and very, very strict. It stayed that way into the nineteenth century, and in some of our states into the twentieth.

By the 1700s, English litigation was tragicomedy, comic in its pompous theater and its formulary rites, tragic in the poison to the law that emanated from it. Plaintiff started with his Declaration. It had to fit precisely an established form of action, evolved through fiction and accreted precedent from some aged writ. The rigor of the pleading affected not only the plaintiff, who had to squeeze his grievance into the inelastic form, but also the defendant. If he wished to rest the contest on the facts, defendant set up his Plea. The Plea might be a curt denial, but then it had to be the particular one that fit the form of action: *nul disseisin* (plaintiff had not had possession); *nihil debet* (there was nothing defendant owed); *non est factum* (there was no such document, or covenant); *non assumpsit* (defendant had not undertaken, when contract actions came about); *not guilty* (for trespass, action on the case, and trover, flaunting their criminal ancestry). These two or three words created a "general issue" and the matter was ready for trial.

But defendant might defend without denial. Plaintiff's Declaration might speak the truth but not the whole truth. Defendant's Plea would then be that while the allegations of the Declaration were true so far as they went, they did not go far enough; there were other circumstances that neutralized those allegations. The situation seen as a whole, defendant said, precluded judgment for the plaintiff. This was a Plea in Confession and Avoidance. Plaintiff could then come back with further allegations of his own, which he asserted overcame defendant's effort to avoid. Each succeeding pleading thus became more special: the case drew nearer some narrow question of fact. This process was accordingly called "special pleading."

The term has come into nonlegal, pejorative use, and been distorted. Dictionaries define it as captious argument, argument stressing elements helpful to the arguer and omitting those that go the other way. Perhaps the resemblance of "special" and "specious" has led to this confusion, aided by the ill repute that common-law pleading earned. Then we flattened the dictionary definition and spread it out. It is now used to describe any dishonest argument, and even to describe nothing more than the urging of one's own interests. Thus from an annual convention of the Association of American Publishers, a gathering of literary people, it is reported that "when it comes to copyright law, everybody—publishers, teachers, librarians, movie makers, recording companies, performing-arts societies, public broadcasters and cable-TV people—is a 'special pleader.' "

□

When common-law pleading was in full blossom, there could be a long and tangled vine. After Declaration and Plea in Confession and Avoidance, plaintiff's response was Replication, to which defendant might make Rejoinder, which could be met by Surrejoinder. Defendant might then interpose Rebutter, at which plaintiff could volley Surrebutter. It was all by formal statement. None of it was testimony.

At any stage, either party might deny the other's last preceding statement. Denial, called Traverse, closed the pleading and posed a question for the jury. Or either party might Demur, which closed the pleading and posed a question for the judge. The demurring party was taking the position that the other's allegations, even if admitted to be true, amounted to a legal cipher. When defendant demurred, he was saying that the plaintiff's pleading could not lead to any remedy the law allowed. When plaintiff demurred, he was saying that defendant's pleading set forth no recognized defense. Demurrer offered to stake the outcome on the proposition that everything the other side alleged, conceding it were proved, added up to nothing in the law.

Traverse meant "not so; you lie." Demurrer meant "So what?" Confession and Avoidance meant "Yes, but . . ." Defendant's choices are essentially the same today, though the style is different.

Traverse or Demurrer was climactic. Traverse meant the facts must be determined. Issue, it was said, was joined, and the next step was the trial. Demurrer was resolved by judicial ruling on the law. The ruling was the end of the case, except as appeal (in the modern sense) came into being. If the lawyer made an error, his client got no chance to plead again. If the wrong form of action was selected, or the allegations were stated in a way that did not fit the form, and defendant then demurred—that was it, forever, though on the facts which could be proved rather than the facts as pleaded plaintiff should have won. On the other side, suppose the reality supported the defendant and could very well be proved, but defendant's lawyer thought that plaintiff, even with all his lies, had failed to plead a cause of action, and hence the lawyer picked demurrer as the quicker, less expensive course. If he was wrong in his view of the law—that is, if the judges took a different view—a false claim would be enforced. So also a false plea, when it was the other way around.

Plaintiff's mistaken choice of form of action, defendant's mistaken choice of plea, mistakes in choice of words by either party, a wrong bet by demurrer that one's adversary was mistaken—any of these would end the litigation, with no decision on whether, in the real world somewhere distant from the pleadings, plaintiff had a worthy claim or defendant had a sound defense.

Traverse led to trial directly; there were not the intervening procedures that we have today. At the trial, the pleadings dominated. If the evidence varied from the declaration, even though the facts as proved showed plaintiff had a valid claim, plaintiff lost his case. The same for the defendant who proved a good defense, but not the one he pleaded.*

□

In the beginning, pleading was oral. Plaintiff stood up in court and recited his declaration; defendant then recited his defense. This made it no less formal. The recitation must be just right. Pleadings began to take written form in the fifteenth century, and before the end of the sixteenth writing was required. Until the eighteenth century, the official entries had to be in Latin. An Act of 1731 permitted English lawyers to write English.

Common-law pleading was not entirely whimsy, or the obfuscating ritual of a temple priesthood. Its valid purpose was to define a question for the jury. The need to discover and express the real dispute between the parties is fundamental to any legal system. The need is not restricted to the law. Most arguments—in politics, in business, at cocktail parties—can be ended by a lucid statement of the issue. If it exists. Usually the passionate debaters are debating different questions. If there were a method of clarification like common-law pleading, it would reveal this. It would show that each speaker is addressing an issue of his choice. If—a rare occurrence—they happen to be talking to a single point, the realization of it will ordinarily end the discourse (though not necessarily the clamor); it usually comes down to a question of personal values or a question of fact, and such questions ordinarily cannot be resolved by the antagonists themselves. The resolution (assuming that they want one) requires reference to an outside source, an authority: a book, a map, a priest, a bartender, a respected friend perhaps. In

---

The perils of the common-law pleading system, and the lengths to which judges might go, in later years, to rescue the mistaken, are illustrated in this reminiscence of a nineteenth-century American lawyer:

 I came near losing a case on a Policy of Insurance by declaring in Assumpsit. When the Policy was produced at the Trial, the defendant's counsel insisted that it had a Seal and so the Action should have been Covenant. There was, indeed, a mark on the paper as if it had been stamped with a Seal or something like it, but the impression was faint, and the Judge, looking at it without his glasses, said he could see no Seal, and denied the Motion for Nonsuit.

the common-law system, if the question is one of fact, the reference is to a jury. If it is one of values—that is, a question of law —the reference is to the judge. Some method of untangling issues is necessary, and in our common law the method, for some seven hundred years, was the method just described.*

□

It is characteristic of Anglo-American law that the parties move the matter forward. The litigants not only fight it out, but, subject to some ground rules, mark the field of battle. The court is passive until called upon to make decision. In recent times this has been modified, but only modified and only in very recent times.

The Roman system and its descendants were quite different. In the Republic, a magistrate supervised definition of the issue, then sent it over to a judge (who was not strictly an official, but one of a chosen group of citizens). Later, in the Empire, the controversy went directly to the judge (who by this time was thoroughly official), and only on the parties' sketchy descriptions of their respective claims. There was no formal statement of the issues; the judge did both the sorting out and the resolution of the questions.

The common law, in contrast, aimed at nonprofessional appraisal of the facts, by a group of neighbors. The judges saw their function as restriction of plaintiffs to established forms of action, to ruling on the legal sufficiency of pleadings if there was demurrer, and to the monitoring of trial. (In the earliest times, the judges' principal function, as we have seen, was declaring the appropriate mode of trial—compurgation, battle, or ordeal—and deciding who must undergo the test. Once trial by jury was established, that function disappeared.) Since the task of finding truth was thrust upon a group of amateurs, the questions put to them, it was thought, needed careful preparation. The litigants, through the pleading process, must develop an issue of fact, chaste and clear, for the jury to consider.

If the parties chose to meet on a field of law, if the gauntlet was demurrer, the jury could go home. The judge could say, on

---

* *Apart from the equity system. Established in the fifteenth century as a liberal device to relieve the rigidity of common-law procedure, it too descended into formalism. Its procedure, though, was quite different. Its history, already touched on, will be given in a later chapter.*

conceded allegations, whether the elements of a cause of action existed in the pleadings; there was no need for trial. But if there was traverse, if the case must turn on facts, the jury played its role. The question should be the kind the common man is well able to decide—a simple who-is-telling-the-truth? Then the good people of the vicinage can say verdict for the plaintiff or verdict for the defendant, and the dispute will be disposed of, nicely.

The glory of common-law pleading, its apostles said, was that it worked without official intervention to produce this limpid issue. But somewhere in the evolution of the common law the match of fact and theory ended. The fully developed system owed less to theory than to other things.

One was what the most thunderous reformers felt was at the core: the enhancement of the mystery for selfish reasons—the aim of bench and bar to keep their private playhouse a place where insiders could be cozy and outsiders could only press their puzzled noses against the windowpane. There was a great deal of that, of course, but this kind of criticism has a weakness, one it shares with all analysis that concentrates on groups or forces so intensely that the components—human beings—are ignored. The average lawyer was not venal in his adherence to the system. He scarcely could be; its difficult abstruseness favored the most skillful, and the most skillful are by definition not the average.

For the most part, bench and bar clung to the system simply because they were used to it, and regarded proposals for change with uneasiness, if not anxiety. But some had a more positive feeling. They seemed to have been in love with pleading, or at least to have found a deep aesthetic pleasure in its artful exercise. These artists were apt to lead the bar and occupy the bench. They published treatises and form books, and these were slavishly adhered to by those who felt, correctly, that they did not know as much. That meant most practitioners. In the eighteenth century, one maestro wrote:

> The science of special pleading is an excellent logic. It is admirably calculated for the purpose of analyzing a cause —of extracting, like the roots of an equation, the true points in dispute, and referring them, with all imaginable distinctness, to the court or jury. It is reducible to the strictest rules of pure dialectics, and tends to fix the attention, give a habit of reasoning closely, quicken the apprehension, and invigorate the understanding.

The most-quoted evangelist was the nineteenth-century barrister Henry Stephen, whose encomiums included this:

> This system, known by the name of *Pleading*, of remote antiquity in its origin, has been gradually moulded into its present form, by the wisdom of successive ages. Its great and extensive importance in legal practice, has long recommended it to the early and assiduous attention of every professional student. Nor is this its only claim to notice; for, when properly understood and appreciated, it appears to be an instrument so well adapted to ends of distributive justice, so simple and striking in its fundamental principles, so ingenious and elaborate in its details, as fairly to be entitled to the character of a fine juridical invention.

Legislative disestablishment did not end the true religion. As late as the turn of the twentieth century, after most states had adopted a new system, The *Harvard Law Review* declaimed:

> Common law pleading was the mill of justice in which an undefined, obscure mass of fact was ground down to clear and distinct issues ... The matchless precision of the old system, the growth of centuries of legal experience, has been replaced by a looseness of which the chief effect is to put a premium on ignorance and sloth.

But what moved admirers of common-law pleading to lyrical devotions moved its critics to nausea. Stephen had organized his book according to the purpose and effect of the various rules of common-law pleading. The American Ballantine followed the plan:

> Serjeant Stephen's masterly *Treatise on the Principles of Pleading* has doubtless led many lawyers to admire the old system of pleading as a true science founded in principles of the soundest reason and closest logic adapted to the ends of analysis. But, if Stephen had been somewhat more candid, he would have classified many of the rules of pleading under headings indicating tendencies quite the reverse of those which he adopted. He would have had to adopt such headings, for example, as (1) rules which tend simply to the nonproduction of an issue; (2) rules which tend to conceal the specific issues; (3) rules which produce duplicity and multifariousness in the issues; (4) rules which tend to produce uncertainty and vagueness in the issues; (5) rules calculated to introduce obscurity, confusion and perplexity

in the pleading; (6) rules which tend to cause prolixity and delay in pleading; (7) rules which perpetuate historical anomalies and frivolous technicalities; (8) rules which make pleadings turn on doubtful and uncertain distinctions not founded in practical sense or policy; (9) certain miscellaneous, arbitrary, and irregular rules to entrap pleaders and defeat the purposes of pleading.

There were two things wrong with the system. One was something proponents and detractors both tended to ignore. Most of the debate, pro and con, had to do with special pleading. But not all common-law pleading was special. Alongside the delicate process of confession and avoidance was the gross encounter of the general issue. If defendant's first response was simple traverse—non assumpsit, for example, or nihil debet—the case was ready for the jury. This was quick and simple; it appeals to those who scorn "legal technicalities." (The quotation marks are used because the phrase is fatuous, implying as it does that a mechanism which needs to be adjusted to numerous complexities can be made to work without technique.) But the general issue gave very little definition of what it was the jury must decide. Some of the allegations in the declaration might be true, others might be false, and defendant with his smug denial was putting plaintiff to the proof of every one of them. If pleading's purpose was to facilitate the trial and the preparation for it, this hardly did the job. It fit the popular notion of good law: curt, comprehensible, and obviously simple. It was also, perhaps a bit less obviously, very nearly useless.

On the other hand, special pleading was torturously slow. As it grew, it sprouted rank requirements and often worked injustice. The job of special pleading, theoretically, was a tidy sort of sculpturing. The job of special pleading, realistically, was much too often maneuver. The obscurities that developed, the penalties imposed for lack of skill or knowledge, the creation of a game with esoteric rules—these wandered far from a root idea that had much to recommend it.

The root, I think, went deep, deeper than the jury trial. Recall that feature of early law which from the modern point of view, we are told, turned things upside down. Judgment came first, then came trial. The judges decided which of the litigants should be put to his proof, and what the proof should be—compurgation, battle, or ordeal. With that decision, all judicial work was done. Our books uniformly present this as a strange (to modern eyes) inversion. Maitland says it is a "startling proposition" that in the early days "judgment preceded proof." Another scholar calls it an "odd paradox." But why is it odd to clear away legal questions first, decide which facts are relevant, and then proceed to proof? Proof is usually the more arduous part of litigation. It was arduous in the early days because of the violence to body or soul it carried. It is arduous now, because of its gluttonous consumption of time and energy and because it is usually dull.*

It was the method of proof that was primitive, not the procedural sequence. Common-law pleading, I suggest, simply continued this approach, the jury verdict replacing the sacral modes. Nor has it ever been abandoned. "Trial judges"—judges in the courts of first instance as distinguished from appellate judges—still do their most significant work before the trial begins. They make rulings during trial, and there are motions decided at the close of evidence or even after verdict (which seek to take the case away from the jury or overturn its verdict). Most major rulings, however, are made in advance of trial. Although today there is much less pleading, motions and other pretrial procedures take its place, and judicial decision operates all along the way. Indeed, few cases ever get to trial, and those that do are often settled in the course of trial, before verdict or decision. During the 1970s, in the federal courts, less than nine percent of civil cases reached trial. My guess is that the percentages are lower now, and even lower in the state courts.

So, in contemporary litigation, apart from appellate review, judicial decision has its main effect before the trial begins, if not by ruling that results in final judgment, then by ruling that induces compromise, or by ruling that shapes the trial. For the most part, judgment precedes proof—Maitland's "startling proposition"—just as it did in the ancient system. There is nothing odd about it.

Another kind of procedure is, of course, conceivable. The trial could come first. The facts could be determined before the

---

* *Most trial work puts a premium on long investigation into, and careful assembling of, a mass of detailed facts. The trial itself is exciting—a civil trial can be a great pleasure for the lawyer opponents—but the preparation can be drudgery, and very often the principal ingredients of success are attention span and immunity to boredom.*

court applied the law. This would have the advantage of presenting the legal questions in full context. It would have monstrous disadvantages: the expense of trial in every case instead of just a few; in most trials a leaden cargo of immaterial evidence; dockets impossibly crowded.

I have urged—against the contrary impression often given by historians and nearly always by writers of historical fiction—that ancient peoples were significantly different from ourselves. Yet this is a point on which I think our ancestors less different than we are told: they are closer to us in legal procedure than in other modes of thought. They differ in their insistence that the proof be left to magic, not in their idea of the proper sequence of the steps of litigation. The emphasis on pleading at common law was in this regard a natural outgrowth of an older order, an order we still have with us.

□

In addition to the good aspects of common-law pleading, its logic and its grace, and the great advance at first it represented; in addition to its bad, the hubris of the bench and the selfish interests of the bar; in addition to the pleasure of the artful craftsman—something further must be entered in the tale. It is the wayward energy of closed systems. What was appropriate and indeed ingenious at the start of the common law became inappropriate as it went along. The evolution of common-law pleading was as though computers were breeding computers. (If that last should ever happen, count on having dumb computers.)

This degenerate progress of pleading was spectacular and long-lived, but it is otherwise not extraordinary in the law. A legal invention, created to deal with a practical need, takes on a personality and runs away from home. It puts on fancy clothes and moves into a twenty-room house full of halls and stairs and bad design. Its origin as ancillary aid is forgotten or ignored; the means becomes the end. It is thought to have a value all its own.

Not extraordinary in the law, or elsewhere. It runs all through the world of intellect. A good mind produces a new important insight. The insight becomes a school of thought. Disciples are fierce in its defense, much fiercer than the founder would have been. They expound and harden it. Philosophy meets faith. Gautama Buddha urges a righteous atheism; his followers make him a god. Jesus preaches a simple and kindly life; his preaching leads to the huge unkindly Christendoms of Byzantium and Western Europe, slaughterers of heretics. Karl Marx, were he alive, would undoubtedly denounce most of those who today declare that they are Marxist.*

Other examples can be found among government agencies, state and federal. Some of them, of course, perform their delegated functions well. Others seem to exist only for themselves. Citizens meant to be beneficiaries are supplicants, and reason yields to the-way-we-do-things. The deterioration of the federal agencies was aided by the flight of intellect from Washington after World War II. In Truman's elected term, one of the best brains in the administration was the President's, an antic state of affairs which his successor managed to correct without improving his subordinates.

Or a very grand example: the Assembly of the United Nations. Conceived as a restraint on aggression and an aid to international justice, it has evolved into something that exists only for itself, itself being a stage for unusually hypocritical propaganda. Perhaps this process can be halted. Turning back the clock, however, is always difficult, especially when turning it back means betterment.

□

The writ system reached maturity fairly rapidly, and then lived on and on. Senility was its longest stage of life. Common-law pleading had become "a science to be cultivated" within a hundred years after the first Writ of Novel Disseisin was issued. The catalog of forms of action, including those derived from Trespass, was completed by the middle 1500s. Thenceforth, until the legislation of recent times, the common law depended for its nourishment principally on masticable precedent and fiction.

With perfect taste and logic, the Original Writ itself became a fiction. A plaintiff could start an action without a visit to the clerks of Chancery; defendant was not suffered to deny that a writ had been obtained. But the structure of civil litigation continued to be called "the writ system," and properly. The form of action was the chrysalis within the writ; it did not matter the integument was shed. The system came over to America; the

---

* *Sigmund Freud, for various reasons, has been spared the apotheosis. One reason is that all living writers owe him royalties. We may, as the Lord's Prayer enjoins, forgive our debtors, but we do not easily forgive our creditors, let alone exalt them.*

dominant colonists were Englishmen and an essential part of Englishry was the common law.

In the prime of life—if size is considered prime—the system was declared abolished. It happened rather abruptly, as legal history goes. In the nineteenth century, Parliament in England and state legislatures here, influencing each other, enacted its demise.

Efforts at reform began at the close of the eighteenth century. People in general had long felt that the bench and bar had a vested interest in keeping things mysterious. People in general were right, although, as pointed out above, there was more to it than that. Blackstone gave the system magniloquent exposition. One of his pupils gave it brilliant, revealing dissection. Jeremy Bentham had attended Blackstone's lectures; let those who teach know that the eager student is not always a teacher's blessing. Popular resentment was given philosophical support by Bentham, a novelist's advocacy by Dickens, and Parliamentary impetus by Brougham.

The first response of British bench and bar was to make things worse. The ostensibly reforming Hilary Rules of 1834 changed traditional procedure by rendering it in some ways more intricate than before. (We'll show these bleeding liberals.) The movement for reform somehow staggered on, receiving a positive charge from events occurring in America. Improvements came from Parliament's Common Law Procedure Act of 1852, and basic alteration was effected by the Judicature Acts of the 1870s.*

In America things had never been as bad. Procedure varied from colony to colony, but in the seventeenth century it was nowhere very elaborate. Puritan dissent extended to the legal system, and there was righteous purifying in the Massachusetts colony. Elsewhere in the spread-out settlements justice was extremely local, and the judges were part of the community. Procedure therefore tended to be rough and ready. So had it been in

---

The Hilary Rules are a nice example of the fake revolution, something presented as upheaval that is aimed at keeping things the way they are. In Mao's China it was called Cultural Revolution.

I will not attempt to describe contemporary British civil procedure. There are differences from the American, but, as compared with traditional common-law procedure, the two are much alike.

the Anglo-Saxon communal courts, which functioned in an environment in some respects quite similar. This is not to say that colonial justice was in essence different from that of the mother country. Though their judges were often laymen, they knew the forms of action. A case in which the court was asked to make defendant give back the plaintiff's horse was recorded as an "action of detenew." Englishmen carry the common law in the pockets of their brains.

In the eighteenth century, colonial society grew more sophisticated, and so did its legal procedure. The English system, then reaching near its apex or, if you wish, groping for the bottom, was adopted (or approximated; there were local variations). The process continued after independence. Blackstone was revered. American law books were based on English sources. The authoritative work on pleading was that of Joseph Chitty. (Remember him? Ashford's lawyer?) Chitty's treatise went through eight American editions, and can be found in working law libraries today.

But, as one might expect, there was antithesis. The homely justice of the early days was not long past. The leaders of the new nation were rationalists; they felt no tie to ceremony, or to vestiges of ancient forms. The American Revolution, after all, had been a revolution. The rebels might regard themselves as transplanted Englishmen, but they surely were not fond of everything English. (They explained it to themselves by proclaiming allegiance to things they said had formerly been English, things truly English.) Blackstone was the lawyer's Book of Common Prayer, but legal atheists read Jeremy Bentham and it was mainly they who led our thought. Francophiles among them advertised the spare elegance of the Code Napoléon. The economy was moving from agricultural almost purely toward a mix with industry and commerce. Businessmen do not take to litigation the way landholders do; they have neither the tradition nor the leisure for courtly combat. Over all there hovered the ideal of simple classic symmetry, afterglow of the Enlightenment.

Halfway through the nineteenth century, reformers gained a victory. It may have been a pale reflection in America of the graver European conflicts. At least there is coincidence. In 1848, when the Continent was in revolutionary turmoil, here we had subversion of our pleading system. It was the first rebellion against the system in six hundred years.

In that year, fourteen after the nonsense of England's Hilary Rules, New York enacted the Field Code, a valiant attempt to clear away the mess the common law had made. It was named for its principal author, David Dudley Field. He came from a gifted family. One brother was the Cyrus who would later lay the transatlantic cable, make possible instant communication between the Old World and the New, and become the subject of a pretty bad poem one had to learn in grade school. Another was Stephen Field, who moved to California and got the California legislature to accept his brother Dudley's creature. (Stephen later had a long career on the United States Supreme Court.) The new procedure then worked inland from both coasts. Missouri adopted it immediately, providing a handhold in the middle. Within twenty-five years more than half the states had copied the Code. Other states held aloof, working toward procedural reform in their several ways and at their several paces. By the time of the First World War, most states had taken the New York model whole or made other considerable changes in procedure. A few preserved their common-law pleading largely unreconstructed.

None of that few were west of the Alleghenies except Illinois. Louisiana, first settled by the French, had, and has, a system with antecedents in the Continental civil law. New Jersey did an interesting, schizoid thing. In 1912 it enacted a radically new process, influenced by English innovations, for its "courts of law," but continued to reject one of the more successful of the Code reforms, the absorption of the equity system. It kept its courts of law and equity separate, and to this day, after another great leap forward in 1948, New Jersey still has its "Chancery Division." Delaware is even more traditional: it still has a Chancellor.*

The Field Code was part of a larger effort to codify the law entirely, substance as well as procedure. Field and others of like mind never managed to get a state legislature to go beyond procedure. Later on, however, starting near the turn of the century, and chiefly under the sponsorship of the American Bar Association, a disgusting organization at the time (which has undergone a radical transformation in recent years), some portions of the common law were expressed in statutory form and offered to state legislatures for adoption. The main motive, probably, was to aid the large corporations that were the Association's favorite clients; doing business in many states, they would benefit from such legislation. But consistency in the laws of the different states is in general helpful. The Uniform Com-

The Code decreed the abolition of the forms of action. It merged the separate courts of common law and equity. It facilitated "joinder" of causes of action and of parties. The common law had limited plaintiff to the particular form of action that he chose, and he had to choose the right one at his peril; now several claims and several legal theories could be combined. And several parties with different but related interests could be brought into the action. The number of pleadings was reduced to two or three: a "complaint" by plaintiff, an "answer" by defendant or, if he chose, a demurrer (sometimes called a "motion to dismiss")—that neat method of posing the legal question was not abandoned—and in most states plaintiff's "reply." The answer took the place of all the pleas.

The central command of the Code was magisterial, pure, sonorous:

> The distinction between actions at law and suits in equity, and the forms of all such actions and suits, heretofore existing, are abolished; and there shall be in this state, hereafter, but one form of action, for the enforcement or protection of private rights and the redress of private wrongs, which shall be denominated a civil action.

The only writ required to start this civil action was a brief summons that would let defendant know he had better come to court. The complaint would be a plain statement of the facts that plaintiff thought entitled him to legal remedy, not the hazardous recitation of an implacable form of action. Defendant's pleading would be similarly factual, informal, straightforward. The formulary phrases need no longer be recited. Just tell us, Mr. Plaintiff, in factual synopsis, what your grievance is. And you, Mr. Defendant, just tell us, simply, where you think he's wrong.

This seemed a strong fresh breeze. The complaint, said the Code, apart from names and a demand for money or other relief, need only contain

> a statement of the facts constituting the cause of action, in ordinary and concise language, without repetition, and in

---

mercial Code, for example, which deals with bills and notes and checks and such, has been widely adopted; so much of business is interstate that uniformity in this field is patently desirable, and codification, though subject to different judicial interpretation in different states, makes for uniformity.

such a manner as to enable a person of common understanding to know what is intended.

Nothing fancy, nothing recondite, just something all of us can comprehend. Only "the dry, naked, actual facts," as the leading treatise on code pleading put it.

□

When the legislature decrees new law, we usually get new law. Subject to the glosses courts are apt to put upon a statute, the law is generally taken to be what the legislature says it is. The difficulties of criminal-law enforcement aside, most statutes are fairly effective. Not this one.

There was some effect, of course. Putting common law and equity into one court increased efficiency, although the unified courts regarded the unified complaint as presenting either a case at law or a case in equity, and changed their mental robes accordingly. Limiting the number of pleadings saved time, although some sharpening was lost. And there was considerable movement away from the Draconian penalties imposed on pleading that did not fit precisely the shape and measure of the forms of action. As revolution, though, the Field Code was not a great deal more successful in the law than was the European turbulence in politics. Counterrevolution set in just as firmly, though more subtly.

It was due in great measure to the same factors that had produced the common-law enormities. To some extent, lawyers and judges were protecting their hoard of arcane learning. To some extent, more innocent, habit put a headlock on reform. The momentum of the great closed system could not be halted all at once. Bench and bar contrived to make the Code seem almost something that had never happened. And in one respect pleading worsened; complaints and answers grew much bulkier than their common-law equivalents had been.

This counterrevolutionary force did not include all judges and lawyers; it was only most of them. There were, especially at first, a number who tried to give the Code its intended consequences. They believed in it, or believed that legislation ought to be obeyed. They were eventually overwhelmed. This is characteristic of reform; the tide rolls in again. Seldom to the point from which it was repelled, however. Pleading would never be quite the same.

But the failure was not the fault of the bench and bar entirely; it was also the fault of the Code itself. The codifiers had sought to melt down the separate forms of action into a single "civil action" and put great stress on facts. But the Code went on to say the plaintiff's pleading should set forth the facts that constitute his "cause of action." "Cause of action" came to be treated as something very much like "form of action." Perhaps the similarity in sound and cadence helped carry the concept over, and for this the draftsmen might be blamed. Lawyers proceeded to prepare their complaints, and courts demanded that they should, so as to state the elements of the old-time forms. The lawyers' habits probably induced the courts' demand as much as the demand controlled the pleading. Mediocre judges tend to think of how-things-are as how-things-have-to-be.

Moreover, the Code contained a constitutional infirmity— small c, that is—a philosophical problem that opened the way to mischief. Field's creation sounds like a healthy reform. It exudes democracy. It seeks to get away from what lawyers call words of art, which the layman cannot understand. It seeks to deal instead in facts, which anyone can understand. There is something reassuring and protective about the word itself. We say "in fact" when we mean to bring discussion down to earth; we will focus on the simple truth. A "matter-of-fact" approach excludes the treacherous highfalutin. Empirical devotion to facts is the basis of modern science; and we all know that modern science brings nothing but benefit. We already knew in 1848.

The trouble is that there is hardly anything less matter-of-fact than the definition of a fact. The concept is concentric. Events and conditions can be described in words increasingly inclusive, in an infinite number of smaller or larger ways, more specific or more abstract. (I speak for the law alone, but I imagine the problem extends to every mode of thought.) The pleader, commanded to state his case in language "ordinary and concise," would not seem to disobey when he uses terms summary and broad: when he says no more, for instance, than that plaintiff and defendant made a contract. Nor, on the other hand, when he fixes on the story's hard details: each word that plaintiff and defendant uttered when they met to make their deal. If the latter was the kind of fact contemplated by the Code, the complaint would be immense, something like a transcript of the evidence. If the former, the complaint would assume a legal conclusion— that a contract resulted from the conversation—and it would tell the defendant and the judge almost nothing of the proof and legal theory plaintiff planned to offer at the trial. So the courts, interpreting the language of the Code, directed pleaders to avoid, on the one side, "conclusions of law" and, on the other, "evidentiary" allegations. No conclusions, no statements of law, no inference; but nothing in the pleading that is merely evidence. To say that plaintiff and defendant made a contract can reasonably be called a conclusion of law. To recite every word of their conversation can be said to be pleading evidence. But these examples are at opposite ends of the scale. There is too much in between.

In an effort to give more guidance, the courts and legislatures turned to the phrase "material facts." That helped a little, but very little. "Material" is itself an elusive notion. The only attempts at definition that did not end in wilderness ended in tautology. "Material fact" was defined in terms of what it was not —not evidence, not conclusion.*

The one statement about a case that can with some assurance be called pure conclusion of law is "judgment for plaintiff" or "judgment for defendant." (And then only at the moment it is rendered. Entered into history, it becomes a statement of fact.) Anything else has strains of fact. "Defendant purchased a quantity of goods," "defendant failed to pay sums due," "defendant trespassed on plaintiff's land," "defendant endorsed said promissory note," "defendants constitute a monopoly," "the said Jane Jones is plaintiff's agent," "plaintiff holds a license under defendant's copyright," "plaintiff's patent has been infringed," "defendant slandered plaintiff," "the publication is obscene," "the order is a prior restraint"—in one sense these are conclusions of law, in another statements of fact.

Move to the other end of the spectrum: "Defendant, at 11:54

---

* *"Material" was the favorite adjective of the later codes, but there were interesting variations: "ultimate facts," "substantive facts," "issuable facts." The casting about for adjectives reminds one of the legislative search for synonyms in antiobscenity statutes. The Comstock Act started, in 1873, with "obscene, lewd, lascivious, indecent." In 1909, in a resolute afterthought, Congress added "filthy." Meanwhile, judges thought of other synonyms. The liquid l was the favorite letter; "lustful, lubricious, libidinous" were added to "lascivious" and "lewd." The sound suggests that somewhere within the judges' souls, despite the condemnation, sex meant music and romance. Contrast the scornful f and the hostile k of the principal word condemned.*

P.M. of the third day of May in the year 1976 on the northwest corner of Fifth Avenue and Forty-fourth Street, in the City, County and State of New York, moving his shoulder and arm with considerable vigor, propelled the knuckles of his right hand in a forward and upward direction, intending that they should come to rest on the left side of plaintiff's nose, and defendant, successfully carrying out the intent aforesaid, made contact between the knuckles aforesaid and the nose aforesaid, so that . . ." The medical details follow. Is this too evidentiary? On the other hand, would "defendant assaulted plaintiff" be too much a conclusion of law? "Assault," after all, is a common-law concept, defined in thousands of rulings. Or is "defendant punched plaintiff in the nose" the kind of ultimate fact the pleading should contain? Plain enough, but a bit too ultimate? Should defendant not be told when and where and how? Plaintiff may have been mistaken; the blow may have been struck by someone hiding behind defendant. Or it may have been an accidental brush. Or defendant at the time may have been in Philadelphia. Details of time and place would help. What sort of proof should defendant be prepared to meet?

Take an example less violent:

You go to buy a car. The ritual haggling finished, the salesman having descended in stately steps to the price his boss has told him he must get—or perhaps you hate to haggle and agree to pay the price the salesman first demands, so that he goes home that night ill at ease and wondering whether life has any meaning—there arises the question of color.

"Blue," you say.

"We have," the salesman recites, "Royal Blue, Teal Blue, Blue Jean Blue, Lonesome Train Blue, Union Blue, Confederate Blue . . ."

"Confederate Blue?"

"Yeah sure. Why not?"

"Okay."

". . . Funky Blue, Television Baseball Outfield Blue, and two kinds of sky blue—Just Plain Sky Blue and Los Angeles Sky Blue."

"What's the difference?"

"All of them?" The salesman looks put upon. "Some cheap bastard stole my chart."

"No. Just the two sky blues. What are they?"

"That I know," the salesman says. "Los Angeles Sky Blue is mostly a nice gray-and-yellow."

"I think I'd like Just Plain Sky Blue."

"Fine. Sign here. Congratulations."

You sign, and some time later, in fact a good deal later, the salesman phones to say your car has come. You go to pick it up, and the color is not what you expected. "That's not sky blue," you say.

"It's Just Plain Sky Blue in our catalog," says the salesman.

"Your catalog is color-blind," you say.

"I put a check next to Just Plain Sky Blue on the contract form," the salesman says, "and you signed it. Besides, you didn't say you had to have Sky Blue. You only said you thought you'd like it."

You ask for your deposit back. The dealer refuses. You get a lawyer and bring an action. Since you live in a code-pleading state, your lawyer must allege the facts—not evidence, not conclusions, just-the-facts-please. What does he put in your complaint? That defendant breached the contract? It would be concise, as the Code directs, but it seems a conclusion of law, a judgment you want the court to reach. That defendant failed to deliver the car as ordered by the plaintiff? This also is concise, but it still sounds pretty conclusory; it tells very little about the actual dispute. That the car was not sky blue though plaintiff made it a condition the car should be sky blue? That the car was not Just Plain Sky Blue though plaintiff demanded Just Plain Sky Blue? Does the lawyer add a description of what in common parlance Just Plain Sky Blue must be understood to be (in the absence of a color chart)?

Maybe your lawyer ought to quote you and the salesman verbatim. That could hardly be called conclusory, and it would give the court and defendant plenty of information, but would he not be pleading evidence? And what does he claim is the effect of the conversation? Does he add that shades of blue are significant? That in the circumstances "I think I'd like" means "Give me what is specified or the deal is off"? That a car of a different color is a horse of a different color? These things tell a lot about what the issues will be, but are they "fact"?

In a code-pleading state, if plaintiff's lawyer puts too much into a complaint, defendant can make a "motion to strike" before he serves his answer. This delays the case for a while, which the plaintiff will not like, and it makes the plaintiff's lawyer appear a poor pleader, which the lawyer will not like. But he can easily explain to his client that overpleading is the better part of valor. On the other side of the almost unmarked trail—more precisely, a trail thickly marked with indecipherable precepts—there is quicksand. If the complaint contains too little, if it puts the case too broadly, if it speaks in "conclusions" instead of "facts," plaintiff will be held to have "failed to state a cause of action." Then the defendant can demur (or, in the language of the later codes, make a motion to dismiss) and the complaint will be rejected "for insufficiency." Dismissal meant the case was done and lost, unless the court granted leave to serve a new complaint.

Under the present codes, the courts usually do grant leave or, by making the dismissal "without prejudice," permit the plaintiff to bring another action on an acceptable complaint. But even though amendment is permitted, time is consumed in the making of the motion, the decision on it, and the preparation of a second complaint; only then does the defendant's time to answer start to run. Meanwhile, defendant sits back and holds on to the money or whatever else may be the subject of dispute.*

And if amendment is not permitted, dismissal, though without prejudice, can be disabling, even fatal. Defendant must be found and process served again. Plaintiff gets discouraged. A witness may move away or die or simply change his mind. Defendant may go bankrupt or skip the jurisdiction. Even something such as this can happen: a statute of limitations may run out between the date the first action was begun and the date of service of the new one, so that plaintiff is left with no remedy at all, whatever the merit of his claim.

The kind of allegation a court might call conclusion of law and therefore insufficient was very hard to predict. The highest court of Connecticut, for example, ruled that "transfer in fraud of creditors" is a statement of fact, but "mental capacity" to make a gift is a statement of law. It made these two rulings on a single day, each decision unanimous. Neither opinion made any reference to the other. Apparently the judges saw nothing odd about the couple, nor any reason to note that "transfer," "fraud," and "creditor" might be legal concepts, nor that the condition of

---

Conversely, an ill-conceived motion to dismiss does not end the case for defendant. Under the codes, he is then permitted to answer. From a plaintiff's point of view, this was hardly progress; it gave defendant an opportunity for another tactic of delay. Demur first, even if the complaint seems pretty sound. Lose the motion, and then have time to answer.

one's mind—a very old person had suffered apoplexy—might be a medical fact.*

A statement circumambulates a set of events or conditions. It may encompass too little and thus be evidentiary. It may encompass too much and thus be pale conclusion. Somewhere in between one may find "material fact." But this means making a proper choice from the set of concentric circles. How to make a proper choice cannot be prescribed in terms of a general, all-purpose, automatic rule.

The natural result is that whenever there is any doubt the lawyer throws the allegation in. He may think it conclusion of law, or he may think it evidence, but he can't be absolutely sure and fears to leave it out. Understandably reluctant to risk dismissal, he would rather deal with a motion to strike. Code pleading produced much longer documents than common-law pleading ever had.

This does not mean the idea was totally unworkable. As elsewhere in our law, a rule can take its meaning from case-by-case adjudication. The courts, as I have said, are used to drawing lines; it is their business. But this distinction is especially difficult, and for all the good it does it is not worth the bother.

The goal of code pleading might have been attained—or at least the courts could have come close enough to make a fairly good system of it—if the problem had been approached in terms of function and context. What may be evidence in one case may be material fact in another; what may be material fact in one case may be conclusion of law in another. It depends upon the particular situation out of which the case arises, and "it depends" is not evasion. The question should be viewed, each time, in the light of the law's purposes. Pleading should give enough information, without undue prolixity—"enough" and "undue" get their meaning from what follows—so that (1) the opposing party can meet the charge and get ready for the trial, (2) the jury will have clear issues to decide, and (3) the court is given, at the outset, some idea of what the case is all about. Code pleading stressed the first purpose, common law the second; the third is not much of a problem. Under the Code, the judge's instructions

---

* The question had to do with reviewability on appeal rather than with pleading, but the criterion there involves the selfsame pair of notions: conclusions of law are reviewable; findings of fact are not.

were counted on to make things clear to the jury, and the main object of the pleading was to give the opposing party sufficient information so that he would know what to admit and what to deny, and be able to marshal his evidence and his legal argument. He ought not be led to meet one kind of case and find himself confronted with another at the trial. Defined in terms of these functions, "material fact" supplies a decent rubric.

But American judges and lawyers of the nineteenth century and the early twentieth—nearly all of them—did not like to think in terms of function. They liked to think in terms of concept. The instigators of the Code were Benthamites; most of those who practiced under the Code were Blackstonites. While the rest of America was being intensely practical, the courts clung to their conceptual addiction. They loved to pronounce orotund rules and make plump statements of principle.

This did not mean that decisions were never functional. As we have noted in another chapter, the court's opinions often had little connection with the results they reached. A line of cases could be seen to come out right—that is, good for practical purposes and in accord with justice—although the opinions were full of overbroad rules and thoroughly inconsistent. On the other hand, the inutility of the concepts often got the courts confused, and their looseness made corrupt decision easier. Things would have been much better if intellect had been in tune with instinct.*

---

* *Here again, with apologies to those who may have seen it, a bit from* The End of Obscenity, *repeated because, though it does not deal with pleading, I know of no example that more clearly demonstrates the courts' addiction to useless concepts along with their striving for good practical results:*

> *This was impressed on me very early, at the beginning of my second year in law school, when I was writing something for a law review. It was in the field that is called, rather charmingly, the law of conflict of laws—which has to do with choosing the law to govern a transaction that has roots in several states, where the different states would treat the transaction differently. The particular question related to a living donor's trust and the restrictive rules that sometimes invalidate such a trust. The beneficiaries may live in one state, while the trustee administers the trust*

The frustration of Code objectives came not only from the mulishness of bench and bar and the frailties of the Code itself. The legislators took a hand. Reforming legislatures frequently dislike the reforms they enact. They vote for measures which in their heart of hearts they oppose, because the public demands the legislation, or because its proponents are well organized, or for some other political reason that goes against all private inclination. So when a chance to negate what they have done arises, they are quick to take it.

New York, the leader of the revolution, was also the leader of the counterrevolution. (Except perhaps for Florida, which executed a smart about-face. It adopted the Code during Reconstruction and three years later restored its common-law pleading system. But this may have been less a matter of legal thought than an expression of racist feeling.) The change from common-law pleading had been deemed so fundamental as to require amendment of the New York Constitution. The amendment directed the legislature to appoint three commissioners "to revise, reform, simplify, and abridge" existing pleading and procedure. It was this that led to the appointment of the Field Commission. Its draft provided, as we have seen, not only that pleading be put in plain and concise language, but also that it be expressed "in such a manner as to enable a person of common understanding to know what is intended." This was part of the Code as the legislature enacted it in 1848. In the very next year, the legislators, having gotten round to reading their creation and apparently having been shocked, amended the Code to expunge the

---

in a second, the property is located in a third, and the donor himself was a resident of a fourth. There was a jumble of contradictory opinions calling on "established principles." Some courts picked one state, some another. But I was struck by the fact that in every case the court picked a state whose laws would make the trust valid. The judges, it seemed, were worried about the children for whose support the trusts had been set up, and while they could not quite bring themselves to say that this determined their decisions, it was the plain meaning of what they had done, and they could be counted on to do it again, no matter what legal theory might be.

There are not many situations in which a rule is so well hidden or so clear once it is uncovered, but the caricature illustrates an important feature of our judicial system.

quoted words. No person of common understanding need apply.

Then they really went to work. In the next two decades the New York Legislature added so many extensions and embellishments that the spare and simple plan was completely lost to view. In 1870 another commission was appointed; its work resulted some years later in something called the Throop Code. It contained almost exactly ten times as many sections as the Field Code. New commissions were appointed in 1895 and 1900; each made a report which the legislature rejected. After several more commissions and reports, something called the Civil Practice Act emerged in 1920. This, with changes, lasted about forty years. The most recent New York renovation came in 1962.

The self-defeating legislature is a familiar character in this part of legal history. It accepts a broad brave plan of reform at the urging of reformers, appoints a distinguished committee, and empowers it to draw a radical design, which the legislature passes into law. Then the legislature hacks away at the clean new structure, and hammers back cupolas and gazebos the reformers thought they had cleared away. Code pleading, in its various stages, has always been a rather ugly structure.*

The legislative appointment of the commissioners included instructions, and among them was "the abandonment of Latin and other foreign tongues, so far as the same shall by them be deemed practicable." To this day, in New York, plaintiff must make a prima facie case, and witnesses are brought to court by subpoena; briefs may be filed by amici curiae; someone who handles his case without a lawyer appears pro se; decisions are rendered per curiam; and until about forty years ago there were proceedings by mandamus and certiorari, these last two being terms that lawyers still use even though the statute doesn't.

11

The Old New Rules

The next idea in the history of the pleading was to get rid of it altogether, or very nearly altogether. Escape the deadly strict requirements of the common law and the puzzling demands of the Code, and let the written statements that start a case be curt descriptions of claim and defense. Remit the functions of issue-definition and disclosure to other mechanisms, less formal and more practical than pleading.

The twentieth-century movement for reform was led at first by Roscoe Pound of Harvard. It reached fulfillment, or about as close to fulfillment as such efforts can come, in the Federal Rules of Civil Procedure. In 1934 Congress responded to the academic agitation and authorized the Supreme Court to compose a new system for the federal courts. The Court appointed a committee. The chief draftsman for the committee, the principal author of the Rules, was Charles Clark, dean of Yale Law School, later an appellate judge, one of the best we have ever had. The Court promulgated the Rules in 1938. Since then a number of states have copied them. Because of these echoes in state judicial systems, and the fact that so much important litigation takes place in federal courts, the Federal Rules, though far from all-pervasive, can be said to be the dominant style of American civil procedure.

Though this jurisprudential rebellion started at Harvard, by the 1930s, when real changes in the law occurred, there was more creative legal thought at Columbia and Yale. Not unusual. Batons pass. The avant-garde tends to rest at the place it has advanced to. Columbia's intellectual vigor was aided by the remarkable minds that came out of New York City's ghetto, that other ghetto. They were kids too poor to live away from home, and came to Kent Hall carrying lunches in brown paper bags and marvelous learning in their heads.

□

The new design is called "notice pleading," from one of its basic features. The role of the complaint is slight compared to the code complaint or the declaration of the common law. Its only purpose, in the view of purists, is to give some general notice of what the case is all about. The Federal Rules require no spelling out of any form of action or cause of action. The complaint starts by giving the basis of the court's jurisdiction (something peculiarly important in the federal courts, with their limited jurisdiction). It ends by saying what the plaintiff wants, the "prayer" or "demand for judgment." In between, there need be only "a short and plain statement of the claim showing that the pleader is entitled to relief." This, the drafters of the Rules intended and most federal courts agree, means a summary recital, in the broadest terms, of the events from which the grievance has arisen. Defendant's pleading is to be correlatively terse.

If the complaint or answer nevertheless appears to be defective, or if there is something the pleader wants to change or add, leave to amend is freely granted. Indeed, within a specified time, pleadings can be changed without the court's permission. Each party is to learn the specifics of the other's claim or defense not from the pleadings, but from discovery procedures. The issues are drawn, and the court informed of the nature of the case it will have to try, in a pre-trial conference of the judge and the attorneys, and through certain pre-trial motions.

The discovery procedures are varied and effective. Each side must furnish the other, on demand, with all its records and documents relating to the case. Written interrogatories may be served to which written answers must be given. There can be oral examination, under oath, in advance of trial, not only of the parties but of other people who may have some useful information. The examination is called "deposition," and laymen caught in litigation have learned that the word means something other than the taking down of Jesus from the Cross (though they may feel there is connection). Discovery is not often limited or defeated. The timeworn cry of "fishing expedition" is still heard but rarely listened to. Springing surprise at trial—the introduction of evidence the other side does not expect—is no longer a tolerated tactic. The old close-to-the-vest poker game, with all its second-rate cleverness, is over.

At the pre-trial conference, the opposing lawyers meet with the judge and under his governance articulate the issues. The conference also provides a ripe occasion for settlement. The judge usually gets to know enough about the case to reach a rough appraisal of the merits. (For clarity's sake: Here I am talking about preparation for a trial; in an earlier chapter I mentioned the varying degrees of antecedent knowledge possessed by appellate judges at the time of argument.) It also gives him occasion to use the prestige of his position to induce a compromise. Sometimes, in my opinion, the prestige is overused; the lawyer may accept a settlement not because he thinks it is just, but because he fears persistence may offend the judge. The fear may focus on the case itself, the consequences of having a thwarted judge presiding at the trial. Or—and this disgraces both judge and lawyer—he may fear in general to offend a judge. On the other hand, calendars are much too crowded and the judge-induced settlement at pre-trial conference is an effective, if imperfect, method of uncrowding them.

The "motion for summary judgment" is designed for the situation in which documents and affidavits establish the facts so clearly that there remains no "triable issue of fact." The questions of law are decided on the motion, and final judgment can be reached without having to go to trial. Where it does not result in final judgment, the motion can still do much to clarify the issues. For one thing, it impels each party to put his best foot forward. For another, partial summary judgment can be granted, which means some questions are disposed of and those left for trial accordingly reduced. The device was invented in England in the middle of the nineteenth century, imported to America by several states and then made part of the Federal Rules.

When at the trial the proof does not conform to what the parties pleaded, but shows some other valid claim or defense, the pleading is simply deemed amended. If the opposing party says this takes him by surprise, he can be given time to get over it; the trial is adjourned for a while. The formerly fatal "variance" is curable.

Thus pleading, which occupied so prominent a place for more than half a millennium, becomes a minor element in litigation. The law forsakes a great pernicious art.

□

That was the plan. It has not been wholly carried out. The fly-wheel keeps on turning. The perfunctory pleadings envisioned by the Federal Rules are rare. Once again habit hinders reform. This time habit has reinforcement: many states, including the largest, have held to their own pleading and procedure, or adopted only parts of the Federal Rules, or adopted them only lately, and lawyers trained in their own state practice carry their ways to the federal courthouse when they go there.

The winsome nuisance of our dual state and federal system. Each state follows its proud and stubborn course. Illinois retained common-law pleading until the middle of the twentieth century, when it enacted a design something like New York's. Maine moved from common-law pleading to a slightly modified copy of Federal Rules, almost skipping the middle step entirely. New York is possibly the most disheveled and erratic. During the first decades of the Rules, its federal Court of Appeals had on it the most forward-looking, as well as some of the best, of all the federal judges. Meanwhile, New York State pleading and procedure remained a turbid mess of code pottage, and the most recent effort at reform leaves major differences between the state and federal practice, this despite the fact that New York lawyers are in the federal courts more often than those of any other state. That last is because New York is still the first or second home of most of the largest corporations, and because the business of communications, a fertile ground of litigation, is centered in New York.

The phrase "cause of action," though it is mentioned no-where in the Federal Rules, did not leave the vocabulary of courts and lawyers. Some states, adopting the new procedure, added a graceless anomaly: the complaint must contain "A short and plain statement of the claim"—verbatim from the Rules—"constituting the cause of action"—verbatim from the Code. In the federal courts some judges have decided that the complaint must set forth a "legal theory," which is very like a cause of action, which as we have seen is very like a form of action.

Eventually, of course, a plaintiff must show that the facts he proves fit into some rule of law that entitles him to judgment (and the same holds for defendant and his defenses), but there is nothing in the nature of things that demands this be part of the pleading. Sometimes it is apparent from the face of the complaint that there is no chance the plaintiff will prevail; no matter what might be proved in support of the allegations, it cannot amount to anything that would entitle him to judgment. Then and only then, if the path of notice pleading is followed, should a complaint be subject to demurrer. But this is not the same as demanding that a spelled-out legal theory be stated at the outset. The Rules do not require it, and everything in the Rules implicitly negates it. Nevertheless, some judges still insist.

Another thing that blurs the Rules' ideal is the use of pleading as a vehicle of argument. Usually the complaint and answer give the judge his first acquaintance with the case. So lawyers often put in more than contemplated by the Rules—things they think will make their presentation more appealing—and write the complaint or answer as though it were a kind of brief. And sometimes the argument is addressed not to the court but to the public. If lawsuits are news, they are usually news when they begin and when they end. In the beginning, the only document is the plaintiff's. This gives the lawyer an opportunity, of dubious propriety, to argue his client's case in the media. A particularly revolting aspect is the exaggeration of the damages sought. They usually bear no relation to what the lawyer expects to get, but journalists by custom make this wholly artificial number a prime feature of the story.

A case in which I have recently been engaged (for defendant, not for plaintiff) started with a complaint over twenty thousand words long, not counting the exhibits "attached and made part hereof." It is not an antitrust action or some other forest of intercorporate litigation; it is a libel action, not more intricate than most. The case is brought in the federal courts, whose Rules —repeat—demand "a short and plain statement of the claim."

Despite the divagation, there has been sizable change. The congenital hanging back of bench and bar has not completely disappeared, but the Rules are to a large extent observed as they are written. This time reform took hold, not perfectly but better than before. There were several reasons. One was that law school teaching got better and spread out widely, so that many new lawyers arrived at the bar with an understanding of the older systems' failings. Another was that scholars had been put on the federal appellate courts by that admirer of scholarship, Franklin Roosevelt. (Compare William I and Lanfranc.) The year of the Federal Rules, 1938, fell in the middle of FDR's terms of office; the year of the Code, 1848, was the year Zachary Taylor and Millard Fillmore were elected. Finally, there is the twentieth-century hankering after novelty, a trait of the times that has had important consequences, a number of them good.

Roosevelt's combination of high-mindedness and low-down clubhouse politics—a blend that was just right for the great crises of the period, Hitler and the Depression—was shown in his appointments to the federal courts. He paid off local politicians by accepting their favorites as district judges, but he was careful to select lawyers of quality, usually, for the appellate courts. The result was that a number of cases were corruptly or ineptly decided by the district courts, while Constitutional and other federal questions were in the main well handled. An ironic sidelight is that attorneys for New Deal agencies often preferred a district judge who came to the bench under Coolidge or Hoover to one the New Deal put there. The former might be politically conservative, but more of a true lawyer, and hence more willing to accept a reasoned argument and enforce the law. Because the Supreme Court itself rarely has points of civil procedure presented to it, the Circuit Courts of Appeal have been the chief interpreters of the Rules, and Charles Clark himself became a judge of the Second Circuit.

□

Two cases decided early in the reign of the Rules will illustrate the change. Each is extreme, and might have gone the other way, but neither could have been decided as it was under the prior pleading systems. One has the singing name of *Dioguardi versus Durning*. Durning was the Collector of Customs of the Port of New York. Dioguardi was a native of Italy, not entirely at home with the American language, not at all at home with American civil procedure. He sued *pro se;* he either could not get or did not want a lawyer. He asserted a number of grievances against the Collector, all growing out of his importing some obscure merchandise he described as "tonics." Obscure, that is, like most of the case, if all one knew about it came from reading the complaint. The United States Attorney moved to dismiss.

One thing was clear: the Collector had sold the merchandise at public auction. Nothing else was clear. The district court granted the motion, saying the complaint "fails to state facts sufficient to constitute a cause of action." The judge was hanging on to code-pleading concepts. What happened next is described in the Court of Appeals opinion:

Thereupon plaintiff filed an amended complaint, wherein, with an obviously heightened conviction that he was being unjustly treated, he vigorously reiterates his claims, including those quoted above and now stated as that his "medicinal extracts" were given to the Springdale Distilling Company "with my betting [bidding?] price of $110: and not their price of $120," and "It isn't so easy to do away with two cases with 37 bottles of one quart. Being protected, they can take this chance." An earlier paragraph suggests that defendant had explained the loss of the two cases by "saying that they had leaked, which could never be true in the manner they were bottled." On defendant's motion for dismissal on the same ground as before, the court made a final judgment dismissing the complaint, and plaintiff now comes to us with increased volubility, if not clarity.

The court reversed, and firmly. It emphasized the difference between the district judge's approach and the approach of the new Rules. Perhaps it was so firm because the opinion was written by the main author of the Rules, but two other superb lawyers joined in the opinion, Augustus Hand and Jerome Frank.*

Clark's opinion said:

It would seem, however, that he has stated enough to withstand a mere formal motion, directed only to the face of the complaint, and that here is another instance of judicial haste which in the long run makes waste. Under the new rules of civil procedure, there is no pleading requirement of stating "facts sufficient to constitute a cause of action," but only that there be "a short and plain statement of the claim showing that the pleader is entitled to relief" . . .

The District Court does not state why it concluded that the complaints showed no claim upon which relief could be granted; and the United States Attorney's brief before us

---

* *Jerome Frank was mentioned in an earlier chapter. Augustus Hand was a cousin of the famous Learned Hand, who sat on the same bench. As a judge, Augustus Hand was no less admirable than his more celebrated cousin, and was quite possibly his superior. This does not deprecate Learned Hand, who had a fine legal mind and one of the best prose styles our country has produced. But the primary business of judges is judging, and a retrospective view suggests that Gus was right in his judgments more often than Cousin Learned.*

does not help us, for it is limited to the prognostication—unfortunately ill founded so far as we are concerned—that "the most cursory examination" of them will show the correctness of the District Court's action.

We think that, however inartistically they may be stated, the plaintiff has disclosed his claims that the collector has converted or otherwise done away with two of his cases of medicinal tonics and has sold the rest in a manner incompatible with the public auction he had announced. . . . Of course, defendant did not need to move on the complaint alone; he could have disclosed the facts from his point of view, in advance of a trial if he chose, by asking for a pre-trial hearing or by moving for a summary judgment with supporting affidavits. But, as it stands, we do not see how the plaintiff may properly be deprived of his day in court to show what he obviously so firmly believes and what for present purposes defendant must be taken as admitting.

In referring to "what [Dioguardi] obviously so firmly believes and what for present purposes defendant must be taken as admitting," the court was emphasizing that the motion to dismiss, directed to the complaint alone, is the good old demurrer, and the demurrer, as we have seen, must concede the truth of the pleading it addresses.

Following this decision, the United States Attorney moved for summary judgment, and got his judgment. Dioguardi again appealed, but this time the court affirmed. Having gone to the facts, and shown them by affidavit and document, the Collector was able to prevail. This is the way the Federal Rules contemplate it should be done, and the court was giving the United States Attorney, and the district judge, and all the rest of us, a lesson.

The other case is more precisely a group of cases, at the end of World War II. The plaintiff was Chester Bowles, late of Madison Avenue, the Bowles of Benton & Bowles, subsequently Ambassador to India, at the time the Price Administrator. He had made an extraordinary move from huckstering to genuine public service. The defendants were a number of the major oil companies.

The Emergency Price Control Act of World War II had a peculiar legislative background. The best description of the legislative intent of most senators and representatives is that they intended not much price control. They really wanted none. They identified—some by nature, some corruptly—with businessmen, large and small, who hated to see so grand an opportunity slip by. Roosevelt pushed them hard, however, and they could think of no very good reply to the most telling argument for anti-inflation measures: that if American sons were required to expose themselves to gunfire, American fathers might be required to expose themselves to lower profits. So they voted for the legislation.

Not, however, without doing what they could to make its enforcement difficult. One of the enforcement devices the statute provided was a treble-damage action, in which consumers or the government might sue for three times the amount of the overcharge. At the same time, Congress imposed a statute of limitations designed to cripple the action. They required it be commenced within a year from the day the particular overcharge occurred.

A crafty joker. The economy was vast. The enforcement staff was small. Price regulations for certain industries were necessarily complex. The major oil companies, along with a lot of other people, had been ignoring the ceilings. They found evasion especially easy because they sold so many different products and used esoteric pricing systems. The oil giants have been accused of being villains in our present energy troubles. I have no knowledge of the truth of the present accusations, but I know for sure they were villainous then.

The government had a limited number of lawyers and investigators to deal with these huge malefactors. The number was limited by the budget Congress allowed the Office of Price Administration. Enforcement was also hampered by the fact that high government positions were often filled by men who were executives of the oil companies on leave of absence, or by men who hoped to become such executives after they left the government. They were not so much regulators of these corporations as corporate representatives in Washington.

Most of the ceilings were hung from the seller's prior practices and prices, and could be determined, ordinarily, only from the seller's documents. The seller was supposed to maintain certain records for the purpose, but even with these records the job of enforcement was difficult, and if they were kept poorly or, as often happened, not at all, enforcement depended on research into the seller's own price history. The government would have the task of establishing not only the prices that were being charged, but also the prices that should have been charged. The investigation required to do such a job could not be done in time to catch all the violations if they had to be specified at the time when the action was filed. If anything like a code complaint had to be used—if the "facts" of the violations had to be pleaded—the one-year limitation would be wiping out year-old violations faster than the government could find them.

So the enforcement lawyers at OPA, reading the new Rules closely, invented something that came to be called the "open-end complaint." The complaint cited the pertinent price regulation, alleged the defendant had failed to keep required records, and then, without listing the violations, simply said the defendant had sold petroleum products "at prices in excess of the applicable maximum prices provided by the regulation." It ended by asking three times the total of the excess charges, whatever they might turn out to be.

Here was a complaint that ignored the specific overcharges that would have to be shown to prove a "cause of action" and did not even say how much the plaintiff wanted. Under the principles of code pleading, it was plainly subject to dismissal. It was far too abstract; it had no "facts"; it was as conclusory as it could be. Grossly inadequate even under the new system, most lawyers would say—ridiculous, laughable. Indeed, the oil company lawyers—their house counsel, the large law firms they retained in each city where they were sued, the specialists they brought in to lead their litigation—started out by laughing, literally.

But the courts, after some backing and filling and hard argument, sustained the open-end complaint. Once the pleading was accepted, OPA investigators were able to find, through discovery in the action itself, the particular breaches that had occurred within the year preceding the filing of the action (along with others occurring thereafter). As long as they proceeded with reasonable diligence, they were free of time restraints. They could end their frustrating race against the statute of limitations and do a decent job under the aegis of the court.

It could not have happened under the codes, or under the common-law system that preceded the codes. And even with the new federal system, this was pushing the concept very far. The petroleum industry journal denounced the iniquity of the open-end complaint. Large-scale dishonesty did not stand in the way of righteous indignation. The oil companies were furious. Some senators and representatives, their best efforts unaccountably defeated, must have been furious too.

☐

The Federal Rules, however, are not a blessing unalloyed. Their failure has nothing to do with departure from the older pleading; it lies in what the discovery procedures have become. To a great extent they are beneficial, and in some cases (like the price-control litigation) they are vital, but in many cases they are wasteful and in many others they are used as an instrument of injustice.

Depositions devour money. They can use solid weeks of lawyers' time, which translates into thousands of dollars, sometimes tens of thousands of dollars (when a law firm uses a senior partner and an associate or two to attend each deposition), plus other thousands for the stenotype reporters who record the questions and answers. This is not only a hardship on the party against whom the discovery is directed; often it is inefficient from the point of view of the attacking party. A great deal of the product is scarcely worth the work. But since deposition is available, lawyers are afraid to disregard it. The tool is there; it must be useful. Or they use it because every other lawyer seems to. The practice of law is not immune to the deadly decrees of fashion.*

These are uncalculated abuses. There is another, peccant sort. By conducting long depositions and demanding the produc-

---

* In a recent libel case, plaintiff's counsel took the depositions of the defendants over a number of days which, put together, amounted to more than six solid weeks. The transcript of the testimony covered four thousand pages. At that point they paused, because there was dispute as to whether certain other areas ought to be explored. Defendants' discovery was still to come. There were four defendants, three whose positions largely overlapped. My firm represented the fourth. To keep expenses down, we did not attend the depositions of the other defendants. This is an unusual way to handle a case, and maybe a handicap, but in my judgment the saving in legal fees outweighed the litigating detriment that might ensue. The client, a publication whose quality matched its net profits—inversely, naturally—was happy to accede. (This, it should be noted, was not a situation in which plaintiffs' counsel were employing the stratagem of burdening their opponents; rather, they had made the judgment that methodical, exhaustive discovery would be beneficial to their case.)

tion of many documents, the side that has more money can create such trouble and expense for the other that continuing the litigation becomes uneconomic or even impossible. It can be done by either side—plaintiff crushing defendant with expense or a defendant crushing plaintiff. Frequently a good claim is not pressed or a bad one not resisted simply because it costs too much to sue or to defend. Wealthy litigants, corporate or individual, have a justice-murdering advantage. This, of course, has always been true, from the time when a rich man could gather oath-helpers or hire the ablest champion, through the time when he retained the most knowledgeable pleaders, through every reform yet devised. But pre-trial discovery, granting its other virtues, exacerbates this sore.

Why has this been allowed to happen? The Rules give judges ample supervisory power over discovery, power that could be used to keep it within reasonable bounds. There are, I think, two reasons. One is that judges feel they have more important things to do. Most federal judges are overworked, partly because of the unimaginable increase (as lawyers fifty years ago might have tried to imagine it) in both the number and the complexity of cases; partly because Congress, profligate elsewhere, is stingy in providing instruments of justice; partly because Presidents are political; and—a product of those three—partly because there are incompetents on the bench, so that good judges have more than their fair share of work. (It is a product of all three because the overwork and the relatively low pay tend to keep good lawyers off the bench even when appointments are not entirely political.) Their time taken up with crucial motions, judges try to avoid the time-consuming supervision of discovery. Decisions on the scope of discovery, with rare exceptions, seem minor. The problem is that in cumulative effect the scope of discovery is major.

The second reason is much less specific. The attitude toward pre-trial discovery is in harmony with the currently fashionable desideratum of unrestrained disclosure. This is an obese creature that intrudes on various aspects of our culture. It waddles about, impersonating art.

The reader may suggest another reason—that lawyers deliberately make things more toilsome than they need be in order to maximize their bills. This, of course, is part of the common wisdom about the profession. I have seen this sort of thing happen, but not seen it very often. (There is an especially horrid manifestation of it in the breaking up of marriages, where some lawyers will worsen the distress of the parties by trying to gain inconsequential points, and thus base a higher fee on "victory.")*

The job deliberately inflated is, I believe, an exception. But lawyers are often inefficient, and—particularly among large firms acting for large corporations—addicted to overkill. The motive, however, is to do the best job for the client, and to win. The criticism to be made is that a more realistic appraisal of the situation and the substitution of ingenuity for drudgery would do the job more cheaply, and usually do it better.

No system of procedure can be wholly satisfactory. Common-law pleading and the Code each had its good features; the Federal Rules, on the whole, are better. I would suggest, as something still unsatisfactory but probably an improvement, that the style of federal pleading be retained, but that the courts exercise much closer supervison over depositions and other discovery, and hold them down. This would not be for the reasons given in the past—that a plaintiff must be able to prove his case before he starts, that business secrets should be closely guarded (a sort of commercial pudency), that a litigant may keep his weapons hidden in the game of litigation. The object, rather, would be to observe the principle of diminishing returns, and to treat the tactic of attrition as foul play.

There are, of course, just claims which without discovery can be but dimly seen. My suggestion does not mean that the probing necessary to such cases be disallowed. It means only that capacity to spend money should not determine legal rights and liabilities. If it is argued that the application of such standards involves some difficult judgments, one may ask why judges bear their honored name.†

□

That, I think, would be improvement. But the problem of the cost of litigation is a broader one, and the best response lies

---

* The common wisdom is supported, naturally, by legend. For example, a lawyer, having hired a bright new junior attorney, goes off on a holiday. On senior's return, junior announces proudly that he has worked hard and wound up three estates that have been lying around the office for years. The news, of course, is disaster; the lawyer has lost his steady income.

† In recent years the use of "magistrates"—official assistants to the federal judges who hear disputes as to the scope of discovery—has to some extent alleviated the problem. Not nearly enough.

elsewhere. A dozen years ago, in another book, I offered the conceit that litigation should be an expense of government, not an expense of those who litigate. Not only the defense of those accused of crime, but also all respectable civil litigation. It met with widespread silence.*

The point may be made that in a capitalistic society it is fitting that those with more money should get the better things, including a better brand of justice. Apart from the historical fact that "capitalistic society" is an anachronistic concept (whether used by the Right or the Left), the moral fact is that certain things are too important to be distributed according to money. Justice is at least as much a public obligation as schools or parks or highways. It is strange that people have to pay for it. Lawyers should be truly, as they are in theory, officers of the court, compensated—like judges, marshals, court attendants—by the government, not by their clients.

I use the word "respectable." False or trivial claims should not, of course, be permitted to inundate the courts. A screening board could winnow out demands patently dishonest or foolish or otherwise not worth litigating. At this threshold, no adversary advocates would be needed or allowed. There is, of course, the possibility of threshold error. But if your claim did not get by the initial test, you would nevertheless be free to sue at your own expense—which means only no worse off than you are now. The difference is that what at present is a necessity in every case would become a luxury in a few.

Counseling apart from litigation could for many purposes— business purposes primarily—remain a private business, like that of English solicitors. Here too, however, there is public obligation, and, to an extent that need not be detailed, advice outside of court should be provided free of charge. The citizen's understanding of his legal rights and duties ought not be a function of his wealth.

---

* Since that time, there has been increasing recognition, in special situations, of the need for free legal service, both service paid for by the government and service voluntarily contributed by the bar. Worthy as the effort is, it misses the main problem. It is directed toward the needs of the poor, and constitutes a form of welfare. God knows the poor need legal assistance, but so does everybody else, and the cost of litigation is a hardship on all except the tiny number, corporate or individual, that compose the very rich.

It may be said that advocates need money to fuel their fires. It is not so. The desire to win is as strong a motive for the litigating lawyer as the desire to get rich. Usually it is stronger. If that special kind of competitive urge does not exist—the characteristic wish to express aggression in this socially useful form— then the person ought not be a litigating lawyer, and will not likely be a good one. There is empirical evidence of the validity of these last comments: anyone who has been opposed by a lawyer for a government agency—that is, a government lawyer who is not a political hack—will know that the opposition is just as fierce as that provided by a lawyer engaged in private practice.

Salaries, of course, should be high; a high skill is required. The cost of a given lawsuit would nevertheless probably diminish. There might be more litigation, but that would result from the fact that those who are at present deprived of the aid of courts and lawyers would then be getting some, and that can hardly constitute objection. There is a better than even chance that the total expense to society would be smaller, not greater, than now. The lawyer-hours might be less, even with more litigation, if lawyers concentrated on the task at hand and not on impressing clients. But far more important are the intangible gains, not only to the individual but to society at large. Our democracy depends on citizens who feel they have a stake in it. Frustration of just claims enervates the citizen. If we are not utter skeptics— if we accept the premise that good and evil have reality at all —then, in the category of evil, injustice has a prime place. It is also, in its deadening discouragement, a peril to the democratic order.

The suggestion may be described as a socialist measure. No fundamental political dispute need follow. We already have a semisocialist economy. Many services are now provided by the government, others by monopolies so closely controlled as to be colonies of government. This occurs naturally when the service is thought to be essential. Surely the service of justice is essential.

☐

"Consumer" attacks on the legal profession have lately come into vogue. To some extent, they are warranted. To some extent they are misguided, for reasons explained in a moment. To some extent they are disingenuous, postures assumed for political purposes or simply for personal prominence. They come both from the outside and from within the profession itself.*

They take two principal forms. One has been the demand, recently successful, that the legal profession give up its traditional ban on advertising. The argument is that if law firms advertise, clients will get better, cheaper services. The argument is weak. There is, to begin with, the general truth (which many who favor the change would themselves assert in other fields) that advertising, more often than not, is bad, not good, for consumers. Specifically, advertising, which can be helpful as applied to some services and products, is quite unsuitable here, except for routine services which paralegals could provide—services for which three years of law school are certainly not needed. The nature of nonrudimentary legal work is such that it cannot be evaluated except on the basis of intense association. It is a wise client, and a rare one, who knows whether a lawyer is giving him his money's worth. He surely cannot tell from an advertisement whether he will be well represented, or whether the work to be done will merit the prices advertised. Advertising is dishonest on most of what it hawks; so far as the law is concerned, it would communicate little that is useful even if it honestly tried.

The Supreme Court's removal of the profession's self-imposed restraint was put on First Amendment grounds. It is part of the Court's recent extension of the Amendment to include commercial advertising, a rather ugly distortion of a guarantee whose beginning had to do with liberty of conscience. The amendment protects, certainly, speech and writing on the con-

---

* President Carter has joined in the attack, charging in upside down. He asserts the individual lawyer is devoted to the welfare of his individual client, and that, the President says, is fine. But organized lawyers, the bar associations, are devoted to the welfare of lawyers, and that, the President says, is awful. Right side up, the fact is that in many cases lawyers put their own interests ahead of those of their clients. This, together with their tendency to put both ahead of social duty, is what is bad about lawyers. So Carter is wrong on the first count. Also on the second. Why should an organization not be interested in the welfare of its members? Does the United Auto Workers union exist to serve the interests of General Motors? In fact the organized bar pays more attention to the needs of society at large than most other occupational groups.

duct of government and other public affairs, and, with hardly any strain, literature and art. When the concept is imported into the sale of goods and services, however, there is an unappealing disharmony. What we are dealing with is commercial puffery— not so much free expression as free private enterprise.

The First Amendment, treated for about a century and a half as a fragile wicker basket that could take no heavy burden, has in the last decade been treated as a garbage van. This is educational and saddening. Educational, because it illustrates the pendulum swings of history, and the dangers of doctrine, and the tendency of doctrinaires to fight past wars. Saddening, because it prepares the way for reaction and puts real freedom in peril. The courts, which thirty years ago regarded as ridiculous the proposition that the First Amendment protected the publication of "obscene" books, now find in the First Amendment reason to sanction advertising by lawyers; to treat writhing as a form of speech; and in the name of democracy bar the Commonwealth of Massachusetts from controlling the use of corporate funds to influence elections. It is not just the courts, of course. Vogue is everywhere. Local officials in a suburb of New York refuse to take action on a complaint that a television network has deceptively fed liquor to schoolchildren, saying that any move against the network would infringe the First Amendment.* Meanwhile, a government agency, the Small Business Administration, denies loans to publishers on the ground that it would constitute government interference with the press, and thus contributes to the stilling of the small voices which the Amendment intended to be heard.

□

Another attack on the legal profession takes the form of a demand that lawyers devote more of their time to nonpaying or low-paying clients. The unavailability of legal service to the many people who cannot afford it is, as I have been saying, an insufferable denial of justice. But the solution does not lie in imposing what amounts to an additional tax on lawyers. So long as the practice of law is part of the private sector—a condition I would change—it should be subject to no duties or imposts that other occupations do not share. Working time for most lawyers is

---

* *I am not criticizing the making of this television program; I do not know the facts. The point here is the fashionable, thoroughly superficial, invocation of the First Amendment.*

interchangeable with money. Compelling the lawyer to give up part of his working time without remuneration, if not regarded as a tax, can only be regarded as involuntary servitude. One might with equal reason—probably with better reason—demand that bankers, plumbers, professional athletes and union leaders give up part of their revenues (without income tax deduction).

If a lawyer chooses to render service free of charge, and many lawyers do, that is another matter. There are no restrictions on charity, among lawyers or other groups. It is not as though, given the ethos of our economic system, lawyers earn more than they should. Ordinarily, the talent, experience and energy that go into the practice of law would yield a better money return if it were directed elsewhere. The wealthiest law school graduates are those who leave the practice of law. The tax that ought to be imposed to provide decent legal service for everyone should be imposed not upon a single group, but upon the community at large, and that is part of what I have urged in the paragraphs above.

There is implicit in the agitation—either as conscious belief on the part of those who attack or as a necessary implication of the proposals made—the premise that lawyers are more reprehensible than other people who work for a living. The premise is wrong. Lawyers in general behave slightly better than most occupational groups. There is another judgmental basis, however, which is valid: slightly better is not enough. A profession that concerns itself with law and justice should be considerably better than most.

□

In a way—an important way—pleading has come full circle. The complaint, the initial pleading prescribed by the Federal Rules, bears a close resemblance to the early writ. Each is a compact statement of the wrong the court is asked to right. After an answer equally terse (if the Rules are followed), the rest of the litigation is proof and argument. The minuet of common-law pleading, the long exchange of positions taken, belongs to a middle period.

It is like a row of family portraits in which, dissimilar faces intervening, there appears a striking repetition. Hidden genes, preserved, suddenly make their presence felt. Compare the Writ of Novel Disseisin with the open-end complaint. Each names the plaintiff and defendant. One identifies the land, the other the business regulated. One simply says the defendant deforces the plaintiff; the other simply says the defendant violates the regulation. In each instance, after denial, the parties can proceed to proof.

But is there more than an arresting similarity? Why so much attention to the ancient writs? They have an antique charm, but what is their significance?

Considerable. It is threefold. For one thing, they were the means by which civil litigation was taken away from feudal courts and drawn into the king's courts. Their better brand of justice established the central judicial structure in which the common law evolved.

For another, they brought the jury trial to civil litigation. There was no jury in the feudal or ecclesiastical courts, or in the old communal courts. Nor would there be a jury in any court of any country outside Britain and America, until, quite recently, some to some extent have borrowed the device. The ancient Frankish custom disappeared from France when the Plantagenets lost Normandy.*

For a third, the writs informed the substance of the law. Each writ determined, once the facts were found, the legal result that followed. If, for instance, plaintiff's ancestor held the land when he died (as the Writ of Mort d'Ancestor said) and if he died after the limiting period began (as the writ said) and if plaintiff was his heir (as it said), then plaintiff would get the land. That is a substantive rule, shaped by the writ itself. The rules, of course, have changed, but there the common law begins.

The power of the writs and their forms of action has been expressed in two celebrated sentences. One is Sir Henry Maine's:

> So great is the ascendancy of the law of Actions in the infancy of Courts of Justice, that substantive law has at first the look of being gradually secreted in the interstices of procedure; and the early lawyer can only see the law through the envelope of its technical forms.

Maine's statement, startling when it appeared in 1883, is in fact an understatement. Yet it is still not fully accepted. A more recent, and very good, historian was quoted in Chapter Six: "Henry . . . only offered new procedures." They were new pro-

---

* There might have been some use of something like a jury in the ancient courts of Sweden, but it was long ago abandoned.

cedures, to be sure, but they were more than that. They were procedural in setting up the apparatus by which the remedy was sought, but the plaintiff got his remedy only if the facts as proved filled out the architecture of the writ. The Register of Writs made up a table of grievances the common law would recognize and act upon. The form of action prescribed the things the plaintiff must allege and prove, as well as the process that went with it.

The law residing in custom and tradition already occupied three places. One was the law of crimes—treason, murder, rape, mayhem, arson, robbery, and the other breaches of the peace. Another was the feudal law: the relationships of king and vassal, vassal and lesser lord, lord and man. The third was local custom, enforced as law by the communal courts. But all three would be absorbed and suffer change, and new law would be added by the royal Justices and clerks, and then by advocates, and by Acts of Parliament. The law of England, and so the law of America, would be the law available in the royal courts. As we have noted, it is this realmwide application that gives the common law its name.

The law of property, the law of tort, the law of contract— each was constructed piece by piece, and the writs with their attendant forms of action were the pieces. Naturally they drew on antecedent concepts. No beginning is pure, excepting the Creation (and even there the Lord had chaos to work with). Before 1166, people had an idea, for instance, of what "seisin" meant. But with the triumph of the royal judicial system, seisin came to mean precisely—no more, no less—whatever it was the new possessory actions would protect.

Hence to say that substantive civil law was "secreted in the interstices of procedure" does not quite convey the dominance of the writs. They were the textbook of the law. It was much less subtle than the present-day connection, the half-hidden relationship between modern substance and procedure, mentioned in *Taxonomy.* Here the relationship—perhaps better called identity—was explicit. "The envelope of forms," with slight exception, was nothing less than a summary statement of the common law.*

---

* *The exception arises from the fact that in its "infancy" the Register of Writs did not occupy the entire field of royal civil justice. Proceedings by "bill" continued for a while—"plaints,"* querelae, *the old improvised beseechings of the king.*

The other famous aphorism is from Maitland: "The forms of action we have buried, but they still rule us from their graves." As Maine's fine sentence is an understatement, Maitland's is an overstatement. The forms of action do not quite rule us now, and their rule was never absolute. They were amenable to change, at first by fiction and to some extent by statute, later by statute more than fiction, and always by skillful play with precedent. They maintained their rule only by compromise and concession, and partial abdication. At any given moment the forms of action might seem rigid, but viewed in a fourth dimension they were wonderfully supple.

And now the forms of action as such have disappeared. Whether or not the prettiest plans the reformers dreamed of have been realized, whether or not their plans were best, no matter how heavy the inertia of the bench and bar, one thing is clear: no form of action need now be pleaded. Nor at the date when Maitland wrote. By the time the nineteenth-century changes got under way, jurisprudence had come to distinguish substance from procedure (though it would later make the distinction less stark), and the idea was gaining strength that if the plaintiff seemed to have a right and defendant had infringed it, the court should strive to find a remedy. At the present time, if the court, looking to what it regards as substantive law, sees that plaintiff sets forth a legal right and says defendant breached it, plaintiff will not be sent away because there is no ready form.

Then what does Maitland's sentence mean? How do the forms of action "rule us from their graves"? In this way, to this extent: The common law has gone through centuries of development, within the forms of action. Analytically, remedy should come after right, procedure follow substance, but historically our rights grow from a mulch of dead remedies, and their growth is naturally affected.

The common law is subject to alteration, as were the writs and the forms of action from which it rose. But not without some tie to precedent, some warrant in the past—except rarely, and then not entirely, and mostly in our Constitutional law. Apart from truly novel legislation, the statement of facts required by the Code, and the claim the new Rules look for, reflect one or another of this historic group of forms. So even if the procedural revolutions had been thoroughly successful, even though eventually they were very near successful, the forms of action, though driven out of pleading, would remain in the bones of our law.

Maitland gives a laconic example: ". . . why do we talk today of 'real' and 'personal' property? Any answer to this question must speak to us of absolute forms of action." It needs a bit of expounding: The distinction between real estate and personal property seems—and not just to lawyers—fundamental, something found in nature. But a system of law could quite easily do without this particular distinction, and set up other classes of things owned. Different kinds of land could make up different categories: farm land, city blocks, the crust of mineral deposits. And the same could be done with different things the law lumps together as personal property: bolts of fabric, computers, stock certificates. And some things now separated as "real" and "personal" might join in a single class; in our transient population, attitudes toward the house one lives in and one's motorcar are often much the same (quite apart from the fact that the mobile home makes them physically the same).

Varying social and practical considerations apply to rural land and urban office buildings, to urban office buildings and urban low-cost housing. Outside the cities with their special problems, food-bearing soil might be treated differently from grazing soil, and both of them differently from surface valuable only for what lies beneath it.

If you sell your house, your furnace usually stays with it, but your washing machine does not. The law's distinction is between what is attached to the land—the house, unquestionably, and, questionably, the things attached to the house—and what is not attached, the latter called "movables." But the furnace and the washing machine are both of them pieces of machinery, both far removed from the idea of "land." And how about the built-in beds and desks of certain modern homes? Careful lawyers do not rely on the law's distinction; they specify in their contracts of sale which items the seller may take with him and which items must remain.

The concepts, then, are not metaphysical; they were fixed by the forms of action. To be sure, people viewed land and goods as different things before the common law emerged, but the writs and the forms of action hardened the distinction. The disparity between real estate and personalty would be less prominent in the law were it not for the forms of action. They were created one by one, and at the time of their creation those that dealt with real estate and those that dealt with goods and coin and other movables were concerned with very different interests. The distinction between land and personal possessions was clearer then, more easily recognized, more strongly felt. Present-day law makes the cleavage deeper than it ought to be, for no reason other than its history.

□

The writs themselves no longer exist. In the eighteenth century they went out, fittingly, by way of fiction: the allegation that a writ had been issued could no longer be traversed. Then they were explicitly abolished by the statutes of the nineteenth century, in both England and America.

Their forms of action, however, have not vanished. Though they constitute only one of the several elements that have made our present law, they are deep within it—"dug in" might be more accurate than "buried"—and if they do not rule, they surely guide and counsel. Our legal rights change constantly; some have died, new ones have been born, old ones have been altered. But they cannot deny their consanguinity to the writs the kings' clerks issued. Much of the content and the character of our law is owed to those little writings.

12

Equity

By 1300, as we have seen, the three great courts of common law are well established. They remain, however, fingers of the royal fist. The Justices act as king's delegates. "In the name of the king" is not at first formality.

Hence petitions to remedy a wrong can bypass the Justices and be addressed directly to the throne. There they will go to the Chancellor, the premier royal aide. In the early days, sometimes called Justiciar, he was viceroy, and ruled England when the king was on Crusade or in his French dominions. In the later Middle Ages, he is more a man of words than action, but even though the clash of arms drowns out the softer voices of the time, the Chancellor retains his status and much of his former power. A simple way to define his office is to say he handles things that have to do with writing, no small matter in the governing of a largely illiterate people to whom the written word is magic. (No small matter still, television notwithstanding.) He is the Great Clerk of medieval England.

The Chancellor and his assistants form a secretariat; it is called the Chancery. They issue the writs that start the actions in the courts of law, and it is to be expected that other legal matters will be referred to them. If you want some royal justice, these are the people you have to see.

Etymology, often misleading because of the way we move our words around, here helps give the picture. The Latin *cancellus* meant grating, and hence *cancellarius*, "doorkeeper." "Chancellor" is medieval English-French for *cancellarius*. Another branch of royal administration is the Exchequer, the king's treasury, his checkerboard tax-collecting and disbursing office, which itself gives rise to a court of law. Chancery does the reading and writing, Exchequer does the arithmetic.

The petitions for something other than a regular writ, in the main, are of two sorts. In the one, petitioner asks the king to rule against himself. This is not as strange as it appears. The king has acted through his men, who may be overzealous, and the king will not lose face if he disclaims their depredations. Besides, petitioner in such cases is likely to be someone high in the social order. Typically, the royal officers have claimed escheat. They say that a vassal who held certain land directly of the king has died without heirs; hence the land must revert to the king as feudal overlord. Then petitioner appears and says it is not so: I myself am heir, a living heir. But Common Pleas, King's Bench, Exchequer—none of them can help me. Their writs do not run against the king.

It happens not infrequently. The king's men are apt to grab land any chance they get. Not likely they will incur the royal frown if they take too much rather than too little. But outraged heirs, we can assume, are for that reason too many to ignore, and some of them important. A regular procedure is developed: the Chancellor considers the petition, and if he recommends, the king sends the case to the Court of King's Bench for a trial by jury. Escheat is a peculiarly feudal phenomenon, and these complaints die out along with feudalism.*

The second tapping of the reservoir of royal justice involves disputes not with the king, but between one subject and another. According to petitioner, the regular writs do not meet his crying need. The procedure is different from that of the established courts. The petition is a direct descendant of the old *querela*. It is called a "bill," like a petition addressed to Parliament. (The same word is, of course, still used for a legislative proposal.) The several governmental functions, as we have seen, are at this time not clearly differentiated. It is also called a "bill of complaint" or, later, simply "complaint."

Here we have two branches. One we may call personal, the other institutional. In the one, the petitioner says the process of the courts is being abused or perverted. "He is poor," as Maitland puts it, "he is old, he is sick, his adversary is rich and

---

* *Escheat, though rare, still exists, and has not changed its name. When there are no heirs or will, the property goes to the state.*

powerful, will bribe or will intimidate jurors, or has by some trick or some accident acquired an advantage . . ." Such cases are a large part of the Chancellor's work down through Tudor times, but in the seventeenth century they stop. They allow too much unfettered power to the Chancellor, and Parliament, finally supreme, will not permit it.

The other difficulty, the institutional, gives rise to Chancery's enduring jurisdiction. It is not that the remedies of the courts of law are being badly used, but rather that, though used at their best, they are simply inappropriate or inadequate. Perhaps there is none that suits some novel feature of the social structure. Or the closest writ is insufficient in the special circumstances, the variety of situations needing remedy having grown with the economy. Nothing in the Register will fit the case; or the kind of judgment the writ affords works poorly or not at all.

For the first hundred years of the common-law system, the Chancellor and his clerks have great freedom to design new writs or alter old ones. In the fourteenth century, as we have seen, this freedom encounters barriers. In part, they are set up by an adolescent Parliament, which, when barons hold the upper hand, resists extensions of the royal power. In part, they represent a changing attitude on the part of the royal Justices. The courts of common law seem less eager to expand their jurisdiction. If the variant writ the clerks have issued seems too far out of line, the Justices will reject it. Perhaps the Justices feel overworked; business has got too good. Perhaps it is the gravity of precedent, a settling into familiar grooves. In any event, the easy entertainment of new writs slows down.

But the Chancellor, acting for the king, can if he chooses exert the underlying power. As time goes on, he chooses more and more. He may be genuinely concerned about petitioner's plight. Or he may wish to enlarge this wing of his office. Very likely both. Though arising from an institutional defect rather than a particular abuse, the petition here, like all *querelae*, is a highly personal entreaty. The bill is "couched in piteous terms." The king is begged to lend his aid, "for the love of God and in the way of charity."

Until midway in the sixteenth century, the Chancellors are ecclesiastics; hence the church courts are the model. The Chancellor orders the person of whom complaint is made to appear before him, under pain—*sub poena*—of some punishment if he fails. The order is different from the common-law original writ, which states the gist of plaintiff's grievance. Defendant is merely told to show up, to answer the complaint. "Answer" means just that. Under oath, and sentence by sentence, defendant must stand and respond to each allegation of the bill.

It is an adversary procedure, like that in the courts of common law. But the Chancellor is a more active figure than the Justices of those courts. The Justice is essentially an umpire, though a princely one. He lets the parties draw the issues and the jury find the facts. He is bound by existing law (in theory always, and usually in practice). The Chancellor, in contrast, asks questions of the parties and finds the facts himself; there is no jury. He is not bound by fixed rules. The Chancellor will decide both what has happened and what to do about it. His disposition of the case follows conscience and good faith (in theory always, and like enough in practice).

If he decides in favor of petitioner, he will issue a "decree." It will forbid the defendant to do something he has been doing or is threatening to do. That is, the Chancellor will enjoin him. As the characteristic remedies of the courts of common law are the judgment awarding seisin of land and the judgment for damages, the characteristic remedy of Chancery is injunction.

□

A fundamental difference in method between common law and equity is written into our federal Constitution and those of most of the states. The Seventh Amendment preserves the right of trial by jury "in suits at common law, where the value in controversy shall exceed twenty dollars." The draftsmen and those who voted to adopt the Bill of Rights meant common law in its narrow sense (as it is used in most of this chapter) as distinguished from what went on in Chancery. So our courts still need to know whether the issue raised is one that would in former days have been heard in one of the courts of common law, in which event either party can demand a jury, or in Chancery, in which event neither can demand a jury. With modern rules permitting joinder of various claims, occasionally a jury will be called to try one part of a case while the judge himself will try another.

The disregard of the jury was not that firm at the start; now and then the Chancellor would send a question to a court of law for a trial by jury. When that practice stopped, the Chancellor sometimes impaneled a jury himself, though he did not feel bound by its verdict; the present-day judge, dealing with a suit for equitable relief, may do the same, and, again the same, this jury's verdict is advisory, not binding.

As early as the fourteenth century, people began to speak of a Court of Chancery, apart from the rest of Chancery. Through that century and most of the next, however, the Chancellor was still acting for the King-in-Council, here as well as elsewhere. He acted with more and more autonomy, though, and by the year 1500 (a date convenient for historians, and not without good reason) the autonomy was complete. For his judicial work, the Chancellor had a regular staff of assistants, and he issued decrees in his own name, not the king's. By the end of the sixteenth century, Chancery was big business, and by the early seventeenth century there were more than fifteen hundred suits a year.

"Chancery" and "Equity" as the name of the court will in later years be fairly interchangeable. "Equity" will also denote the power the court wields and the body of substantive rules it eventually constructs.

As ever, improvised responses to specific occasions are gradually reined in. Procedures are fixed and principles stated. In the full development of equity, its decree will take various forms: an order to carry out an agreement, as distinguished from damages for its breach, where the subject is something deemed unique, sale of land especially ("specific performance"); the nullification or rewriting of a document which, because of fraud or mistake, does not say what the parties meant to say ("rescission," which cancels it, or "reformation," which alters it); a command to a fiduciary to tell exactly what he has done with his beneficiary's property ("accounting"); tolerance toward the delinquent mortgagor, enforced against the mortgagee ("equity of redemption"); the marshaling of the assets of an insolvent and their distribution to creditors ("equity receivership"); an order to defendant to act rather than refrain from acting ("mandatory injunction").

The "mandatory injunction" is addressed to situations that cannot respond to negative decree. Forced inaction will not remedy the situation; defendant must be ordered to do something. Yet the injunction in the beginning was only a restraint, and so the Chancellor, until recently, felt obliged to put his decree in the traditional negative form. Hence the mandatory injunction ordered the defendant not to allow the continuance of a state of affairs he had created. An owner of waterfront property builds a wall across the beach down to the low-water mark. He likes to think of the beach as his, and is much disturbed by people walking by. It is not his, however. From mean high tide on down, the beach is public property. The court will enjoin the maintenance of the wall. In plainer language, the court is telling defendant to get busy and tear his wall apart. While this form of decree is still used, courts no longer hesitate to issue direct affirmative orders.

But sometimes an affirmative order will not work and a negative decree may accomplish a positive result. It happens with employment contracts. It is used not in the ordinary kind of employment, but only when the services are "unique"—that is, when a replacement will not do. Take a famous musician (classical or pop) or a famous athlete (any sport will do), a star whose appearance can be expected to draw fans to the concert hall or the ball park. If the performer, dishonoring his contract, refuses to perform, it is hard to say how many tickets will go unsold; damages are too "speculative" to support a judgment at law. So equity intervenes. But how? It cannot order the delinquent to do his job. There is an uncomfortable suggestion of involuntary servitude, even though this servitude began as voluntary and the contract will make the slave a millionaire. So equity will not command him to carry out his contract, but it will enjoin him from singing a note or swinging a bat for any employer other than the one he signed with.

□

I mentioned that "equity" denotes the court itself, the power it wields, and the substantive law it enforces. The word appears in all three senses in this chapter; the context will show which. It has at least three meanings more: the value of a piece of property excluding the amount of the mortgage; the residual interest of shareholders in a corporation, after the claims of bondholders and other creditors; and, in simple English, simple fairness. "Courts of law," in accordance with long usage, will refer to the three English judicial institutions other than Chancery and to their American descendants (although in a wider sense, of course, a court of equity is a court of law). The colonies did not carry over the trinity of Common Pleas, King's Bench, and Exchequer as separate courts, nor, naturally, did the states, but we have had our separate "courts of law" and "courts of equity." (And, varying from state to state, other divisions of jurisdiction: vertically, criminal–civil, and horizontally according to the seriousness of the crime or the money value of the civil matter.) Delaware, as mentioned, still has a separate Court of Chancery. New Jersey kept a separate court until 1947 and still has a Chancery Division. Massachusetts started without a court of chancery, but by legislation granted equity powers to its law courts. Until

1938, the federal courts had a separate set of procedural rules for cases in which the remedies of equity were sought.

After a judgment in a court of law, the losing defendant had to pay the money or get off the land or return the goods. If he refused or failed, the sheriff swung into action (or crept, depending on the sheriff) armed with a "final writ" that gave him his instructions. Throw defendant off the land, distrain defendant's chattels and turn them into money that will satisfy the judgment, take the thing replevied and deliver it to plaintiff. Chancery enforced its decrees in a different way: the losing defendant must obey the Chancellor's order or go to jail. He can stay there and rot until he is ready to comply. He keeps the keys to the jail in his pocket, as the maxim has it, but he cannot draw them out until he yields.

It is said the common-law judgment operates *in rem*, it has to do with things, while the Chancery decree is *in personam*, it goes against the person. The force of the decree is aimed straight at defendant rather than his land or goods. As usual in the law, the distinction is not tidy. When the sheriff comes round with his judgment at law, the person will feel a twinge or two. And a decree of equity can for practical purposes determine ownership of land—that is, deal with the thing. But whatever the overlap may be, equity's favorite weapon, jailing for contempt, is personal *par excellence*.

Equity's ultimate place was nicely described by the nineteenth-century American Justice Story, writing at a time when courts of Chancery were still separate. (What a fine name for a Justice, if I was not wrong in saying that every case is first of all a story.) Schematic presentations of the law—which lawyers like so much, and laymen even more—are or should be suspect. But Story's scheme is good. The jurisdiction of equity, he wrote, has three parts: exclusive, concurrent, and auxiliary. Take prominent examples. As to trusts, equity has exclusive jurisdiction. Then concurrent: some kinds of fraud, not all, are covered by the common-law action of deceit; for others relief in equity is needed. Finally auxiliary, as when a party in an action at law goes to Chancery with a bill of discovery to find out what his opponent will rely on at trial. All three, since Story wrote, have been folded into our unified courts, but these remedies have only sloughed their Chancery skin; they have kept their equitable tissue.

□

I mentioned a maxim. Equity has a number of them. Its developed doctrines—the abstractions of principle from decided cases —often took the form of statement not at all abstract. There is much imagery in equity. "He who seeks equity must come with clean hands." That is, defendant may have been behaving badly, but if plaintiff in their dealings has himself been tricky or overreaching, Chancery will ignore them both. "Equity will not aid those who slumber on their rights." Conversely, "Equity aids the vigilant." The specific statutes of limitation that apply to actions at law do not apply in Chancery. The Chancellors, however, impose their own demands for promptness, demands characteristically flexible and adjusted to circumstance. If plaintiff has let the state of affairs to which he objects go on too long, especially if others have been led into some action or inaction on the assumption it would continue, the Chancellor refuses to hear the complaint, though plaintiff would have won if he had brought suit promptly. "Equity will not concern itself with trifles." (Or, sometimes, "Equity will not stoop to pick up pins.") Plaintiff may be altogether right and defendant altogether wrong, but the whole thing involves two shillings; don't ask the Chancellor to bother. "Equity regards as done that which ought to be done." Documents containing mistakes are ordered changed to reflect the parties' real intention; the law courts generally followed the letter of the instrument. "Equity delights to do justice, and not by halves." (Also, somewhat narrower in scope, "Equity abhors a multiplicity of suits.") Call all who have claims in the subject matter into Chancery and avoid future litigation. The old law courts heard two parties only, plaintiff and defendant, even though the situation was one where others had obvious interests and would probably start another litigation later. "Equity suffers no wrong to be without a remedy." No matter there is no precedent; if in good conscience plaintiff ought to have some help, the Chancellor will help him. This last is a bit misleading, at least from the time that equity became a system, but it is indicative. The Chancellors felt less bound by precedent than the judges at common law, and in really outrageous cases they were always willing to act. (That is, if they were proper honest Chancellors).

These maxims are all alive today, though their expression has lost color. They are less fixed rules than guides to judgment, in cases where the remedy sought is one the Chancellors used to give.

□

The main source of Chancery's jurisdiction, we have seen, was the grievous situation in which the courts of law refused to act because nothing in the Register of Writs applied. There were also cases in which injustice ran the other way: the law courts, tracing their geometric patterns, would render a judgment for the plaintiff which in fairness they ought not to. Now it is defendant-at-law who goes to Chancery, where he becomes complainant. The injunction forbids the defendant in Chancery, who was the plaintiff in the court of law, to carry on his case at law. Here, ineluctably, there is high and mighty conflict. The Chancellor is much too polite to enjoin their Honors: he never says they must bow to his decree. But by stopping a party to the action he is actually stopping judges; the courts of common law rely on parties' energies for their motive power.

In its beginning, equity was what its name implies, and to a considerable extent it still is: "justice" as opposed to "law," a reach for fairness in the particular case as distinguished from enforcement of general rules. In other chapters I have pointed out the danger to real justice that inheres in both these concepts: the hurt done by the sharp corners of an angular legal structure, the hospitality to tyranny that lies in easy disregard of rules. Both ideas are needed—adherence to abstractions that override the inclinations (bad or good) of those who make decisions, attention to the requirements of special situations. From time to time, one or the other becomes too prominent. Then there is clamor for its counterpart.

In the reign of Henry II, system is required, and he provides it. In the fourteenth and fifteenth centuries, that system becomes both crotchety and venal. The common law is sometimes unrealistic even when its courts are honest, and all too often they are not honest. They quail before power, and they trade judgments for money. It is a time of "livery," when great lords employ armies of retainers—sometimes thousands—and tell the judges how to judge. It is also a time when sheriffs, for a few shillings, will supply juries made to order, while decent jurors are intimidated by important men who come to court and make their wishes known. Chancery offers rescue. The Chancellors are relatively honest, and the royal power is greater even than the power of great lords.

Then, in time, the balance swings the other way. The monarch rather than the aristocracy becomes the enemy of freedom, and the discretion of the Chancellor is easily abused. John Selden, the seventeenth-century scholar-rebel, makes his famous statement: "Equity is a roguish thing. For law we have a measure, know what to trust to: Equity is according to the conscience of the Chancellor, and as that is larger or narrower, so is Equity." It is as though the standard of measure called the "foot," says Selden, were not a fixed length, but rather the Chancellor's foot, which will vary according to who happens to fill the office. "The Chancellor's foot" becomes the symbol of the unreliability of equity.*

☐

We have been speaking of civil controversy. Under the Tudors there were other expressions of the royal judicial power. They established a criminal court that used no jury and exerted a criminal jurisdiction outside the common law. It served, at first, a useful purpose, antidote to the creaky inefficiency and corruption to which the courts of law had come, indeed a popular institution. But some of the crimes it prosecuted were political; it became the court for traitors, and "traitor" can merely mean opponent, opponent of royal policy. In the end, under the name Star Chamber, it was the feared instrument of royal arrogance. There was also the Court of High Commission, formed to root out heresy. A likely pair, Star Chamber and High Commission: treason and heresy go together. When treason consists of words, it is hard to tell them apart. When treason is confined to words, our First Amendment (as it has in recent decades been construed) says it cannot be a crime. And, in the United States, heresy has never been a crime; this guarantee is in another

---

* *Selden was a practicing lawyer, legal historian, Parliamentary hell-raiser, and all-around antiquarian. He was twice sent to the Tower, where he spent his time studying and writing, the scholar in him perhaps relieved by the respite from the distractions of hurly-burly politics. He gave us a succinct, homely description of the idea of the constitutional monarch: "A King is a thing men have made for their own sakes, for quietness' sake, just as in a Family one man is appointed to buy the meat." The range of his scholarship is impressive; among his works, for instance, is* Uxor Ebraica, *a treatise on marriage and divorce among the Jews. It was written when, as the* Encyclopaedia Britannica *delicately puts it, he "lived under the same roof with" the widow of the Earl of Kent, a situation that may have stimulated in this man of humble origin an interest in exotic sexual arrangements.*

clause of the First Amendment. But in the centuries before the colonies rebelled and wrote our Constitution, both heresy and treason-by-words were crimes in England, prosecuted often and punished horribly. The Chancellors collaborated; they aided the monarchs, in bad works as well as good.

The fact that the Chancellors were Keepers of the Great Seal added to their authority. All important documents required the Seal—invocations of Parliament, treaties with foreign powers, royal charters and grants, writs initiating actions at law, the Chancellor's decrees. The medieval mind, as we have noted, liked to deal with tangibles; it had difficulty separating the concept from its physical embodiment. The thought clung to the Seal. The stamping was itself regarded as an exercise of royal power. An instrument bearing the Seal was conceived to be effective even though the content of the instrument might be contrary to the king's wishes. Even much later, in the reign of George III, the Seal was used to keep the government operating in periods of royal madness. The man who was both Chancellor and Keeper of the Seal, next to the monarch himself, was the most important person in the realm. That is, saving rebellion.

Rebellion comes. It is not the old-time push and shove of great nobles and the claimants to the throne, the competition for personal power that hogs the road of medieval history. Around 1600, real revolution starts—meandering and hesitant at first, revolution nonetheless. There is no rising of the masses. The instigators are the lawyers and the landed gentry and some of the wealthy merchants. In a sense it is the old struggle between Crown and aristocracy, but only in a sense. The opposition here is lower, broader. And in the end, the distant end, the rebellion will serve the people.

Here we have reversal. In the past the enlargement of royal power has generally been advantageous to the lower classes. The aristocracy has been their chief oppressor. The reign of Henry II is the prime example. The lords, temporal and clerical, had imposed a lawless tyranny on a subjugated populace; Henry subjugated the lords and brought the rule of law to people (or took a long strong stride in that direction). Now the Stuarts want autocracy; the gentry want rule of law. And rule of law, in time, is bound to benefit the many rather than the few. Never mind the personal interests of the individual antagonists, or their immediate aims; these rebels are fighting for ideas that form the basis of our modern democratic structure. Many of them consciously.

James I insists the royal power is absolute. Christ is God's Vicar on Earth; each monarch is His minister. James therefore rules by Divine Right, and frustration of his wishes is both heresy and treason. Though cast in religious terms, the statement is political. Later in the century religion itself seems the issue. The outcome shows that it is not. The Established Church and radical Protestantism manage to lie down together. What changes is the British Constitution.

It may appear a strange setting for a revolution, but the first uprising is in the courtroom. From the time the common law emerged, there have been some lawyers who said that royalty must live within it. Now more say it. Is James right? Is the king supreme? Or is he too a subject, subject to established law?

The common law becomes the ground the rebels stand on, and Lord Justice Coke is its champion. Chancery is the embodiment of royal judicial power, unbound by common law, and Lord Chancellor Ellesmere is its champion, soon joined by Francis Bacon. The lawyers argue. The center of the monumental struggle is a point of procedure, something to which the word "technical" might be applied today. It is a question of jurisdiction—a contest in civil litigation between Chancery on the one side and on the other the courts of common law. The power of Star Chamber also is involved, and the Court of High Commission. However, they are dealt with incidentally; the principal opponents are equity and common law. Then religion grows large in the thought and words of the contestants (though it is hard to say which way it points, to freedom or oppression). The powers of Parliament are engaged, and finally the clash of arms. But in its inception this rebellion is a clash of lawyers, fought out in private lawsuits.

All during the sixteenth century the power of Chancery had been debated, in the courts and in the press (the press then being mainly treatises and commentaries). One large part of the jurisdiction Chancery claimed—the case in which a plaintiff in a court of law was using the law unfairly—obviously involved an interference with the law courts' operations. Those same courts had in the past sent writs of prohibition against proceedings in the ancient courts they conquered (communal, feudal, ecclesiastic). Now something very similar was being done to them.

In the first decades of the seventeenth century, this conflict became grand politics, deadly politics. Superficially, the Chancellors seem right. There ought to be a remedy for abuse of legal process, a way to right a wrong inflicted by unbending rules. But there was more to it than that. Granted that the courts of common law could be the scene of grave injustice, yet with all their defects they spoke for the rule of law. Chancery spoke for the rule of James. In 1609, Ellesmere made it plain: "The monarch is the law."

There were instances in which Ellesmere issued injunctions against the carrying forward of cases in the law courts, and others in which Coke issued writs or judgments designed to thwart the Chancellor's decrees. In most cases, when the Chancellor decreed injunction, the defendant in Chancery (who was the plaintiff in the law court) obeyed, dropping his action at common law or abandoning a judgment already won. In some, the defendant in Chancery disobeyed and the Chancellor jailed him, and then the law court tried to free him with a writ of habeas corpus. Almost always, on the particular facts, Ellesmere was on the side of justice, the equitable side.

For example, *Courtney versus Glanvil*, where Glanvil had sold Courtney a jewel worth £30 for £360. (There were other facts that aggravated the fraud, but these are the essentials.) Glanvil got a judgment for his overreaching price in a court of law, and Courtney went to Chancery, which decreed the deal should be undone: Courtney get his money back, Glanvil get his jewel. Glanvil refused, and Ellesmere sent him to jail. Glanvil's lawyer applied for habeas corpus. Coke held that though Courtney had "much matter of equity in his favour," the judgment at law had been given, and must stand unless Parliament itself would give relief. Glanvil was released. (The wry charm of history: in this critical case the cheating plaintiff, carrying the banner of the common law, bears the name of the first great treatise on the common law.)

Eventually, judgments and decrees flying back and forth like missiles, James referred the question to Francis Bacon, then Attorney-General, for opinion. Bacon gave the answer that James wanted: Chancery's injunctions could nullify the judgments of the courts of common law.*

---

* *Bacon, who had perhaps the best mind in a time and place of very fine minds, was also the most paradoxical of a group of paradoxical men. It is hard to conceive how an intellect so grand and a character so mean could have been housed together. While he was toadying to the King, and arguing propositions he must have known were wrong, and as Lord Chancellor accepting bribes, he was also contributing important new philosophy. But*

The struggle produced high theater in a case entitled *Colt and Glover against The Bishop of Coventry*. It had to do with the revenues from a church office, and who had the right to grant them. The bishop claimed by grant from the King himself, Colt and Glover from other sources. They brought an action in a court of law. James sent a letter to all the Justices instructing them to halt the action. Coke went right on hearing the case and sent a letter back. Coke wrote: "That in case any letters come unto us contrary to law, that we . . . go forth to do the law, notwithstanding the same letters." All twelve Justices of the three courts of common law signed Coke's letter and sent it to the King.*

James summoned the Justices. He had Bacon and Ellesmere present to tell them how wrong they were, but the King himself began. He denounced Coke's statement: it was "very undecent and unfit for subjects to disobey the King's commandment." Then James took the letter and tore it "with a violent gesture." The Justices went to their knees.

But, kneeling, Coke continued to argue. Bacon and Ellesmere answered. Finally the King demanded of the Justices whether they would ever do such a thing again. Eleven said they would not: if the King or his Chancellor ordered them to stay proceedings, proceedings would be stayed. Coke alone refused to yield. Still on his knees, he gave this answer: "When the case shall be, I will do that which shall be fit for a judge to do."

That finished Coke as Lord Chief Justice. It also impelled James to publicize the point. He performed the seventeenth-century equivalent of commandeering the networks. On June 20, 1616, he called the chief men of the realm to Star Chamber. His coming "was announced a long way off with trumpets." He appeared in full regalia—purple cloak, crimson robe, jeweled sword, crown upon his head. The gold-tipped mace preceded him; there was a large complement of supernumeraries, adding crowd and color. The scene was full of majesty.

James spoke:

---

there are Coke's jarring inconsistencies, and then, of course, we have that petty hateful bit of writing, Shakespeare's will.

In school we had a little book that said Bacon died testing the preservative value of snow on poultry. Nobody knew whether this meant he died of pneumonia or ptomaine.

* The time was not too distant when the three courts had been viewed as one, and so, on important or difficult cases, the twelve Justices—here again the magic number—sat as a single court.

Kings are properly judges, and judgment properly belongs to them from God: for kings sit in the throne of God, and thence all judgment is derived. It is atheism and blasphemy to dispute what God can do; so it is presumption and high contempt in a subject to dispute what a king can do.

On July 26 James issued a decree. The symbols, the color, the trumpets notwithstanding, the decree was no diapason of Divine Right. Instead, and characteristically—not of James but of England—it was a ruling in the litigation. The Chancellor was directed to "give unto our subjects upon their several complaints such relief in Equity (notwithstanding any former proceedings at the Common Law against them) as shall stand with the true merits and justice of their cases, and with the former ancient and continued practise and precedency of our Chancery."

The judicial principle endured. The royal doctrine it was meant to serve did not.

☐

Coke moved to Parliament, and so did the struggle. If the Crown was not subject to the common law, was it subject to the Acts of Parliament? In older terms, was it King or King-in-Council that ruled the realm? The terms were now not quite the same: the Council had been an assembly of the greatest barons; the House of Commons, by now the more powerful House, was mostly a middling gentry. But the question was no different: did the monarch have the final word?

As a judge, Coke had been unwilling to give Parliament unfettered power. He had declared in *Bonham's Case* that an Act of Parliament was void if it contravened the common law. This was the first instance of what has become so prominent a feature of American government—judicial nullification of legislative acts because they clash with higher law. Here the higher law is our Constitution. Coke would have given the same status to the common law. That is, until he left the bench and entered Parliament.*

Just as he was a savage prosecutor on the side of the Crown when he was Attorney-General, and then the brave standard-bearer of the common law when he was a Justice in the courts of common law, Coke became the exponent of Parliamentary supremacy after he joined Parliament. In his earlier years, as Attorney-General, ". . . he started a series of State prosecutions

The first instance, *Bonham's Case*, and in England the only instance. Once the conflict with the throne was settled, Acts of Parliament would be supreme in Britain. The British Constitution, unlike the American, is unwritten; it is only a settled form of government. It has had substantial stability; drastic alterations do not frequently occur. But when the will to change exists, the mechanics of change are easy. Since the end of the seventeenth century, Britain has seen the extension of the suffrage, the enervation of the House of Lords, and the negation of what was left of royal power. These, of course, were important changes, and there have been others, but each has been made effective by Act of Parliament alone. There is no need, as in the United States, to ignite and operate the ponderous machinery of Constitutional amendment. By simple legislation the British Constitution could be transformed tomorrow. It is as though the Congress, by one-vote majorities in each House, even without a Presidential signature, could declare the Bill of Rights a nullity. Theoretically, Parliament can deny free speech; allow any sort of search and seizure; take the vote away from women; take it away from Jews and blacks; confiscate property without compensation; let courts convict on mere suspicion; authorize the use of torture to extract confession. Parliament can, but it has not. On the contrary, the Acts of Parliament have moved toward wider suffrage, a more even distribution of wealth, greater liberty, more humanity—in short, toward the cluster of concepts we call democracy. But nothing in the British Constitution forbids a different course.

---

for libel [of the royal government] on a large scale. The theory he advocated was that all comment on the doings of authority was unjustified; the remedy of those aggrieved was to be sought in the courts or in Parliament." That is, no one should be allowed to question the conduct of the government unless something the government did gave him a right to sue in one of the forms of action, or unless he could get legislation under way in Parliament, a Parliament which at the time was dominated by the sovereign. Start a lawsuit or get a member to offer a bill; otherwise, don't say or write a critical word. This, of course, strikes at the heart of the freedoms for which Coke later boldly fought. Self-interest seems conjoined with principle—changing principle—throughout his long career, and hence his loyalty to principle is suspect. Yet the style and tone of his later arguments do not have the sound of self-interest. Some people get better as they get older.

□

Even in the contest between Parliament and Crown, the courts remained a battlefield. A climactic lawsuit took place in 1637. Again it was heard by the assembled dozen Justices of all three courts of law. Its name is *The King against John Hampden in the Case of the Ship Money.*

Charles I was now king, and needed money badly. By old custom the sovereign could require the port towns to provide ships for coastal protection, or give cash instead. Using this as precedent, Charles imposed a tax on the entire realm. The assessment on John Hampden was twenty shillings. He refused to pay. He argued that only Parliament could impose a new tax except in times of "instant danger and actual invasion." Mere apprehended danger, though apprehended by the King, Hampden's lawyers said, was not enough. (Note that the selfsame concept, differently expressed, was used three centuries later to limit certain exceptions to the First Amendment—"clear and present danger.") The King could not, they urged, by his own cry of alarm supersede the normal processes of law. The Justices decided in favor of Charles, but by the narrowest majority— seven with him, five with Hampden. Considering they had been appointed by the Crown, this victory was, in practical effect, a shattering royal defeat. Within five years there was civil war, and in 1648 Charles was put to death.*

---

* *Hampden was typical of one sort of man, other than the lawyers, who was making the revolution, the intelligent and stubborn country gentleman. Another was the religious zealot. A third, which included Cromwell, was both. From Lord Clarendon's description of Hampden:*

> *For the first year of the parliament, he seemed rather to moderate, and soften the violent and distempered humours, than to inflame them. But wise and dispassioned men plainly discerned, that that moderation proceeded from prudence, and observation that the season was not ripe, rather than that he approved of the moderation ... After he was among those members accused by the King of High Treason, he was much altered; his nature and carriage seeming much fiercer than it did before. ... And without question, when he first drew his sword, he threw away the scabbard ... He was rather of reputation of his own country, than of public discourse, or fame in the kingdom, before*

Argument in the courts, argument in Parliament, a call to arms, regicide, the Lord Protector Cromwell, Restoration, and finally Glorious (and bloodless) Revolution. The Stuarts are defeated, and their doctrine of Divine Right. So are the Puritans, asserting a Right equally Divine, though this Divinity has different ideas of government. At the end of a century of armed and unarmed conflict—most of it unarmed—there is a muddled compromise. Great Britain becomes a limited monarchy, and a limited democracy, and, most of all, for about two hundred years, a limited oligarchy. After World War I, both monarchy and oligarchy are enfeebled, and after World War II they are politically dead or dying; they live on mainly in a social sense, in Britain's class distinctions.*

The masses do not profit much, immediately, from the seventeenth-century turmoil. But the gentry are committed to a set of principles that are preconditions to a government by people. These principles give ideological fire to the American rebellion, and are carried further and made explicit in our written Constitution.

It is not our Bill of Rights alone that reflects the seventeenth-century British experience. The body of our Constitution, in addition to its thematic separation of powers, contains provisions for impeachment and restrictions on trial for treason. And *The King against Hampden* probably contributed to the inclu-

---

the business of Ship-money; but then he grew the argument of all tongues, every man enquiring who, and what he was, that durst, at his own charge, support the liberty and property of the kingdom, and rescue his country, as he thought, from being made a prey to the court.

Clarendon himself was a royalist, but sufficiently objective to write thus favorably of an antiroyalist. He was the ablest of the Restoration councillors, but ability can be a handicap when put at the service of a stupid ruler, and objectivity a positive peril. He ended his life in disgrace and exile. Like those expelled from Washington in recent years (though for utterly different reasons), he wrote his memoirs, which today, in similar circumstances, might bring two million dollars.

* *The British class system, the most unattractive feature of an otherwise admirable society, has withstood all democratic winds. Contemporary political change seems to involve not the erasure of classes, but only a different allocation of power.*

sion of the clause that gives Congress the sole power to declare war, a proposition disrespected these past decades by King John and King Richard and King Lyndon in between.

□

It is easy to focus on "property" in the triptych of "life, liberty and property" to which the seventeenth-century rebels were devoted—to say that the triumph was antidemocratic because the Levellers' movement was defeated and those who gained the most were the wealthy Whigs. This is a current view. It is wrong, I think. For one thing, "property" did not mean what it came to mean in the late nineteenth and early twentieth centuries, when courts were nullifying social legislation because, they said, the legislative efforts to make things better for the masses infringed the hallowed right of property that belonged to owner-employers. Rather, it was seen, in one important aspect, as a materialization of liberty, visible expression of a preserve of rights that royal government had no warrant to intrude upon. It was seen as other things too, of course, but this was a large part of what the rebel leaders had in mind. It was also something different from the power-land of feudal times. Indeed, the purchase and sale of property had been a lever to break the bonds of feudalism.

The seventeenth-century conflict, like most political conflicts, had uncongenial alliances on each side. Not all who fought the monarchy had aims we would approve, not all the royalists were mean or unattractive. But for the future the chief winner was enlisted with the rebels. That winner was the rule of law, autocracy its vanquished enemy. The essentials of democracy—freedom and equality and self-government—cannot live outside the law. Democratic concepts were voiced all through these struggles, and they did not disappear when the Whig aristocrats took power. They supplied much of the ideological content of the American agitation.

That the common law of Coke contained grave inequalities does not mean that inequalities were fewer, or less grave, under the royal absolutism he opposed. He and Selden and Pym and Eliot and the others were not fighting for the inequalities; they were fighting for the law. Once that battle was won, other elements of democracy could begin to make their way. As they did.*

---

* We may note a beneficent irony. Probably the most important ideological factor in the progress toward a more democratic system once the rule of law was firm—more important than the

□

Through all this and beyond, the victory of equity was sustained. Several times later in the seventeenth century, in the courts and Parliament, there were efforts to undo James's decree of 1616; none of them succeeded. Coke was on the good side politically, the side that later won. Bacon and Ellesmere, politically, were on the bad and losing side. But Bacon and Ellesmere won the argument about the courts, not only in the eyes of James but in the eyes of history. Despite Coke's reputation, Bacon, I suggest, was the abler lawyer. Bacon's advice that the other courts must yield to equity's injunction remained the law after the opponents of the Stuarts triumphed, and it remains the law today.*

Equity, however, was a gracious victor, a tolerant victor; even, one might say, a timorous victor. It did not employ its weapons wantonly. It gained the power to interfere with the processes of common law, but it would not exercise the power unless complainant was entitled to judicial help and the courts of law could not supply it. A tight mechanism needs a safety valve; Chancery was in the main content to serve that function. The Chancellors intervened only when the injury could not be fended off or compensated by a judgment of the law courts. Except where statutes are addressed to special situations, a plaintiff who seeks the remedies of equity must show that "there is no adequate remedy at law."

Two centuries after James's decree, equity had a victory of another kind. The procedural reformers of the nineteenth century took as their model the formless form of action of the Chancellor, and sought to substitute its looser ways for the stylized

---

slippery doctrine of "natural rights" —was utilitarianism. And, though Francis Bacon is not named among the utilitarians, his philosophy clearly signals the path they later took. In some ways, he anticipated Bentham by a couple of hundred years. Bacon's writings pointed in the direction precisely the opposite of his actions as a politician, and had consequences more abiding.

* Coke, a specialist, could cite more cases than his contemporaries, and this accounts for his reputation as the greatest English lawyer. But he cannot, in this fast company, be considered brilliant. He was out-argued not only by the philosopher Bacon, but also by the man-of-action Raleigh. Coke's courage is exciting, not his homework.

pleading of the courts of common law. They drove home their point with their terminology: plaintiff's initial statement would be called "complaint," not "declaration"; defendant's would be an "answer," not a "plea." Then, in the twentieth century, pre-trial discovery, an invention of the Chancellors, became a prime feature of civil litigation.

But it is all a victory of law. By the time John Selden speaks, his statement is an overstatement. The day is past when the Chancellor considered each case a fresh problem, which he must solve as though there had never been another like it. From the reign of Elizabeth forward, the Chancellors no longer are ecclesiastics, with a single short exception in the reign of Charles the First. They are lawyers, and, politics aside, they respect the common law. The early case-by-case-what's-right-in-this-case becomes a set of principles, though with a leaven of discretion. The Chancellors' feet will grow or shrink no more than other judges'.

Until they became an arm of royal politics, the Chancellors probably always felt they were acting according to the law of England; they were only trying to give effect to the essentials of the law in circumstances where, for some specific reason, the motors of the other courts sputtered or would not start at all. Chancery did not, except in the Stuart period and a bit before, think itself an adversary of the common law.

By the second half of the sixteenth century, cases in the Court of Chancery began to be reported, and once we have something written, we have something that can be consulted, and once we have something to consult we have a precedent. (Precedent can also be a memory, and until the nineteenth century, judicial opinions often contained statements of what the judge remembered of another case in which he was judge or lawyer, but writing is necessary to a thorough precedential system.) By the end of the seventeenth century, equity is itself a legal system.

The application of principle, however, remains appreciably more flexible in equity than in the courts of law. The earliest petitions had asked for a royal boon the Chancellor as royal surrogate might if he wished bestow, and this survives in fainter form as an equitable discretion. The later Chancellors, more than the judges of the law courts, could still address themselves to the special features of each case. For disputes that have their antecedents in petitions to the Chancellor, present-day courts can with a freer hand grant or withhold relief, or tailor it to circumstances. For those that have their antecedents in the forms of action of common law, there is a continuing tradition that urges the courts to respond to a given sort of situation in a given way.

Again, however, it is a matter of degree. On the law side, judges can expand rules or contract them when particular circumstances have force enough. And the jury is an effective, if sometimes foolish, improviser; jurors can, and do, disregard the instructions they have been given, and the judgment usually stands. On the other side, equity's discretion is not unrestrained: decrees can be reversed for "abuse of discretion"—that is, for wandering too far from equity's own precedents. And its history, as we shall see, is full of juridical failures, as much as that of the law courts, sometimes more.*

---

* *"Discretion" is a "word of art" (that is, a word that has taken on special meaning through continued use in a discipline) in another, unrelated part of the law. It frequently appears in contracts that are meant to give one party or another complete control over some aspect of their relationship. For example, in a new venture one party is to do the work and the other is to put up the money; the contract may provide that the one is given "sole discretion" as to the design of the product, the other "sole discretion" over how much is spent in promoting it. As this chapter is being written, I have received a draft of a proposed contract in which the lawyer on the other side demands that his client have control over something as to which my client wants to have a voice. The draft arrives with a clause stating that, on this aspect of the deal, the other party is to have "soul discretion." I answer that spiritual decision, though estimable, is a bit too unpredictable for a matter of this kind.*

It is a fine season for typos. My partner has dictated a memorandum on the possible outcome of a criminal trial; he gets back a neatly typed page in which it is said that assuming a sympathetic attitude on the part of the jury, the case is likely to end in "a quibble" (that is, a verdict of not guilty).

Again, I am given a contract to read because the two corporations concerned simply have not been able to get along; they have engaged in a continuous series of disputes. The contract includes, as nearly every contract does, a clause specifying how long the arrangement is to last. Such provisions are usually cast in standard language, as is this one, almost. They say something like "This agreement shall commence on January 1, 1978 and terminate on December 31, 1982" or "The term of this agreement shall be three years from . . ." Here, however, the

□

That was the theory, a lovely theory: one juristic institution with a set of rules, not frozen, capable of growth, but definite; another institution ready to meet the cases where those rules might work injustice, yet subject to some rules of its own, flexible but not capricious. That was the theory; what was the practice? Ah, the practice. By the time of *Jarndyce versus Jarndyce,* the deficiencies of equity were ancient. Dickens wasn't bringing news.

For one thing, though theory and origin matched nicely—equity indeed began as a stand-by source of justice for the failures of the common law—the Chancellors were soon busy setting up a new branch of substantive law. It was the law of what we now call trusts, in the fiduciary, not the cartel, sense. They were at first called "uses."

In the age when Chancery got started, land, by far the most important form of wealth, could not pass by will. Personal property could, and the church courts enforced those wills, but personal property, including coin, was relatively insignificant. Some testamentary control of land had been possible in earlier days; it had ended in the thirteenth century. Two reasons are generally given for its disappearance. One is the developing common-law rule that transfers of land required a physical act, the act called "livery of seisin." The other is that a will might be used to defeat the lords' feudal benefits. At the death of the landholder, his lord came in for various cuts of what descended to the heir—a pay-

---

parties have signed a document that says: "Disagreement shall continue in full force and effect for . . ." A mechanical error, one may presume, but prophetic.

The practice of law is especially rich in charming typos; the seriousness of the occasion makes the pratfall all the more engaging. Ordinarily the mistake is caught before the document reaches final form, so that only the lawyer gets the pleasure. But not always, as the last example shows. There are others. A friend tells me of a letter he has received which refers to a party who has not stirred himself to respond to an attack as "lying doormat." Once I was given a memorandum dealing with a tax on business income; it said the tax was measured by "grocery seats." (You must pronounce it.) It evoked a more leisurely, pre-supermarket era, when a body could have a moment's rest while discussing produce and prices with the man behind the counter.

ment called "relief," "wardship" if the heir was minor, some other benefits. If there was no heir by blood, the lord got it all, by escheat (as he also did by forfeiture if the owner's death had been a punishment for felony).*

A third reason may be suggested. In the absence of a will, land would usually descend in one piece, by primogeniture, which had advantages. For a feudal government, the balkanization of domains would make control more difficult. For the owner, primogeniture suited the urge to dynasty. Most men wanted their estates kept whole; they felt their land should extend as far as possible, even though they lay beneath it. The custom of primogeniture continued long after the law ceased to require it. Even when the time arrived when owners could, if they chose, divide their lands, they usually chose not to.

But not all men felt that way, or at least they felt some conflict. They might love their other children, or think it unbecoming to leave impoverished offspring. They would want to supply a dowry for a daughter, give part of the land to a younger son, provide for illegitimates. These things can now, of course, be done by will, but until 1541 the law did not allow it. So someone —we do not know his name—hit on the device of transferring land during one's lifetime to a friend (by livery of seisin) on the promise of the friend that he would hold only naked title to the land and give the use and profit of it to the daughter or younger son or anyone else the donor thought to care for.†

---

* These feudal benefits were based on the theory that the relationship between lord and man was personal, an exchange of the protected use of the land for services. When the man died, he could no longer render services and the deal had come to an end. The lord could then grant the use of the land to anyone, not necessarily to the dead man's son. Ordinarily, the heir stepped in, but the theory allowed the lord to exact a toll.

† The widow was entitled by law to a portion of her dead husband's lands so long as she lived. This was her "dower," whose echo we hear in "dowager." The widower had a correlative right called "curtesy" in all his dead wife's lands, but only if there had been a child in the marriage, born and "heard to cry alive." These rights, altered, appear in modern statutes that provide an "indefeasible share" for the surviving spouse, overriding stingy wills that specify something less. The statutes vary from state to state; the share can be as little as a third of the decedent's real estate (in New Jersey, for example), which amounts to noth-

The inventor probably built on what he knew of an earlier invention (as inventors generally do). The Franciscan friars swore not only personal poverty but, unlike other orders, communal poverty too. Other monks might own nothing as individuals, but their abbey could be rich, and the abbey supplied their needs—an early, and often splendid, expense account. But how will the poor Franciscans live? Like this: someone seeking to save his soul will give land to the local community, on the community's promise to hold the land "to the use of" the local branch of the order.*

The religious device was turned to family purposes. But suppose the friend was false. The common law had no way of enforcing such arrangements. The law of contract was still to come, and when it would come the remedy would be a judgment for damages, which, except as threat, could not serve these ends, and even as threat could not serve them well. The Chancellor, though, could order the trustee to keep his promise. The transaction had been a solemn one. The beneficiaries were holy men or family; the corpus was usually land. A trustee's failure to do what he swore to do when he received the seisin could be seen as something deeper than a tradesman's abandonment of an arm's-length bargain. It amounted to breach of faith. The Chancellor was a churchman, and the church courts were accustomed to punishing breaches of faith.

As soon as the device gained Chancery's approval, it began

---

ing if the wealth is stocks and bonds, or, in community-property states, as much as half of everything he or she has earned for an indolent spouse.

* The word "trust" came in later. It means the same as "use." They are simply bracketed by different prepositions: "to the use of," "in trust for." Maitland takes pains to demonstrate that "use" in this sense comes not from the Latin usus, which means use, but from opus, which means work. This is not significant for legal purposes; it merely emphasizes the trustee's role as grantor's agent. Maitland's scholarship, however, illustrates a wider lesson: we tend too quickly to assume a meaning because of similarity of sound. Words currently suffering this distortion include "vagary" (which does not mean something vague), "viable" (which does not mean there's a way), and "parameter" (which does not mean perimeter). (Though by the time this note is published, they may, they may.)

to be used for reasons other than family fairness, less sympathetic. One was evasion of debt. Creditors could go against your land, but once in trust it was no longer legally your land; it belonged to the trustee. A nice balance could be worked. Defeat your creditors by putting part of your land in trust for children, whom you dominate, so that you can take the income; put the rest in trust for a clerical order and save your cheating soul.*

In general, trusts were in tune with the times. They were part of the dismantling of the feudal structure. But they had their bad side: fraud of creditors, and, from the point of view of feudal overlord, defeat of ancient expectations. So in 1536 came the Statute of Uses, which undertook to abolish trusts of land. (There could still be trusts of personal property.) The statutory device was simple: when anybody received land "to the use, confidence, or trust" of another, he would be deemed totally seised of it. His right would be entire, and hence he could not be forced to carry out the grantor's wishes. Five years later landholders were permitted to do directly something they had earlier accomplished through the trust device: the Statute of Wills allowed land to be handed down by will, so that younger children and other objects of affection could be provided for.

But trusts by then were wanted for other reasons. A faithful trustee would prevent the dissipation of a profligate's inheritance. Defeat of creditors is ever popular. So lawyers hacked away at Parliament's Statute of Uses. If the grant imposed active duties, such as collecting the rents and paying them over to the beneficiaries, the Chancellors ruled the Act did not apply. Someone came up with another idea: convey the land to one friend, who is to hold it to the use of another, who is to hold it to the use of the person whom the grantor wants to benefit. Under the statute, the first friend must get full seisin, but with the statute thus satisfied, is not the second friend in the position of trustee? Don't be a wise guy, said the courts of common law; the intent of Parliament, even though they may not have thought of such a situation, is that the second friend should get full title. The

---

* There were elaborations. For example, you might convey to a number of trustees, and empower them to appoint others, and keep the thing going on indefinitely, controlling the disposition of your land through generations. The law eventually put limits on this posthumous building of wealth—"the rule against perpetuities" and "the rule against accumulations."

Chancellors gave in on this, and the decision held for about a hundred years. Then during the Restoration, Chancery ascendant, unrestricted trusts of land resumed.

Trusts still are widely used, though the testamentary difficulties are long gone. A common object is to manage funds for those the donor deems unable to do the job themselves. These beneficiaries are usually minors, though sometimes they are grownups whom the donor seeks to protect against improvidence or merely wishes to insult. But probably the main contemporary motive is the ancient one of thwarting the overlord, now resident in Washington: trusts are a prominent tax-avoiding device.

So to the original *ad hoc* helping hand, where, specifically, the common law had failed to work, there was added a generalized catering to a social wish, the creation of a new body of substantive law. This was, by and large, not bad. The bad departure from Chancery's genesis lay in its own procedure, the way the court was run. I have described the defects of procedure in the courts of common law. Chancery was worse.

□

In the beginning, the method was expeditious. The defendant, remember, was subpoenaed and made to answer, orally, the charges plaintiff lodged against him. Then the Chancellor decided who was right and issued a prison-backed decree. Soon, however, it became the practice to write out the complaint and the answer, and by the sixteenth century everything in a Chancery suit was put in writing—not only pleadings but all the evidence. This had advantages and disadvantages. Writing could make the case clearer, and preserve it for subsequent scrutiny— as a precedent, or as a memorial of the Chancellor's ability and honesty (or their absence). On the other hand, there was no opportunity for cross-examination before the Chancellor, no observation of the witness. These opposing factors did not stay in balance. The requirement of writing became a ravenous monster.

If there had to be papers, there had to be copies, and copies, of course, were by hand. By the time Chancery was full-fledged, there were papers of all sorts—complaints, answers, petitions, pleas, demurrers, motions, interrogatories, responses, briefs, references to masters (delegates of the Chancellor), the masters' reports, exceptions to reports, and the various orders all along the way. Copies were needed, but the problem was that copies were made by the Chancery clerks and paid for by the parties, and the clerks viewed copy-making as a business, an uncontrolled monopoly. The number of copies required had no relation to need; for example, the lawyer had to buy a copy of his own papers. Sometimes if the document was important, two copies were made by two different clerks, and both had to be bought, even though the party himself had the original. The clerks charged by the page and stretched things out. They added recitals, used wide margins, put large gaps between lines, and inserted "dashes and slashes" to consume more space. In 1627 (which was no different from other years) a writer noted: "I did see an answer . . . of forty of their sheets which [recopied in normal writing] was brought to six sheets."

This kind of extortion at least was evenhanded. More pernicious was the sale of favors. The favor might be a favorable decree—very easy when a court is merely doing what is right in the oh-so-special circumstances. Or, probably more frequent, one would have to give a bribe to get the court to take some step that should have been taken anyway—pay merely to have a motion decided, never mind the outcome. One of the reasons equity got started was corruption in the courts of law. Within a century it had its own.*

Second to the corruption, and feeding it, was the overload. It is astonishing, but despite the vast increase of cases in Chancery from the fourteenth to the nineteenth century, the court continued to have only one judge—the Lord Chancellor himself. There were masters who conducted inquiries, and clerks aplenty, but every case in the end must be taken to the Chancellor. Half a millennium passed, and still one man had to make all final decisions. In the middle of the seventeenth

---

* Corruption is the worst crime—worse than robbery, arson, mayhem, worse than rape and murder. By starving law enforcement, it feeds these other crimes; it is the progenitor of lawlessness. More: through its example, it debilitates the conscience. It poisons our society; it poisons our souls. (Pick the one you feel the greater evil, according to your religion.) The litigant who uses influence to affect the outcome of a case, and the judge who bends to that influence, are our most heinous criminals. How can we respect the law when we find calculated injustice in our halls of justice? And without regard for justice, without respect for law (brother though not twin), our civilization cannot function. Anyone who tries to fix a traffic ticket is damaging all of us.

century, "it was confidently affirmed by knowing gentlemen of worth that there were depending in that court twenty-three thousand cases, some of which had been there depending five, some ten, some twenty, some thirty years and more." There would be a century's further accretion to the time of *Jarndyce versus Jarndyce*.

There was both free-lance bribery and institutionalized graft. The offices of master and clerk were sold by the Chancellors, and because they were so profitable they brought excellent prices. One source of profit was the money paid into court in cases where funds were the subject of the suit. The funds were turned over to the Chancellor's chief assistant, the Master of the Rolls. He was under no obligation to account for interest, so he used the money for his own investments. Since large sums were involved, and they stayed in court so long, this was big business. It took the South Sea Bubble to end the practice; if the Masters had been more prudent in their investments, it would not have ended then. In the subsequent investigation, one Master testified he had offered five thousand pounds to gain the office, but the Chancellor had held out for guineas.*

Then there was the system devised by the main clerical assistants, a group known as The Six Clerks. (They themselves were assisted by another group known as The Sixty Clerks.) In the eighteenth century, when salaries had been added to the fees paid by litigants (that is, fees as distinguished from bribes), the Six decided that each of them could act for all the others. So each went to work for two months of the year, and each drew a whole year's salary. Ten month's holiday is nice, a splendid paid vacation, but a sixth as much work was done as should have been done (assuming that anything much was done at all).

Then there was the number of times a case could be heard. Every issue in the suit could go to a master for inquiry, one time or more, then to the Master of the Rolls, to the Master of the Rolls again for rehearing, then to the Lord Chancellor, to him again for rehearing, and occasionally beyond the Chancellor to the House of Lords. At each stage except the last, additional

---

* *That is, five thousand times twenty-one shillings instead of five thousand times twenty. It is difficult to take inflation into account and translate this into modern money, because the social structure was so different. But in present-day dollars this is probably somewhere in the hundred thousands.*

evidence could be offered. And all this followed the pleadings, commissions, interrogatories, depositions, and the rest of the almost endless nonsense.

Pleading was not the gravest of equity's problems, as it was for actions at common law. But that is not to say it was no problem. Though its complaints and answers were in a way the models for the codes, they were hardly simple. Equity pleading of the early nineteenth century, according to the foremost American commentator of the time, "requires various talents, vast learning, and a clearness and acuteness of perception, which belong only to very gifted minds."

Finally, there was the personality of certain Chancellors, some corrupt, some conscientious to the point of paralysis. Lord Eldon, Chancellor at the start of the nineteenth century, is the prime example of the latter. While litigants spent more money litigating than they were disputing over, while estates shrank to nothing as suits among their claimants went on and on, while heirs grew old and died before they could lay hands on their inheritance, Lord Eldon pondered. In part, it was his need "to consider so carefully each case that permanent and final justice should be done"—an engaging will-o'-the-wisp. In part, as Holdsworth says, it was

a dilatory habit of mind which tended to grow upon him, at a time when the expanding population and commerce of the country were bringing into still stronger relief the defects of the court. A judge should, it is true, take time to consider a doubtful case. But Lord Eldon would often express a clear opinion after hearing the argument, and then, as Campbell says, "he expressed doubts—reserved to himself the opportunity for further consideration—took home the papers—never read them—promised judgment again and again—and for years never gave it—all the facts and law connected with it having escaped his memory." Yet Romilly, from large personal experience, said that however long he took to consider a cause, he had rarely known him differ from his first impression.*

---

* *Eldon is also known, in America, as a figure in the history of obscenity law. In the* Ulysses *case, Judge Augustus Hand mentioned the "foolish judgments of Lord Eldon . . . proscribing the works of Byron and Southey . . ."*

The scandal that was equity—the name itself was bitter irony—continued into the nineteenth century with scarcely any abatement. There were anguished outcries from time to time, and proposals for reform. Commissions of inquiry were conducted, and reports of abuses made. A number of bills to alter things were introduced in Parliament; they never were enacted. Corruption and murderous delay continued to infect the system, varying only in degree, and survived the seventeenth-century triumph of the common lawyers. With one short-lived mad exception: Cromwell made an ordinance. It had many good features, which Cromwell ungratefully took from the Parliament to whom he cried, "You have sat here too long for the good that you have done. In the name of God, go!" But Cromwell's ordinance left nothing to the discretion of the commissioners who were supposed to enforce it. And, among its other products of the military mind, the ordinance commanded that every case should be heard and determined in a single day. The cure for taking thirty years was a fiat to take one day. Obviously it could not work and did not last.*

Soon came the Restoration, which restored all equity's old bad habits. The Glorious Revolution did not change them. Finally, around 1830, after a Whig return to power, reform began. (The voguish deprecation of the Whigs was once perhaps a needed caveat to readers of Trevelyan and Macaulay. It has now become distortion.) Equity began to resemble what it started out to be. At about the same time, reform of common-law procedure got under way.

Things have since improved. Our courts today, of course, could be far better than they are, but they are far better than they were. The present judicial system (even with its stains of corruption) is immensely superior to the brittle process of the courts of common law and the deadly tedium of Chancery (with their equal or greater stains).

Theory eventually triumphed over practice. Despite its re-

---

* *Those of us enamored of radical solutions, who will never settle for anything less, might pause here for a moment. For some abuses, radical change—change that goes to the root—is needed. For others, it cannot be successful. Each problem has to be considered on its own. Commitment to a style—radical, liberal, conservative, reactionary—may provide a poultice for one's internal pains; it does not help society's.*

maining faults, equity is now much closer to the ideas from which it sprang than to the practices to which it fell.

◻

The kind of injunction we usually see in the news is the "preliminary injunction," also known as "temporary injunction" or, less commonly, "interlocutory," "interim" or "provisional." It is granted on motion, near the beginning of the lawsuit, well before trial. Ordinarily it is done on paper evidence—affidavits and documents—though once in a while the court will hear oral testimony. Since a full trial cannot be had immediately, and since there is not likely to be much more evidence when it is reached, and since the kind of case in which injunction is sought concerns a wrong from which the plaintiff is suffering right now and every minute—for these reasons, a fast remedy, even without full exploration of the matter, is frequently appropriate.

Many cases end with the decision on the motion, but not all, and the plaintiff who wins the motion but loses at the trial will be liable to defendant for any damage the restraint may have meanwhile caused. To cover this possibility, he must usually post a bond. If the judge suspects that something wrong may be going on, but is not sufficiently persuaded to enjoin defendant without full trial, he may deny the motion but direct an early trial, ahead of other cases on the calendar.

An even earlier sort of injunction may be issued. It is usually called a "temporary restraining order" and fills the time between the start of suit and the decision on the motion for preliminary injunction. It may be granted *ex parte*—that is, on the affidavits and argument offered by the plaintiff's lawyer only, without hearing defendant's side. The reason is that a contested motion, though not elaborate as a trial, always takes some time. The parties must marshal evidence, and brief and argue the law, and the judge will probably need several days to study the facts and the law. (It is not the only case he has.) The *ex parte* procedure may seem unfair, and often is, but the judge who grants the order does so with the thought that, for the relatively short period involved, less harm will be done by restraining the defendant than by permitting him to go on doing what the plaintiff says he is doing. (Unless the judge grants it because a fix is in. Sorry, but this is an ever present possibility in too many courts, and on something as discretionary and explicitly uninformed as an *ex* *parte* order it is very difficult to distinguish honest error from crookedness.) Here again a bond is usually required.*

In all of this, contested or one-sided, the court "weighs the equities" and considers relative hardship, sometimes called "the balance of convenience." How much benefit to the one side, how much harm to the other? Suppose defendant is about to sell and deliver something that plaintiff says is his, and once out of defendant's hands it will be hard to get it back, while if defendant just holds on to it, tangled claims of ownership can be sorted out in due time. Why not grant the interim restraint? On the other hand, suppose defendant is engaged in a course of conduct that plaintiff says infringes some right of plaintiff, but when the motion is made defendant is already so far along in what he is doing that things cannot be undone without great cost. Here "the equities" suggest that plaintiff wait a while.

Example of the former: defendant is giving a valuable painting to someone about to leave the country. Why not keep the painting at hand while ownership is determined? Example of the latter: plaintiff sees a film which, he says, plagiarizes a book he has written. If the film is already being shown in theaters, the judge is not likely to order the showings halted on a preliminary motion; interrupted distribution can cost millions. The Copyright Act gives the court power both to enjoin infringements and to award damages, and, unless the plagiarism is obvious, plaintiff will probably have to rest content with the prospect of damages or injunction at the end of the case.†

Indeed, good legal advice in the movie case will recommend that plaintiff make no motion. Unless the lawyer feels close to certain about the ultimate outcome, his client-plaintiff may have to pay huge damages if the court, better informed by the trial, concludes the temporary order was improvidently granted.

Suppose, however, the film has not yet been released. The loss involved in postponement of distribution is much less than that involved in interruption. Indeed, there may be no loss at all, the best timing for presentation of a film (or publication of a

---

* *The willingness to act* ex parte *varies from court to court. For example, the New York state courts are readier to do so than the federal courts that sit in New York.*

† *He may, however, get both. Statutes can and do depart from equity's rule that it will not act if there exists an "adequate remedy at law." The Copyright Act offers a tray of remedies, and the court can choose one or more.*

book) being largely a matter of luck. The likelihood of getting the order at this point will accordingly be much greater.

There is another factor, equal to the consideration of the injury, to the one side or the other, that may be done by the granting or denial of the interim order. It is the judge's estimate of how things are likely to look after they are fully litigated, his preview of "the merits." He makes a tentative appraisal, subject to revision after trial. M for estimate of merits and H for relative hardship, and Mh = mH.

□

In colonial America, equity went through a reprise of the part it played in seventeenth-century English politics, in a different, lower key. The Lord Chancellors in England had been instruments of Stuart monarchy. Courts of Chancery in the colonies were instruments of whatever monarch the mother country had —Stuart, Orange, Hanover—or were looked upon as such. The fact that Chancery employed no jury contributed both to the reality and the feeling. The jury was an expression of democratic striving. It still is, somewhat, but it was much more then than now. In some colonies, the royal governor was himself the Chancellor. And the Chancellor held court, usually, only in the colony's capital, while the common-law judges rode circuit, bringing justice "to every man's doorstep." In America, as in England, there were complaints about Chancery's slow pace. Though the situation here was not nearly so extreme, the action at common law, even with its special pleading, was faster.

With the Revolution, the political aspect of equity disappeared. Not long after, as has been mentioned, some of its procedure became a model for reform. Then later, in the last quarter of the nineteenth century and in the first quarter of the twentieth, equity again became political. The injunction was put to fierce use against labor; equity became Chancellor Fink. This ended with the 1932 enactment of the Norris–La Guardia Act. (Odd couple in collaboration: grand old Nebraskan and the Little Flower that grew out of the sidewalks of New York. Misfit combinations are often needed to effect reform.)

That particular perversion of equity is over, but the injunction continues to be used for purposes political, now generally for liberal ends. A traditional equity defendant was a neighbor doing something disagreeable enough to constitute a nuisance. Recently, defendant may be an industry, and the suit involve a larger nuisance, against which environmentalists invoke the aid of equity.

Among injunction's modern uses, there is often an agency of government on one side or the other. The government invokes the aid of equity to enforce a regulation, or a citizen asserts the Bill of Rights against something government officials are doing and asks the court to stop them. The theory is that it is not the government, but one of its employees, acting ostensibly pursuant to law but in fact illegally, who has deprived the plaintiff of his rights, and so it is an individual and not the United States that is sued.

It is only where a statute specifically permits it that there can be litigation against the government itself, as distinguished from the individual officials. Here again old doctrine: the sovereign may not be sued except with his consent. At first, as we have seen, the courts of common law would not hear claims against the king, but the Chancellor, alter ego of the king, might graciously entertain them. Later, legislative permission was required. An example of suit against the sovereign specifically allowed: a taxpayer, claiming after audit that the Treasury asks too much, may pay the tax and then sue in the district court to get his money back. (He has the alternative of resisting the payment and going to the Tax Court, a special tribunal for federal tax questions.)

The doctrine is hard to reconcile with the concept that the sovereign is not above the law. But think of the mess that would be made if every citizen with a real or fancied grievance could take the government to court. The statutory exceptions, plus the liability of individual officials who go beyond the law, constitute a compromise which, if conceptually unsound, does make practical sense.

The Civil Rights Acts provide for both injunction and damages. Courts, however, are loath to stick an individual with money liability for what he does as an official. Often he has acted on an honest misconception, even though his version of his duties is far wrong. So the case ends usually with injunction, which itself establishes the point that those who sued want made. But sometimes damages are won.*

---

* Thus the Case of the Bad Coffee, in 1977. A New York judge sent out for coffee, pronounced it terrible when he tasted it, had the vendor brought in handcuffs to his chambers, and delivered his gustatory judgment then and there. The vendor brought suit

Even when the official is not so obviously misusing the power of his office, the provision for damages is helpful. It is an unlikely but ever present risk for the official who might otherwise be cavalier about the citizen's rights. In 1964 the district attorney of New York's Nassau County started an obscenity prosecution against the publishers of *Evergreen Review.* He seized almost all the copies of the magazine, ostensibly to use as evidence in the prosecution. (The bindery was in his county, in the town of Hicksville. *Sic.*) The publisher argued that while the district attorney was entitled to bring his prosecution (though not to win it), his taking all the copies was an attempt to suppress the magazine without judicial hearing, and hence a violation of the First Amendment for which the Civil Rights Act of 1868 afforded remedies. (The Act had a different provenance; note the date.) A three-judge federal court, after hearing lengthy argument, issued a preliminary injunction commanding the return of all the copies. This disabled the pending prosecution; all the evidence was gone. The part of the publishers' complaint that sought damages was left for trial. The district attorney gave notice of appeal to the United States Supreme Court from the preliminary injunction. The publisher's lawyer settled the case by offering to drop the claim for damages if the district attorney would abandon his appeal and promise not to recommence the obscenity prosecution. The district attorney dropped the appeal and made the promise, the *Evergreen Review* got distributed, and that was the end of the matter.

So the injunction can be an effective remedy when the citizen sues to enforce his rights against the government. It is usually feeble when the government sues the citizen. The government enforces its laws mainly by criminal penalties— prison, fine, occasionally forfeiture, and—as this is written, maybe—capital punishment. It also employs the civil suit—that is, injunction, revocation of a license, and, under a couple of statutes, an action for treble damages. As an enforcement device, the injunction is often an anti-enforcement device—especially under an administration sympathetic to big business and hostile to the regulatory laws it is supposed to administer. It offers a way to make a showing of law enforcement while letting the mis-

---

in the federal court under the Civil Rights Act, and testified that the judge had screamed at him. The jury awarded $141,000. The price of coffee during 1977 had reached unprecedented levels, and apparently in this jury's view coffee with scream was extra.

creant corporation escape the harsher and therefore more effective penalties. Usually all the government's injunction says is that you must not do it again; if you repeat your violation, you will be punished. Probably punished, that is. Often in contempt proceedings the result is nothing more than another warning; the defendant is permitted to "purge itself of the contempt" by coming into compliance. Be nice from now on, the injunction says.

There is an adage in the law of tort (about as reliable as other adages) that every dog may have one bite. The idea is that the owner is not liable unless he has reason to believe his dog is vicious. Until man's best friend demonstrates he is not a friend to all, the owner may assume that he is gentle. The injunction as an instrument of law enforcement operates much the same way. Several companies that together control a certain market conspire to fix prices. The Department of Justice charges into court and bravely demands an injunction against violation of the Antitrust Acts. The court, after the companies (which can afford high-priced lawyers to contend with the government's low-priced lawyers) have made a long contest of it, may issue an injunction. More often, somewhere along the way the case is settled: the companies, "not admitting guilt," enter into a "consent decree."

Either way, the main achievement is a ruling that if the defendants do the thing again, the government can go to court again, and, if the government succeeds again, the defendants will be held in contempt. This means they will pay a sum fixed by the court, since corporations cannot go to jail. The sum almost never does much damage to their balance sheets.

Altogether a nauseating parody of law enforcement. A slap on the wrist for large-scale violation of the law, a cluck-cluck-tut-tut-you-really-mustn't for social harm far more damaging than a burglary of jewels (to take an example that will put a man in jail for several years). How much deterrence is there for other corporations, tempted to fix prices in their other markets? Injunction used this way gives a President who does not like existing Acts of Congress a way to blunt their force.*

---

*That "decent, honest person," for example, Gerald Ford. Interesting, schizoid character. As President, he was a selfish politician merely, not the mixture of selfish politician and altruistic leader we have a right to expect (and very often get). As congressman he was worse: his attack on Justice Douglas was delib-

Another weakness of the injunction as an instrument of law enforcement is that equity traditionally acts only against things already in existence or obviously threatened, and ordinarily the threat can be proved only after some injury is done. Burglars rarely advertise coming attractions.

It may be said that injunction nevertheless performs a useful regulatory function. Statutes that deal with our economy are often vague, often ambiguous—sometimes because of poor draftsmanship, sometimes by reason of the complicated nature of the things they deal with. A suit for injunction can serve to clarify the statute; the defendants may honestly believe that what they are doing is not illegal. But there is a better device for the purpose: the action for declaratory judgment, a twentieth-century innovation (by statute) that permits a court to declare the law in a particular situation even though the plaintiff asks no money damages or injunction or any other sort of sanction.

Not that injunction is always feeble. A serious enforcement agency and a serious court can occasionally use it to good effect. If the individual executives of the corporation are made defendants, the suit takes on real meaning. Nobody likes to run the risk of punishment for contempt, and the shame of the judgment of lawlessness, even though there are no penal consequences, means something to some people, especially when, as in the General Electric case, they live in Scarsdale.

☐

The orders of government regulatory agencies are similar to injunction. In some respects, they are weaker: jail is one step farther away. If the violator persists, the agency must get a ruling from a court before the stage is reached where further violation constitutes contempt. In other situations, they are stronger. The courts have developed doctrines of "administrative regularity" and "presumption of administrative expertise" that makes these orders hard to overturn. And if resistance in the courts will cost a lot of money—as, for example, when a zoning board infected with bias or corruption refuses to grant one resident the sort of variance it grants to others—a bad administrative order may simply go unchallenged; the individual householder, unlike a corporation, usually cannot afford the litigation.

erately unfair. Yet he did give off an air of decency. The sort of man, it said, whom you would like to have for a next-door neighbor. Which should have been his career.

Let me mention once again the enforcement of wartime price control. You may wonder at the repeated use, in illustration, of the adventures in the courts of a government agency thirty years defunct. There are two reasons. One is that the new-fangled Office of Price Administration ran into ancient procedural problems. A modern protagonist in timeless situations serves well as illustration. The other is that the subject matter is not really dead; it is only hibernating. Modern free-enterprise economies cannot avoid inflation. Voluntary controls are contradictory and unfair—unfair because they penalize those who try to be good citizens, contradictory because our economic system depends on the profit motive. So, sooner or later our free-enterprise system will add to its other restrictions on free enterprise a pattern of price control.

Injunction was one of the tools that Congress gave the Office of Price Administration during the Second World War. The agency was trying to cope with immense and critical problems, trying to keep inflation from wrecking the American economy, the economy that was the strongest soldier in the war, stronger even than British gallantry and gift for espionage, than Russian strategy and numbers. Then the Supreme Court decided—war or no war, problems of enforcement notwithstanding—that equity is equity, and the kind of demonstration required of a private suitor who wanted the Chancellor to help him guard his property was required of a government locked in battle with Hitler. The hurdles a plaintiff must clear before the Chancellor would enjoin, say, enforcement of a contract alleged to have been unconscionably obtained must all be cleared by the Price Administrator before the Court would lend the aid of its decrees to his generous price controls.

In the particular case in which the decision came, the Price Administrator proved specific over-ceiling sales. The Supreme Court nevertheless held that since the defendant had alleged good-faith attempts to comply with the regulation, there must be a full trial to see if that was so, and if the trial court thought it was, there could not be injunction. The ruling put a heavy further burden on an overburdened agency. It was a difficult litigating chore to disprove intention to comply. The violator's heart might have been pure, even though he slipped up now and then. (These wartime businessmen always seemed to slip up, hardly ever down.)

The decision was remarkable. For one thing, it was unanimous. For another, the main opinion was written by the liberal, almost-always-progovernment William Douglas. There were two concurring opinions, one by Owen Roberts, a conservative who thought the majority should have gone even further in favor of the defendant, and one by Felix Frankfurter, who shied away from total agreement with what Douglas had to say, but agreed with his central point—that the Price Control Act, in Frankfurter's words, "does not change the historic conditions for the exercise by courts of equity of their power to issue injunctions . . ."

In fact, Congress, giving way to the administration's arguments that something effective was needed, had done exactly that—removed the "historic conditions." At least, the words of its statute surely seemed to. It said that if the Price Administrator showed that the defendant had violated a price regulation, "a permanent or temporary injunction, restraining order, or other order *shall* be granted without bond." I have italicized the word "shall"; in ordinary language, in this third-person context, the word means that something has got to be done. The principal guide to the meaning of a statute, the courts have told us over and over again, is the ordinary meaning of its words. So once the violation was proved—whether the violator had been acting in bad faith, good faith, or with a mind devoid of moral content—Congress was instructing the courts to issue an injunction. An injunction, after all, only tells the defendant not to do it again.

Other Acts of Congress, dealing with other fields of regulation and enacted before the war, had used quite different language. They used "may" instead of "shall" (the court might issue an order, but didn't have to) or provided that the order should be granted "on a proper showing" (leaving it to the court to decide what constituted a proper showing) or simply gave the court "jurisdiction to restrain violations" (implying that the court need not exercise the jurisdiction). The legislative history of the Price Control Act showed the Congress had considered discretionary provisions of that sort and rejected them.

The Supreme Court was impermeable to reason. It seized on the phrase "other order." In its context, the phrase appeared to be intended to make the remedy stronger, not weaker—to invoke equity's ancient power to fashion whatever decree might be most effective, not to declare its helplessness. Under the Supreme Court's labored interpretation, "other order" meant "no order."

How could such a good bench do such a bad job? The conservative four who had consistently opposed New Deal legislation were gone. There were some mediocrities on the bench—

both right and left—and Frankfurter was past his prime, but five of the Justices were outstanding lawyers: Rutledge, Jackson, Black, Douglas, and Chief Justice Harlan Stone. If, on the face of the statute and on its legislative history, the Act had appeared to give defendant an out, we would expect to see these five Justices use their legal ingenuity to make the statute stronger. Here the statúte's language and its history favored the government's position. To reach its bad result, the Court had to strain the other way. How come?

Once again we have to guess. One factor, it seems, was that the government allowed the issue to be tested in the wrong case. The defendant was the Hecht Company, owner of Washington's favorite department store. Not that the Justices had overdue charge accounts, but this is our friendly neighborhood dry-goods merchant, not some distant corporate monster. And though the Hecht Company had violated the law, its infractions were less serious than those of many others, while its efforts to comply were patently more serious. "Hard cases make bad law": this was a nearly perfect example of that much misunderstood aphorism. (It means a case where good law goes in one direction and one's sympathies in the other, so that the judge renders a decision that sets a bad precedent.)

Why did the OPA pick this case? Could it have been because it was handy? Did an overworked staff appreciate a defendant within walking distance (where one might, by the way, find time to do a little neglected shopping)? Not likely. Probably it was only the momentum of the administrative machinery: the thing just got started and nobody thought to stop it until too late. Whatever the reason, the Justices were presented a case that had poor color.

This widened the way for advocacy. Supreme Court decisions, as well as those of courts below, often turn on the imagination and the art of the lawyer for the one side or the other— less on the basis of oral argument than is generally believed, but more on the basis of the briefs than is generally believed. (This despite the impression one gains from the media that Supreme Court decisions are the product, entirely, of the facts, the precedents and the Justices' political views.) Charles Horsky, lawyer for the Hecht Company, was known for his skill. But the lawyers for the government were also very good, and they included Thomas Emerson, a truly first-rate legal mind.

More likely the decision simply manifested the ever present risk of low-grade judicial performance. The best batters now and

then strike out, the best pitchers hang a curve, and—more difficult to understand, but it seems to be nature's way—a whole
team, the best of teams, becomes a collection of clowns on a
particular day. Courts too, even the most august, and the most
deserving of our respect. And here our Supreme Court displayed
a special weakness: its winsome but naive infatuation with legal
history. Equity arose out of social need, and throughout its history responded to changes in social need. At the very least, it did
in theory, and if, as the Court decided, the idea of equity was
crucial, theory was all that counted. The need might be miscon-
ceived, as in the period of the labor injunction, but it was the
larger social view that shaped the rules of equity. The attention
the Chancellors had devoted to particular circumstances does
not negate the point: it simply reflected society's demand for a
source of particularized justice to ameliorate unheeding rules of
common law. The social need in the case before the Court was
for judicial aid against inflation.

Moreover, the ways of a court of equity were surely not
unalterable. Equity always had to yield to legislation. Nothing in
the rules or tendencies of Chancery could withstand an Act of
Parliament. Was an Act of Congress entitled to less respect? Not
unless there was conflict with the Constitution, and in this case
there was none. Congress could punish the violation as a crime;
obviously Congress could make it an occasion for injunction.
Some states had done away with Chancery altogether. Could not
the nation—especially in wartime—modify Chancery's operation?

Bad, bad scholarship, by the usually sound but often hasty
and sometimes muddled Douglas, and by the formerly brilliant
Frankfurter, and by the others who went along. We may feed our
wonder by observing that Frankfurter and Stone had been distinguished teachers of the law, Frankfurter the best-known lecturer
at Harvard, Stone Columbia's dean.

Finally, the American attitude toward the war did not have
the single-mindedness that present television documentaries
suggest. Roosevelt understood the war, and Churchill understood the war, but most Americans did not. Churchill had an
easier time rousing his people; the wolf was at their door. The
wolf was three thousand miles from Washington, and even farther from Chicago. Why go to war to save the Jews? Hitler was a
nasty man, of course, but, on the other side of the ledger, he was
out to get the Communists. There was, on the part of many Americans, more enthusiasm about fighting the other wolf, the slanty-

eyed sneaky one; Hearst had long since warned us of the Yellow Peril.

Communism contributed to this attitude in two ways. Anti-Communism had been one of the most potent forces in American politics in the decade past. Joe McCarthy and Richard Nixon did not invent it; others had been in the business earlier, from the end of the First World War. These politicians and others like them, and most of the press of the thirties, had been working, with great success, to persuade America that Communism was a synonym for any kind of economic legislation. A solid minority of the citizenry was sure it was, another minority knew better, and the balance was caught in stays, fluttering between the right-wing propaganda and Franklin D. Roosevelt's charm. Unless you happened to be the recipient of legislative benefit. Then you made distinctions. The farmers approved of price supports and other pro-farm measures; they regarded the rest of the New Deal program as the work of Communist devils. And the opposition to Roosevelt's domestic program carried over to "Roosevelt's war." *

There were, of course, some Communists working in government agencies. Their influence was even less than that of their brethren in that other focus of anti-Communist frenzy, Hollywood, where the Communists made their presence felt by occasionally sneaking in a line of pro-union dialog, or, in a Western, making an Indian a good guy. (Once we were in the war, with the Russians as allies, it was okay for films to be slightly pro-USSR, and some of them actually were.)

Roosevelt was bent on saving the American form of government from whatever was going to replace it if the economy got any more chaotic. People born afterward usually do not fully understand how deep the Depression was. Historians have lately been pointing out what was obvious to those who were not diverted by the contemporary clamor—that the New Deal was shoring up the capitalist system while its opponents were doing their best to sap it.

The opponents, as I have mentioned, were rarely total opponents; they favored those features of the New Deal that put money in their pockets. This created some antic alignments. For instance, the Rural Electrification Administration, which brought farmers the affordable electricity that the power companies denied them. I think REA had some Communists in it; at least, once in a while in its corridors I heard a voice proclaim

Then the press. Ah, the press! Conqueror of Richard Nixon. Guardian of our liberties. Savior, through the First Amendment, of the nation. That is, recently. These things can be said, with honest accolade, of the press of the 1970s. Also of the 1770s. But in between, the record of the press is spotty.

In the half-century leading up to World War II, "spotty" is too good a word for it. Most of the press fell into the hands of men who regarded it primarily as an instrument with which to gain wealth and exercise power. They twisted the news to promote the interests of the part of the population (including themselves) that was accustomed to running things. Not all the time, or all the press, but nearly all the press, and usually.

I am not—I suppose it has to be said—arguing for a weaker First Amendment. We must recognize, however, that freedom of the press is not a total delight. Leaving control of mass communication in the hands of those who have capital enough to operate it as a business is a good thing only in the sense that it is better than the gross alternative of government control. Something in between serves our freedom better, and something in between is what in fact we have.

It was not just Mr. Hearst, and Mr. Scripps and Mr. Howard, and Colonel McCormick and his brother-in-law Mr. Patterson. (The last two owned the newspapers that had the largest circulations of any in the nation: *Chicago Tribune* and *New York Daily News*.) It was nearly every owner of every small-town newspaper. They were anti-union, anti-leveling-of-income, anti-efforts-to-make-big-business-honest, anti-welfare. They presented all this to the people as anti-Communism. And—Lord Almighty—didn't they hate the Roosevelts and their damn New Deal.*

---

something like "Lenin said electrification must precede socialism." At the same time, one of the agency's chief sponsor-defenders in Congress was Representative Rankin, a thoroughgoing fascist. On most matters, Rankin was anti-Roosevelt, an ally of other congressmen who were fighting to protect the power companies and other corporations from the Securities and Exchange Commission and similar Communist schemes. But he represented a congressional district whose rural voters just loved the federal handout they were getting.

* *The fact that Roosevelt kept on winning has been cited for the proposition that the press cannot control the people. It goes along with the democratic faith that the people have good judg-*

□

So the Supreme Court—confronted with a hard case, obtuse on the relevant legal history, caught as always in political currents —decided that the "historical" attributes of equity must trammel the Price Administrator's suits for an injunction. This broad holding extended beyond the Hecht case. There were other traditions of Chancery that could blunt the force of the statutory injunction. One of them soon made its presence felt.

Most price ceilings were set according to the seller's prices on an earlier given date. This was the plan used for the initial broad control, until there might be time to work out specific

---

ment. I share the faith. That is, I believe the people are intelligent—"intelligent" being a relative word that in this context means that people have intelligence enough to govern themselves better than most tyrants will. (An occasional tyrant does a better job, but the odds are very much against it, and the gamble, considering what can be lost, is atrocious.) Intelligence, however, is not enough: good choices are required, and good choices depend on knowledge of the facts. The media, by definition, are the principal source of that knowledge. They can filter the facts, select the facts, twist them a bit, simply falsify —whether, as in the 1930s, they do it from their secure baronies ("overmighty subjects" once again) or, as in the early Nixon period, in fear and trembling of central power. (Spiro Agnew's real complaint was not that the press was unfair, but that it was not unfair enough—the other way, of course. Most of the press knew Nixon's real nature while it was still treating him with respect.) Lincoln concluded only that you can't fool all of the people all of the time. Given control of the media, you can fool a sufficient number an awful lot of the time. In the Roosevelt period, enough of the truth—the essential truth (he himself manipulated facts)—got through the filter. There were three reasons, in addition to his personality: radio was available, and he knew how to use it; he and his supporters were brighter than the opposition; truth, abstracting other factors, is always an advantage. Yet the press was powerful. Roosevelt continued to get elected, but if the press had been neutral, his majorities would have been as vast in 1940 and 1944 as in 1936, and if the press had been as biased in his favor as it was against him, there would have been no contest. That last would have been most dangerous of all.

ceilings appropriate to specific industries. All prices, with various qualifications and exceptions, were to be held to what they were on the chosen date, under the General Maximum Price Regulation, known with affection and revulsion (by its designers and those for whom it was designed, respectively) as "General Max." As things turned out, specific ceilings were so difficult to fix that for most businesses this tie to date remained the mode throughout. So record-keeping was crucial, not only to determine the prices the seller was now charging in the period of control, but also, from the seller's past, the height of the ceilings themselves.

Toward the end of the war, returned from undistinguished military service (I had been taught to fly an airplane, to no purpose whatsoever), I became head of an office in the OPA called the Special Litigation Branch. (I had had three years' experience at the bar; lawyers better qualified were filling higher posts, or making too much money fighting the government to consider joining it.) In the cases this branch handled, I found I had to deal with lower-court judges whom the Supreme Court had meanwhile smothered under the Chancellor's robes.

Injunction, with all its weaknesses, was a necessary supplement to the other enforcement tools. Treble-damage actions were slower, and consumed too many staff hours to be used against all violators. Criminal prosecutions had those same problems, plus the task of proving guilt beyond a reasonable doubt to jurors who often shared defendants' view that this was a time to make money. The OPA sought injunction not only where there was proof of over-ceiling sales, but also where sellers violated the record-keeping rules. And in the latter type of case, it asked for decrees that would not only order record-keeping but also enjoin price violations.

In the traditional suit for injunction, a decree will not be granted unless the specific thing complained of is already in existence, or plainly about to happen. The trustee is using the trust property for his own benefit, not for the beneficiary. The seller of real estate, under contract to sell, has announced he will not deliver the deed. The faithless employee is disclosing his employer's trade secrets. Neighbor is building a fence that rests on your property, not his. The court enjoins the diversion of trust assets, decrees specific performance of the real-estate transaction, restrains the blabbermouth employee, orders removal of the fence. Given the traditions of equity on which the Court insisted, how could we get an injunction against selling over ceiling, when there was no proof of over-ceiling sales? The fact that proper records had not been kept did not prove that defendant was charging too much. Would the judges issue a decree, enforceable by imprisonment for contempt, commanding the defendant to refrain from charging more than lawful prices, when there was no evidence that he had ever sold a single thing for more than its lawful price?

Of course, the judge would probably order the defendant to establish and maintain the required records. A New York federal court had done just that. But such a decree was not much help. The OPA would have to deploy its frail investigative staff a second time and, now that records were available, and assuming they were honestly prepared, perhaps find evidence of over-ceiling sales. This done, it could start another litigation to get another decree—a price injunction in addition to the record-keeping injunction. Only then would the stage be set for contempt proceedings on over-ceiling sales.

If, in contrast, the OPA could in a single trip to court win a broad injunction against all violation of the Act, simply on a showing of record-keeping violation, the instant threat of punishment for contempt might turn the profiteer into law-abider without additional expenditure of depleted enforcement energy.

Yet, as defendant's lawyers argued, equity traditionally did not enjoin except when it was proved that the conduct sought to be enjoined was happening or could confidently be expected to happen unless the court stepped in. Here we could make no claim of either: we simply couldn't say, although we might suspect. In the words of the appellate court:

> [Defendants contend] correctly, that there was no allegation made against them charging them with violation of price ceilings. Therefore, they say, they should not be enjoined for what nobody has ever claimed they did or threatened to do.

Just twelve months earlier, the Court of Appeals for the Second Circuit, which sits in New York, had held in favor of this contention. Now we were in the Third Circuit, only ninety miles away in Philadelphia, and the facts were nearly identical. I was given the case to argue. I felt I was being play-doctor, with a switch: we were opening in Philadelphia after a New York tryout had flopped—the first time since 1787 that New York had been out-of-town to Philly.

I thought that OPA in its prior cases had been too diffident. Some of our lawyers had let pass too easily the description of record-keeping delinquency as a "technical" violation. Failure to keep records, I argued, amounted to a disregard of the law more serious, not less, than over-ceiling sales. It was a larger kind of misconduct; over-ceiling sales were merely a subspecies. If the seller did not keep the necessary records, there could be no control at all. This total flouting of the law justified, indeed demanded, an injunction against any violation of the Act. Defendants like these were total outlaws. So far as wartime price control was concerned, I said, they might as well be conducting their business on Mars.

Judicial plagiarism of lawyers' ideas and words, I have mentioned, is a welcome sort of robbery, one the sensible victim prays for. It happened. The court's opinion said: "Whatever [the defendants'] state of mind may have been, the effect was as complete a disregard of the wartime control statute as if they were operating at the North Pole." This, of course, was long before our explorations into space, and the court may have felt the reference to Mars was *outré*, permissible perhaps for an advocate in the heat of argument, but a bit too wild for a court's opinion. Make it more moderate, less fanciful, more judicious and judicial. Let's just say North Pole.

The court granted the broad injunction. The defendants could be punished for contempt if they sold at prices over ceiling, though there was no proof of over-ceiling sales. Chancery, in this case at least, was back where it belonged, making special dispensation where plaintiff showed a need.

□

So equity, a body of remedies and rights, arose from an autocratic attempt to deal with the deficiencies of the existing system of private law. It is now an integral part of private law, and also a part of public law. In the latter role, it works both on behalf of government against the unlawful citizen and on behalf of the citizen against unlawful government.

13

Evidence

Most of us have experienced the courtroom trial in fiction—novels, films, the theater, television. Those who are not lawyers are often mystified by some of the things that happen. Mystified, but compliant: they accept what they see or read as the way the arcane thing must be. Much as the landlubber reading a story of the sea will accept the alien terminology, which, for all he knows, might be only the author's practical joke.

Lawyers are mystified, too, but for a different reason; the puzzle is why producers for our two mesmerizing screens, the big one and the small one, insist on doing things so wrong. It would seldom diminish the dramatic interest—more frequently enhance it—to do them close to right. (Lately there has been improvement, probably because some producers have discovered that paying for legal advice is only a drop in the budget.)

One aspect of these fictional trials that ought to set the viewer wondering apparently does not. It is those continual objections to testimony, especially the leaping lawyer hollering, "Irrelevant, incompetent, and immaterial!" If the witness has something to say that may possibly shed light, why is he not allowed to say it? The layman does not hesitate to criticize other aspects of the law. Yet he humbly takes these odd constraints as entitled to respect, even though his intellect, if put to work, would raise some serious doubts.

The rules the lawyer's cry invokes are known as the law of evidence. It has a visage that seems to come from an ancient time, when there was dread to make the unknowable known or utter the ineffable. But in fact it forms a young part of the law; it came into being a scant two centuries ago. Blackstone in his *Commentaries* gave little notice to the subject, and Edmund Burke, in the impeachment trial of Warren Hastings (first Governor General of British India) was able "to argue down the rules of evidence." But in the next one hundred and fifty years the subject grew enormous. The much used leading treatise squeezes into ten fat volumes.*

The textbooks tell us that these rules are a product of the jury system. The thesis was first advanced in the 1890s by a fine legal scholar, James Bradley Thayer. (Or first elaborated; it is usually hard to say, of any idea, who should get credit as author.) It was perpetuated in the treatise mentioned, written by another three-name Harvard law professor, John Henry Wigmore. And it is followed in the lesser handbooks on the subject. There is, no doubt, much truth in it. At common law, once the pleadings had produced an issue, everything was left to the jury's verdict, and the judges were naturally concerned that the jury have before it only good reliable proof. (Probably, in ruder terms, the judges distrusted the clods they thought the jurors to be.) But though the use of the jury had much to do with the creation of our evidence rules, it is not, I think, their only source. There are other major tributaries.

One is the adversary scheme itself. If we wish to learn the truth by leaving it to litigants to provide the court with facts— if we are to have our trial by combat, with evidence and argument instead of lance and shield—we must lay down some rules. Certain kinds of proof will be admissible, other kinds will not, and this will be by standards the litigants can know. These standards must be stated and available not only in the course of trial, but also before and after: before, so that contestants may prepare; after, so that the fairness or unfairness of the contest may be shown.

The inquisitory system has not this need. The magistrate-inquisitor can simply follow his nose. He can ask whatever questions he believes may help him ascertain the facts. No point in imposing rules upon himself. But if we are to have a match of litigants, not every question may be asked, not every document received. Instead of magistrate-inquisitor we have an umpire-judge. So the weapons must be specified and the field of combat

---

* *This book, as I have warned, is no compendium of law, and this chapter offers nothing like a thorough digest of the rules of evidence.*

marked. What constitutes appropriate evidence will be the product of several vectors, the jury not the least of them, but the very
fact we are playing a game demands the game have rules. Some
of the rules will relate to pleading, some to conduct at the trial,
some of them to proof. This holds true whether or not a jury is
involved.

Then there is the time-and-energy factor. The court has lots
of work to do: this is not the docket's only case. Even if it were,
it would have to stop some day. The court cannot sit and hear
everything each party fancies may work to his advantage. Jury or
no, contest or inquisition, there must be an end of things. Every
inquiry that depends on evidence (as distinguished, say, from
tea leaves) must impose restrictions. The inquirer will now and
then politely call a halt. Or not politely: Don't hand me that; it's
the kind of stuff that doesn't prove a thing. Or even testily: How
you do go on; think I've got all year? These interruptions,
roughly, are the rules of evidence.

Finally, there is the element I mentioned in trying to account for the grotesqueries of pleading—the machine valued for
itself, with its priest-mechanics who want to make their sacred
knowledge inaccessible to laity. The huge mass of precedent and
statute that constitutes the law of evidence would be less huge if
its votaries carved fewer graven images.*

There have been counterefforts recently. The Federal Rules
of Evidence (a younger brother of the Federal Rules of Civil
Procedure), and statutes in many states, have sought to rid this
branch of the law of its accumulation of recondite, wasteful, jus-
tice-denying fine points. The very character of what reformers
are attempting to excise—the intricacy, the impertinence, the
divorce from the world outside the courtroom—suggests the inadequacy of Thayer's scarcely-ever-questioned explanation. A
law of evidence that needs such surgery must come, at least in
part, not from concern that juries will be misled, but from a
way-to-play-the-game approach in which clever use of precedent
becomes a Holy Goal. Plus the more respectable objective of
doing things efficiently.

When the codes combined common law and equity in a single form of action, procedure was amalgamated not only at the

---

* One might think it not simply the location—once the site of an
establishment of the Knights Templars—that has produced the
names of two of the four governing societies of English legal
practice: Inner Temple and Middle Temple.

pleading stage but also at the trial. The new pleading was more equity than law, the new trial practice more law than equity, but both would draw on both. With this important difference: cases that would have been brought in courts of common law would still be tried by jury, while those that would have been brought in Chancery would be tried by judge alone. But though the established law of evidence would be used less rigorously in nonjury cases, it would permeate all litigation. As the rules of evidence emerged, the Chancellors had announced that they applied in equity. This sets another difficulty for the Thayer thesis, unless we assume the Chancellors were singularly obtuse. The assumption is unwarranted—some corrupt, some too slow, but hardly a one obtuse.

The most recent revisions of the law of evidence make no distinction between jury and nonjury cases. Each, of course, involves the adversary system; neither can afford a leisurely wandering among the facts; for each, reformers try to shake the clutch of priestcraft.

☐

Yet for two parts of the familiar three-part cry there really are no rules. Materiality and relevance are for practical purposes the same, and neither can be broken down into useful classes. With the indulgence of the reader, I repeat something from an earlier book:

> "Immaterial" adds nothing to "irrelevant." There is some fine conceptual distinction, but lawyers cannot seem to remember what it is. It makes a pleasant parlor game, or rather office game, to ask trial lawyers to cite an example of something that is material but not relevant, or relevant but not material. Added to the asserted lack of competence, they give us the standard incantation, which has its source in our deep fondness for trinities and the rhythms of magic.

When we search for a definition of materiality, we find the pronouncement that it excludes testimony that goes outside the issues fixed by the pleadings. But this is subsumed in the requirement of relevance: testimony addressed to points that are not in issue surely is irrelevant. And even the theoretical distinction disappears in the modern system of generalized notice pleading. So we are left with relevance and competence.

The concept of relevance, however, cannot give birth to rules. Since all creation is a causal web, every happening is related to every other. The question is: how closely? Exclusion for irrelevance involves a quantitative judgment. We must draw a line between related-closely-enough and related-too-remotely. The latter is legally unrelated, which is to say irrelevant.

In each instance an individual appraisal must be made. Does the evidence adduced confuse the issue? Is it beside the point? These are considerations that enter every interchange of information, every dialog, every argument—not just those in the courtroom. Experience may build appreciation of the requirements of trial efficiency. But even that familiarity will not produce sharp-edged principles easily applied. Whether particular testimony is no more than a distraction, whether it has some bearing on the thing to be decided, whether it has enough bearing to be worth the attention of judge or jury—the answers to such questions are a matter of "logic" or "common sense" or whatever else you may like to call it, a faculty exercised by all of us, on and off, every day, all day long. (Less in the night.) It is not a subject that professionals alone can know. It is not capable of division into classes that will give a lawyer guidance. It is special to the law only in this respect: the degree of relevance demanded is measured at one end against the litigating need to find things out and at the other against the need to get the litigation done.

Competence is different. Certain kinds of proof presented are more reliable than others. Here we encounter the don't-hand-me-that-stuff objection. Not that it doesn't prove a thing, but rather that, though it may, it does not have enough "probative force." So here we can define classes, and formulate some rules. The challenge to competence asserts either that the sort of statement offered falls outside the categories deemed sufficiently reliable or that the sort of witness who will present it does. ("Competent" is sometimes reserved for the kind of person allowed to be a witness, with "admissible" used to describe the kind of statement permitted, but "competent" is also used for both.)

Evidence is mostly oral or documentary. The former is testimony—words spoken in court by a witness sworn. The latter is writing that may be introduced—correspondence, contracts, memoranda. Sometimes physical objects are evidence—a sample of the goods delivered, the patented device, the alleged murder weapon, "the rent and bloody garments" of *Ashford versus Thornton*. These are called "real" evidence, not because they have more reality but in the sense of *res*, a thing. In recent years we have had the creatures of technology: photographs of the hole in the sidewalk in which plaintiff tripped and fell, a tape of a damning conversation, occasionally a film. And once in a while the judge or jury will leave the court and go see the place whose construction or topography is important to the issue; this bears the good plain name of "take a view." But most evidence consists of words—words spoken from the witness stand or written before the parties come to court.

There are also hybrids, product of pre-trial discovery: testimony given on deposition and transcribed, and written answers to written interrogatories. These can in proper circumstances be read into the record at the trial or, when there is no jury, simply handed to the judge. It is permitted, for example, when the deponent is an adverse party. Or when by the time of trial the witness is beyond the jurisdiction, that is, beyond the reach of a subpoena, and cannot or will not attend—sometimes not just outside the state, but in the Great Beyond-the-Jurisdiction (a circumstance not too infrequent, given the time that litigation takes). They can also be used to impeach a lying witness who is forgetful (a serious disability for a perjurer); his testimony at the trial can be contradicted by his deposition.

The law of evidence, then, is a matter of who may speak and what they may say, or, with documents, what may be read and for what purpose. It is usually stated in negative form—exclusionary rules, generalizations of what the courts will not listen to or read or look at. Certain people will not be heard: children under a certain age, for instance, adults certifiably deranged. Certain documents are unacceptable: a copy, for instance, when the original can be obtained (the "best evidence rule"). But most of the law of evidence has to do with the purpose for which a document not wholly unacceptable may be used, and—there is much more of this—what a witness who takes the stand will be allowed to say.

□

We must be careful to distinguish between "admissibility" and "weight." The fact that evidence will be heard does not mean it will convince. The trier of the facts—the juror, or the judge in a nonjury case—will assess it, compare it with conflicting evidence in the case, decide how well it fits his own ideas of what is plausible and what is not. Weight, like relevance, cannot take the form of rule. Rather, as its name implies, it requires judgment in each instance. This witness is allowed to speak on the point, but how believable is he? (The usual legal term is "credibility.") And what is the significance of his testimony? The same reckoning is made of documents. The piece of paper has probative value enough to be admitted, but how heavily does it press on the scales of verdict?

The rules of evidence, as I say, focus on exclusion. The twentieth-century trend has been to trim down the rules—to permit more testimony to be heard—and to rely instead on the ability of judge or juror to assign the evidence its proper weight.

☐

The basic exclusionary rule confines evidence to "fact." The law's present method of seeking truth is empirical. Ordinarily a witness may not give opinion or inference or deduction, or supposition however plausible. It is not coincidence that our rules of evidence began to take shape in the same century—the seventeenth—as did modern scientific method.

The subjunctive is not wanted; the indicative is the mood approved. Not what a person involved in the event would have done—no matter how naturally or probably—but what the witness witnessed. Trials are based on sensory perception. When? Where? Who was there? What happened then? What did you see or hear (or smell or taste or feel)? These, for the most part, are the only questions a witness may be asked. Inference and deduction are the work of judge and jury. The courts want our primary sensations (which are often enough askew) and not our cortical appraisals (strained through another distorting screen).*

It suits our prevailing epistemology, which puts such stress on fact. Yet I have had to say "ordinarily" and "for the most part" in the paragraphs above. There are two related reasons. One is in the nature of things; the other is explicit in the law. In a sense, a final sense, all "facts" are matters of opinion; the only difference is that what we commonly call opinion comes less directly from our eyes and ears than what we commonly call fact. But it is only opinion in its everyday sense that the rule excludes. Even here the law must make exception. Opinion in its everyday sense

---

* Here, as elsewhere in the law, threads that make a modern tapestry stretch far back. In an age when there was nothing like the modern trial and witnesses were used for quite another purpose, courts were demanding that they restrict their statements to what they had seen or heard: they must speak de visu et de auditu.

may be central to the dispute; the right result in certain cases will depend on estimate, assessment, analysis, or prediction which the judge and jury are ill equipped to make. The law's solution is to allow statements of opinion if they are given by people specially qualified as experts on the subject, qualified by study, training, or experience. Their statements are called "opinion evidence" or "expert testimony."

When a lawyer seeks to have such testimony taken, he puts the witness on the stand and asks him questions whose answers he hopes will demonstrate knowledge and experience. The judge then rules on whether the witness is sufficiently expert, and if he rules favorably the witness is allowed to give opinion. The process is called "qualifying the witness."

Actions for physical injury involve such testimony. The amount awarded is supposed to reflect the severity and permanence of the injury. So physicians take the witness stand and give their medical opinions. Sometimes there is a need that property be priced. The estate tax, for instance, is levied on the value of what is left to heirs. The amount of cash and bank deposits is a matter of fact. So too is the worth of stocks and bonds actively traded on exchanges. But when we come to real estate or jewelry or paintings, or a going business, value can only be opinion. Here again there are people the law accepts as experts —real-estate brokers, jewelers, art dealers, financial analysts— and their opinions are admissible. (The lively market in paintings since the end of World War II, and their use as a medium for investment, has almost moved them out of the opinion category and into that of stocks and bonds. This particular cultural renascence owes far more to the Internal Revenue Code and its golden infant, the capital gain, than it does to any heightening of our aesthetic sensibilities.)

In the literary-censorship cases of the 1960s, opinion evidence was crucial. The then recent *Roth* decision, a thumping defeat for libertarians (except in hazy retrospect), had held antiobscenity statutes constitutional, and set forth a definition of obscenity which, the Court said, merely summarized the existing law on the subject: a work was obscene if, considered according to its impact on the average person and in the light of contemporary community standards, its dominant appeal was to prurient interest. The only thing new in the definition was the substitution of "prurient" for the other similar adjectives that had theretofore been used.

Two years later came the trial of *Lady Chatterley,* in which the principal defense was that the Roth case did not, could not, mean what it seemed to mean. Defending the book and its publisher, I argued that the First Amendment protected any work that had discernible social value, no matter how lustful or prurient, no matter how offensive, no matter how violative of community standards; and that literary merit was a significant social value, there being little enough around.*

Assuming the argument would be accepted, the fact still had to be proved. To show the book in question had such merit, critics were called to testify. Not to testify it was not obscene; literary people had been used that way in the past, to my mind unjustifiably. The standard practice in earlier cases was to have the witnesses say their responses in reading the book were intellectual solely, without sexual arousal, and hence the book in question was not obscene. This was not only disingenuous; it failed to fit the new argument. For one thing, I was trying to get the courts to hold that sexual arousal—which until then had been the test; it was what "lewd" and the rest came down to—was irrelevant if the book had any literary value. For another, the question whether the book was or was not obscene was the final legal question, the responsibility of courts and not the critics; if my opponents and the trial judge missed this point, the higher courts, I felt, would not. Once value had been established, the conclusion that the book was not obscene would follow (if the argument succeeded), but that was for the courts, not the witnesses, to say. Our witnesses would be giving opinion only in

---

* *The argument now seems ancient. In 1959 it was brand-new and, to many judges, outrageous. The prevailing view was that well-written obscenity was the worst kind (because, those judges reasoned, it would be the most effective). The courts' acceptance of the new argument turned the thing around. "Social value" moved rapidly from new idea to accepted legal concept to conversation piece to cliché. Toward the end of the progression, an editor at a publishing house not known for the quality of its product told me of a negotiation with a literary agent. The agent was trying to get her to publish a manuscript the editor regarded as a trashy but salable sex novel. As part of the negotiation, the editor said the manuscript was junk. The agent protested; he argued that, really, it had social value, some actual literary merit. "Don't worry," said the editor, "we can work around it."*

the field in which they were expert—literature—and not in the field in which the judges were expert—law.

In the *Lady Chatterley* case, there were only two such witnesses, Alfred Kazin and Malcolm Cowley. Before asking their opinions of the book, I took them through their education, the posts they held, the highly regarded literary criticism they had published. The judge ruled they were qualified to give opinion evidence on the merit of the book.

The cross-examination of Cowley provided a rather merry illustration of what is expert testimony and what is not. One of the government lawyer's tactics was an attempt to embarrass and fluster the witness. He asked Cowley to direct his attention to a sexual passage in the book, one of Lawrence's most detailed and fervid. The lawyer gave him time to read it, and asked Cowley to say "whether it is a complete description; in other words, from the beginning to the end of it, there is no doubt left in the mind of the reader. . . ." Cowley seemed to have some difficulty with the question. The government lawyer pressed on:

Q. Would you agree that he probably omitted no detail in the description of the act . . . ?

It would not be well to have this line of questioning continue, and so I rose to call attention to the rules governing expert testimony. I made my objection:

MR. REMBAR: I don't know that Mr. Cowley is qualified in this area.

There was a large courtroom audience. When things had settled down, the government lawyer abandoned his maneuver and went on to other things.

Here again the pedigree is old. Well before the present form of trial emerged, courts recognized the worth of expertise. In a fourteenth-century case, the Justices summoned surgeons to say whether the victim's wound was a sufficient dismemberment to support a charge of mayhem, and in a fifteenth-century case they summoned scholars to tell them the exact meaning of a Latin word. There were as yet no witnesses in the modern sense; these were assistants to the court, something like the *amici curiae,* the friends of the court, whom we hear about today. But the idea was there, and later, when our evidence system was established, it supplied a basis for the use of expert witnesses to give opinion testimony.*

☐

Next in importance to the empirical stricture is the hearsay rule. In broad statement it is simple: a witness shall speak only of his own perceptions, not of someone else's, and a document is evidence only of itself, not of things outside itself.

Unless the words are themselves a relevant event—defendant's epithet in a slander suit, the promise in an action on an oral contract—a witness may not testify to someone else's words. (There are exceptions we will come to.) He may speak only of what he knows directly, not of what another person told him. Or two other persons, or three, or more, even though the witness says that all of them agree. Somebody must be in court, have immediate experience of the happening, and, exposed to cross-examination, be willing on oath to describe it. We have turned our backs on the sort of information that in the early days could make a man ill-famed and supply the basis for conviction of crime at Clarendon, and later for a jury verdict. "What everybody knows" is not evidence.

That last must carry a caveat. The caveat is not really an exception to the hearsay rule; it operates outside the testimony system. Certain things that everybody knows, or can easily ascertain, will be taken into account though there is no one on the witness stand. The device is called "judicial notice": the court will take notice of these things despite the fact there is no proof in the usual legal sense. Judicial notice has to do with information generally regarded as indisputable, or available in records whose accuracy is not questioned—that Canada lies north of Mexico, for instance, or that a certain debate took place in Congress on a certain day. (Or, in earlier centuries, that the earth is flat and there are witches who cast spells.)

The amicus *idea itself has undergone a change. Originally, the theory was that someone with no interest in the outcome of the litigation would submit information or legal comment helpful to the court. There are judicial statements to the effect that if the proffer came from a person with a partisan view, this was reason to refuse it; the* amicus *must be truly a friend of the court and not a friend of the cause. Today, however, almost all* amici *are people with an ax to grind, for their own reasons trying hard to influence the decision.*

It is the basis of a Lincoln story, his defense of William Armstrong, "popularly known as 'Duff' . . . a youth of bad habits." Duff was the son of Jack Armstrong. This Jack Armstrong was not the model for the All-American Boy of the same name, but another sort that populates our literature: the bested bully redeemed. He had been the arrogant local champion who forced young Abe to fight when Lincoln was a clerk in Offutt's country store. Abe outwrestled Jack, who in accordance with the script became Lincoln's staunch and loyal friend. (It works so often: Robin Hood and Little John, Dink Stover and Tough McCarthey, and the manly pairs in the films of the thirties and forties, and even Penrod and Sam.) Duff was a disappointing scion. One day he quarreled with a man named Metzker; they had a serious fight. That night Metzker was killed, and the grand jury indicted Duff for murder. Though Duff was represented by a lawyer of considerable local reputation in criminal matters, Duff's mother asked Lincoln to try the case. Lincoln, who had little experience in criminal law and almost no spare time—he was in the midst of the Douglas debates—felt friendship's obligation and took over the defense.

Another man, who had not been at the matinee but joined the evening brawl, had been convicted of manslaughter for his part in it. Lincoln's contention was that this other man had caused the death. The chief witness for the prosecution swore he saw Duff Armstrong hit Metzker "with a slungshot" (not a slingshot, but a weapon with a flexible handle and a heavy metal head, quite capable of causing death). When? asked Lincoln. About eleven o'clock at night, the witness said. How did you see it happen? By the moonlight, the witness answered. Lincoln then presented a published authority on the phases of the moon (by one account "a calendar," by another "an almanac"). It showed that on the fatal night the moon was only slightly past its first quarter, and went below the horizon seven minutes after midnight. At eleven o'clock this slender moon was very low in the sky. The witness could have had only a very dim view. Duff Armstrong was acquitted. No claim was made that the statement in the almanac (or calendar) was hearsay. It was, of course; but it is the kind of thing that comes under the head of judicial notice.*

The story is no Lincoln Legend. It is recounted in detail in a book published in 1906 by F. T. Hill, who had spoken both to the district attorney in the case and to an associate, then still living, of Armstrong's original lawyer. Later tellers of the tale

□

The reasons for the hearsay rule are plain enough. We know from daily life that what one hears from others is usually entitled to less credit than the testimony of one's own eyes. And cross-examination cannot perform its function if the witness is only quoting someone else; the person quoted is not in court to have his statement tested.

Secondhand information, as the rule assumes, is often unreliable. Often, but not always. And sometimes there is no other way to get the facts. So the rule excluding hearsay has its exceptions, numerous and large. The Wigmore treatise takes two hundred and fifty pages to expound the hearsay rule. It then takes nearly a thousand more to teach us the exceptions. We may note a few.

A statement that could only have hurt the one who uttered it is likely to be true; hence a "declaration against interest" may be repeated in court by anyone who heard it. A witness may testify to a "dying declaration"—the identification of the killer by the expiring victim; the theory seems to be that a man about to meet his Maker will be careful to speak the truth, or (a rationale that takes in atheists too) that he may as well tell the truth because he will not live to reap the benefit of lying.

Documents have no eyes, and except as they themselves are facts, they are hearsay necessarily. But again there are excep-

---

were less careful. For example, they confused "slungshot" with "slingshot." (If it had been the latter, Lincoln would have been given another defense: how could Armstrong have had the accuracy of David in that darkness?)

The case is interesting also as an illustration of a point borne in on me on more than one occasion: a first-rate lawyer, untutored in a specialty, will do a better job than an expert with less all-around ability. This is especially noticeable at trial: a lawyer with relatively little trial experience is often more effective than an experienced, even celebrated, "trial counsel." Leonard Boudin, for example, did an outstanding job in the trial of Dr. Spock, where the doctor and his various "co-conspirators" were represented by various lawyers. A good mind can overcome unfamiliarity with procedures and practices. Which in turn illustrates the proposition that the law is less occult than generally supposed.

tions. One is the "shopbook rule." Records regularly kept in the course of business are generally admissible to prove the truth of what they contain. Accurate records are important to the businessman, and routine reduces the risk of tampering. The name of the rule shows its nineteenth-century origin; it might now be better named the computer printout rule. The nineteenth was the century in which both the hearsay rule and its exceptions bloomed.

Some documents, however, are facts, and as such will be received. That is, the writing is accepted as evidence of its own existence and effect, not to prove the truth of other things. The document expressing an agreement that is the subject of a suit —the "contract"—is of course admissible. (That it indeed expresses the agreement is an inference which can be refuted, as we shall see some pages hence.) To illustrate the distinction: The particular document, admissible in the contract action, may happen to recite that one of the parties has bought some land from X. Now suppose another action, between that party and X over the ownership of the land. Here the recital is hearsay, and the document is not admissible (ordinarily); it is not the subject of the land-ownership action and would be offered to prove a transaction outside itself.

Again, a newspaper has a report of an altercation that ended in a broken jaw. Lacey, the story says, called Lucas a liar and a thief, following which, the account continues, Lucas threw a rather good left hook that landed on Lacey's jaw. Lucas sues the paper for libel. Not for what it said about the violence—Lucas is rather proud of his punch; he didn't know he had it—but for printing Lacey's epithets. (He sues the paper rather than Lacey because Lacey hasn't much money, and the repetition of someone's else's words can create liability under traditional libel law. Besides, Lacey may deny he said what he said.) The newspaper story is of course admissible; it is the subject matter of the case.

In a separate litigation, Lacey sues Lucas for assault and battery, and offers the newspaper to prove his claim. It plainly says that Lucas delivered the first and only punch, and the reporter is known for his journalistic integrity. But here it is not admissible; this is secondhand evidence of the blow alleged. Let Lacey himself, or the reporter, or someone else who was there, come to court and tell what happened, and be cross-examined. The mute piece of paper cannot answer questions. This is different from the libel suit, where the report is offered as evidence only of the fact that it exists.*

Here again the censorship cases afford an illustration. In addition to the testimony of the expert witnesses, I submitted reviews and essays dealing with the book. My opponents objected: the reviews and essays were pieces of paper only, purporting to reflect what someone said. Utter hearsay. Where was the cherished chance to cross-examine?

They were not far wrong in crying hearsay. If the documents were offered to establish the truth of the assertions they contained—that *Lady Chatterley* was good Lawrence, that *Tropic of Cancer* contained excellent writing, that *Fanny Hill* could proudly stand in the ranks of the early novel—they were hearsay sure enough. They were the carefree statements of people not present at the trial, safe from the scrutiny of the court, from the possibility of perjury. That is, my opponents were right if the reason for the admission of these documents was to prove the truth of the appraisals they contained.

I offered a different reason. Whether or not their contents were correct, the very fact that such essays and reviews existed was relevant. If a book had no importance, it would not receive such treatment in the press. Its publication might be reported as a curiosity, or as the occasion for prosecution, but it would not be the subject of serious comment in established literary journals. Their existence was what I wanted to prove, not the truth of the opinions they expressed. This was not hearsay; the documents spoke for what they were, not for what they said.

In each case the court accepted them. Their acceptance brought a bonus. Once evidence is admitted, the trier of the facts does not confine his gaze to certain aspects of it. The views expressed in those documents were hearsay in the law of evidence, but the possibility that cross-examination could induce the critic to abandon his appraisal of the book would seem to the judge remote. So the printed views, inadmissible as such, very

---

* *Documents do not ascend the witness stand themselves. They must be identified, and the basis for using them given. A human witness is shown the piece of paper, tells what it is, and by his answers to questions may establish its admissibility. Once received in evidence, the document speaks for itself, but in order to be received it must be spoken for. In the case supposed (unless these facts are conceded) there must be testimony about the newspaper and its publication.*

likely affected the judgment. The hearsay crashed the gate. It had no ticket of admission, but it got through on a "He's with me."

□

I speak of the judge. There were no juries in these cases. I sought to avoid them, and managed to. The present use of the jury has been the subject of a large literature. It is strongly condemned and defended. The jury, we have seen, helped form the character of our law; it also helped save England from the terrors of the inquisitorial system used elsewhere in the world. The question is whether it serves us well today.

Its defenders call it democratic; it is still, they say, *vox populi* if no longer *vox Dei*. Its detractors say it is only the voice of certain groups of people, chosen usually according to the lawyers' ideas of who will help them win, people vulnerable to advocates' tricks that have nothing to do with justice, people controlled by their biases—the all-white jury punishing an innocent black in the South before, say, 1950; the all-black jury freeing a guilty black in the urban centers of the North after 1960 (or a mostly black jury with two or three intimidated whites). The argument is overstated. The cynicism is fashionable. Like most fashions, it was stale by the time it became one. A significant number of jurors are interested in justice, and try hard to bring it about.

The detractors add that a jury trial takes much more time than a trial before a judge alone. The overloading of the courts is doubly bad: it contributes to our current lawlessness by crippling law enforcement, and it is grievously unjust to the individual, whether he is an accused who must sit and wait for trial or a civil litigant who must abandon a rightful claim because it takes too long to have it heard. And even if a jury trial could be promptly had, it is far more expensive, both to the litigants and to the state, than a trial without jury. Finally—it must be said—most juries are not good at what they are supposed to do. (This is no condemnation of democracy; neither are most legislatures, those other incarnations of "the people.")

But the jury helps the law in two important ways. One is that it mitigates corruption. Jurors have, of course, been known to take a bribe, but by and large there is worse corruption in the judiciary. Political payoffs, favors for a friend, are easier done than passing cash to a stranger. The crooked judge gives better money's worth unhampered by a jury.

The jury's other contribution to the law is elasticity. A jury can achieve justice in hard cases without distorting the law. A judge must give his reasons, and his reasons, when the particular case won't come out right under the governing rule, may produce an infelicitous precedent. The jury, on the other hand, gives no reasons. And while jurors are supposed to follow the instructions of the judge, who spells out the law for them, there is no telling whether in fact they do. Often they do not, sometimes for bad reason—prejudice, stupidity. But other times they have good reason—justice in a situation where the pertinent rule of law works poorly. The best broad principles, as I have said, must fail in certain cases. So the rule is nicely preserved in the judge's charge, while justice is nicely done in the jury's unheeding verdict. The jury gives the law some give.

The arguments for and against the jury both are powerful. I favor its continued use in criminal cases; it is a safeguard for the accused that ought not be abandoned even though it is expensive. I favor its abolition in civil cases; here it is not worth the cost.

Generally, the litigant has some choice. In civil cases, a jury will not be called unless one side or the other asks for it; in criminal cases the accused may waive a jury. (Whether the prosecution can insist upon a jury when the accused would rather not have one is a question whose answer varies from state to state; it can in the federal courts.) In civil cases, the choice is enlarged by the choice of the kind of complaint; equity, as we have seen, works without a jury, and sometimes a plaintiff can proceed either by a route that started in the courts of common law or by another that started in Chancery.

On freedom of the press, juries are sometimes good, more often bad. Peter Zenger was acquitted by a New York colonial jury, and concepts of freedom were thereby strengthened, in defiance of the judge's charge. But there the jury gave expression to prevailing local sentiment. Our Bill of Rights protects the individual against our majoritarian government. The First Amendment, particularly, is a shelter against prevailing sentiment. It protects talk and writing the majority would rather not hear or see. When most citizens approve of what is said or written, there is no need for the guarantee. When they disapprove, they tend to snub the guarantee, which is, after all, an abstraction. The freedom most people are interested in is only freedom for themselves. At the time of *Lady Chatterley* and Miller's *Tropics* and *Fanny Hill*, the majority favored suppression, a very large majority. Most people wanted to read the books, or, rather, read parts of them, but they also felt these things they liked should not be openly published.

□

I mentioned, as a reason for the hearsay rule, the lack of opportunity for cross-examination. Cross-examination is a large subject in itself, but not so large as the place it occupies in the public mind. Probably because of its dramatic interest, it is thought of as the major part of trial, and commonly in common speech all questioning of witnesses is called cross-examination. This is a solecism: the word "cross" means examination from the other side—the side other than the one that brought the witness to the stand. The questioning of one's own witness is simply "examination," or, if a distinction is to be made, "direct examination." Judges and lawyers often drop the word "examination" and refer elliptically to "direct" and "cross." *

The purpose of cross-examination is to weaken the testimony the witness has given, or, at best, negate it, or, less spectacular but highly useful, to do no more than clarify ambiguous responses. The cross-examiner seeks to show inadequacy of observation, confusion, bias, inconsistency, even contradiction. The dramatic interest, of course, arises mainly from the contest between the witness bent on maintaining his position and a lawyer bent on destroying it. The audience, at a real trial or a fictional one, loves the plangent clash and wants to see the witness bleed, or the lawyer bleed, or, even better, both. The contest can be good-humored, or at least courteous, but it is often drenched in hostility. The cross-examined witness is typically a cross examined witness.

The fight is fine; it suits the adversary system. But it should stay cool, and its function kept in mind. Petty triumph is not the goal. Both witnesses and lawyers are vulnerable to detrimental urges. They get angry, they get happy, they play to the audience, they give expression to impertinent emotion. The lawyer should do nothing whose aim is personal gratification. He must watch out especially when he begins to enjoy himself a lot.

Yet lawyers are tempted to continue cross-examination beyond the point where it serves their cause, and sometimes they

---

* *There are situations in which a lawyer is allowed, by ruling of the judge, to cross-examine his own witness—where the witness unexpectedly turns hostile, and the lawyer asserts surprise.*

ride it over the edge of defeat. A few years ago there was a trial in which a crucial question was whether certain employees had been discharged because of their activities on behalf of a union. If they had, the company would be required to reinstate them, with considerable back pay. The employer was a publisher of books and a magazine. The organizing union was the Amalgamated Meat Cutters. (An odd reaching out for jurisdiction, unless the magazine were *Hustler*.)

One of the discharged employees who had been active in the organizing drive was a brother of a friend of the company president. The president had sent a wire to his friend saying that the brother's conduct was "outrageous and disloyal." On cross-examination, the president testified, without elaboration, that the wire did not refer to the employee's union activities. The union lawyer, intelligent and hard-hitting, asked what was "outrageous and disloyal" about the employee's conduct. The implication of the question, of course, was that it could only have been something the employee did on the side of the union against the management's interest. The president did not meet the question, but instead spoke of his friendship with the employee's brother, and rambled on. He claimed that the employee's services were not valuable and that he had been in effect a guest of the company. The lawyer would not be diverted; he pressed for examples of misconduct. The president's replies became a shade more responsive but still quite vague. He said he felt the employee's behavior was destructive both to the company and to the employee himself. The lawyer pointed out that these replies were evasive: the witness had failed to give a single specific instance in support of his vague assertion.

At this moment, the cross-examiner had done his job. The clear impression was that the employee's so-called disloyalty must have been pro-union activity, because the president had given no other explanation. But for one reason or another—perhaps because his clients were murmuring happy approval, perhaps because the lawyer himself was enjoying the game so much —he simply couldn't stop. He demanded, scornfully, that the witness give him an instance, just one instance, of disloyal outrageous behavior.

So at last the witness did. The employee, he said, had been openly handling illegal drugs in the company offices. That could easily have created trouble for the company, an anti-establishment publisher in a sensitive public position. It was indeed behavior destructive to the company and to the employee himself, as the witness had said. It constituted ample reason for the firing, and had nothing to do with the union.

The cross-examination rather than the witness was defeated. The credibility of the company president was preserved. Some sympathy for the company side was gained. The president's friendship for the employee's brother had made him reluctant to reveal this bit of information. It had been forced out of him by the incisive, relentless cross-examiner, spurred on by his cheering clients.

The same point is made by a story from an earlier time, a story probably apocryphal, but there is some wisdom in the Apocrypha. In an action for assault and battery, plaintiff claimed defendant had bitten off the plaintiff's ear. Plaintiff's lawyer called a witness who testified in rather general terms that what was charged was true. Then the defendant's lawyer cross-examined. Taking the witness through the answers he had given on direct, the cross-examiner made it clear that there was no specific evidence in what had been related. And then he buttoned it up: "That's all very well," the lawyer said, "but did you actually *see* the defendant bite off the plaintiff's ear?" "No, sir," responded the honest witness, "I did not."

Here was the moment, as in the labor case, where the lawyer could have done nothing more brilliant than sit down. But here again, in full cry, he was unable to. "Then how can you possibly testify that the defendant bit off the plaintiff's ear?" "Because," the witness answered, "I saw him spit it out."

Two more notes on cross-examination—on "leading questions" and "answer yes or no." The question that puts words in the witness's mouth and leads him to the answer the lawyer wants is forbidden, generally, on direct, but allowed on cross. The theory is that the lawyer should not suggest to his own witness, who is presumably eager to cooperate, testimony the lawyer would like to have. On cross-examination, however, when the witness can be presumed to be antagonistic, the leading question makes it possible to confront him with a view of the facts, in the form of a question, inconsistent with his own. There may be illumination in the witness's attempt to reconcile the two versions, or explain away the seeming inconsistency, or in his acceptance or rejection of what the question leads to.

When a case is tried by a judge without a jury, the rules of evidence are looser. The judge will usually permit some leading questions on direct. They save time. It takes longer to go through a series of unslanted questions, and there may be little doubt as to what the answers will be. In one such case, I waited, quiet, while my opponent fed some leading questions to his client-witness, the plaintiff in the case. But after a time it seemed to me his questions became abstract, too leading, too far removed from the normal search for evidence, even under the loosest view of the rules. I got up and said I was finally moved to make an objection, or, better, a proposal: why didn't plaintiff's counsel state what he felt to be the version of the law and the facts most favorable to his client's claim, and then ask his client whether he agreed?

Finally, "Answer yes or no." There is the notion that the witness must. He need not. Very often, though, he ought to. Most questions can be answered simply, and the witness will only hurt himself by fencing with his questioner. He is not supposed to argue; that is his lawyer's function. For the sake of efficient trial procedure, the judge will cut him off, and from his own partisan point of view he should not go on talking when a yes or no will do. The cross-examiner may be delighted to have him give a larger answer than the question calls for. It could include a statement damaging to the side for which the witness speaks, or yield some useful information that the lawyer would otherwise not get, or open the door to a line of inquiry that the rules would otherwise foreclose.*

But sometimes a yes or no won't do. The situation is not that simple. Then the court will allow the witness to give a longer answer, which is neither yes nor no. It happens often.

Let's say that plaintiff, an author, complains that defendant, another author, started to collaborate with plaintiff but then went off and did a book on his own, using plaintiff's ideas. Defendant admits all except the use of plaintiff's ideas. Defendant is on the stand, being examined by plaintiff's lawyer:

Q. Did plaintiff prepare an outline of the book?
A. Not *the* book.
Q. All right. An outline of *a* book.
A. Yes.
Q. Did you see that outline?
A. Yes.

---

* *I long for the opportunity, when yes-or-no is appropriate and the witness is discourteous (having missed out on childhood lessons), to demand that he respond with a proper "Yes please" or "No thank you."*

Q. Did you use that outline in writing your book? [Pause.]

Q. Answer the question. Did you use that outline in writing your book?

A. Sort of. In a way.

Q. In a way? You mean you did.

A. No, I didn't. [Another pause.] Not really.

Q. Did you use the outline or not? Answer yes or no.

A. Uh.

Q. Well?

A. Yes and no.

Q. That's ridiculous. How could you have used it and not used it? [Satisfied smile to the jury.]

A. Well, I was short of paper one day, so I took the outline apart and used the backs of the pages to type on. Except for two pages that I used to shine my shoes with.

Q. Oh.

□

In the earliest days of our law there was no testimony in the sense in which we use the word. It would have been presumptuous; the facts were found by God. Once the issue was fixed, the judgment was pronounced by the outcome of the ordeal, or its variant the battle, or by the ritual recitations of compurgators —the ways in which the Lord His legal wonders did perform.

The concept of the witness had a place in law, but not in the sense of one whose testimony was weighed in court. Certain solemn transactions needed witnesses in order to take effect. These were witnesses invited to attend the event, not witnesses who, in court, thought back to something they had chanced to see. The event might be the sealing of a written instrument, or the granting of a charter, or the endowment of the bride at the church door. People present for the purpose could later swear the transaction had occurred. They had a function like that of the present-day notary before whom one's signature is acknowledged, or the people who write their names alongside the signatures of the parties to a contract, or those who attest the making of a will.

But not exactly. Modern witnesses to the execution of a document can be called, if needed, to testify at trial. These ancient witnesses had a different role. They came to court just to enable plaintiff to have his case considered. It was one of the various things it took to get an action started. The claim itself was not enough to start the wheels of justice turning. Something more was needed, such as the offer of one's body (or the body of one's champion) when battle was appropriate, the presentation of the "mainour" (the stolen goods) in a prosecution for theft, the display of the wounded limb (or its absence) in a case of mayhem. So here the plaintiff needed a train of witnesses to gain admission to the court. They were called *secta* in law Latin, a *suit* in law French—literally, those who followed plaintiff into court. They took no part in the trial itself, which, with a rather small exception, would be by compurgation, battle, or ordeal.

The small exception was this: Sometimes the plaintiff brought *secta* who were not pre-appointed witnesses. They came to court to swear that the story plaintiff told was true. They were not the oath-helpers who swore that the litigant was a truthful man, but people who swore they knew the facts. And sometimes the defendant brought *secta* of his own to swear in contradiction. The judges would then make a decision. At first the decision was not a final judgment, but only the usual decision of our primitive law—an allocation of the burden of proof: whether plaintiff or defendant would have to offer to fight, or face ordeal, or gather compurgators. Nor was the decision based on any questioning of the suitors or appraisal of their testimony. It was done by counting the suitors and weighing their importance in the community; the decision went in favor of the party with the greater number or the greater prestige of suitors.

Then, in the thirteenth century, we see some cases of this sort where the sacral modes are dispensed with, in favor of something less divine. The judges question the opposing suitors, and the final judgment seems to go off on which group offers statements more consistent or more detailed. The judges in these instances are judging credibility.

This questioning of suitors happens only now and then. Most of it takes place while jury trial is settling in and things are still confused. The most frequent example is the case of the "would-be widow"—not the lady who would her man were dead, necessarily, but one whose man might well be dead. She wants to take her dower in his lands. There are two possible reasons for the use of questioning in this situation. One is that widows are thought entitled to speedy justice. The other, more plausible, is that the jury can rarely have any knowledge of whether a man who has gone beyond the seas—to fight in France, for instance, or on Crusade—is alive or dead. As with other archaic procedures, this one lingers on until the nineteenth

century, though rarely used and later only for the would-be–
widow case.

It might have grown into a system of rational trial, though
one quite different from what we have now. And quite different
from its contemporary jury trial, altogether inconsistent with it.
(We have seen that consistency is not a feature of our legal history.) The Justices are not relying on the jurors' own information;
instead, they are trying to find out for themselves what happened, by asking people who offer testimony. It seems a prom-
ising beginning, but it would have come to a bad end. It is alien
to the adversary system—the Justices do the questioning—and
it does not need the jury.

It is quite literally alien. English scholars of the thirteenth
century have been studying Roman law. The Romans did not
depend on divination. They wanted the mundane facts, and they
got them by official interrogation. "Inquisition" was not at first
the hateful word it has become. It meant that the magistrate
inquired—a better way to learn the truth than by seeing which
champion could unhorse the other or whether burnt flesh would
fester. And better, too, than rendering a verdict based on ill-
repute.

It was in its application that the word took on its present
connotations. Innocent III prescribed *inquisitio* as a procedure
to root out heresy. The procedure to begin with was unfair: accusations were collected which the suspect did not hear. Later it
got much worse. This churchly version of seeking truth was gradually adopted by the temporal courts of the Continent.

Imposing reason on people who are not ready for it can have
harmful consequences. (A variation of that sentence can be applied to current history: change "reason" to "democracy.") Examining witnesses was much more rational than leaving things
to the rumor or the bias that might move a medieval jury. But for
those who ruled in medieval times this rational way of reaching
judgment was, unaided, often insufficient. It might even seem
beside the point. So the Continental courts, ecclesiastical and
temporal, found a supplement. Suppose you decided to get rid
of an opponent or a troublemaker or somebody you simply didn't
like, and there was no evidence against him. You got the testimony the inquisition required by torturing the defendant until
he confessed, or torturing other witnesses until they said whatever you wanted. Then, possessed of the necessary answers to
the questions, you had complied with the procedure. If the de-

fendant died in the process, the vexing problem was even sooner solved. This is what England, with its ruder legal notions, managed to escape. It used torture as a punishment, mostly under Good Queen Bess and other Tudors, but (with some exceptions which were departures from the common law) not as a method of deciding cases.

Inquisition in its original sense must have appealed to Bracton and other scholars. It offered something intellect could appreciate, instead of the mystical tests, and it could be a stronger, fairer test of the truth than the secondhand information on which a jury verdict might be based. Add to it the use of suitors. Let the judges question them, compare their answers, and arrive at a conclusion. The old "trial by witnesses"—by counting them—supplies a convenient form; let what we have retrieved through our Latin scholarship give the form new content. We will have a fine new wine in an old but useful bottle.

To the educated jurists of the 1200s, this would have had the heady aroma of progress. Hindsight tells us that in all likelihood the progress would have been toward evil. England's system of criminal prosecution in the centuries that followed, relatively fair, relatively humane, might have become the horror whose prime example is the Spanish Inquisition.

For a moment the questioning of witnesses was sometimes used, and then it disappeared. Why? Perhaps it went like this: Few Justices were the scholar Bracton was, and there were not many scholars of any kind, in or out of the law. Hardly any litigants would have knowledge of Roman law, and most of them viewed all innovation with alarm. They knew the use of suitors, but this was not that use. To make the questioning of suitors the trial itself would seem a perversion of old ways, not only strange but unbecoming. In contrast, the jury as an instrument of trial was by then familiar. As mentioned several chapters back, it had long been available as a purchased privilege for civil dispute, and under Henry II it had become a matter of right in certain forms of action. When ordeal for the trial of crime was abolished by the Lateran Council's 1215 decree, trial by jury was the substitute rushed in. Judicial interrogation of the suitors was tried in that same century. Possibly it found no foothold because the ground was already taken. It is as though English litigants in civil cases and English officials in trials of crime were saying to the coterie who admired Roman law, "Thank you very much, but we have been given a replacement for the older modes of trial, and we have grown fond of it."

The ground was taken, but only freshly taken. This is one of history's more evident might-have-beens. Except for Henry and his improvising, the contemporary interest in Roman law might have won the day. The classical scholarship had an important general effect: it helped direct the law into rational paths. But the fact that the new learning came a little after Henry, not before, meant that the form of trial in England would be quite different from the form of trial on the Continent. It is an exciting race of ideas. By a split second in history—half a century—one system beats another. Except for this narrow victory, we should not have had our celebrated jury trial.*

☐

At the start of the jury trial for crime, the mode is semi-sacral still: the verdict of the people of the vicinage is deemed divinely inspired. But they are people after all, and have people's liability to reason (approximately equal to their liability to unreason). They will tend to use the faculties they use in daily life. That is, most of the time they trust their senses—what have they seen, what have they heard? And use a quotidian habit of thought: if this has happened, then that must follow; how could this have happened but for that other thing?

Still, for several centuries, testimony is rare. In criminal cases, the jurors construct their verdict out of their own knowledge, knowledge they have brought to court. In civil cases, each of the lawyers, conveniently unsworn, gives his version of the facts. The jurors may mix their impression of these unsworn con-

---

* *The original* secta, *the suit of witnesses, has left a faint and comic trace. The requirement that plaintiff support his claim at the outset, whether by witnesses or otherwise, was gradually discarded. This would follow naturally when the trial itself became a matter of observable proof rather than invisible heavenly management. Suitors were no longer needed, and their use became a memory. Yet the formula remained, a vestigial appendix to the high etiquette of the pleading that developed. Into the nineteenth century, as late as 1852 in England, plaintiff's lawyers were still writing, at the end of their declarations, "And thereof he produces suit." By that time, most people—including, probably, most of the lawyers who wrote the words—were thinking of "suit" as having the meaning of "sue" and "lawsuit." Not infrequently, with the aid of ignorance, we synthesize sense from nonsense.*

tradictory statements with what they already know, or have heard, or can pick up on the outside even while the lawsuit pends.

The rule that later occupies most of the law of evidence, the hearsay rule, is a long time coming. When it comes it marks a dizzy turnaround. For a couple of hundred years, except when jurors happen to have personal knowledge of the event, hearsay is precisely what they go on. That this was not then thought remarkable is shown by the fact there was no word for it. "Hearsay" does not enter the language until the sixteenth century.

One who sought, or submitted to, the verdict of a jury, was said to "put himself upon the country." It was not poetic image. Early England was almost wholly rural. The man or his claim would be judged by those who inhabited the countryside around him. But England changed. More land came under cultivation or was used for pasture, towns multiplied in size and number, the society was less simple. In 1215, the jury could be counted on to know what went on in the neighborhood, or at least what people said went on. In 1415, this was less often so, in 1515 even less. The jurors still came from the vicinage—as they still ordinarily do—but by then the vicinage might be a populous place with a great deal going on. The jurors needed to be informed; the trial did little to inform them.

When Henry II made jury trial a regular procedure, and his seisin actions became the bulk of civil litigation, people in the neighborhood would remember who occupied the land at the date the writ referred to. When, half a century later, trial by jury was extended to the trial of crime, people in the neighborhood were likely to know a good deal about local violence. But in the next three centuries civil litigation went far beyond the writs of seisin; there were the many legal conflicts engendered by the nation's growing industry and trade, for which new forms of action were devised. And crimes were less likely to be visible events, dramatic in their interruption of daily life. The common knowledge of the vicinage became inadequate for many cases, probably for most.

Occasional attempts were made to adjust the old idea to new conditions, by choosing juries that had special information. Near the end of the thirteenth century, in a case that turned on how things were done in Florence, a jury was drawn from Florentine merchants resident in England. In another case, "A Jew had his trial [by a jury] of Jews; and they were sworn upon the five books of Moses, holding in their arms, and by the name of the God of Israel, who is merciful." (A curious display of sympathetic tolerance; a few years later Edward I expelled the Jews from England.) There were other such adaptations. Defendants accused of selling bad food went before a jury of fishmongers in one instance, a jury of cooks in another. The common law's erratic personality: these forays into sensible administration came when *peine forte et dure* was in high vogue.

Such patchwork could not cover all the many cases where jurors were no longer in the midst of things, acquainted with what went on. Evidence was needed, to supplement their meager personal knowledge, or to provide a basis for their verdict when they had no knowledge at all.

It came first in the form of documents. Here confusion lent its helping hand. We have noted the early cases in which a sealed instrument was presented to the court. If its authenticity was not challenged, it would be enforced according to its terms. If its authenticity was challenged, there would be trial in one of the sacral modes. Later, when the regular writs came into use, a document might be offered in support of the writ. In some forms of action, derived from the old sealed instrument procedure, the document was conclusive. In others, the courts began to allow the jury to consider the document, not for conclusive effect, but for the bearing it might have on the matter in dispute. The latter was the use of evidence in the modern sense. The fact that courts were long accustomed to receiving documents, though for a different purpose, must have aided this development. Either there was some fuzzy thinking or there was deliberate disregard of the distinction by forward-looking judges, or, most likely, there was a bit of each—confusion transitive and intransitive.

The seisin actions, which for a while were the main business of the courts, played a special part in the move from document-itself-the-ultimate-fact to document-as-evidence. A transfer of land required "livery of seisin." Transferor and transferee went on the land together, and the former handed something of it to the latter—a clod of earth, a growing twig. There would ordinarily also be a writing—a "deed" describing metes and bounds, the payment made or to be made, the conditions of the tenure. The livery, however, was the essence, and the deed alone was not considered proof of livery.

In the older legal practice, this would have been an appropriate occasion for the use of preappointed witnesses, requested by the parties to observe the happening on the land. But Henry's writs provided that seisin questions be determined by the jurors. (Perhaps wise buyers sent out invitations, offering refreshments, and hoped that if the purchase was later put in doubt, some of the guests might happen to be called as jurors.)

If the jurors said there had been a livery, the main question was disposed of. But how about the conditions? On this, the deed, though not conclusive, would seem at least an indication of what the parties had in mind. And so the document came to be accepted as evidence of the terms on which the livery was made. Not, as in the ancient action on the seal, an adamant expression of the whole transaction, but (once the main fact—transfer—had been settled by the jurors' prior knowledge) as an aid to determine price, description, and other corollary matters.

This distinction between the document as the fact itself and the document as evidence, plain enough in the thirteenth century, is often lost sight of today. Contracts govern much of our lives, and most people think of the typewritten paper, with parties' signatures appended, as "the contract." It is not. The contract is a set of disembodied rights and duties, the writing merely evidence of it. In most cases, it is good enough evidence so that the distinction makes no difference, but nonlawyers—and many lawyers—tend to accord the piece of paper a power it does not possess. It is open to a litigant to show that the document was not meant to have the effect it seems to have: it was never delivered (in a jurisdiction that still requires delivery as well as signature), or there was a mutual mistake, or it was induced by fraud, or it was just a joke, or for some other reason the parties never really intended to establish the relationship described in the physical instrument. Then the courts will either order it reformed to express the real intention of the parties or simply not enforce it; the "contract" is no contract.

☐

Oral testimony came later, and harder. Despite the ever more apparent need for it, and despite the analog of documents, the taking of testimony did not become the major part of trial until the end of the sixteenth century. Why did it take so long? One theory ascribes the lag to the efforts of courts and Parliament to guard against certain social evils of the age. The jury system was susceptible to interference and disruption—specifically, to "maintenance" and "conspiracy."

These are a legacy of feudalism. The central government does not have power enough, the local lords too much. There are kings of England during this time who are strong men, successful in ventures of their own, but none who are strong governors. Not one deserves respect as the ruler of the nation, though most histories accord them some. Between Henry II and Henry VII —three hundred years—being monarch means being first among the feudal gangsters, a shaky Boss of Bosses.

Hence juries are subject to intimidation. The local magnate has his private army, those who wear his livery. He comes to court and makes his presence felt. Or he sends hard hired hands. The threat is obvious. If someone offers to give testimony, for one side or the other, and he is recognized as the magnate's man, the jurors know which way to vote. Only the brave and honest juror will follow the facts and his conscience. So the king's Justices must regard the use of witnesses as a dubious aid to truthful verdicts.*

Another kind of corruption also shows its feudal antecedents. Litigation is a substitute for armed conflict; Henry II deliberately made it so. But the memory of what it replaced remains —everything from the freeholder's fracas to the magnate's civil war. The battlefield has changed, but the attitude carries over: all's fair in war and litigation. The assault is made by legal process, and every trick employed. To the extent that witnesses in the modern sense are used—and to some extent, unsystematically, they are used from the thirteenth century on—they are like as not misused. "The origination and prosecution of suits that were based upon purely invented facts and supported by . . . perjury seems to have ranked almost as a recognized profession." So again the Justices must doubt the value of testimony.

The king's Justices, most of them, sought to save the integrity of the royal courts. So did the better Parliaments. The remedies were harsh. "Conspiracy" and "maintenance" were made crimes. Conspiracy, literally, is "a breathing together": a group had plotted to pervert the judicial process toward some wrongful end. The prohibition was meant to guard the weak against the

---

* *"Livery" here, of course, has a far different meaning from the word used a few paragraphs ago, despite their single Old French root—"something given." Here it means the identification worn by the magnate's men, which could be anything from a whole uniform to a simple badge.*

strong and preserve the legal system. In recent years, it has sometimes gone the other way—a swollen charge that may infringe First Amendment guarantees, as in the trial of Dr. Spock. (I refer, of course, to the use of the charge to quench dissidence, not to the government's attempts to contend against industrial conspiracy.)

Maintenance meant instigating or supporting litigation, and it has that meaning today. But today it usually refers to a lawyer's promoting a lawsuit in order to get a fee ("ambulance chasing") or to a nonlawyer's promoting a lawsuit for compensation from the lawyer ("fee splitting"). In the times we speak of it was a much more serious thing.

In their efforts to save the integrity of the legal system, the Justices enlarged their definitions of conspiracy and maintenance to the point where acting as a witness was perilous. One who was asked what he knew of the matter—by the judge or the jurors—was warranted in answering. But one who offered his testimony unbidden, or at the bidding of a litigant, might be declared to be an intermeddler, and severely punished. The safest course was to stay away. The twentieth-century soldier's maxim applied perfectly: keep your mouth shut and never volunteer.*

□

---

* The words "maintenance," "champerty," and "barratry" were, and are, all used to describe the activities the courts and Parliament tried to stop. Champerty is a species of maintenance, the kind in which the outsider shares the award: etymologically, he gets a "part" of the "field." "Barratry" is a word of wider meaning. It comes from a double Old French source, and according to the Oxford English Dictionary it "intimately blends the two ideas" of deceit on the one hand and fighting on the other. It appears in the sixteenth-century Holinshed's Chronicles in its nonlegal sense: "Such barretors are used to take monie to beat any man, and againe would not sticke to take monie of him whom they had so beaten, to beat him that first hired them to beat the other." The word also refers to maritime mischief of various kinds—setting false signals on shore, for example, so as to cause shipwrecks whose cargo the villains will pillage (which, early in the nineteenth century, constituted the first commercial development of the Florida beaches.)

But the threat of punishment for conspiracy and maintenance can hardly have played so great a role as it has been assigned. Granted there was great corruption, these antidotes do not themselves explain so sparse a use of testimony. Keeping witnesses out of court would not prevent the local strongman from making his wishes known, nor stem the flood of unjust litigation. Jurors were not insulated; indeed, they were supposed to draw information from outside of court, even while the case was under way. The opportunities for pressure were ample whether or not a show of force was made by having witnesses appear.

Other reasons must be sought. The principal one, I suggest, was the medieval lack of confidence in humanity. In God we trust, not man. So strong was the reluctance to rely on human faculties that an early compilation of the laws of England declared, in the tone of a Bill of Rights, that no one should be convicted of a capital crime on the basis of human testimony. These are *Leges Henrici*, the Laws of Henry I—grandfather of Henry II—who gave his realm a better-than-average rule in the early 1100s.

A century later, when the jury system had been introduced, this distrust of man-made ways of seeking truth did not disappear. It was necessary to think of God's voice as present in the voice of the countryside. Moreover, from a more earthly point of view, England had something that was pretty good, and relatively very good. *De Laudibus Legum Angliae* ("In Praise of the Laws of England") was written in 1470 by Sir John Fortescue, an ex–Chief Justice of the Court of King's Bench. Ex, because Fortescue was a Lancastrian, and at the time the House of York was taking a turn on top. (Another instance of how those thrown out of office turn to writing books.) Fortescue was a booster, as the title of his book makes clear, and was bent on proving the English system better than that of other countries, France especially. He is persuasive. He says the juror-witnesses of England were far more reliable than the partisan witnesses on whose testimony the judgments of the Continental courts were based. The testimony of two men was enough to support a judgment in the courts of France. Fortescue is scornful: "Slender, indeed, in resource must he be thought, and of less industry, who out of all the men he knows cannot find two so void of conscience and truth as to be willing, for fear, favor or advantage, to go counter to the truth in anything . . ." In contrast, Fortescue continues, the English jury system means there will be twelve witnesses, chosen by a high public official, from among men of property in the neighborhood. They are not partisans but independent men, and in any case subject to challenge. If for some reason they ought not act, they will be replaced. "Here no one's cause or right fails by the death or failure of witnesses. No unknown witnesses are produced here, no paid persons, paupers, strangers, untrustworthy, or those whose condition or hostility is unknown . . ."

Not a bad critique; just better suited to an earlier time. Fortescue, though he was probably expressing sentiments still powerful, was not keeping pace with events. The jurors of England themselves supplied the facts, but by his time they must find them mostly in thinned-down rumors and in their appraisal of the versions given them by counsel. As the society grew less stark and simple, what was "known" had less validity, and the contentious statements of counsel were more difficult to value.

□

For whatever reason, the kind of courtroom trial so familiar to us, so much part of our culture, is something very recent. Its evolution is long and slow. There are the snags and sandbars, the eddies and cross-currents, that we see all down the river of the law. Almost from the beginning of the jury system, cases can be found where witnesses in the modern sense are used. One sort is that in which a question comes up about the conduct of the trial itself. This appears as early as the thirteenth century. Jurors, as Fortescue pointed out, were subject to challenge, on a ground that would of course be good objection now: they had a stake in the outcome. Or, a reason with an older ring, because of past misconduct they had "lost their law," were not "lawful men of the vicinage." If the challenge was disputed, the court might call for testimony. Another use of witnesses on the fairness of the trial had to do with confession. A report remains of an early case in which the accused claimed his confession was extorted, and the Justices sent for his jailer and fellow prisoners to tell the court what happened.

I have mentioned the lawyers' recitation of the facts. Pleadings in the early years were oral, and they might be lengthy. The later prohibition against "pleading evidence" did not exist, and each advocate, though he had no firsthand knowledge of the facts, told a story he felt would serve his client's interests. By the fourteenth century, they were bringing along people to swear that what the lawyer said was true—something close to modern testimony.

There was also the now-and-then appearance of witnesses who fit no special category—miscellaneous volunteers who for one reason or another could penetrate the net of maintenance and conspiracy. Here we see once more the casual, cursory track of the law. Perhaps some judges were less concerned about maintenance and conspiracy; perhaps some judges were less vigilant; perhaps it seemed in the circumstances that the testimony would undoubtedly be honest; perhaps some judges felt the old method simply was not working and the jury ought to have the facts. From the records that come down to us, the instances cannot be reconciled; there is no comprehensive pattern. What can be seen is the growing recognition that the jury in its original incarnation—that knowledgeable group—is no longer a reality.

Meanwhile, the triumph of the Tudors forced local strongmen to calm down. Private wars were ended. King-in-Parliament became thoroughgoing government. (Under Henry Tudor—each Henry Tudor—it was much more King than Parliament.) Just when the need for testimony in litigation was becoming obvious, the need for its discouragement receded. In the sixteenth century, reliance on witnesses in the modern sense rapidly increased. Finally, in the time of young Elizabeth, in 1562 and 1563, statutes were enacted that gave the courts of common law authority to summon witnesses at the instance of a litigant. (Chancery, as we have seen, already had its *sub poena*, a device the courts of common law adopted.) The statutes not only made it possible to bring the neutral or unwilling witness into court; they also protected him from prosecution. Testifying could hardly be a crime when the court demanded it.*

Even then, and for another hundred years and more, the jury kept its ancient essence; it was itself a body of witnesses, who need not rely on the testimony they were offered. They could draw on what they knew from other sources, or thought they

---

* *There is a reflection of this in present-day litigation. The expenditure of time apart, people are still reluctant to be witnesses, though now the reluctance is based not on fear of prosecution but on fear of making enemies. Often an individual or a corporation, asked to testify or produce documents, will ask that a subpoena be served. The aim is diplomatic—to avoid appearing to be a friend of the one side and thus an enemy of the other. The witness wants to be able to say he had no choice.*

knew. In the eighteenth century this was a dying concept, but it died slowly. What we regard as bedrock in our legal system, that evidence given in court is the sole legitimate basis of verdict and decision, is less than two centuries old. Not until 1816, precisely half a millennium after trial by jury became the dominant mode of trial, do we find an unequivocal statement from an English judge on what we today regard as given: that the juror "should enter the box altogether uninformed on the issue which he would have to decide." American courts had reached this stage only a few years earlier.

Two lessons may be learned from this. One is the danger of the genetic fallacy. If we looked only to the genesis of the jury, we should think its character the very opposite of what it is today. Jurors are now expected to come to court strangers to the case before them, with no taint of prior knowledge or opinion. In the beginning they were expected to base their verdicts on their own knowledge of the case, however fragile or ill-formed. The other lesson has to do with the nature of traditions. We think of them as building only gradually, in the measured march of centuries. In truth, most that we regard as immemorial were not long ago brand-new.*

□

Once the use of testimony becomes regular rather than occasional, questions naturally arise as to what is worth listening to

---

* The law of free expression provides two nice examples of Instant Tradition. The first criminal prosecution for publishing an obscene book occurred in 1727. There was no anti-obscenity statute on which to base the prosecution. However, the King's Attorney-General argued, and the court agreed, that publishing an obscene book was a crime at common law—that is, an act criminal from ancient times by custom and tradition. Since there had never before been such a prosecution, this particular tradition must have lain quiet and unnoticed for all those many centuries.

On the other side of the coin, there has been a huge expansion of First Amendment doctrine in the last fifty years. The present reach of the Amendment would have seemed remarkable not only to those who voted for the Bill of Rights, but also to almost all Americans before the First World War. Yet evangelical proponents of a bloated freedom preach an immemorial legal right.

—who will be a reliable witness and what limits there should be on what he has to say. So the law of evidence begins, though for quite a while it is hardly law but rather a bundle of varying decisions made at various trials, unreported, mostly unrelated (except as memory serves), with no established principles. Toward the end of the seventeenth century some general tests emerge, but a hundred years later the subject still is small. The nineteenth century, with cases now thoroughly reported, sees a powerful maturation of the rules of evidence. The mid-twentieth sees their relaxation—that is, in civil cases. The rules stay firm for the criminal defendant, indeed grow firmer. Here we have an interesting reversal. For a long time, the criminal defendant got less protection from the rules of evidence and procedure than the civil litigant; at present he gets more.

I have referred briefly to some of the rules of evidence. I intend, as I have said, no rounded treatment of the subject. It is the idea of legal evidence, rather than the rules which from time to time have governed it, that this chapter is concerned with. But a few more features may be noted.

The application of the rules will vary according to whether the case is tried by jury or by judge alone. In civil litigation, there is no jury if the issue is one which could have been heard only in Chancery before its shotgun wedding with the common law (a wedding that resulted in a cool propinquity rather than a selfless union). Nor, though it be a claim that comes from the courts of common law, if each party waives his right to jury. Once a law of evidence came into being, the Chancellors accepted it, and present codifications—the federal most prominently—make no distinction between jury and nonjury trials. Yet there is a difference. Judges put more trust in their own appraisal of the evidence. They feel that they, much better than the average juror, can sort out what is relevant and what is not, and which testimony speaks to reason rather than to bias. They are, in general, right. Hence very often in a civil nonjury case, when there is objection to the evidence offered, the judge will say, "I'll take it for what it's worth." (This is no paraphrase; it is exactly what they usually say.) Instead of stopping to consider the rules of evidence, the judge will let the testimony be given or the document introduced, and after the trial is over, when he is mulling his decision, assign the evidence its appropriate weight (or weightlessness). In criminal trials, no jury is required for offenses considered minor. "Minor" is defined by the sentence that may be imposed. Here too there is a difference between jury and nonjury trials, but the judge will be stricter on admissibility than in a civil case.

Appellate courts cooperate. The trial judge will not be reversed by reason of his having listened to inadmissible evidence if there is enough admissible evidence to support the decision he hands down (unless his opinion shows he relied on inadmissible evidence). The acceptance of that same evidence in a jury trial may produce reversal.

In earlier days (though probably not in the earliest) judges spoke freely to the jury. They commented on the evidence while it was being given, a kind of ongoing critical review. The judges said what they thought of the credibility of witnesses and the significance of their testimony. During the nineteenth century, in the United States, this practice was disapproved by the courts themselves, and in some states forbidden by statute. It lingers, however, in more or less subtle abuses of judicial power. Some judges will indicate to the jury—by facial expression, gesture, tone of voice—what they think of the witness. If and when the record of the trial becomes audiovisual instead of transcript, this abuse may bring more reversals on appeal.*

The basic formula is this: questions of law for the judge, questions of fact for the jury. The judge rules on procedural points that come up in the course of trial, and on the admissibility of evidence. Then, at the end, he gives the jury instructions as to the substantive law that governs the case; that is, he "charges the jury." When the theory works, the judgment is the neat result of pressing the facts as the jury finds them into the matrix of the law. This, like almost everything we have been speaking of, is subject to qualification, and the prevailing practice is to allow the judge, in making his charge, to comment, judiciously, on the evidence.

The older style probably left the jury less confused, if more vulnerable to the judge's wishes. The charge now tends to be lifeless, difficult to relate to what has transpired, often rather boring. The trial judge is afraid that if he departs from instructions approved in earlier appeals, he may encounter the embarrassment of reversal; so the jury gets a set of canned instructions, hard to listen to. On the other hand, this very fact makes for greater jury freedom; the judge has less influence on the verdict.

The change has not been as great in England, where judges still make remarks about the testimony as it is being given.

Which—back to the first hand again—may not be such a good idea, depending on your estimate of the quality of juries.

□

In the beginning, jury verdicts could not be judicially reversed or set aside. The remedy was "attaint." The rendering of a wrong verdict was made a crime. The jurors were prosecuted and tried by another jury, usually men of a higher station. The penalties were severe—prison, heavy fines, forfeiture of property, usually all three. This, in rough rude form, was our first appellate review.

It fitted the nature of the early jury. Unlike their modern counterparts, these jurors were not responding to evidence; they were supposed to be people who knew. A wrong appraisal of evidence is only a mistake. A wrong statement of what happened —sworn—is perjury. As time went on and it became unrealistic to assume that the jurors knew the facts, and as the use of witnesses became more frequent, attaint was seen to be unfair, and convictions for attaint with its harsh penalties were difficult to get. It gradually disappeared.

Our present appellate review has two main antecedents: the "writ of error" of the courts of common law, which at first was limited to points of procedure and later took on other points of law, and the "appeal" employed in Chancery, which was close to a thorough rehearing. Today's appeal is, in most instances, something between the two. Chancery gives us the word (which has no historical connection with the ancient criminal action), but the writ of error gives us most of the theory. The theory, in general, is that the upper court corrects only mistakes of law; finding the facts is the job of the court below.

There are three reasons why appellate review is thus limited. One lies in the original concept of the jury's function: total power on questions of fact. The verdict, like victory in trial by battle or proper recital in compurgation, was the sole determinant of facts. In later centuries, this was modified, but there remains in the law the idea that the jury should have great, if no longer absolute, power to decide the facts.*

The jury's power was limited at the trial level by devices that seem to have been developed during the sixteenth century and still exist in one form or another. They were the demurrer to the evidence, the motion in arrest of judgment, and the motion for judgment notwithstanding the verdict. The first asked the trial

The other reasons are more a matter of logic than of history, and apply to both jury and nonjury cases. The jury or the judge in a trial without a jury, "sees the demeanor of the witnesses" and hence is in a better position to appraise credibility. This, of course, does not apply to documents, and in some jurisdictions, if the findings are based on documentary evidence alone, the appellate court need not incline at all toward the trial court's view; it can read the impassive papers as readily as did the court below. Even as to oral testimony, this reason may disappear if technology is used in the way mentioned some paragraphs ago —if electronic recording, both audio and video, is substituted for, or becomes a supplement to, the present court stenographer and his transcript. (It is already being done in Alaska. Numb fingers, probably.)

Finally, the main responsibility of appellate courts, both by legislative direction and by their own tradition, is the husbandry of the law. The several lower courts in the jurisdiction may differ on how a statute should be interpreted or on how the common law should be applied to new situations; the appellate court will settle the point and try to keep the law clear and consistent throughout the jurisdiction. A poor appraisal of the facts by the trial court will seldom have any consequence beyond the particular case (though that is consequence enough to those concerned). Unless the trial court has gone wrong on a question of law, it is an expensive use of appellate time to reexamine the judgment. Litigating over and over again to make sure an individual dispute is properly resolved is not worth the social cost, as the history of Chancery shows us.

---

judge to rule that, with all the evidence in, and taken at its best, no claim that the law would recognize had been shown. The second asked the judge to rule, after verdict for the plaintiff, that plaintiff was not entitled to it. The third asked him to rule, after verdict for the defendant, that plaintiff nevertheless ought to have a verdict in his favor. Such rulings were not frequent; the inclination to leave things to the jury was strong (once the pleading stage was over) and it is strong today. And in one situation, which the next paragraphs bring us to, there is no interference with the jury's power. The older motions are now usually replaced by the motion for a directed verdict, which may be made by either side; the case will be taken from the jury and decided by the judge when he is persuaded that on the evidence adduced there is only one reasonable conclusion.

But whether or not the higher court is authorized to review the findings, in fact it often does. Appellate judges are generally inclined to want to see a controversy come out right. (Too much inclined, I would say. In their bumbling efforts, they mess up the law, and by that create injustice in other situations, including some that never get to court; the law has frequently been muddled by their shortsighted groping for justice.) Here the doctrinal excuse is that a verdict or decision "unsupported by evidence" or even "against the weight of the evidence" is legally erroneous. The theory, which has little logic to support it, is that it was an error of law for the trial judge to have let such a verdict stand.

We end with something in between. The main rule here is best stated as a tendency. There is a tendency to go along with the court below—jury or nonjury—on its findings of fact. Probably the most useful formulation is that the upper court accepts the findings of the trial court if they are within the range the evidence allows, even though the appellate judges feel that they themselves would have gone the other way.

So the hearing on appeal is not, as many think it is, a second chance to present one's case to another, higher court. It may lead to a second chance, in the court below, if the decision on appeal is a direction to hold a new trial. But the appellate court does not reexamine witnesses or receive additional evidence. To the extent the appellate court goes into the facts, it takes the evidence as it finds it in the record—twice removed from reality, once by the process of trial itself, removed again by the fact that what appellate judges see is not the trial itself but a paper-and-ink history of it. (Appellate courts may try to read between the lines, but they are not obliged to, and often the effort is presumptuous and results in a misreading.)

Atop this pyramid of appellate courts sits the Supreme Court, supreme in a very important but strictly limited realm. It can review decisions of the federal courts, but no decisions of the state courts except those that involve a federal statute or some provision of the federal Constitution. This means that the Supreme Court has nothing to do, can have nothing to do, with most of the law that governs the lives and fortunes of most of us. The law of contracts, the law of torts, the law of marriage and divorce, your job, your house, your compensation for injury, your punishment for the commission of crime or protection if you are innocent—these are all governed by state law mostly, in cases the Supreme Court rarely, very rarely, hears. Even where its jurisdiction exists, the Court exerts it in only a tiny fraction of the cases it is authorized to hear—those it considers most significant for the law at large. It intervenes to settle new or unsettled questions of constitutional law or federal statutory law, or because it wishes to change or confirm earlier decisions on these subjects. (In departing from its own precedents, the Court observes some limits, observed differently by the Court in different periods, and least of all by the "conservative" Burger bench.)*

So the Supreme Court is less interested in the particular facts than most appellate courts, and its style of review most closely approaches the old concept of writ of error. Yet even here there is, occasionally, departure. The Court will on occasion dig deep into the record for tiny nuggets of fact. This is called "review de novo," meaning that the Court will make its own findings of fact without deferring to the judgment of the trial court, ignoring the question whether the findings of the trial court are within the range of the reasonable. Here the Supreme Court will have no inhibition about disagreeing with the trial court on fact as well as law. Typically, this happens when the evidence may determine constitutional right, as on the "facts" affecting due process in the treatment of one accused or on the "fact" of value in an obscenity case. The Court will use the term "constitutional fact," an interesting ontological concept.†

---

* In the last two decades, Supreme Court decisions have come to play a much greater part in the lives of the mass of citizens. This is because of a greater awareness of the Bill of Rights, and an expansion of the meaning of its provisions. The most prominent examples are the integration cases and the First Amendment cases. The statements in the text above nevertheless remain valid, though to a lesser extent than if they had been made twenty-five years ago.

† We think of appeal to a second court after trial is over and judgment rendered as a fundamental right. Even to a third or fourth court: "I'll fight this case all the way to the United States Supreme Court." But appellate review is relatively recent in our law. In fact, only a minuscule fraction of all litigation reaches the Supreme Court, and very little gets to the highest courts of the various states. The Supreme Court's appellate jurisdiction is subject to regulation by Congress, and, as the Acts of Congress have long been construed, the Court hears only the cases it feels like hearing. Appeal to the intermediate federal courts,

□

In criminal trials the rules of evidence are not evenhanded. They are strictly enforced against the prosecution, and liberally interpreted when the defense presents its case. Criminal trials were never evenhanded; for most of our legal history they were heavy-handed the other way. What we tend to think of as the natural rights of the accused are in fact quite recent inventions. But one feature of the early jury trial, the unassailability of the verdict, eventually worked in defendant's favor. Later, as we have noted, the trial judge could in civil cases give judgment that went against the jury's verdict, and there was also some chance of upsetting the verdict on appeal. But while in criminal cases the judge can take the case away from the jury and order a dismissal, nothing can be done about an incorrect acquittal, even an incredible acquittal.

After attaint fell into disuse, judges might still, on their own, fine or imprison juries for rendering verdicts the judges felt were obviously wrong, but this did not happen often. Then came Star Chamber, a good deal of whose business was the punishment of juries. Star Chamber, however, disappeared in the upheavals of the seventeenth century, and at last the celebrated *Bushel's Case* put an end to all penalties for wrong verdicts, unless, of course, corruption could be shown. William Penn (the same) and William Meade had been charged with unlawful assembly. They were acquitted, and a furious royalist judge fined the jurors, Bushel among them, and put them all in jail. On habeas corpus, the jurors were released and the sentences annulled. Part of the reasoning of the Justices assembled was that a jury might have knowledge of which the judge was ignorant; the old concept of the juror-witness was still vigorous. But even when that concept died, the result of *Bushel's Case* survived as a rule of law: ac-

---

and appeal in the state judicial structures, is a privilege provided by statute or by state constitution, either of which can be changed. It is not, as most of us assume, something in the Bill of Rights. Due process gives us a day in court; it does not give us two. The states are free to have a single-level system, with everything concluded the first time round and no appeal whatever. (The United States Supreme Court could review such federal questions as might be involved, but most cases involve no federal questions.)

quittal in a criminal case is final. Convictions may be reversed, and so may a judgment for either side in civil litigation, but acquittals stand.

This meant, in practical effect, from 1670 on, that jurors, though convinced the facts were as the prosecution charged, could let defendant go if they liked him, or did not like the law on which his prosecution was based, or thought the circumstances justified the crime, or felt the law was not what the judge in his charge said it was, or ought not be. In the eighteenth century, this was stated doctrine, in America if not in England: juries in criminal cases could decide both fact and law.

At the time of the Revolution, and for some years after, it was widely believed in America that the law was often too rigid, encrusted with too many rules that had long since lost their reason. (This was no doubt true.) There was also strong sentiment that the common sense of the common man would serve the purpose better than any fixed rules of law. (This was not true, never has been, and, barring an extraordinary change in human nature, never will be.) The sentiment was probably the product of three conditions. One was philosophical—the tenets of the Enlightenment with its emphasis on Natural Law. The other two were special to America—resentment against the Crown-appointed judges, proconsuls of a distant monarchy, and the habits of self-reliance developed in a sparsely settled New World. The idea became explicit that the jurors were also judges, at least in criminal cases: they could decide the law as well as the facts, and treat each case as justice might demand. This persisted into the nineteenth century, and got reinforcement from the Jacksonian triumph. About the same time, however, with the nation growing and memories of foreign tyranny receding, the need for settled principles became apparent, and doctrine began to turn the other way. By the end of the nineteenth century, in the federal courts and in all but one or two states, it was accepted that the jury's function is to find the facts and then apply the law as the judge has laid it down. And today lawyers and judges think of this as though it has always been the way.*

But though now the rule is clear that juries must obey the

---

* The "one or two states" is meant literally. Under the Maryland constitution, juries are told that the judge's instructions are "advisory" only. Indiana has a similar constitutional provision, but a decision of its highest court seems to have interpreted it away.

judge's instructions, it does not follow that they do. In civil litigation, a jury's verdict that is shown to go against the law (or severely against the facts) can be overturned and a new trial ordered or judgment given for the other side. Nothing like that can happen in a criminal trial that ends in a verdict of not guilty. We have a firmly stated perfectly plain rule of law, quite unenforceable where acquittals are concerned. In fact though not in theory, the jurors are free to do as they please in favor of the accused.

But the jurors are not told that they can do as they please. The judge will not inform the jury of their freedom, nor allow counsel to. This may seem strange, and wrong. I agree it is strange, but I do not think it wrong.

It is an odd corner of the law. In a criminal case, the judge (as in a civil case) tells the jury what the law requires, but a verdict for defendant, no matter how unwarranted, cannot be corrected (as it can in a civil case). If the jurors happen to know that an acquittal is irreversible, they can thumb their noses at the judge. If they happen not to know, they may still, perhaps with some anxiety, contravene the judge's charge and release a guilty defendant, but they are less likely to. In some degree at least, they feel constrained to do as they are told.

Should things be left to such accidental knowledge? Should not the jury be informed that though the law, on the proven facts, requires a conviction, they may, if they wish, pay the law no heed? Is not defendant entitled to have the judge tell the jury the truth? "This is the law, and if you find the facts to be what the prosecution says they are, you really ought to convict. But if you decide you would rather not convict, nothing will be done about it. Here are my instructions; you may ignore them."

In 1970 some people who wished to make a statement against the war in Southeast Asia broke into Dow Chemical offices and vandalized them. (They chose Dow because it was the manufacturer of napalm, proceeding on the view, hardly questioned at the time, that this particular device for killing people was more heinous than the others.) At the trial, the defendants, honorably and bravely, did not deny the essential facts, or that what they had done was illegal. They argued instead that the war was wrong, that what they did was an appropriate protest, and that the jury should be instructed that whether or not there had been a violation of the criminal law, it could and should acquit.

There was no question that defendants broke the law. There

was no question either that they were nobly motivated. The prosecution had no problem of proof; the defendants brought reporters and photographers to the scene of the crime to record it. They engaged in the crime as a protest, and meant to use the trial to publicize their protest.

We heard a good deal about "political trials" during the Vietnam War, generally from opponents of the government policy who complained of being persecuted. The term was also applied to trials in which the defendants' main purpose was to make a political point. In its true sense, a trial can be called political where the crime alleged is an attack on the regime (the trial of Walter Raleigh, for example, or the Stalin purges) or where the object of the prosecution is not the crime it names but some ulterior political end (the Dreyfus case, as we know, and very probably, at least in part, the case of Sacco and Vanzetti). There was little of this in the Vietnam period. In the Dow Chemical case and others, the defendants loudly broke the law, and it would usually have been an abuse of criminal administration not to prosecute them. Almost all the trial courts abided by the requirements of due process, and appellate courts corrected them when they failed to, or when the prosecution came into conflict with the First Amendment—as in the Chicago Circus and the trial of Dr. Spock. A couple of trial judges behaved badly (and got reversed), but by and large our courts persisted in being courts of law. They generally gave defendants more leeway than strict rules would have allowed, while refusing to let their courtrooms become political broadcast stations. Altogether, a rather impressive display. Do not confuse the perfidy of the Executive with the dutiful performance of most of the Judiciary during a difficult time. Nobody went to prison for something he didn't do.

The defendants in the Dow case were found guilty. They appealed and had their convictions reversed.* The convictions

---

* *The ground on which the protestors' conviction was reversed presents a question interesting in itself, though it is not the question we are concerned with here. Defendants wanted to represent themselves. The trial judge wanted defendants to be represented by counsel because he felt the proceedings could be better controlled if he was dealing with lawyers rather than with the defendants themselves; he was concerned to prevent a repetition of the outrageous parody on which the team of Hoffman & Hoffman (Hoffman, J., and Hoffman, Abbie) had collaborated in the then recent Chicago conspiracy prosecution.*

were reversed because the defendants wanted to appear *pro se* —that is, to act as their own lawyers in the trial—and the trial court, while it granted them considerable latitude in speaking for themselves, insisted that they also have lawyers. Two of the three appellate judges ruled that forcing the defendants to have the assistance of counsel was reversible error. At the same time, two of the three (not the same two) ruled that the trial court correctly refused to give the instructions the defendants asked for.

Excellent judges were sitting. On the point we are concerned with, which is called "jury nullification"—the accepted clumsy term for the jury's freedom to ignore the judge's charge —they wrote strongly conflicting opinions. Judge Harold Leventhal's view prevailed, because Judge Adams joined with him.

Defendants cited both the Constitution and an Act of Congress granting a right to have counsel. (The crime took place in the District of Columbia, and so federal law applied.) Leventhal and Adams said that since the Act implicitly gave defendants the right to dispense with counsel, it was unnecessary to decide the Constitutional question. Bazelon said defendants had the right both under the Act and under the Constitution. Adams went on to say that though the right existed, it had been waived by the defendants' disruptive behavior at the trial, and since he agreed with Leventhal on jury nullification, he voted to affirm the conviction. The Act had been passed by the very first Congress, in 1789. It was signed by President Washington one day before Congress proposed the Sixth Amendment, the part of the Bill of Rights on which defendants based their Constitutional claim. The Sixth Amendment gives the accused in criminal prosecutions the unqualified right "to have the Assistance of Counsel for his defense." Does the Constitutional right to have a lawyer necessarily imply a Constitutional right to refuse to have one? The question at this date is open, though most earlier decisions assumed the answer was yes. The earlier cases were decided not long after the time when a felony defendant had no right to counsel at all, so it seemed plain he could dispense with counsel if he wanted to. At the present time, however, there are two contrary considerations: concern for an orderly court procedure in cases where defendants plan to be obstreperous, and concern that the particular defendant may not know what's good for him.

Chief Judge David Bazelon was the dissenter on this point.*

Both Leventhal and Bazelon reviewed the history. In England, though jury disobedience did not reach the level of explicit doctrine as it did in young America, people knew that at times juries did acquit even though acquittal was inconsistent with the law as given them by the judge. Such verdicts were especially prominent during the eighteenth and early nineteenth centuries, when Acts of Parliament imposed capital punishment for many crimes thought not grossly wicked even by the standards of the time. There is no record showing how many times, when defendant's guilt was proven beyond a doubt, juries brought in not-guilty verdicts because they could not bear to see him hang for a minor crime. But we know from various sources that the feeling existed, and had its effect on verdicts; all we do not know is the numbers.

In 1831 the jurors of London submitted a petition to Parliament protesting the overuse of capital punishment, saying, ". . . juries feel extremely reluctant to convict where the penal consequences of the offense excite a conscientious horror in their minds, lest the rigorous performance of their duty as jurors should make them accessory to judicial murder." A petition submitted a year earlier by the bankers of England carries the probative force of specific selfish interest. The bankers asked that capital punishment for forgery be abolished because it made conviction difficult "and thus endangers the property which it is intended to protect."

In America, the most familiar single instance of jury nullification is the Zenger case, where the jury acquitted in the teeth of instructions from the judge which, applied to the undisputed facts, clearly required conviction. In the early nineteenth century, there were acquittals that went against the plain instructions of the judge in prosecutions for seditious statements (the First Amendment was then but a child), and just before the Civil War in fugitive-slave prosecutions. In the present century, dur-

---

* *These parts of the opinions were not obiter dicta. Because of the ruling on the pro se aspect, the case was going back for a new trial (unless the government dropped the prosecution). The trial court would need and follow guidance on how to charge, and hence the decision on whether it should call attention to jury nullification constituted holding in the strictest sense.*

ing Prohibition, juries often let violators go. When the automobile became an instrument of death, juries were reluctant to return manslaughter verdicts against reckless drivers. Most jurors themselves were drivers, and the auto had become a totem if not indeed the principal god in our technological pantheon. (A god can use a human sacrifice now and then.) This led to statutes putting homicidal driving into a special category of crime, with lesser penalties than other negligent killing.

The acquittals in the sedition cases, the fugitive-slave cases, and the Prohibition cases proceed from the belief the particular law itself is wrong. Then there are cases where the jurors have no objection to the law but decide it has no application to the case before them: a bartender's serving a drink (post-Prohibition) to a World War II teenager who was in our Army or Navy and had the uniform to prove it; or a husband's striking his wife, when the jurors thought the damage slight and the whole thing "just a family quarrel." Then there are cases where the jurors subscribe to an "unwritten law" they believe ordains exceptions. Thus the tolerant view of retaliation by the victim of an assault, and the acquittals, more common in some parts of the country than in others, and by now archaic, where the outraged husband, in hot blood, murders the man he finds with his wife. Finally, and overlapping, there are what we may call empathy cases—acquittals of statutory rape (not forcible rape, but intercourse with one deemed too young according to statutes that vary widely—the age of twelve in one state, eighteen in another) where the defendant himself is young, or the complainant though young in years is not young in experience or appearance. There is empathy, too, in the motorcar manslaughter cases. If the jury feels that there but for the grace of God go I, it is apt to add its grace to God's.

All in all, a rather large list. So why not tell the jurors that they have this power, a lenity they may exercise? Leventhal had some difficulty in explaining why, if the power does exist, juries should not be told of its existence. Bazelon called for "candor." He was too courteous to say it bluntly, but his opinion implicitly makes the charge of hypocrisy. He went on to argue that a jury carefully instructed would do better than one left to guess at the dimensions of its power. Instruct the jury that it may disregard the law, he prescribed, but also that it should save this freedom for really deserving cases.

An appeal to candor is powerful, but it may obscure a deeper truth. In my view, Bazelon's eloquent arguments are not sound. They ignore the other, darker side. The jury's license to acquit against the law is matched, almost, by a license to convict. Discussions of jury nullification always speak in terms of acquittal, but juries can be unlawfully vicious as well as unlawfully lenient. The case may go to the jury under instructions that they should convict only if they find such and such to be the fact, but if they convict for another reason, the verdict will not be upset. Not so long ago, in cases too many to mention, the defendant was convicted, in reality, not of murder or rape, but of being black. Or of being a foreign radical (Sacco and Vanzetti). Or of being Jewish (Leo Frank in Georgia). If the testimony is conflicting, there is small chance of showing that the verdict was based on bias rather than on a fair appraisal of the evidence. And even if we look only at acquittals, the mercy that tempers justice is not always a lovely thing: the correlative of what has just been mentioned was the ready release of white men for crimes against black victims.

Describing the sort of charge he favored, Bazelon said it "would speak in terms of acquittal, not conviction . . ." But if candor is our criterion, then the jury should be told not only that it is free to acquit the guilty, but also that it can condemn the innocent with no large likelihood that its verdict will be reversed. Along with the good acquittal, this sort of candor would encourage the bad acquittal and the bad conviction.

Moreover, if the freedom-in-fact were turned into freedom-as-explicit-law, the juror would have an added burden which is neither fair to the citizen called upon to serve nor an aid to sensible law enforcement. Told about his great power, the juror would rightly hear the instruction as making it his responsibility, rather than the law's, that the guilty suffer punishment. And the burden can be more than psychological. Consider the juror who wishes to follow the law, though he knows that a verdict in accordance with law will be unpopular in his community: if unconfined authority to acquit or convict were explicitly his, he would have a greater storm to face.

There are counterparts outside the law. Consider the rearing of children. Not every transgression will be discovered. Parents know it and children know it. The perfectly behaved child is rare, and very likely ill. Some rules laid down by parents will normally be breached. This does not mean that parents should not lay down the rules. Nor that they should add qualifying footnotes that contemplate there will be breach and imply acceptance of it.

The understanding parent would be properly distressed if he thought the child complied in every instance. Yet the understanding parent does not say, "This is how I expect you to behave, but I also wish to point out that because I cannot know everything that happens, you have freedom to misbehave." The child will misbehave when the temptation is strong enough to overcome the inhibiting effect of the parental rule, but he should do it with keen knowledge that what he does is not approved. The sound child will feel a tug of restraint even as he breaks the rule. Things make more sense that way.

So they do for the jury. When for one reason or another the pull toward acquittal is strong enough, the jury will go against the law. But the sound jury does this with an awareness that it ordinarily ought not to. It will save these departures from the law for what it regards as extraordinary occasions. I am speaking of a conscientious jury. If the jury is biased or venal, it is obviously harmful for the judge to tell the jury that it has a permit to ignore everything he has just said to them.

We tend to make "hypocrisy" too broad a word, carrying its scornful connotations to regions where they are not condign. The problem of jury freedom may tell us something about the limits of candor, a quality now held in higher-than-ever esteem. The word, after all, comes from a word meaning whiteness. There are situations that call for color. The candor fad, of course, extends beyond the law. In the current literary world, for instance, published itching and scratching is often mistaken for art.

□

Earlier in this chapter, describing kinds of documentary evidence, I mentioned the affidavit. It is a written statement made on oath. The word is direct from Latin: it means "he has made an oath." The one who makes it is called "affiant" (the accent on the second syllable). In an older use, the word included a deposition; an affidavit usually begins by reciting that the affiant "deposes and says," and it may call him "the deponent." But in its current use an affidavit is quite different from a deposition. A deposition is the oral testimony of a witness, a witness subject to cross-examination, given outside the trial, written down and transcribed. An affidavit is a prepared statement, a composition;

there is no opportunity for cross-examination; the countervailing weapon is an affidavit from the other side.

Affidavits had their origin in Chancery, where all evidence presented to the Chancellor was for a long time written. In the modern combined procedure, with all its pre-trial motions, affidavits have come to play a major role. Civil litigation, as I have mentioned, rarely reaches trial. It can end on a question of law that emerges from the pleadings, or on motions for summary judgment, or motions for some interim order such as temporary injunction. Excepting the first—where the pleadings themselves cast up the legal issue that disposes of the case—these pre-trial contests involve the use of affidavits. From them the court determines the facts, and, having heard the arguments of law, reaches its decision. Other, less dispositive motions are also based on affidavits. And the so-called "quasi-judicial" proceedings of our administrative agencies ("quite" would be more accurate than "quasi") make extensive use of affidavits.

No one can be compelled to give an affidavit; there is nothing equivalent to the subpoena that produces oral testimony. Hence they come from parties to the litigation, or outsiders willing to contribute to the case. The usual practice is for the lawyer to ghost-write the affidavit. He gets the facts from the affiant and prepares a first-person narrative. The affiant may, of course, require changes before he swears and signs; the lawyer may have misunderstood something the affiant said, or may have gone further toward the point the lawyer would like to make than the affiant wants to go. But the writing is almost always the lawyer's. Hence most affidavits are constructed of a stilted jargon that could not be anyone's natural telling of the story. There is nothing improper in this practice; it is recognized that the lawyer does the drafting. It is just poor lawyering; the closer the affidavit to the affiant's own style of speech, the better impression of truth it gives.

But occasionally an affiant will participate in the drafting. The affidavit then becomes collaboration, not merely an as-told-to. This produced an atypical affidavit in a situation typical of the early 1950s.

Isaac Barnett Mailer, an accountant with the War Department whose job was under Civil Service, one day got a notice from the Civil Service Commission. It told him that there was "reasonable doubt" as to his loyalty. Such doubt required he be fired.

The reasonable doubt, the notice said, was created by the

fact that Mr. Mailer had a "continuing close association" with a person who, according to "reliable information," was a "concealed Communist." The person with whom Mr. Mailer was accused of associating was his son, Norman Mailer. I. B. Mailer was told that he could file an answer to the charge. He could also if he wished (and, the notice seemed to say, if he dared) obtain a hearing before a Loyalty Board. This was at the deepest point in the McCarthy trough. Such hearings rarely cleared the accused employee. Representing Mr. Mailer, I submitted his answers to the Commission's questions, together with affidavits from several respectable people attesting to his character and reputation. But such affidavits do not impress inquisitors. The only significant affidavit would be that of the person with whom Mr. Mailer was said to associate, and from whom his guilt derived.

Norman Mailer is not only the writer that he is, but also an excellent untrained lawyer. He would be among the very best if he turned pro. It seemed a good idea to collaborate. The affiant and the lawyer each wrote paragraphs, and each rewrote parts of what was written by the other, and argued a bit—not much—about the final version. Most of the affidavit, with minor editing, follows:

State of New York   )
              : ss.:
County of New York)

                        Norman Mailer, being duly sworn, deposes and says:

    Since there is no direct charge against my father other than he is my father, it seems to me that I must offer a statement about myself and my relationship with my father before he can clear himself.

    I understand that the standard to be applied is whether "there is a reasonable doubt as to the loyalty of the person involved." This extraordinary inversion of the normal standards of justice, coupled with the weight which is attached to the parental–filial association, requires that the government employee take extraordinary measures in his defense. Among such measures is his establishment not merely of his own innocence, but also—unless he is that psychological and social abnormality, the man who has completely dissociated himself from his family—the innocence of members of his family. The result is that persons who, in the language of lawyers, are "strangers to the proceeding," must come forward with a statement of their private views. This, it seems to me, can be a hardship and a serious invasion of personal liberties. In my own case it happens it is not. My political views have already been given repeated public expression.

It seems to me that any "defense" must be separated into two compartments: (1) have I ever influenced my father —directed, cozened, implored or otherwise sought to control him by our "continuing close association"? (2) does the "reliable information" that I. B. Mailer's son is a "concealed Communist" possess any reliability or information? . . .

My father is a man of conservative stable temperament, and though we have many of the relations proper to a father and a son, I think I may say with assurance that he has never had any political influence upon me nor I upon him, nor for that matter have I ever made any attempt to so influence him. He is not in the habit of ever speaking about the details of his work, nor have I ever had any interest in asking him about his work. Our political ideas are in great disagreement, and I should like to submit to the members of the Loyalty Board the notion that disagreement between fathers and sons is a human phenomenon which has been long remarked. To put it another way, may I be so forward as to ask any member of the Loyalty Board who has children to consider whether his children possess sufficient influence and control over him to be able to lead him into activities or attitudes unnatural or repugnant to his own outlook or temperament?

Now to the charge that I am a "concealed Communist." . . . Nothing could give me more pleasure than to be able to confront my accuser or accusers. I suspect, however, it is not nearly so simple to clear oneself of the charge that one is a concealed Communist. The questionnaire submitted to my father contains the following sentence: "For your information, a concealed Communist is one who does not want himself known as a Communist and *who would deny membership in the Communist Party*." (My underlining.) Gentlemen, I must ask you . . . to consider how difficult it is for any individual once accused in this manner to avoid being judged automatically as one kind of Communist or another. For notice: if the accused admits being a Communist, he is a Communist; if he denies being a Communist, his denial is irrelevant to the issue, since the heart of the accusation is that the accused is in the habit of making such denials.

This is not to say that the Loyalty Board should have no

interest in Communists who deny that they are Communists. Obviously, in the discharge of their governmental function, the Board is bound to consider the concealed Communist as dangerous as, if not more dangerous than, the open Communist. But the Loyalty Board must appraise the charge that an individual is a concealed Communist at its true value. This is not merely to save the rights of the individual, but also to prevent the process which the Board administers from destroying itself. If the Board were to consider such an accusation to be anything more than an accusation—that is, if the Board were to regard the charge itself as a basis for "reasonable doubt"—the accused would be denied his defense in advance. Indeed, . . . the loyalty process would lose all meaning as an investigative procedure; once the accusation is made there would be nothing left to investigate. Consequently, I must assume that the charge itself is to be given absolutely no weight as evidence, and that only if there is substantial evidence apart from the charge should there be any reasonable doubt in this matter. It is such evidence, and not the charge alone, which the accused should be called upon to deal with. If anything has been offered to the Board which purports to be such evidence, it is false, and I should be told what it is and given an opportunity to disprove it.

For it is a very serious matter to be called a "concealed Communist," more serious I should judge than simply to be called a "Communist." A concealed Communist is in effect a spy. Thus by the doubtful virtue of an accusation which feeds upon itself, there is imposed upon me the burden of establishing that I am not guilty of an offense which carries the gravest consequences.

The irony is that I am one of the few people (apart from that rare creature, the candid professional politician) whose political beliefs have been made entirely a matter of record. . . . The result of my writings so far as I have been able to determine them is that I have influenced exactly no one. Nonetheless I have been open to misinterpretation. The Communists for some years now have been calling me a Trotskyist; the Trotskyists call me a "so-called splinter Socialist"; the splinter socialists call me an anarchist; the anarchists call me a capitalist; and that representation of capitalism which to whatever extent is embodied in my accuser or accusers sees fit to call me a Communist. . . .

I would ask the Loyalty Board to consider whether, in the light of my own written record, it is conceivable that I should be a concealed Communist. Let us suppose that a young writer publishes a novel which makes him a figure of some importance in the literary world, and that the Communists thereupon woo and win him. Presumably he could serve them in one of three ways: he could declare himself openly to be a Communist, and thereby lend his limited prestige to the Communist Party; or he could secretly commit himself to the Communist Party and, more or less subtly, slant his writings so as to make Communism appear attractive; or he could secretly commit himself to the Communist Party, and seek to achieve a literary or journalistic status where he could exercise some influence on editorial policy and public opinion. But is there any sanity in the assumption that the Communist Party would have him do none of the three? Can it be said rationally that he would openly espouse political ideas which could only serve to persuade his readers that Communism was bad, and which at the same time, by its dissident and unpopular nature, would destroy any chance of his being accepted in the policy-making circles of influential publications? Is it conceivable that the Communists should want to accept his public damning while he disables himself from rendering them any private service?

So, gentlemen, the situation as I see it is exactly this: is my father, who has no political agreement or sympathy with me at all, to be deprived of his means of making a livelihood within the government (and the government is to be deprived of the services of an experienced and competent professional) because his son is—not, as the charge claims, a "concealed Communist"—but admittedly and openly a dissident from the conventional and generally accepted attitudes about America and its position in the world today? . . .

If further evidence of my parent's patriotic allegiance to this country is necessary, I would suggest that some secret recording device be installed in my parents' home. On those occasions when I continue my "close association" with my parents, such as those evenings when I visit for dinner, the following conversation could probably be heard between my father and myself:

THE TIME: (one of those rare times when politics is discussed.)

NORMAN MAILER: I think the whole thing in Korea is hopeless. It's a pilot-light war. Ignorant Americans and ignorant Orientals are just butchering each other.

I. B. MAILER: I don't know where an intelligent boy like you picks up such idiotic rubbish.

FAN MAILER (the mother): Don't call him an idiot.

NORMAN MAILER: Well, he's not so smart himself.
I. B. MAILER: I never talked to my father the way you talk to me.

Sworn to before me
this 7th day of
January, 1953.

[signed] Norman Mailer
Norman Mailer

[signature and seal
of the notary public]

    With a degree of arrogance that might have been risky but I felt was appropriate, we showed little gratitude for the offer of a hearing that was so kindly made. We took the position that I. B. Mailer ought to be cleared on the affidavits alone, and asked for a hearing only in the event that the Commission should fail to see that this was so. This, of course, was tactic, an advocate's bravado. But—an extraordinary event in those morbid times—the Commission cleared I. B. Mailer without even holding a hearing.

14

The Rights
of the Accused

We have tracked the civil lawsuit to its present place. In the beginning, civil justice and criminal justice were not so separate as they are today, and the law was more concerned with keeping order than with what we now call civil claims. Hence the first few chapters of this book dealt principally with trial of crime. We may end where we began, at the methods society uses to determine guilt or innocence. Not all of criminal procedure, not nearly. Rather, some features of it, certain safeguards our law extends to those accused of crime.

We are proud—rightly—that our system affords these rights; and we regard them—wrongly—as naturally part of that system, ancient and honored axioms. In fact, except for jury trial and the indictment that precedes it, they are quite recent, and hardly axiomatic. Other legal systems do without them, as did ours not long ago. Taken together, they put a kindly thumb on the scales of justice, on the side of the accused. But the scales not long ago were tipped the other way.

Take, for instance, defendant's right to counsel. Court decisions of the last fifty years have step by step come to this conclusion: the state must provide a lawyer to any defendant, too poor to hire one, who risks a prison sentence.

The first step was taken in the case of the Scottsboro Boys, seven young blacks accused of raping two white girls. It was 1931, Year II of the Great Depression, when a great many people wandered around the country, looking for work or just looking. A fare-free mode of transportation was the freight train. In a gondola car of a slow freight chugging through Alabama were three insufficiently segregated groups: two white females, nine white males, and a larger number of black males. A fight, in the Supreme Court's careful neutral words, "took place." It ended with all the white males but one thrown off the train. How the fight started and what happened afterward were matters of dispute.

The ejected sent word ahead. A sheriff's posse stopped the train, seized nine of the blacks, and took them to Scottsboro, the county seat. There was a large crowd there to meet them. In the words of the Court again: "It does not sufficiently appear that the defendants were seriously threatened with, or that they were actually in danger of, mob violence; but it does appear that the attitude of the community was one of great hostility." The girls said the blacks had raped them. On this charge, a capital offense, nine of the blacks, in three separate sets, were tried, each trial completed within a single day. The juries found seven guilty. The judge sentenced them to death. There was some participation of lawyers on the side of the defense, but no clear designation of counsel, no single lawyer with clear responsibility.

The Supreme Court held that in the circumstances—a capital offense; a hostile environment; defendants "young, ignorant, illiterate"; a crime "regarded with especial horror in the community where they were to be tried"—the trial court's failure to appoint counsel for defendants, with specific responsibility from the start of the proceedings, was a violation of the due process clause of the Fourteenth Amendment. Hence the convictions could not stand.*

New trials were held. Defendants were represented by volunteer counsel, the most prominent being Samuel Liebowitz of New York, a name and point of origin also regarded with especial horror in the community where defendants were tried. A second conviction in a trial of two of the seven was again set aside by

---

* Of the nine Supreme Court Justices then sitting, four were noted conservatives (or notorious; suit yourself) generally thought of as a bloc: Sutherland, Van Devanter, Butler and McReynolds. Sutherland wrote the opinion of the Court; Van Devanter was one of the seven who joined in it. Butler and McReynolds dissented and said the convictions should be affirmed.

The Chief Justice of Alabama, alone of all the Alabama judges, had held for the defendants. This is parallel to what has been noted earlier in this book, the presence of modern minds in medieval times. Here substitute "place" for "time."

the Supreme Court, on the ground that blacks had been kept off
the jury. Finally, four were convicted and the convictions up-
held, but with the death penalty imposed against only one, and
that commuted. By 1946, three of the four had been paroled.
Two years later the fourth escaped, and reached the American
equivalent of medieval sanctuary—the North. Michigan refused
an Alabama demand for extradition.*

There is a provision in the Sixth Amendment that grants a
right to the assistance of counsel when the United States is prosecutor—that is, when a violation of federal criminal law is
charged. But so far as the states are concerned, the Constitution
says not a word about counsel. The Scottsboro trials involved
violation of state law and were conducted in a state court. So the
Supreme Court invoked the Fourteenth Amendment, which provides, among other things: "No State shall . . . deprive any person of life, liberty, or property, without due process of law." The
Supreme Court's holding was that in the Scottsboro situation, in
the circumstances to which the Court called attention, it was a
denial of due process to try a person for his life without supplying counsel.

That is a narrow holding. Suppose no death penalty was
involved. Suppose the crime alleged was a felony less than rape
or murder. Suppose it was a misdemeanor. Suppose it was a
minor offense, less than misdemeanor. Suppose the defendant
was sophisticated, the ambiance friendly, the jury fair, and the
trial judge considerate and helpful. It was a precedent that might
or might not be followed when the facts of the case were different. In succeeding years, the Supreme Court took some steps
forward and some steps back, and then, in 1963, decided the case
of Clarence Gideon. Gideon was tried and convicted on a charge
of breaking and entering a poolroom in Panama City, Florida.

---

* *The fact that they were known as the Scottsboro Boys was
partly a mark of the youth of the defendants, partly the vocabulary of racism. The label would not be used today. They would
be called the Scottsboro Seven, like the Wilmington Ten, the
Chicago Seven, the D.C. Nine, and other groups of defendants
in criminal cases that have political overtones. I tried to trace
this numerical form of designation to its origin, and got as far
back as Czarist prosecutions of the 1870s. But I am by no means
certain that those were the first, and perhaps some nineteen
hundred years ago there was talk of the Calvary Three.*

This is a felony under Florida law, but about as feeble a felony as one can imagine. Gideon, white, had been caught and convicted four times before. He seems to have been rather weak in perpetrating crime, but an excellent jailhouse lawyer. At his trial, he had asked that counsel be appointed for him. The judge politely refused:

> Mr. Gideon, I am sorry, but I cannot appoint counsel to represent you in this case. Under the laws of the State of Florida, the only time the court can appoint counsel to represent a defendant is when that person is charged with a capital offense. I am sorry, but I will have to deny your request to appoint counsel to defend you in this case.

At this point Gideon declared:

> The United States Supreme Court says I am entitled to be represented by counsel.

As a statement of how far the Supreme Court had gone, this was incorrect. The last time the Court had spoken on the subject, in 1942 in a case called *Betts v. Brady,* it had said that unless the death penalty was involved, there must be "special circumstances"—things like those stressed by Justice Sutherland in his Scottsboro opinion—before a state would be obliged to supply counsel for the defendant. In Gideon's case there was no hostility; he was treated fairly; he was not young, ignorant, or illiterate, and there was no suggestion that Panama City was horrified by illegal entries into poolrooms.

So Gideon was wrong when he told the trial judge that the Supreme Court had said he was entitled to a lawyer. But if we accept the jurisprudence that the law is a prediction of how the courts will act, Gideon was dead right. It was self-fulfilling prophecy in the strictest sense: two years after he made the statement, the Supreme Court unanimously held he should have been given a lawyer and overthrew his conviction.

On his retrial, represented by counsel, Gideon was acquitted. Anthony Lewis, in his superb book on the case, suggests that the result proves the point—that the presence of a lawyer made the difference between the first verdict and the second. It seems to me the second jury's verdict can be attributed as readily to other factors. We should not ignore the unhappy fact that some lawyers (many lawyers? most lawyers?) favor highly publicized trials with energies they would not ordinarily expend on minor criminal cases. Moreover, Gideon was by then a sympathetic figure, a winning underdog—or, perhaps more powerful in Panama City, a celebrity—and therefore, in the eyes of the jury, his tale should just naturally end in victory. Not to mention his having put Panama City on the map.*

By 1963, then, anybody accused of felony, capital or not, was entitled to representation. If he could not afford to hire a lawyer, the state, if it wished to prosecute, had to supply one for him. But felonies are not the only crimes; there are misdemeanors and lesser offenses. The point of providing counsel is to avoid conviction of the innocent. Though the punishments may not be equal, is not justice deeply offended whenever one is punished for something he didn't do? On the other hand, is the state to be put to the expense of furnishing counsel for everyone accused of speeding? People charged with minor infractions of the law who are able to pay a lawyer do not always engage one; often they do not think it worth the money. Yet if the rule of Gideon is to be extended to every prosecution, the pauper, for the same offense, would have a lawyer free of charge. And consider the financial burden on the state if it must have a defense lawyer standing by for all the thousands of petty offenses committed every year. Experience has shown that there is difficulty enough in providing counsel for those accused of the graver crimes.

The Supreme Court met that problem in 1972, and drew a line. Repeating the seven-to-two division of the Scottsboro case, but with a different cast, it held that counsel must be supplied if the result of conviction could be a prison sentence. Whatever the label attached to the misconduct—felony, misdemeanor, violation, offense—a lawyer must be provided by the state if one of

---

* *It is doubtful that the absence of a lawyer at the first trial accounted for the result. "Gideon conducted his defense," the Supreme Court said, "about as well as could be expected from a layman":*

He made an opening statement to the jury, cross-examined the State's witnesses, presented witnesses in his own defense, declined to testify himself, and made a short argument emphasizing his innocence . . .

The trial judge had gone further: he said Gideon had done "as well as most lawyers could have done in handling his case."

the possible penalties is imprisonment, unless the judge declares in advance he will in no event impose a prison sentence.*

Justice Powell, who had had experience with the problem when he was president of the American Bar Association, dissented, joined by Justice Rehnquist. Powell stressed the burden imposed, on an already overburdened criminal justice system, by the requirement of counsel in every case from which a term in jail may follow. He questioned the sense of the line that was drawn, pointing out that a large fine can be onerous, and that "losing one's driver's license is more serious for some individuals than a brief stay in jail." Hence he "would hold that the right to counsel in petty offense cases is not absolute but is one to be determined by the trial courts exercising a judicial discretion on a case-by-case basis."

The majority holding was, indeed, line-drawing of a simple, obdurate kind. Powell's was a more finely tuned solution. But the wish to avoid further burdens on the courts hardly supports his conclusion. His plan would require the weighing of factors in each of this ocean of cases, perhaps with argument by the prosecutor on whether defense counsel was needed and decision by the judge (the trial judge or another?), followed, quite possibly, by appeal. (Would the prosecutor himself, who might not be thoroughly objective, argue the question, or would special counsel be appointed to represent defendant on the question whether trial counsel should be appointed?)

The criminal justice system is struggling. It is clear there are not enough judges. But it is not at all clear there are not enough lawyers. Powell would create more decision-making and put an additional load on the judges on the theory that it is hard to find lawyers to defend the indigent. The majority, too, was worried about where to find the lawyers, to such an extent that three members of the majority filed a separate concurring opinion for the sole purpose of suggesting that law school students could "provide an important source of legal representation for the indigent." They must have been thinking of Washington, D.C., where they sat, which has a number of law schools in and around it, or perhaps of New Haven, a small city containing a law school with a large social conscience. But who would serve Emerson, North Dakota, or Escalante, Utah? There are about one hundred

---

* *The case,* Argesinger v. Hamlin, *like Gideon's, arose in Florida. The three most important cases on the subject all came from a small corner of the country.*

and fifty law schools in the United States, obviously not de-
ployed so as to reach each locus of prosecution.

The fact, however, is that there are plenty of lawyers, for this
and other purposes. There are probably too many. The real question is whether the government, state or federal, will furnish the
funds with which to hire lawyers for defendants unable to pay.
It is not a matter of personnel; it is, like most social needs, a
matter of money. Three fewer fighter planes would make room
for the defense of thirty thousand cases.*

Powell mentioned drivers' licenses. There are other licenses
that may be lost as the result of a criminal conviction, licenses to
engage in certain occupations. For some defendants, a short jail
term may well be less damaging than the loss of livelihood. So
Powell's formula has more logic than that of the majority. But
assuming that counsel are not to be supplied in all criminal
cases, the majority's formula quite sensibly sacrifices nice logic
to larger practical needs.†

The Supreme Court in the Scottsboro case found the right to
counsel in the due process clause itself. Subsequent Supreme
Court majorities followed an alternate path to the same result, a
path that had been hacked out for other uses; they decided that
the Sixth Amendment was among those parts of the Bill of Rights
which the Fourteenth Amendment made applicable to the states.
(More about this farther on.) But the Gideon bench leaned heav-

---

* *The thirty-thousand-case estimate includes the range of defenses from the plea of guilty (the correct plea in most cases) to full
trial (much less numerous) through appeal (rarely appropriate
in this kind of case). Remember the Court was dealing with
minor offenses.*
† *Throughout these opinions on right to counsel there runs an
ode to the value of counsel. It seems to me too lyrical; a word of
caution is needed. So much depends on what counsel the defendant gets. There is enormous variation in the competence of
lawyers. There are many cases where a fair judge and an intelligent defendant will do as well as—I daresay better than—a
posturing lawyer more interested in making himself look good
than in making the defendant look innocent. Add stupidity—it
exists—to bad motivation, and one may well conclude that the
particular defendant would be better off without a lawyer. One
is reminded of General Burgoyne's comment, in Shaw's* The
Devil's Disciple, *when, in speaking of execution by firing squad,
he reflects on the marksmanship of professional British soldiery.*

ily on the Scottsboro case as precedent, and the Scottsboro opinion itself drew on previous cases to give due process broad meaning. Those cases had dealt not with procedural rights, but, originally, with the freedom to conduct business as one chose, and later—some Justices gladly, others trapped in their precedents—with freedom of expression. Due process of law, said the Scottsboro majority, included "the settled usages and modes of proceeding under the common and statute law of England" and "fundamental principles of liberty and justice which lie at the base of all our civil and political institutions." The elements of due process, the Court had many times informed us, are familiar, long established, at the core of the common law.

Features of our criminal justice system that are familiar, long established, and at the core of the common law are not hard to find. Everyone must have his day in court; don't put a man in prison without giving him a trial. The French, at the time of our Revolution, were doing exactly that, with their *lettres de cachet*. Don't torture the defendant to obtain a confession on which he can be convicted, something the Spanish were famous for. "Due process of law" forbade such things; their prohibition needed no spelling out. But where in the common law was a right to counsel?

In England, at that time, a man accused of felony had no such right. It was not a matter of being too poor to hire a lawyer. No matter how rich you might be, you simply could not have one. The centuries-old practice was that the Crown used lawyers to prosecute and the defendant defended himself. This had been true even where the hideous penalties for treason might come down. As to treason, a statute changed the common law in 1695. The people who fomented the Revolution of 1688 were, of course, traitors—unless and until they succeeded. Having succeeded, they must have had a vivid memory of what it was like to be on the other side, and been keenly aware of what would have happened if they had failed in their endeavor. This probably accounted for the new Parliament's decision to allow one accused of treason to get himself a lawyer.*

---

* One day before the statute, already enacted, was to take effect, Sir William Parkins was brought to trial. He asked to be allowed counsel, quoting the preamble to the statute, which said it was just and reasonable that the defendant in a treason case have counsel. The court rejected the argument, and expressing some regret, informed Parkins that the old practice would remain in

But that change was for treason only, a rather infrequent crime. As to felonies generally, Parliament let the common law be. Then, as the nineteenth century approached, defense counsel began to appear. It was by intermittent judicial favor, and for limited purposes only. The courts forbade, for example, what modern criminal lawyers make so much of—the final address to the jury. And representation by counsel was in no event a right. It was an act of charity by the judge, from whose denial no appeal could be taken. Not until 1836 did Parliament vouchsafe to those accused of felony the privilege of hiring a lawyer.

During the time when people charged with felony could have no legal representation, those charged with misdemeanor could. The Supreme Court, in these recent opinions, commented on the irony of this, and, in the Court's view, its illogic. The defendant who faced punishments more severe, in greater need of counsel, got none. But the rule was not illogical. The key is in the different points of view. Today we think in terms of defendant's rights. For most of our legal history, those who governed thought in terms of keeping order. Misdemeanors did not disrupt the king's peace nearly as much as felonies, and treason must be obliterated. It was very important that those who committed felonies be punished; it was most important that those who committed treason be punished; it was considerably less important that those who committed misdemeanors be punished. The Crown could afford to allow the misdemeanor defendant the luxury of counsel. But the Crown would take no chances on the more serious crimes. That some innocents might suffer was unfortunate but, it was felt, a necessary incident of governance. The Crown would not run the risk that clever lawyers might make it possible for traitors or felons to escape the force of law.

But note: all this had to do with whether a defendant with money enough would be allowed to hire a lawyer. There was no thought that the government should supply one. When, in 1836, Parliament made secure the right to retain a lawyer in felony prosecutions, it said nothing about cases in which the accused could not pay a fee. The indigent defendant was as defenseless as before. Meanwhile, what was the situation in America?

It was better. Things varied from colony to colony, and then from state to state. Three of the colonies had statutes allowing

---

force for another twenty-four hours. They then denied his prayer for a postponement of the trial. Parkins was tried, found guilty, and executed.

the use of counsel, and two of them, for capital offenses, provided that counsel should be assigned. A fourth reached this liberal conclusion by judicial ruling. The rest of the colonies, however, followed the English practice. After the Revolution, most of the states—not all—either by constitution or by statute, sooner or later granted the right to retain counsel, and some provided for their assignment. However, "as late as 1800, it seems probable that only in New Jersey, by statute, and in Connecticut by practice, did the accused enjoy a full right to retain counsel, and to have counsel appointed if he were unable to afford it himself."

Whatever the precise historical facts may be, it is clear that at the date when the Bill of Rights was appended to our Constitution, the right to counsel was considered something that a state might or might not grant, something that needed express provision, something very far from a maxim planted in our law. The drafters found it necessary, in dealing with the central government, to make explicit provision for the right to hire counsel in the Sixth Amendment. Three quarters of a century later, addressing the governments of the states, the Fourteenth Amendment simply lifted a phrase—"due process of law"—from the Fifth Amendment. It could also have lifted the language of the Sixth. It didn't.

Has the Supreme Court been wrong, then, in concluding that the states are compelled by the federal Constitution not only to allow a lawyer to the accused but even to provide one? I do not think so. The Court has been less than perfect in its reasoning, and, as usual, sloppy in its history, but these decisions do not violate our precedential plan, do not breach the law's continuum. I will give my reasons later.

□

In the general applause that attended the right-to-counsel cases, Justice Black's stark and telling formulation was often quoted: "There can be no equal justice where the kind of trial a man gets depends on the amount of money he has." It is a statement with which I heartily agree. But do not draw the inference that these decisions installed a pattern of equal justice, or even went far to achieve it. They only did a little. Some lawyers are abler than others, and the abler, not always but ordinarily, are the more expensive. The variations are extreme, much greater, say, than the variations among professional athletes. While the differences among the athletes are interesting, the differences among the lawyers are appalling. Your life and fortunes do not depend on the competence of a pitcher or a quarterback (unless you are foolish enough to make large bets); they do depend on the competence of lawyers. In an adversary system, some rough equivalence would be ideal, but, failing that, the brand of justice one receives should not depend on money.

There is also, in the cost of litigation, the number of lawyers used (two heads are better than one, so long as one has power of decision, and three are even better), the employment of investigators, the employment of accountants, the compensation of witnesses (legitimately) for their time and travel. Money talks, for the defense in criminal cases, and for one side or the other in civil cases. It is delusion that appointing counsel for the pauper assures the same quality of defense as a wealthy man can count on.

Moreover, these decisions help only the indigent; they do nothing for the great mass of people between the indigent and the prosperous. ("Prosperous" includes the corporations. Corporate crime is to my mind more damaging to society than the crimes of violence we hear so much about; it kills people less directly, but in greater numbers.) Within that great intermediate class, there are differences in resources that necessarily affect the strength of the defense. If we would divorce the chances of conviction from the funds at one's disposal, we must adopt the outlandish suggestion, made some chapters ago, that the practice of law should stop being a form of free enterprise. There are weaknesses in the proposal, but without it the quality of justice will always be strained by money.

□

It bears repeating that these recent decisions have to deal with supplying a lawyer gratis, and that in the not too distant past the accused was not allowed to have a lawyer, appointed or engaged. But if it seems unfair that the prosecution should have used professionals, trained in law and practiced in persuading juries, while the defendant was left on his own—if that was unfair, consider the use of witnesses.

The most prominent feature of the modern trial, the testimony of witnesses, was nonexistent in the first centuries of the common law, and did not win a major place until late in the sixteenth century. When witnesses at last are welcomed to the courtroom scene, their role in criminal trials is by our lights a strange one. There can be witnesses for the Crown; there cannot be witnesses for the defense. Gradually, by intermittent judicial favor, the accused is allowed to have witnesses to speak on his side of the case. What they say, however, does not amount to testimony: they are not permitted to be sworn. Nor can the accused compel anyone to come to court; the judges do not go so far as to give him the subpoena power that Parliament has given the Crown. Witnesses for the defense must be volunteers, brave and hardy volunteers in the politics of the day. Later, under the Restoration, the courts will issue subpoenas at defendant's request, but still not let him have his witnesses sworn. This is a heavy disadvantage. Whom is the jury to believe? The Crown's witnesses, who give their testimony under oath and run the risk of punishment for perjury? Or the defendant's witnesses, who can say whatever they want, or are bidden to, without fear of legal consequence? Finally, after the Revolution of 1688, real change is made. Testimony by sworn witnesses is granted the defendant by Act of Parliament, first in cases for treason, in 1695, and then for felonies generally, in 1702.

So in this critical aspect of criminal trial, the accused did not draw even with his prosecutor until the very century in which our Bill of Rights was written. Man's memory could run to the contrary easily, without drawing the slightest deep breath. Nevertheless, in the United States, defendant's right to call witnesses and have them sworn was not thought to require mention in the Bill of Rights. It was considered part of due process, and simply was not questioned.

□

In the kind of criminal trial we see today, providing evidence of innocence is one half of the defense; the other is attack upon the prosecutor's witnesses. But need the prosecutor's case depend on the use of witnesses? Is not the accusation, the official conclusion that defendant is guilty, enough to put upon defendant the burden of proving innocence? After all, keeping order and enforcing law is a gigantic task, and a government would not ordinarily waste time and energy in bringing groundless cases. If the government has investigated and come to the conclusion that X has committed a crime, is it not sufficient to give X an opportunity to prove that he has not? One can readily imagine such a way of doing things: governmental investigation without trial, and, if the result indicates that this person has done the deed, official charges followed by an opportunity for the person to clear himself—if he can. It is readily imagined because it exists in much of the world today (excluding places where the accused is given no chance at all). And it existed, more or less, in our own system until not long ago. Into the seventeenth century, the defendant had no right to make his accusers subject themselves to cross-examination, or even to know who they were. And so the Sixth Amendment gave him both those rights, by providing for confrontation.

□

Due process of law, our courts have told us, is a legacy of Magna Carta, the fundamental common law, the Natural Law, the ancient rights of Englishmen, the timeless features of our legal system. We have seen that the rights we have been speaking of are considerably less than timeless; that if they are fundamental, the courts have only recently made them so; that if they are Naturally Ordained, the epiphany is lately come. It is ironic, then, that two other guarantees provided by the Bill of Rights, which speak of features truly long established, have been rather roughly treated. One is our celebrated right to trial by jury. The other is the almost as celebrated interposition of grand jury action between suspicion and trial. The latter is in the Fifth Amendment: "No person shall be held to answer for a capital, or otherwise infamous crime, unless on a presentment or indictment of a Grand Jury . . ." The former appears twice in the Constitution. Article III, Section 2, in the main body of the document, says: "The trial of all crimes, except in cases of impeachment, shall be by jury . . ." Then the Sixth Amendment lists jury trial first among the rights it assures defendants: "In all criminal prosecutions, the accused shall enjoy the right to a speedy and public trial, by an impartial jury of the State and district wherein the crime shall have been committed . . ."*

---

* *"Presentment" is accusation by a grand jury moving on its own knowledge (the way its ancestor, the Clarendon jury, operated). "Indictment" is the more inclusive term. Almost all grand jury action is at the prompting of a public prosecutor (the "district attorney" in many places), and so we rarely hear of presentments. Occasionally, a grand jury will act without the prosecutor's help. Sometimes it will act despite official wish that it should not; when it does this, it is known, informally, as a "runaway grand jury." It happens, typically, when a bold grand jury goes after official corruption.*

One accused of crime has had the right to jury trial since about 1220—serious crime, that is, but at that date all common-law crime was serious. Accusation by grand jury is even older, a half century older. Yet the Supreme Court does not deem these guarantees as much a part of the law of the land as such arriviste intruders as the right to counsel and the right to bring in witnesses. This despite the fact that the men who made our Revolution and wrote our Bill of Rights regarded jury trial as a right of prime importance. They mentioned it specifically in the documents of outrage that preceded the Constitution—the resolutions adopted in 1766 by the Stamp Act Congress, in 1774 by the First Continental Congress, and in the Declaration of Independence itself.

So far as application to the states is concerned, the grand jury guarantee has been given short shrift, or, rather, no shrift at all. The Supreme Court has said that the states are free to abolish the grand jury. It was first said, it is true, in a case decided before the Court began to insert the Bill of Rights into the Fourteenth Amendment. A more recent case, however, in the age of the Court's anxiety to find protections for the accused, silently confirms the earlier holding. A rather peculiar Michigan statute was attacked as violating various safeguards in the Bill of Rights. The convicted defendant made no point of the fact that the statute provided for imprisonment without grand jury action. The Court, overruling a line of Michigan cases upholding the statute, and deciding in defendant's favor, made no mention of this omission except to note it. The Justices do not hesitate to speak on Constitutional deprivations they find in the record, whether or not the petitioner calls attention to them. (In this very case, one of the two grounds on which the Court reversed the Michigan conviction was a ground that the petition for certiorari had not asked the Court to consider.) So it is a fair inference—indeed, an inescapable inference—that the Justices did not deem the absence of grand jury indictment even worth discussing. Moreover, Osmond Frankel, one of the country's best Constitutional lawyers, especially active in this field, argued for the defendant; if he had thought the point worth raising, he would have raised it. We can safely conclude, then, that the oldest right of the accused, the right not to be tried for crime unless accusation is made by a duly assembled grand jury (the action of appeal, now gone, apart) —this right is not so fundamental as to constitute part of due process.

In the late sixties and early seventies, we heard a great deal about the importance of the grand jury as a bulwark of our liberties, particularly in situations that had political overtones, with the usual misdirected calls on history. In its origin, the grand jury was a device directed to a more rigorous law enforcement, something to benefit the government rather than the suspect. Later, under the high-handed Tudors and Stuarts, when Star Chamber prosecution might be begun simply at the Crown's desire, common-law prosecution, which required grand jury indictment, was a safer course for those the Crown looked upon as enemies. But in our recent history the grand jury has been the least important of the accused's protections. Not only are the states free to get along without it, but it has not been used at all in England since 1933. If the trial itself is conducted with what we consider due process, the Constitution does not demand, except in the federal courts, that prosecution be preceded by citizen accusation.

Our Court has given the petty more respect than the grand. The right to jury trial, like other provisions of the Sixth Amendment, has been read into the due process clause—only not entirely. Amendment Six says "all criminal prosecutions." The Supreme Court says "some prosecutions." Article III of the body of the Constitution, which establishes the federal judicial power and puts limits on it, says "all crimes." The Supreme Court says "some crimes."

The right to demand a jury in the trial of crime was established seven hundred and sixty years ago. Indeed, it was both a right and a recommendation, a recommendation impressed with stones. But, though long established, it has also long been modified. When it became the mode of trial for crime in the courts of common law, no crime at common law was minor. Each was a breach of the royal peace—serious to the central government in terms of keeping order, and serious to the accused in terms of penal consequence. And every crime in the courts of common law was felony; there were no misdemeanors. Minor violations were handled in the local courts. Gradually, as we have seen, the courts of common law consumed the local courts. Then, as the population grew, the number of violations grew. And as the economy and the polity got more complex, Parliament passed certain regulatory statutes and declared their breach a crime. The traditional common-law crimes remained, of course—murder, mayhem, rape, arson, robbery, criminal trespass—but there were many new offenses. With the monopolization of legal business by the royal courts, they had to handle not only the major common-law offenses, plus the minor offenses that had been dealt with in the local courts, but also the new statutory violations. The number of cases got so big that jury trial for each and every crime became an unbearable nuisance. It took too much time of the Justices and too often interrupted the daily lives of the good and lawful men of the vicinage.

Under the Tudors things began to change. First, sessions of court were made more frequent, but that hardly solved the problem. "The King's most loving subjects," says a statute of Henry VIII, "are much travailed and otherwise encumbered in coming and keeping of the said six-weeks sessions, to their costs, charges and unquietness." Then, about 1500 (that watershed date again), Parliament, in enacting new statutes, provided in some of them that trial should be by the Justices alone, without a jury.

Coke says there was an instance of this before 1500 in the reign of Henry VII (and finds vindication of the importance of jury trial in the repeal of the statute on that King's death). Modern scholars question this, and suggest the first such statute came in the reign of Henry VIII. The early statutes of this sort dealt with things that in former days had been the business of the local courts—swearing, drunkenness, disorderly conduct. Later, under the Stuarts, there were tax acts and trade regulations whose violations were tried without the intervention of a jury. Then came a flood of nonjury criminal statutes, on subjects ranging from selling liquor in the wrong places to bribery of officials.

By the eighteenth century, we are told in a study by Felix Frankfurter (later Justice, then Professor) and by Thomas G. Corcoran (then his student, later an important New Deal figure), there were "at least one hundred offenses" that could be prosecuted without a jury, some of them carrying heavy fines, with prison for failure to pay. Hence, these scholars argued, the transplanted Englishmen who made the American Revolution and wrote the Constitution thought of trial by jury as a right that applied only in some criminal cases, with a line to be drawn between the serious and the petty.

The Supreme Court has accepted the argument, and located the line. It answered the question first in federal prosecutions, and then carried the answer, in the commodious cart it has made of the Fourteenth Amendment, to state-court prosecutions. Some Acts of Congress have carried only small fines as punishments, and Congress must also provide local law for territories of the United States and for the District of Columbia. So the Court got round to the matter before the recent spate of Fourteenth Amendment decisions. As early as 1904, it hinted that jury trial should be reserved for crimes that might bring down six months or more in prison, and finally, in 1970, it drew the line through a point just one day later—"more than six months," it said. The 1970 opinion took no note of the statement of 1904, but half a year in jail seemed to both benches the place to put the line.

These rulings offer a remarkable insult to our language. (Justices Black and Douglas, it should be said immediately, disagreed with the majority reasoning.) The word "all," used in both Constitutional provisions that assure jury trial, is one of the least ambiguous we have. It is not like "the press" (does "press" encompass "film"?) or "abridge" (does some restriction as to time or place constitute abridgment?) or "free speech" (is the whispering of military secrets what we mean by free speech?)— those First Amendment words leave some room for argument. "All" is a quantitative word. The most precise expressions that we have are quantitative—none, one, two, three, ten million, all. Yet the Supreme Court tells us that "all" means "less than all."

The fatuity is all the more impressive if we follow the respected, and sensible, canon of construction that instructs us, when we assign meaning to the words of a legal statement, to keep in view the entire text—to take in "the four corners of the document." Amendment Five, which immediately precedes the Amendment we are considering, contains the requirement of indictment, and limits the requirement to "a capital or otherwise infamous crime." Those who wrote the Bill of Rights evidently knew how to specify certain crimes when they did not intend to include all crimes. The chief writer of these provisions was James Madison, a very good man with words.

The Supreme Court majority cited legal history, and drew support from the Frankfurter-Corcoran study. Frankfurter and Corcoran relied on two kinds of history. One was the English legislation that permitted trial without jury for certain specified offenses. But this really points the other way; it rules out the possibility that the drafters were merely careless. They were designing a new form of government, and were familiar with past practice. Against this background of some-not-all, the Constitution twice says "all." It surely looks as though the American rebels, overturning many features of the British system, were intent on changing this one too. If they were not—if they wished to keep the British pattern—could not these masters of the language have found a way to do it? Would it not occur to them to write "serious crimes" rather than "all crimes"?

The second sort of evidence offered by the professor and his pupil was the history of the drafting of the Constitution. What their investigations turned up was exactly nothing, from which they drew the conclusion that no change in the British pattern was intended. That is, the fact that no contemporaneous comment was made about these clearly drawn provisions is offered as proof that "all" should be taken to mean "not all."

This exercise in legal reasoning was not only inept but inappropriate. There is no warrant here to call on history. The courts have over and over told us that they will not look beyond the words of a statute unless there is some ambiguity. The Constitution is, of course, a statute. It is true that the Constitution is deemed, quite properly, to have more capacity for adaptive growth than an ordinary statute, and that the Courts have discovered ambiguities in it that to the nonjudicial eye are rather hard to see. But by looking closely one can find them. "All" has no ambiguity, none at all.*

Now there are excellent practical reasons for withholding jury trial from the many lesser offenses. The aching back of our judicial system would be bowed down even further if the time and expense of jury trial went into every minor violation. But the Constitution provides a way to solve the problem. It is the process of amendment. Too slow and cumbersome? Even if it were,

---

* *Another word in the clause we are concerned with can be said to contain some ambiguity: the word "crime" itself. It would be reasonable judicial construction to hold, for instance, that parking overtime, while it should entail some deterring consequences, is not in every sense a crime and hence does not require jury trial. But the Court did not pursue this path. And it is clear, and has been clear for centuries, that "crime" takes in more than "felony." Moreover, Frankfurter and Corcoran leave no doubt that the offenses they are talking about are crimes in every sense. They use the words "crime" and "criminal" in describing the instances in which Parliament dispensed with jury trial. They even say that "some bordered closely on serious felonies." To move to the present day, and the decisions of the Court, no one would doubt that misconduct that will put you in prison for five months is criminal. Finally, the Court itself refers to the trials it has excluded from the jury guarantee as "trials of crime" in the very opinions in which the amputation was done.*

that would not excuse so gross a departure from judicial standards. But the process of amendment is not, in fact, too slow and cumbersome, not in a situation such as this. It is different where the proposal has active opposition, as, for instance, the Equal Rights Amendment. But an ample number agree there need not be jury trial for the minor crimes. Where no organized dissent exists, the Constitution can be amended rapidly. The repeal of Prohibition by the Twenty-first Amendment—to which there was some fervent opposition—took less than ten months. The burden on the judicial system during the brief time needed to change "all crimes" to "major crimes" or "serious crimes" or, if precision is wanted, "crimes involving imprisonment for more than six months"—that burden would have been considerably less important than the damage to the fabric of our law done when our highest Court indulges in such essays in illogic. This is not a case of giving old words the meaning they should take on in a time-changed context. It is a case of utter denial of the meaning of a word—"all"—that has a single meaning in any context. The majority simply decided it could amend the Constitution on its own.

It is interesting that this extraordinary example of judicial arrogance drew its main support from the Court's chief exponent of judicial deference. When Frankfurter ascended the bench, he argued passionately that his brethren much too often went much too far in altering the law to make it what they thought it ought to be. I disagreed with his conclusions on several specific issues, but I agree (who can disagree?) that there must be limits on judicial power to make new law. We ought not be subject to a Dictatorship of the Black Robes, no matter how benign. Here, on the right to jury trial, we had precisely that.

It is something different from simple bad decision. Take an example of the latter: In 1976, the Court held that parts of an Act of Congress that put limits on using money in federal elections were unconstitutional. The basis of the decision was that the restraints imposed violated the First Amendment. That is, the Court held that spending money is a form of speech, and that spending money to influence elections is the sort of freedom the Amendment guarantees. The Court was saying, in effect, that the Constitution guarantees a rich man a greater voice in government than a poor man. That may be fact, but it is not law. (Except in the sense that this decision—which probably will someday be overruled—has made it law.) From political and social points of view, the election-law decision might well have been the worst judicial display since the Court's turn-of-the-century rulings that maximum-hour, minimum-wage statutes violated the Constitutional right to make profits. It perverted the meaning of the First Amendment, and assailed the meaning of democracy. But its vice was different from that of the jury-trial decisions. It is not irrational to argue that there are elements of expression in spending to elect. ("Not irrational," I say; I do not say "right" or "sound" or even "respectable.") It is irrational to argue that "all" means "less than all."

I spend these paragraphs on the jury trial decisions because they contradict the premises of our Constitutional form of government. The power of the Supreme Court is limited by a measure of respect for precedent—a gravitational pull that exerts some restraint on even the most active judicial activist—and by a recognition that law depends on language. The fact that words usually have several meanings gives the Court great leeway. But this was not a matter of choosing meaning. It was an outright denial of meaning, a phenomenon of self-induced illiteracy in the most august, and intellectual, of our political institutions. If we abuse our language to this extent we are damaging our law.

Our law, however, will survive. A living organism, composed of blood and bone and muscle, it heals, so long as the wounds are not too many.

☐

Most of our criminal law is state law. Vastly more criminal prosecution goes on in state than federal courts. So to the average citizen (average reader? average culprit?) it is the rights that the states grant to the accused, or are compelled by the United States Constitution to grant to the accused, that have immediate meaning.

We have considered some of the safeguards for the accused that are expressed in our Bill of Rights, and have been held to bind the states. There are others. Evidence seized in the course of "unreasonable searches and seizures," forbidden by the Fourth Amendment, is excluded from criminal trials. The defendant may not be tried in secret, if he objects, and he may not be kept waiting for his day in court too long; the Sixth Amendment starts by declaring that "the accused shall enjoy the right to a speedy and public trial." (Even the Founding Fathers, good writers all, could have used some editing; consider that word "enjoy.")*

The Fifth Amendment sets forth two guarantees for the accused apart from those that have been mentioned. One is the double jeopardy clause, whose main effect we took note of early in this book; it also reinforces the rule that the prosecution cannot appeal from a verdict of acquittal. The Constitution, incidentally, does not say "double jeopardy"; it says that no person shall "be subject for the same offence to be twice put in jeopardy of life or limb." Note that fines and prison are not mentioned. The courts have remedied the omission, hardly bothering to discuss it. I have seen only one judicial attempt to wrestle with the problem, and that an awkward one. But it would not be unreasonable to argue that imprisonment puts life and limb at hazard, and for a large part of the population the deprivation of money is psychic mayhem. ("It'll cost you an arm and a leg.") The probable explanation for the language used, however, is historical. Most punishments at the time did involve the loss of life or limb, or, as with the pillory or banishment, a risk of loss; imprisonment

---

*The criminal cases in which the courts have expelled the press are cases in which the defendant wanted to keep the event unpublicized. If the defendant wants a public trial, the Sixth Amendment guarantees he will have it. Yet the recent Supreme Court decision affirming a trial judge's shutting of the courtroom doors was in my opinion wrong. (It may be modified or overruled by the time this book is published.) I believe that the First Amendment guarantee must include some right of access. Enabling the people to make the right political choices is generally considered the main reason for a system of free expression (though it is not the only one). To arrive at such choices the people must have access to the facts. This includes the way our institutions of government operate (though there are, of course, some limits, some necessary governmental privacy). In centuries past, the facts were usually apparent; what was needed, and what the government opposed, was comment on the facts. Now we are free to comment, but the facts are hard to find. Society has grown much larger and more complex. There are many more relevant facts today than there were in 1600, in 1700, in 1800, even in 1940. And—quite apart from efforts to suppress them —the facts are buried in the multiple creases of this complicated culture. It is not the Sixth Amendment alone that is involved when a court decides to operate in secret.

as a regular penalty was only getting started; and the phrase itself went back to an even earlier time.

The other is The Privilege—the provision that no one "shall be compelled in any criminal case to be a witness against himself." This means not only that defendant need not take the stand, but also that no attention is to be paid to the fact he chooses not to. Moreover, the clause is read as though the arrangement of its words were different: in other proceedings, which are not "a criminal case," a witness can refuse to testify on the ground that such testimony might be used in a criminal case against him if later on there should happen to be one.

The privilege was prominent in the 1940s and 1950s when Martin Dies, J. Parnell Thomas, Joe McCarthy and Richard Nixon were making careers by playing the Communist game. (More or less successfully. Thomas went to jail; Nixon didn't.) Some witnesses in Congressional committee hearings refused to respond to questions on the ground that their answers might tend to incriminate them. They might indeed. Their activities could have run afoul of various statutes, and during part of the period mere membership in the Communist Party was a federal crime. Hence the Congressional inquisitors, despite their investigatory powers, could not hold the witness in contempt for his recalcitrance. (They could, however, as we know, use extralegal pressures to make the refusal costly, an abuse of power for which the inquisitors should have been prosecuted.)

Two decades later, the privilege came to the fore of public consciousness again, coupled with the right to counsel, in another context. The Miranda Warning entered our culture. (If one can call our television dramas culture. But if potsherds can constitute a culture, why not television too?) "Read him his rights," says Kojak-Columbo-McGarrity. The classier culprits interrupt: "Never mind; I know my rights." Adding, in an episode I hope to see someday, "Miranda versus Arizona, Volume 384 of the United States Reports, page 436."

The Supreme Court, splitting five to four, gave us the Miranda rule in 1966. Briefly, it means that when an arrest is made, a confession by the person taken into custody cannot be used against him at his trial unless, before the questioning starts, he is given an explicit warning—that he has a right to remain silent, that any statement he may make can be used as evidence against him, and that he has a right to the presence of a lawyer during the interrogation.

The rule brings with it some corollary questions. Just when

is one in custody? In the police station, after he is booked? Earlier, when accosted by an officer? Or at some point in between? Suppose he is questioned about a crime that has nothing to do with the offense for which he has been arrested? How does the rule operate when there is a series of interrupted interrogations? It is on these corollary questions that the Burger majority has reversed the direction taken by the Warren majority, without reversing the Miranda rule itself.

□

The reader might like to know what else our Bill of Rights contains. The Ninth and Tenth Amendments in essence say, "We mean it." The Constitution was a grudging grant of specified powers to the central government, and these amendments display the states' anxiety that this be understood. The Tenth, an exercise in redundancy-for-emphasis, declares that powers not delegated are reserved. The Ninth says: "The enumeration in the Constitution, of certain rights, shall not be construed to deny or disparage others retained by the people." It was an Amendment almost totally ignored for two hundred years, until, in the contraception case, three concurring Justices concluded that the privacy of the bedchamber was an unenumerated right. The Eighth Amendment forbids excessive bail and excessive fines and the infliction of cruel and unusual punishments. It has been given attention only in recent years. The Seventh preserves the right to jury trial in civil cases at common law (that is, cases other than those in equity) "where the value in controversy exceeds twenty dollars." This has been held to apply to the federal courts alone; so far as the states are concerned, it serves only as an index of inflation. The Sixth, Fifth and Fourth have been discussed. Another important part of the Fifth is its provision that "private property [shall not] be taken for public use, without just compensation."

The First Amendment we are now very much aware of. For a hundred and thirty years, however, it was scarcely noticed. This was not because there was perfect freedom of speech and press; it was because nobody thought there ought to be. The First Amendment also separates church and state, protects freedom of religion, and guarantees "the right of the people peaceably to assemble, and to petition the government for a redress of grievances." At times in English history, an assembly was considered a riot and the very fact of group petition was treated as a crime.

The Second Amendment says: "A well regulated militia, being necessary to the security of a free state, the right of the people to keep and bear arms, shall not be infringed." The gun lobby likes to quote "the right of the people to keep and bear arms," but the courts have sensibly held that the Amendment has to do only with the maintenance of a militia (that is, a citizen army).

The Third Amendment is this: "No soldier shall, in time of peace be quartered in any house, without the consent of the owner, nor in time of war, but in a manner to be prescribed by law." It got its first significant mention in that same contraception case. The main Supreme Court opinion listed it, along with other sections of the Bill of Rights, as a source from whose "penumbra" a silent right of privacy "emanates." The other Amendments through which the right of privacy softly steals into the Constitution are the First, Fourth, Fifth and Ninth.

The only other judicial context in which I have seen the Third Amendment cited is a 1951 federal-district-court case, an action by the government under the Rent Control Act. Defendant's counsel argued:

The 1947 Housing and Rent Act as amended and extended is and always was the incubator and hatchery of swarms of bureaucrats to be quartered as storm troopers upon the people in violation of Amendment III of the United States Constitution. This challenge has not been heretofore made or adjudged by any court, insofar as our research discloses.

The court, straight faced, replied:

We accept counsel's statement as to the results of his research but find this challenge without merit.

The British Bill of Rights is sometimes described as the progenitor of the American. There is not much resemblance. The British Bill was an Act of Parliament presented to William and Mary in 1689 as a condition of their taking the Crown. Like any other British statute, it was subject to amendment or repeal by later Parliaments—not, like our Bill of Rights, an overriding restriction. Moreover, not much of the British Bill focuses on the liberties of the citizen; it is mainly an assertion of the powers and privileges of Parliament as against the Crown. The British provision regarding free speech, for example, has to do only with what goes on in Parliament. The jury-trial provision is class-angled: the jurors in trials for high treason must be freeholders (that is, owners of land). The only provision that has a marked similarity to one of ours has to do with punishments. It provides the model for our Eighth Amendment, in almost identical language: excessive bail shall not be required, nor excessive fines imposed, nor cruel and unusual punishments inflicted. Drawing and quartering had been the usual punishment for treason in the seventeenth century, which will give you some idea of what the drafters of the Eighth Amendment had in mind.*

□

The way the Bill of Rights has been applied to the states has had a curious history. All sides agree that when it was adopted, at the insistence of those states that would not otherwise join the United States, it applied to the federal government only. The Fourteenth Amendment came into the Constitution seventy-five years later—a product, along with the Thirteenth and Fifteenth, of the Civil War. Among other clauses designed to see that the rebel states should not mistreat those who had been their slaves, the amendment contained the following: ". . . nor shall any state deprive any person of life, liberty, or property, without due process of law . . ." This repeated, word for word, a part of the Fifth Amendment, the only difference being that the Fifth referred to the federal government and the Fourteenth to the states. Other parts of the Fifth Amendment were not repeated, nor were any other clauses of the Bill of Rights.

Now since the Bill contains a number of distinct provisions, it can hardly have been intended that one should be a summary of them all, unless the document said so, which the Bill of Rights does not. Indeed, if due process took in everything else, the Bill could have consisted of a single sentence. Or, if greater specific-

---

* *The adoption of the Bill of Rights, which like other amendments of the Constitution required action by three-fourths of the States, was effected in 1791, when Virginia became the eleventh state to ratify. There were then fourteen. Massachusetts, Georgia and Connecticut, early opponents of the Bill, finally made it unanimous, in 1939. (A great deal of the opposition had come from people who thought the guarantees of the Bill implicit in the body of the Constitution and feared that enumeration of certain liberties might raise doubts as to the existence of others.)*

ity was wanted, the drafters might have itemized such things as self-incrimination, unreasonable searches and seizures, and freedom of speech and religion, and then said, at the end of the Bill, "and other aspects of due process." Or, if they wished to be really precise, they might have started the Bill by saying: "No person shall be deprived of life, liberty, or property without due process of law, and due process of law includes among other things the following . . ." They did none of these. Hence it can be argued that due process of law is just one of several separate guarantees given in the Bill, and its repetition in the Fourteenth Amendment carried nothing with it.

There is, however, an argument that goes the other way. Despite the fierce controversy over how far the concept of due process extends, there is no dispute about the center of the concept. Certain aspects of our legal procedure are regarded as our due. They are a mixture of elementary fairness and traditions in the law. A person accused of crime ought to be informed of the nature of the accusation against him. He is entitled to a public trial which shall not be delayed at the pleasure of the prosecution. He must not be tortured into a confession. These things are unquestioned aspects of due process. Yet each has its own express provision in the Bill of Rights. It is therefore apparent that though the Bill could have been better drafted, due process of law includes at least some of the items listed elsewhere in the Bill. When the words were repeated in the Fourteenth Amendment, they brought these items with them.*

An argument of this sort was made by the first Justice Harlan in a dissenting opinion in 1884. He was the grandfather of the Harlan who sat on the Court from 1955 until 1971. The two Harlans, both of whom belong to the score or so of first-rate men of law who have served as Supreme Court Justices, found themselves in attitudinal disagreement—a skip-a-generation gap. The elder was a prominent liberal on a conservative bench; he dissented from the 1895 decision that "separate but equal" facilities are fair and constitutional (a decision overruled in 1964), saying "our Constitution is color-blind." And he dissented from a 1905 decision that held maximum-hour legislation invalid. The younger, though certainly liberal by former standards, was a conservative in relation to his contemporary fellow Justices. Dissenting in a right-to-jury case, the second Harlan spoke disparagingly of the view that the intent of those who drafted the Fourteenth Amendment was to make the Bill of Rights applica-

A few Justices have taken the view that the entire Bill of Rights was incorporated in the Fourteenth Amendment. A few have taken the view that no specific provisions of the Bill were incorporated, but that the concept of due process includes ideas close to some of those spelled out in the first eight Amendments. The view that has prevailed is in between. It is called "selective incorporation" or "absorption." It means that most, but not all, of the Bill's guarantees are held to govern the states, just as though they had been spelled out in the Fourteenth Amendment.

The Court came to this conclusion by a strange circuitous road. The expansion of the due process clause of the Fourteenth Amendment started not where one would logically expect it, in matters of procedure, but in the Court's invalidation of state legislative efforts to deal with social and economic problems. It paralleled the Court's use of the due process clause of the Fifth Amendment to knock down similar Acts of Congress. The Justices developed the barbarous notion of "substantive due process"—barbarous both in its solecism and in its human consequences.

In the late nineteenth century and the first third of the twentieth, Supreme Court majorities were generally to the political right of Congress and most state legislatures. When social and economic legislation was enacted, it ran afoul of the Justices' fervent devotion to their image of free enterprise. There was an apotheosis of private property and "freedom of contract." The result was that much of this legislation was held unconstitutional. Due process was made to embrace not only the process by which substantive law is enforced but some of the substantive law itself. Harking back to Magna Carta, Supreme Court majorities decided that any Act of Congress must conform to "fundamental liberties," to the "natural rights" of the people. These included the right to hire labor as cheaply as the market would

---

ble to the states. "A few members of the Court have taken the position," he said, and in a slighting footnote cited Hugo Black and "Harlan, J." Grandpa Harlan, that is.

There is a prankish recurrence of names in the Supreme Court's rosters. The two Harlans—each John Marshall Harlan —repeat the name of the early Chief Justice. Harlan F. Stone was on the Court from 1924 to 1946, finishing as Chief Justice. And our two most recent Chief Justices have been the end-to-end Earl Warren and Warren Burger, who overlap only in name.

allow in what was then a buyers' market, to work employees for as many hours as that market would permit, and in general to conduct one's business on the precept of the-public-be-damned.*

In the 1920s, state legislation that impinged on First Amendment guarantees came to the Supreme Court. Some states, responding to the Red scare of the World War I period, had passed statutes that forbade not only action but also talk. The First Amendment is substantive, not a matter of process, but by this time the notion of substantive due process was so firmly entrenched that it was difficult for proponents of the legislation to say that the Fourteenth Amendment did not include the First Amendment guarantees. If freedom to make money was one of the fundamental liberties encompassed in due process, it could scarcely be argued that freedom of speech was not.

In the 1930s, partly because of the evidence given by the Great Depression that unrestricted free enterprise might not be the sacred blessing its disciples had declared, and partly because of new judges on the Court, a radical change took place. The decisions that held social and economic legislation unconstitutional were overruled. At the same time, progressing from the First Amendment cases, the Court began to give personal rights the tender treatment formerly lavished on property rights.

A great debate on the proper role of the Court has come from this. At the one end are those who say the Court must follow the text of the Constitution, and interpret it as any other statute would be interpreted. At the other end are those who say the Court should do whatever is "right," and guide its decision-making according to social needs that exist as each case arises. In between are those (who do not entirely agree among themselves) who hold that the Constitution is not an ordinary statute, that it does no more than set the main outlines of government, and that the judiciary have the power and duty to fill in the open spaces and to engage to some degree (how much is in dispute) in Constitution-making.

So far as the federal government was concerned, the Court destroyed Acts of Congress both by broadening the concept of due process and by refusing to broaden the concept of interstate commerce despite the fact that state boundaries had become irrelevant to our economy. Another weapon used to shoot down welfare statutes was the Fifth Amendment's prohibition against taking private property "without just compensation."

The debate—between the "activists" and those who favor the use of "neutral principles"—is both important and interesting, but it does not, I suggest, have any great bearing on whether the central safeguards of the Bill of Rights are available to people accused by the states. When we speak of criminal prosecution, we are speaking of procedure. It is not a question of what the crime consists of, or whether the legislature may Constitutionally prohibit the conduct it has declared to be a crime. It is a question of the way the rules are to be enforced. There is no stretching of language when we are talking about "process." The issues relate to the kind of process that is due.*

□

"Essential fairness" is the phrase the Justices use, over and over again, in these recent cases, to define the rights encompassed in due process. The use of the phrase is misleading. Fairness is a central component of due process, but it does not define the rights the clause assures. Due process, I suggest, means essential fairness both expanded and restricted by the history of our law.

---

*The pure "activist" position is that text and precedent are meaningless, that judges decide cases according to personal preference, and that the preference is usually formed by enlightened appraisal of social needs (good in the eyes of most activist commentators) or by conservative bias (bad in those selfsame eyes). But courts do not in fact feel free of constraint. Their opinions show their inhibitions. When they strike out in new directions, it is not without discussion of Constitutional text and precedent. Only rarely do they say they are overruling a previous decision, and then they usually justify their course by arguing that the previous decision was wrong, that it was inconsistent with decisions even earlier and was poor reading of the text. No Justice of the Supreme Court has yet felt ready to jettison the explanation of decision that is the function of judicial opinion; none has been content to say, "This is the way the law will be because this is the way it ought to be." Since they feel this need to make sense in terms of precedent and the words of the Constitution, they have only so much tether. They have a great deal, and it is elastic, and opinions are often rationalizations of decisions based on other, unspoken motives. But the rationalization has to be a pretty good one. The thoroughly activist position is unrealistic, for the rather simple reason that no judge wants to look silly.

Consider the treasured right of jury trial for major crimes. There is nothing "essentially fair" in leaving the determination of the facts to twelve laymen rather than one judge. On the contrary, chances of getting fair treatment may be better with a judge experienced in lawyers' tricks and witnesses' evasions. Quite apart from the fact that, as a group, judges have above-average intelligence and hence above-juror intelligence, they are experienced in sifting facts, in observing witnesses, in discounting the scoring of meaningless points. In a word, they are professionals, and have the advantage over amateurs held by professionals in every field. Yet, for the trial of crime thought serious, the Supreme Court tells us that amateur decision is required by due process. The fact is that trial by jury—though it may well be an excellent thing—is demanded not by fairness but by our legal history.

We can go further. Take something not specifically mentioned in our Constitution at all: our adversary system. Let us assume that a state decides to dispense with it. This state will use the method of the Continental law. There is nothing essentially unfair in this. The magistrate may be able to draw nearer the truth through his inquiries than can untrained jurors acting as audience to the performance of lawyers and their witnesses. He is apt to erect a better guard against prejudice. It can be argued that the adversary method, by drawing more energy into the production of facts and the presentation of the law, is more likely to generate fair results. It can be argued in opposition that the adversary method, by leaving so much to the skill of counsel and the financial resources of the parties, is less likely to generate fair results. Yet an attempt to abolish the adversary system would no doubt be held to be a violation of due process. The system is embedded too deep in the history of our law. Here again it is our past, not essential fairness, that defines the concept.

Correlatively, there are elements of unfairness about which due process does nothing. A district attorney makes choices among the crimes he will pursue. He must be given that power; far too many violations of law occur to permit prosecution of them all. Suppose the district attorney for personal reasons hates one crime more than another. Suppose he has a racial bias. Or suppose he is corrupt, for money or advancement. He may devote disproportionate energies to dirty magazines, while muggings go unchecked. Or he may spend all his time on violence, ignoring white-collar crime. He may prosecute easy cases in order to build a record of success, and avoid more important cases where he thinks he may get beat. And even with totally honest prosecutors, the process of selection cannot be nicely adjusted to moral culpability; administrative problems stand in the way. The unlucky few chosen for prosecution may feel, with warrant, that they are catching hell when worse miscreants go scot-free. It is, in fact as well as feeling, inordinate injustice. Yet, assuming there is a basis in law for the particular prosecution, the courts cannot say that due process has been denied.

Due process, then, is not "essential fairness" alone. It includes some things that are neither fair nor unfair, and excludes some things intensely unfair. It combines our present moral and ethical ideas with our legal past. And, so far as the rights of the accused are concerned, the progress of Constitutional law has not been very different from the progress of the common law. The recent expansion of those rights has not, in general, involved the kind of decision that can properly be criticized as judicial amendment of the Constitution. (I need hardly remind the reader that the decisions on right to jury trial require the phrase "in general.")

It is not good law to insist that words must lie inert. Change the ambiance and leave the definition literally the same, and you change the essential meaning. The draftsman who set down the words, and those who voted to accept his draft, could not have imagined all the possibilities of application as new circumstances would come into being. If we would be faithful to the intent, we will expand, diminish, and otherwise alter the effect of the words in these unimagined circumstances. The new circumstances, as I said earlier in this book, can be material (economic, technological), social (the very fact of population growth, for instance) or (call it what you will: philosophical, moral, spiritual) new ways of thought and feeling. The periphery must change with time if we would have the core of the word stay constant. In 1789 due process of law did not mean that the accused had a right to counsel. Today it does, because the world has changed. These decisions do not tamper with the meaning of the Bill of Rights. A failure to arrive at these decisions would.

The fact is this: Nothing is timeless in our law except the idea of the law itself, the idea that we are to be governed by rules and principles and not by unconfined Authority. (The rules and principles can be textually inexplicit, the sum of judicial decision; or they can have fixed texts, as in our constitutions and our statutes.) We do not submit to the wisdom or unwisdom of Prince or Pope or Party Secretary, not to Adolf Hitler or Good King Wenceslas. Of course, individuals mold and alter law, but they do so deferentially—as judges, with deference to past decisions and to new thoughts and attitudes; as legislators and executives, with deference to the existing structure and to the next election; and all three, in the United States though not in Britain, with deference to the text of the Constitution. Sometimes these officials transgress, either mistakenly (the jury trial decisions) or corruptly (the news gives us fresh examples almost every day) or —very rarely—in simple outlawry (Richard Nixon). But in general the idea of law is recognized and respected.

□

The benefits to the accused most often cited as the glories of our system have no specific statement in the Constitution. Nor has any such statement been needed. Their existence is never challenged, and we may safely assume that if a question were raised, they would be held to be part of due process.

They are "the presumption of innocence" and "proof beyond a reasonable doubt." If people were asked the salient features of our scheme of criminal justice, these would probably be named. One thinks of them as basic rules of law, or complementary parts of a single basic rule: everyone accused of crime is presumed innocent, until his guilt is proved beyond a reasonable doubt.

It seems clear enough. It isn't. A gifted writer on the law, James Bradley Thayer, considered the presumption and concluded it could be analyzed away. It is meaningless, he said, except in a sense in which it applies to every kind of litigation. Whether we have a criminal charge or a civil claim, the party trying to get the court to act must make some sort of showing. The plaintiff in a civil suit does not establish his claim just because he makes it. The prosecutor gets no farther merely by lodging his accusation. Each must offer proof. The civil defendant will not be liable, the accused will not be convicted, unless the plaintiff or the prosecutor, as the case may be, gives evidence to the court. Once he does, however, the "presumption" disappears. It is then up to the defendant—criminal or civil—to offer proof to refute the proof against him. This, wrote Thayer, is natural to any litigating system. So the presumption of innocence is not something special to our style of criminal justice. In fact, says

Thayer, the statement of the presumption tells us nothing that is not subsumed in the requirement of proof beyond a reasonable doubt.

Thayer's thesis is attractive, and it cleared away some turbid thought, by courts and commentators. The Supreme Court of the United States, for instance. In a unanimous opinion, at a time when unanimous opinions were still fashionable, the Court declared that the presumption of innocence constitutes "evidence in favor of the accused." This it cannot be. If the prosecutor produces strong evidence of guilt and the defendant stands mute, the presumption manufactures no countervailing evidence on his behalf. Despite the Supreme Court's dictum, neither it nor any other court has upset a guilty verdict in such a situation. (True, the mute defendant in a criminal case is entitled to a jury verdict, and juries, for whatever reason, have power to acquit, but this is not the same as saying there is "evidence in favor of the accused.")

But I cannot quite agree with Thayer. The presumption does say something, though it is poorly named. In fact, it says three things, related but distinct.

To begin with, the requirement that the prosecutor offer proof in court is not a part of nature. Our present legal system demands it. For other systems—for our own at an earlier time— the accusation is enough to cast upon defendant the task of proving innocence. The "presumption" expresses, in this regard, our current way of doing things.

Second, the presumption is a declaration of neutrality. The defendant has been arrested, which itself suggests that he is guilty. (When, outside the evidentiary confines of the courtroom, a statement is made about a criminal record, we hear not only the number of convictions, but also the number of arrests.) Then the grand jury, a body of defendant's fellow citizens, has concluded he ought to be tried. At the opening of the trial, the prosecutor, a public official who ordinarily has no personal animosity toward defendant, assures us he is guilty. He is brought to court from prison, or has been allowed a temporary freedom only on posting bail. When he is seen by us in such a setting, it is hard to put aside a strong suspicion that he indeed is guilty. Where there is smoke, the common wisdom tells us, there is fire.

The presumption of innocence instructs us to ignore all this. Start the trial with an open mind, it says. Pay no attention to the smoke; it comes from irrelevant fires.

The third thing the presumption says is that the accused is

entitled to at least litigating equality with the prosecution. More —to certain special advantages. Compare him with the defendant in a civil case. There are stricter rules on the use of evidence against him. He need not be a witness if he does not wish to testify, and the jury is told to draw no inference from this. Evidence obtained by the government in violation of the Fourth Amendment may not be offered to show his guilt, even though, if the evidence were admitted, the jury would surely find him guilty. (It would not be unreasonable to admit the evidence and enforce the Amendment differently: prosecute the officials who obtained it, for their unlawful search and seizure.) Confessions made in certain circumstances may not be introduced. Finally, there is the standard of reasonable doubt itself.

The presumption is a way to express the sum total of the protections the law erects around the accused. It reminds us that punishment is a serious thing, that we should not prejudge, that on every close question we should favor the defendant. If not itself a rule of law, it at least describes an inclination.

Thayer tells us the presumption "is a very ancient one." Not so. In the beginning of our criminal law, the naked accusation put defendant to the test, and he was convicted by an unhealed burn, an unhorsed champion, a floating to the surface of the pond. There was no room for presumption. Later we had the Clarendon indictment—for practical purposes about as good as a conviction—based usually on hearsay. Then jury trial, but with lawyers for the prosecution and none for the defense, and later witnesses for the prosecution and none for the defense. Add the glowering authority of the Crown, and it is plain that until quite recently the chances of the accused were poor. There was no presumption of innocence. There was, instead, a presumption of guilt.

Then how about the maxim so often coupled with the presumption—that the jury may not convict unless guilt is proved beyond a reasonable doubt? Here we have something we can call a rule, a forceful direction to the jury. The difficulty is that we do not know exactly what the maxim means. We can never be sure that any two jurors will understand it in the same way (if they understand it at all). Or, for that matter, any two judges. How much "doubt" is "reasonable"? Respected legal minds have tried to tell us.

The rule entered the law shortly after 1800. The word "reasonable" seems to have been a successor to "rational"; the jurors were not to convict if they had such a doubt of guilt as rational men might entertain. Then the phrases "well-grounded doubt" and "beyond the probability of doubt" appeared. Starkie, a noted nineteenth-century writer on the law of evidence, added a reference to "moral certainty." In the middle of that century, the celebrated Chief Justice Shaw of Massachusetts uttered the pronouncement most drawn upon in later cases. It made much use of moral certainty. Reasonable doubt, said Shaw,

> is that state of the case, which, after the entire comparison and consideration of all the evidence, leaves the minds of jurors in that condition that they cannot say they feel an abiding conviction, to a moral certainty, of the truth of the charge.... The evidence must establish the truth of the fact to a reasonable and moral certainty,—a certainty that convinces and directs the understanding, and satisfies the reason and judgment ...

What sort of certainty is moral? Does it differ from intellectual certainty? Does "an abiding conviction" mean something more than that the juror feels his present view will last, that he will not change his mind tomorrow? Suppose the juror cannot assign the reasons for his doubt, yet cannot make it go away. Does "reasonable doubt" include the uneasiness we call "intuitive," or "instinctive," or "visceral"? And in the end, ignoring the psychological nature of the doubt, just how much of it is needed?

Chief Justice Shaw, and Mr. Starkie, and others who have written on the point probably have a fairly clear idea of the standard each would use, but the one's idea may not be another's. It is the sort of thing on which language serves us poorly. We can understand, and transmit, the test in civil cases: the evidence, all in all, makes the alleged event more probable than not. But your idea of reasonable doubt may not be mine, and there is no way for you to tell me exactly what yours is.

Imagine a conversation that will take place when someday communication is established with another planet in a distant galaxy. By some undreamed-of marvel, we have instant conversation. That planet, though a bit older and more advanced—actually, it is they who have established contact, and they quickly learn our language—turns out, remarkably, to be very like our own. Very, but not quite. We chat with them about things there and here, and derive pleasure from the fact we have so much in common. One day we get onto the subject of colors.

EARTHPERSON: "Blue is a nice color; we really like blue."

OTHERPERSON: "So do we. Perfect for a sky. And not bad for eyes."

E: "Lots of us like brown eyes."

O: "Go along with you there too."

E: "Of course, red is more dramatic. Terrific in sunsets, and in a log fire."

O: "Yeah."

E: "Yellow is cheerful. We paint some of our houses yellow, and they look real nice."

O: "You're kidding."

E: "No, really. Yellow looks good on houses. We paint the shutters green. You must like green."

O: "Green?"

E: "Yes, green."

O: "How do you spell it?"

E: "G-r-e-e-n."

O: "That spells it all right. But what is it?"

E: "What do you mean, what is it?"

O: "What's green?"

E: "What do you mean, what's green?"

O: "What's green?"

E: "Well, stupid, grass is green."

O: "Grass here is purple."

E: "Guess you've been doing your lawns a couple of eons longer than we have. Got anything that really works on crabgrass?"

O: "No. And I'll overlook that 'stupid.' We're farther advanced, you know, and so we don't engage in petty ego manifestations."

E: "Let's get back to green. Trees and plants put out green leaves in springtime."

O: "Our leaves are orange."

E: "Our oranges are orange."

O: "Great sense of humor you guys have. What else is green?"

E: "Well, you know the color copper roofing turns after it's been weathered?"

O: "Sure. It puts out that lovely brown patina."

E: "Listen. Take a bucket of yellow paint and a bucket of blue paint and mix them."

O: "Coming right up."

E: "Now what have you got?"

O: "Pink. Naturally."

E: "Christ. What's going on here? I mean, what's going on *there?*"

O: "Apparently we don't have your green. Tell me about it. What does green look like? Explain it to me."

Try it. Tell somebody—there being no example on which to draw, no associations to make—what the color green is.

There is almost the same difficulty in trying to tell someone what proof beyond a reasonable doubt is. Some standard lies in the mind of the speaker, but language does not provide a way to transmit that standard to the mind of the hearer, not with any certainty that what is sent will be received. Proof beyond a reasonable doubt is a quantum without a number.

Should we legislate a numerical expression of the proof required? The rule might be that the jury is to find defendant guilty if it appraises the probabilities at eighty–twenty. Or seventy–thirty. Or sixty–forty, or ninety–ten. We would gain in mutual comprehension and precision, and therefore in equal application of the law. With the present vaporous definition, we can be sure that defendants in different cases are judged by different standards, though the juries be well-meaning. But it is highly doubtful that such legislation would ever be enacted. Most of us are comforted by vagueness when we are pronouncing guilt or innocence. We had rather not be asked to think precisely. Still, the established form of jury instruction can be, I think, improved upon. I would abandon "reasonable doubt" and "moral certainty" and suggest a shorter charge:

A verdict of guilty in a criminal case requires more than the degree of proof that can lead you to a conclusion in everyday affairs. No one is to be convicted simply because the evidence makes it more likely than not that he committed the crime in question. How much more likely? A whole lot more likely.

If that last strikes you as too colloquial and hence unsuited to the law (in my view nothing that helps to make a concept clear is unsuited to the law), then you might substitute "very much more likely." Either way, I believe the charge would be better than what the courts are using now.

The problem would be reduced, but, reduced, it would remain. There is no way for a judge to tell the jurors exactly what degree of likelihood the law demands (assuming the judge himself has the proper degree in mind). Unless we go to the numbers.

Whatever its measure, the standard of reasonable doubt is a benefit for the accused. But, considering that we take it for granted, it is a remarkably recent one. Judges of the seventeenth century would have been astonished at such Crown-defying nonsense. Lawyers for defendants were probably urging something like it late in the eighteenth century, but imaginative lawyers are always ahead of the law. Reasonable doubt was not the test when our Bill of Rights was drafted. The rule seems to have been at least in part a product of the revulsion against the use of capital punishment for an extraordinary number of offenses, many of them extraordinarily trivial, a lunacy that reached a peak just about 1800. The causal connection is strengthened by the fact that the courts first uttered the rule in cases involving the death penalty, and not in other criminal trials until some time afterward. By the middle of the nineteenth century, it was accepted as the standard in all criminal cases. That is not so long ago.

□

So most of the things that we consider basic in our criminal justice system, and of which we are properly proud, are only lately made. They came into our law partly by a legislative act, the adoption of the Bill of Rights, and partly by what we have seen to be the way of the common law: lawyers and judges— sometimes reflecting the thoughts of others, sometimes creating their own—have stretched or confined old rules and rulings, and given new meaning to words. Not altogether new, since often what they do is to hold the essence constant as the context changes. I do not suggest that every court decision fits this pattern. There have been many bad decisions, and the actions of the courts in different cases, and the statements with which they justify their actions, are often inconsistent. But by and large there is consistency, along with healthy growth. And our law is a matter of by-and-large. It lives, if I may say so one more time, not according to absolutes, but by degree and extent. Its task is to draw generally sensible lines within the infinite shades of circumstance that constitute our world.

Acknowledgment

This book, drawing on the history of our law, tries to reach some understanding of its nature. At the law I am professional (there is a certificate that says so), at history an amateur.

In college, full of adolescent arrogance, I decided that what might be gained from listening to lecturers could be gained as well from reading what they wrote, and the reading of history need not be done at a university, there being books at other places. This would seem to represent a reasonable, if callow, judgment, except I made an equally reasonable judgment against every other field of study. Foreign languages were not worth precious time because there was so much of substance to be learned, and another language yielded none of the substance but only another form in which to put it. Neither should mathematics be taken; there was enchantment in it, but unless we would be physicists it only taught us games. As to literature, why study it? Wasn't it meant to be read? *Et cetera* (a bit of Latin I picked up in high school).

In law school there was a compulsory course in legal history whose compulsion I managed to parry; it dealt only a glancing blow. But one part of the rationalization for playing ball or looking out the window or doing whatever I was doing instead of what I should have been doing turned out to hold a bit of truth: after a time I began to read some history and got from it a lovely mixture of pleasure and instruction. I found the plots ingenious, and the writing often superb. And there was the bonus of book reviews of history books, essays which often have their own importance; or, when they lack it, may nevertheless sometimes be enjoyed, or at least marveled at, for their competitive displays, fine traceries spun of spite or personal ambition.

Or respected for their honest indignation. (Of which these days we have too little; we substitute apathy or tantrum.) A well-known historian, plainly intelligent and a gifted writer, reviews two books about England. He is an Englishman, and has that modicum of national pride that many good people have. The books to some extent are disrespectful of the English, and this must naturally affect him. His outrage, disproportionate and charming, destroys his usual sense of measure. In a short review in which he handles both the books, he recites his countrymen's accomplishments, and in the course of his recital says:

> "In [British] invention recent decades have produced radar, penicillin, the jet engine, hovercraft . . ."

Hovercraft.

Well, okay, hovercraft. But here we have been concerned with a different product of that country: its legal system. Our law is the law of England, imported and then developed separately. Not altogether separately: English cases continue to be cited as precedents in American courts, precedents not controlling but persuasive, like cases from another state.

The main difference is the presence of our written Constitution and the doctrine of judicial review that has been hinged to it. Courts here nullify Acts of Congress and actions of the Executive (and of state governments as well) when they find them inconsistent with the Constitution. No such thing, as we have seen, can happen in Great Britain. But the law of the United States began in England long ago, and grew there for a thousand years before the United States existed. It must all be considered one system of law—the Anglo-American law, different from that of any other nation.

This book is not meant to be encyclopedic, far from it. It is not a treatise, and has neither the exhaustiveness nor the symmetrical proportions of a treatise. The aim, rather, is to take some features of our legal system—some of the most significant, perhaps; those apt at any rate to reveal its character and personality—and tell how they came to be what they are.

In pursuing that goal, I have become indebted to a great many writers of history and writers on the law, so many that I cannot express my debt to some without silently disclaiming just debts to others. *Expressio unius est exclusio alterius*, said the

Lord Chief Justice Coke: if you name a thing or a person specifically, we'll take it you don't mean others. But I ask the reader to waive the Lord Coke's maxim while, acknowledging a debt much more diffuse, I list some works of legal history to which I am especially obliged:

F. R. Aumann, *The Changing American System* (Ohio State University, Columbus, 1940).

C. H. S. Fifoot, *History and Sources of the Common Law* (Stevens, London, 1949).

L. M. Friedman, *A History of American Law* (Simon & Schuster, New York, 1973).

Sir W. Holdsworth, *A History of English Law* (Methuen, London, 1903, *et seq.*).

J. W. Hurst, *Law and the Conditions of Freedom* (University of Wisconsin Press, Madison, Milwaukee and London, 1967).

F. W. Maitland, *The Constitutional History of England* (The University Press, Cambridge, 1908).

———, *The Forms of Action at Common Law* (The University Press, Cambridge, 1909).

———, *Equity* (The University Press, Cambridge, 1909).

S. F. C. Milson, *Historical Foundations of the Common Law* (Butterworth, London, 1969).

T. F. T. Plucknett, *A Concise History of the Common Law* (Butterworth, London, 1940).

Sir F. Pollock and F. W. Maitland, *The History of English Law Before the Time of Edward I*, 2nd ed. (The University Press, Cambridge, 1898).

B. Schwartz, *The Law in America* (McGraw-Hill, New York, 1974).

J. B. Thayer, *Evidence at the Common Law* (Little, Brown, Boston, 1898).

In addition, I should like to mention several works which, while they do not deal primarily with legal history, bear on the content of this book. They are:

H. M. Cam, *England Before Elizabeth* (Hutchinson's University Library, London, 1950).

N. F. Cantor, *The English* (Simon & Schuster, New York, 1967).

W. H. McNeill, *The Rise of the West* (University of California Press, Chicago and London, 1967).

H. J. Muller, *Freedom in the Western World* (Harper & Row, New York, 1963).

G. M. Trevelyan, *English Social History* (David McKay, New York, 1942).

W. L. Warren, *Henry II* (University of California Press, Berkeley and Los Angeles, 1973).

Yet the list can be misleading. The chief written sources of this book are the materials of the law itself—judicial opinions, early reports of cases (when judges wrote no opinions), legislation (including our grandest statute, the Constitution).

And there are unwritten sources to whom acknowledgment is due—lawyers I have encountered in the practice of law, both those with whom I have worked and those I have worked against. I have learned a very great deal from my friends and from my adversaries and I thank them both.

Some Notes on Sources

2 BATTLE

page
18 The case of *Ashford v. Thornton* is reported in Barnewall and Anderson, *Cases in the Court of King's Bench*, volume 1, at page 25. The quotations from the old treatises appear in the case report.

30 The quotation, attributed to Raimundus de Agiles, appears in Muller, *Freedom in the Western World* (Harper & Row, New York, Evanston and London, 1963), at page 48.

3 TAXONOMY

61 Senator Long's statement is quoted in "Week in Review" of *The New York Times* of March 16, 1975.

63 The baseball case is *Federal Baseball Club v. National League*. Holmes' opinion is reported in volume 259 of the *United States Reports*, at page 200.

63 The vaudeville case is *Hart v. Keith Exchange*. Holmes' opinion is reported in volume 262 of the *United States Reports*, at page 271.

80 Maine's statement appears in his *Early Law and Custom* (Holt, New York, 1883), at page 389.

84 The statement as to the early state legislatures is in Corwin, "The Progress of Constitutional Theory," *American Historical Review*, volume 30, at page 514.

84 *Erie Railroad v. Tompkins* is reported in volume 304 of the *United States Reports*, at page 64.

85 The *Guaranty Trust* case is reported in volume 328 of the *United States Reports*, at page 99.

4 THE HUE AND CRY,
THE FEUD, ORDEAL AND COMPURGATION

103   The quotations in the footnote are from Thayer, "The Older Modes of Trial," in *Select Essays in Anglo-American Legal History* (Little, Brown, Boston, 1908), volume 2, at pages 392–393.

104   The quoted statement is in Fuller and Braucher, *Basic Contract Law* (West, St. Paul, 1964), at page 157.

107   Cristiana's Case is quoted in Stephen, "Criminal Procedure from the Thirteenth Century to the Eighteenth Century" in *Select Essays in Anglo-American Legal History* (Little, Brown, Boston, 1908), volume 2, at page 487.

114   The Maitland statement is in Pollock and Maitland, *The History of English Law*, 2nd ed. (The University Press, Cambridge, 1898), at page 599.

115   The quotation appears in Thayer, "The Older Modes of Trial," in *Select Essays in Anglo-American Legal History* (Little, Brown, Boston, 1908), volume 2, at pages 395–396.

5 THE START OF TRIAL BY JURY

120   The quotation is from Cam, *England before Elizabeth* (Hutchinson's University Library, London, 1950), at pages 70–71.

125   Detailed material on castles of the time is in Warren, *Henry II* (University of California Press, Berkeley and Los Angeles, 1973), following page 208.

127   Cam, *op. cit. supra*, at page 80.

129   The contrasting descriptions are in Cantor, *The English* (Simon and Schuster, New York, 1967), at pages 136–137, and in Duggan, *The Devil's Brood* (Coward McCann, New York, 1957), at pages 37 and 40.

131   A description of the duel between Marshal and Nevers is in Duggan, *op. cit. supra*, at page 175.

131   The quotation on captives is from Duggan, *op. cit. supra*, at page 240. The one on rank and pomp is from Warren, *op. cit. supra*, at page 78.

134   The quotation is from Duggan, *op. cit. supra*, at page 100.

135   The quotation is from Pollock and Maitland, *op. cit. supra*, volume 2, at page 398.

135   The quotation regarding the word "serf" is from Pollock and Maitland, *op. cit. supra*, volume 1, at page 395.

6 GRAND AND PETTY

143   The quotation is from Pollock and Maitland, *op. cit. supra*, at page 139.

147   The details of abjuration are described in Riggs, *Asylum in Anglo-Saxon Law* (University of Florida monograph, Gainesville, 1963).

148   The Supreme Court opinions are in *Trop v. Dulles,* volume 356 of *United States Reports,* at page 86.

154   The case of the recalcitrant magnates is described in Thayer, *Evidence at the Common Law* (Little, Brown, Boston, 1898), at page 56.

160   The quotation is in Thayer, *op. cit. supra,* at pages 89–90.

163   Alcuin's statement is in his Epistle to Charlemagne, quoted in Stevenson, *The Home Book of Quotations* (Dodd Mead, New York, 1956), at page 1480.

165   The quotation appears in Thayer, *op. cit. supra,* at page 73.

7   A LITTLE WRITING

173   The Van Caenegem view is summarized in Bell, *Maitland* (Harvard University Press, Cambridge, 1965), at page 83.

176   The Muller statement is in his *The Uses of the Past* (Oxford University Press, New York, 1957), at page 257.

8   TRANSGRESSIONS, PARLIAMENTS AND TRESPASS

193   The quotation is from Bell, *op. cit. supra,* at page 81.

193   Milsom's statement is in "Trespass from Henry III to Edward III," *The Law Quarterly Review,* volume 74, at page 207.

9   FICTION

211   The *Times* account is in its "Week in Review" of September 12, 1976.

214   The statement of William Rufus is quoted in Pollock and Maitland, *op. cit. supra,* volume 1, at page 87.

220   The Supreme Court case referred to is *New York Times v. Sullivan,* reported in volume 376 of the *United States Reports,* at page 354.

10   PLEADING

227   The quotation is from David Dudley Field, in an article in volume 25 of *The American Law Review* (1891), at page 518.

229   The lawyer quoted is Sir William Jones, in Shipman, *Common Law Pleading* (West, St. Paul, 1923), at page 5.

230   Stephen's statement is in his *Principles of Pleading* (Kay, Philadelphia, 1867), at page 21.

230   Ballantine's rejoinder is in an article by him in the *University of Illinois Law Bulletin,* volume 1, page 1.

238   The treatise quoted is Pomeroy, *Code Remedies,* 5th ed. (Little, Brown, Boston, 1929), at page 640.

244   The two same-day cases are *Hine v. McNerney* and *Farley v. Fitzsimmons,* reported in volume 97 of the *Connecticut Reports,* at pages 308 and 372.

11   THE OLD NEW RULES

254   *Dioguardi v. Durning* is reported in volume 139 of *Federal Reporter Second*, at page 774.

255   The reference is to Frank, *Law and the Modern Mind* (Brentano's, New York, 1930).

267   Maine's famous statement is in his *Early Law and Custom* (Holt, New York, 1883), at page 389.

268   Maitland's famous statement is in *The Forms of Action* (The University Press, Cambridge, 1908), at page 296.

12   EQUITY

281   Selden's statement as to equity is quoted in Holdsworth, *A History of English Law* (Methuen, 1903–1938), volume 1, at page 467.

281   Selden's statement as to the king is quoted in Cantor, *The English* (Simon and Schuster, New York, 1967), at page 429.

284   Ellesmere's statement is quoted in Bowen, *The Lion and the Throne* (Atlantic-Little, Brown, 1956), at page 300.

284   *Courtney v. Glanvil* is reported in *Croke's King's Bench Reports*, at page 343.

285   Coke's letter, James' statements, and Coke's statements are quoted in Bowen, *op. cit. supra*, at pages 371–375.

286   *Bonham's Case* is reported in *Coke's Reports*, in volume 8, page 118.

288   The *Ship Money Case* is reported in volume 3 of *Howell's State Trials*, at page 825.

299   The quotation is from Holdsworth, *op. cit. supra*, volume 1, at page 427.

300   The quotation is from Holdsworth, *op. cit. supra*, volume 1, at page 432.

301   The quotation is from Holdsworth, *op. cit. supra*, volume 1, at pages 437–438.

13   EVIDENCE

331   The Lincoln defense of Duff Armstrong is described in Hill, *Lincoln the Lawyer* (Century, 1906), at pages 229 *et seq.*, and in Frank, *Lincoln as a Lawyer* (University of Illinois Press, Urbana, 1961), at pages 175 *et seq.*

346   The special juries are described in Thayer, *Evidence at the Common Law* (Little, Brown, Boston, 1898), at page 94.

354   The description of the "uninformed" juror is from Pike, *History of Crime*, quoted in Thayer, *op. cit. supra*, at page 170.

361   *Bushel's Case* is reported in volume 6 of *Howard's State Trials*, at page 999.

363   The Dow Chemical case is *United States v. Daugherty*, reported in volume 473 of *Federal Reporter Second*, at page 1113.

14 THE RIGHTS OF THE ACCUSED

377 The Scottsboro Supreme Court opinions are reported in volume 287 of the *United States Reports,* at page 45.

379 Gideon's colloquy with the trial judge appears in the Supreme Court majority opinion, which is reported in volume 372 of the *United States Reports,* at page 335.

381 The Supreme Court *Argesinger* opinions are reported in volume 407 of the *United States Reports,* at page 25.

389 The Michigan case is *Re William Oliver,* reported in volume 333 of the *United States Reports,* at page 257.

391 The Frankfurter-Corcoran article appears in volume 39 of the *Harvard Law Review,* at page 923.

392 The cases referred to are *Schick v. United States,* in volume 195 of the *United States Reports,* at page 65; and *Cheff v. Schnackenberg,* in volume 384 of the *United States Reports,* at page 373.

399 The Third Amendment argument was offered in *United States v. Valenzuela,* reported in volume 95 of *Federal Supplement,* at page 363.

402 The younger Harlan's remark is in *Duncan v. Louisiana,* reported in volume 391 of the *United States Reports,* at page 174.

408 The Supreme Court case is *Coffin v. United States,* in volume 156 of the *United States Reports,* at page 432.

409 The Thayer analysis is in his *Evidence at the Common Law, op. cit. supra,* at pages 566 *et seq.*

Index